CSR, Sustainability, Ethics & Governance

In recent years the discussion concerning the relation between business and society has made immense strides. This has in turn led to a broad academic and practical discussion on innovative management concepts, such as Corporate Social Responsibility, Corporate Governance and Sustainability Management. This series offers a comprehensive overview of the latest theoretical and empirical research and provides sound concepts for sustainable business strategies. In order to do so, it combines the insights of leading researchers and thinkers in the fields of management theory and the social sciences – and from all over the world, thus contributing to the interdisciplinary and intercultural discussion on the role of business in society. The underlying intention of this series is to help solve the world's most challenging problems by developing new management concepts that create value for business and society alike. In order to support those managers, researchers and students who are pursuing sustainable business approaches for our common future, the series offers them access to cutting-edge management approaches.

CSR, Sustainability, Ethics & Governance is accepted by the Norwegian Register for Scientific Journals, Series and Publishers, maintained and operated by the Norwegian Social Science Data Services (NSD)

More information about this series at http://www.springer.com/series/11565

Nayan Mitra • René Schmidpeter
Editors

Corporate Social Responsibility in Rising Economies

Fundamentals, Approaches and Case Studies

Springer

Editors
Nayan Mitra
Founder-Director Sustainable
Advancements (OPC) Private Limited
Kolkata, West Bengal, India

René Schmidpeter
World Institute of Sustainability
and Ethics (WISE)
Cologne, Germany

ISSN 2196-7075 ISSN 2196-7083 (electronic)
CSR, Sustainability, Ethics & Governance
ISBN 978-3-030-53774-6 ISBN 978-3-030-53775-3 (eBook)
https://doi.org/10.1007/978-3-030-53775-3

This Springer imprint is published by the registered company Springer Nature Switzerland AG.
The registered company address is: Gewerbestrasse 11, 6330 Cham, Switzerland

UN GLOBAL COMPACT
Network India

Global Compact Network
UNESCO House, 1st Floor
1, San Martin Marg, Chanakyapuri,
New Delhi - 110021
Phone : +91-11-2611 1071/72
Email : gcnindia@globalcompact.in
Web : www.globalcompact.in

FOREWORD

As the world grapples with one of the worst economic downturns in human memory due to the COVID 19 pandemic, the invisible line between developed economies and rising economies is blurred. The debate between voluntary versus mandated Corporate Social Responsibility (CSR) is passé; the only guiding concern being sustenance for a better tomorrow. The lockdown in the various parts of the world is seeking introspection – of harmonious mindful effort, regeneration of micro, small and medium enterprises; localizations over globalizations and collapsing of the bubble between essential and non-essential.

These are indeed uncertain and most challenging times – and I heartily congratulate Dr. Nayan Mitra and Dr. Rene Schmidpeter for conceptualizing and bringing out this extremely relevant book on Corporate Social Responsibility in Rising Economies, which not only documents the country specific cases of Pakistan, Bangladesh, India, Georgia, Brazil and Poland; but also discusses key issues including meaningful work, responsible food supply chain and the role of responsible education. Most importantly, the chapter on the Future of the UN Sustainable Development Goals in Rising Economies authored by Rene, Nayan and Bonnie beautifully sums up the issues – indeed the world will now align with the 10 UN Principles and the 17 SDGs.

I am certain this book is going to be a milestone for major practical lessons in the near future!

Kamal Singh

Executive Director

April 12, 2020

Foreword for "Corporate Social Responsibility in Rising Economies - Fundamentals, Approaches and Case Studies"

Prof. Danica Purg

Already since the Club of Rome (in 1968), there has been concern about the impact of economic growth without changing the nature of the growth. Globalisation and the rise of economies that were lagging behind could have accumulated social and environmental problems beyond control. The most important global organisation, The United Nations (UN), gave to the world an important message by promoting the "Sustainable Development Goals (SDGs)" by organising corporations behind the UN Global Compact initiative, and the educational world behind the "Principles for Responsible Management Education (PRME)".

It is particularly encouraging and hope giving that the rising economies have fully embraced these initiatives. The World Institute for Sustainability and Ethics in Rising Economies (WISE), bringing together Europe, China and Africa (CBS International Business School from Germany, University of Stellenbosch Business School from South Africa, School of Management, Zhejiang University from China, and IEDC-Bled School of Management from Slovenia) was also established to support them. Furthermore, also leadership and management development institutions and associations in rising economies, such as CEEMAN, CLADEA, AABS, RABE, MBDA, Forum Poland, unified under the Alliance with Management Development Associations in Rising Economies, belong to the strongest supporters.

Therefore, it is not just by coincident that this important publication on Social Responsibility and Sustainability presents the cases and examples of rising economies. It easily shows how in different parts of the world, in various industries the UN SDGs can be concretized. It is my strong personal wish that this book finds the way to many readers, particularly to business leaders and managers in rising economies, but also in the other parts of the globe.

Prof. Danica Purg
President of IEDC-Bled School of Management
President of CEEMAN, The International Association of Management Development Institutions
The Acting Chair of the PRME Steering Committee

IEDC – Bled School of Management
Prešernova cesta 33, 4260 Bled, Slovenia; Tel: +386 4 57 92 500; http://www.iedc.si

Preface and Acknowledgement

We are all currently experiencing major economic and societal changes due to the COVID-19 crises—changes that we need to shape in a positive way. With our actions, each of us show what qualities we stand for: helpfulness, cohesion and solidarity. Now the following applies more than ever: We shape the future of the world together! The strength of mankind has always been to cope with difficult events—we all grow with it. The current crisis is an opportunity for the world because it creates unity, solidarity and the realization that we are all connected to each other. We can expect anything, especially the positive. The positive forces are already stronger because we are starting to shape the time after the crisis together by responsible leadership and sustainable management.

Globalization as we know has been paused—it is now time for reflecting on our strengths. The Corona crisis, of all things, helps us to contain negative social and economic developments that had threatened the spirit of solidarity and humanity before the crisis. The crisis promotes small-scale structures, regional economic cycles and social cohesion, everything that still exists in many places in the world. Based on these micro-structures and local business, we can rebuild our economy and use our strengths together. It is now time to invest more in sustainable business and small-scale structures that make us strong in and after the crisis.

We can all have a positive impact on the world by showing that sustainable economic structures, responsible decision-making, regional circular economy and solidarity practised by everyone ultimately lead to economic and social success. We can show the world that in the end it is human measure and shared values that count and that economic success and social cohesion are not mutually exclusive! The time has come to change the future together for the better and to say thank you to everyone who contributed to this volume of hope and innovative business thoughts. Special thanks go to the brilliant authors who keep inspiring, our families and friends who have been patient with us and all those unexpected helps that were showered on us! We convey our heartfelt gratitude towards Springer International Publishing for providing us this platform to share and contribute on this dynamic issue, especially to Dr. Samuel O. Idowu (Series Editor for Springer's *CSR, Sustainability, Ethics and*

Governance books) for his encouragement and support, and Mr. Christian Rauscher (Senior Editor of Springer) who was always there to guide and advise us.

Everyone can use these good examples from rising economies for a positive change and let us promise: Everyone will look after each other and we will not leave anyone behind. Both rising economies and developed countries need to change together for a better tomorrow—these have been shown to us by the raging Corona virus!

Kolkata, India
Cologne, Germany
In April 2020 – during times of Crises

Nayan Mitra
René Schmidpeter

Contents

Editors and Contributors

About the Authors

Akanksha Jumde is a Ph.D. Scholar at Deakin Law School, Deakin University, Melbourne, for which she has been awarded the Deakin University Post Graduate Research Scholarship (DUPRS). Prior to commencing her Ph.D. studies, she taught at prestigious law institutions in India such as National Law University, Jodhpur, and the Faculty of Law, Delhi University. She has completed her Bachelors of Laws, from ILS Law College, Pune, University of Pune, India, and thereafter an LL.M. (IP and IT law), Franklin Pierce Law Center, University of New Hampshire, USA. Recently, she was awarded the "Young IP Scholar of Asia" fellowship for presenting her research paper at the 4th IP Works-In-Progress Conference, at Singapore Management University, Singapore. Prior to joining academia, she has worked as an IP lawyer at a leading IP law firm in India, and joined academics as the head of the IP Chair at Gujarat National Law University (GNLU), established by the Government of Gujarat, India. She has routinely published in renowned legal journals in India, on various legal topics, and presented papers at several national and international conferences, held at prestigious institutions such as the University of Melbourne and Indian Institute of Management (IIM), Calcutta.

Ameeta Jain, Ph.D., is a Senior Lecturer in Finance at Deakin University. Prior to joining Deakin, Ameeta worked as a lecturer at Delhi University and then at Monash University. She completed her M.Phil. at the Delhi School of Economics and a Ph.D. at Federation University, Australia. She has more than 15 years of teaching experience in economics and finance units and has led unit teams in the development and enhancement of various units. Ameeta is passionate about teaching and has been rewarded consistently for her teaching excellence. She has been the director of property programmes at Deakin, where she was responsible for managing industry accreditation for property courses. She believes in promoting student engagement to promote deeper learning. Ameeta's primary research interest is corporate social responsibility in the banking sector. She is also interested in the changes in the CSR space brought about by GRI and more recently the UN SDG. She has a secondary stream of research in regional resilience. She has published in internationally ranked journals such as *Regional Studies, Australasian Journal of Environmental Management* and *Social Responsibility Journal.*

André Nijhof, Ph.D., is Professor of Sustainable Business and Stewardship at Nyenrode Business Universiteit. Much of his recent work has focused on embedding long term-value creation in the core processes of an organization. Andre is a visiting professor at the UN-mandated University for Peace (Costa Rica) and project leader for a 4-year teaching and research programme with the BGMEA University for Fashion and Technology in Bangladesh.

Arabinda Bhattacharya is a Former Associate Professor of the Department of Business Management, University of Calcutta, where he has taught for the last 40 years. He completed his M.Stat. (Master of Statistics) from the Indian Statistical Institute in 1974. He obtained M.Phil. in Economics from the Centre for Development Studies, Trivandrum, affiliated to Jawaharlal Nehru University, New Delhi. He has also done FDP (Faculty Development Programme) in Management from the Indian Institute of Management, Ahmedabad. His research interest is in the area of organization behaviour and market research. He has published several research papers in the national and international journals and has supervised numerous research scholars in their doctoral work.

Bonnie Lewtas fell in love with islands on her first overseas trip to Hawaii at the age of 11. She was fascinated by the stunning landscapes, slow-paced lifestyle and magnificent ecology, but disturbed by the hotel and tourism industry's needless degradation of the local environment. Determined to find a better way, she dedicated her career to uncovering innovative ways for island hospitality to become sustainable. Her work has taken her around the world and especially to the Caribbean including the British Virgin Islands, Grenada, Barbados, and more. In 2017, on the island of Dominica, Bonnie was hit by Maria, a category 5 hurricane that tore the country to shreds overnight. This was a wakeup call that if island economies are to survive, the time for action is now! Exactly 1 year later, on the anniversary of the hurricane in an industry stakeholder meeting on the island, she launched her company TurtlCo. The company, based in Amsterdam, helps islands become more self-sufficient and resilient against natural disasters by implementing innovative energy, water, waste, food and wildlife conservation strategies. When not trying to ward off climate change in the Caribbean, Bonnie works as a consultant for Greening the Islands in Sicily, the province of Friesland on the EU INTERREG Islands of Innovation project, as well as supports several up-and-coming technologies like TwingTec's containerized airborne wind energy solutions.

Charles Eller, Ph.D., is an experienced educator and has worked on several continents in various management positions in the hospitality industry. His main research interests are in longitudinal studies about graduate outcomes especially in the hotel sector of the industry.

Christopher Stehr, Ph.D., is a Professor for International Management at the German Graduate School of Management and Law (GGS). He studied Political Science and Business Administration at Ludwig Maximilian University of Munich. After receiving a scholarship of the German-Japanese-Academic Burse for his doctoral thesis on globalization he worked as project manager at the Research Institute for Applied Knowledge Processing in Ulm with a focus on applied research within the topics of sustainability and entrepreneurial globalization of enterprises. As an assistant professor at the Institute for Corporate Management of the University of Ulm, he founded successfully Polymundo, a globalization consulting company especially for small and medium-sized enterprises. The focus of his engagement is to accompany enterprises during different change processes in the areas of human resources, internationalization, intercultural management and digitization. He teaches strategic management, global business challenges, CSR and research methods at different national and international MBA and Ph.D. studies (Rennes Business School, Andrassy University for example). He is an author/co-author/editor/co-editor of more than 100 scientific publications including several books on CSR (*CSR in China*, Springer/2015; *CSR und Marketing*, Springer/2017; *CSR in Brazil*, Springer/2018; *CSR in Poland*, Springer/2019). He initiated the Heilbronn Declaration a voluntary self-commitment between different SMEs and MNEs with a focus on CSR and its successful implementation.

Florian Urbański (Diplom-Betriebswirt FH) is a Sales Specialist and Customer Representative at BFZ Sp. z.o.o. as well as Intercultural Trainer and Workshop Coordinator for the WrOpenUp Foundation. He studied Business Administration in the Biberach University of Applied Sciences and has experiences in sales, marketing and project management as well as in youth and adult education. Main scientific interests are in intercultural communication and competence, Polish-German business relations and projects of corporate social responsibility.

Jubin Jacob John is a doctoral candidate at the La Trobe Business School. Jubin is an SAP-certified professional currently researching in the area of sustainable supply chain management. He has worked/consulted in several industries including electrical engineering, telecommunications, entertainment and education. He has published in the area of fresh produce supply chain management and education, and his research interests are in the area of augmented reality, blended learning, sustainability and supply chain management.

Maia Shekriladze, MBA, is a native Georgian having Diploma in International Business—Intercultural Studies (2008) and MBA in General Management (2017). Her MBA thesis was on "Corporate sustainability in the globalized world, developing a tool to measure corporate sustainability of SMEs of the home improvement sector in Germany", which was successfully presented at the USASBE Conference in January 2018 in Los Angeles. She is passionate about the following topics:

intercultural competence, ethical management and business ethics, corporate social responsibility and corporate sustainability.

Majid Khan is currently pursuing his doctoral degree at Massey Business School, Massey University, New Zealand. Broadly, his research focusses on how business organizations report corporate social responsibility, and how institutional environment shapes the reporting behaviour especially in developing countries. In particular, his Ph.D. research investigates how and why institutional pressures of conformity lead business organizations to decouple reporting of CSR from its actual practice.

Mari Kooskora, Ph.D., is a Head of the EBS Centre for Business Ethics, researcher and trainer who has expertise in business ethics, CSR, sustainability, leadership, corporate governance, diversity, public relations, organizational behaviour, social entrepreneurship and related fields. She has teaching and training experience in Estonia as well as in Finland, Lithuania, Latvia, Slovenia, France, Switzerland, Norway, Sweden, the UK and Canada for more than 20 years. She is the author of research papers published in nationally and internationally recognized journals and has given numerous conference presentations. Her main research interests are ethics and responsibility in business and leadership, sustainability and women in leadership. As a board member of CSR Forum Estonia and member of European Business Ethics Network (EBEN), EABIS CSR Research Network, IESE BS Alumni, Business and Professional Women Estonia and earlier also Transparency International Estonia and several other international networks, she is actively contributing to the development of more balanced and sustainable business and leadership.

Martin T. Knopp is a research associate at the Institute for Compliance and Corporate Law (ICU) at the German Graduate School of Management and Law GmbH (GGS) in Heilbronn and a Ph.D. candidate at Zeppelin University in Friedrichshafen. He is also working for the Interdisciplinary Center for Compliance, Integrity and Law (CIL)—a cooperation between the GGS and the Zeppelin University in Friedrichshafen. His research areas are corporate compliance, corporate crime, corporate governance and corporate (social) responsibility. Martin T. Knopp obtained a Master of Laws (LL.M.) in International Economic Law at the University of Augsburg, a Master of Laws (LL.M.) in State and Administration in Europe at the German University of Administrative Sciences Speyer and a Master of Mediation (MM) at the FernUniversität in Hagen.

Meeta Sengupta, FRSA, board member and founder/investor, is a writer, speaker and advisor on education with a cross-country perspective on policy, skills and pedagogies. She has written extensively on school systems and impact, pedagogies and processes, assessments and outcomes, teachers and leaders and education gaps and funding. She is a Fellow of the Royal Society of Arts (FRSA), and a Salzburg Fellow, among other affiliations. She has been a regular columnist and op-ed writer including the *Forbes* blog, the *Times of India* blog, the *Daily Pioneer*, the *Indian*

Express, *DNA*, the *Hindustan Times* and more and has been quoted in the *Voice of America*, *DNA* and many other publications across media. She has been a keynote speaker and panellist at national and international gatherings, on television and now online events. She has advised organizations including highly ranked think tanks and universities. She is also the Founder of the Centre for Education Strategy that runs projects such as the School Safety Campaign, the Communities as Learning Aids, #Eduin (online conversations on education issues) and more. Meeta Sengupta is a keen writer, observer and a builder of communities and institutions.

Nayan Mitra, Ph.D., is the Founder-Director of Sustainable Advancements (OPC) Private Limited that broadly aims to promote the Sustainable Development Goals (SDGs) through advocacy and implementation (www.sustainableadvancements.com). Under her leadership, Sustainable Advancements has established itself as a holistic institution of international repute in the area of corporate social responsibility (CSR), sustainability and corporate governance—coaching, consultancy and research on one side and developing and promoting innovative, responsible and sustainable products on the other. Dr. Mitra is a Ph.D. in the subject of CSR (Management); is editor of the books *Corporate Social Responsibility in India: Cases and Development after the Legal Mandate* in India (2017) and *Mandated Corporate Social Responsibility: Evidence from India* (2019) with co-editor, Dr. René Schmidpeter; and is Academic Council member and Science Board member in International Academic forums. She works closely with some of the eminent corporations and civil societies of India and is a pro-bono member of the Advisory Council and Board of some of the eminent NGOs in India, whose work has received global recognition. Dr. Mitra was a finalist of the Chevening Gurukul Scholarship for Leadership and Excellence (2013) by the British Deputy High Commission; recipient of the prestigious Author Award at the Indian CSR Leadership Summit three years in a row: 2017, 2018 and 2019; adjudged as one of the 25 most impactful CSR Leaders in India 2019 and many other international awards for her contribution to CSR; and recognized as an Exceptional Woman of Excellence at the Women Economic Forum, 2019 (New Delhi, India). A staunch believer and proponent of women's empowerment (#SDG 6), she is the Kolkata Influencer for Womennovator, 2019–2020; Mentor at Aspire for Her; and an active member of All Ladies League, Kolkata.

Navin K. Veerapa, Ph.D., is a Visiting Professor of Marketing at Saint Mary's College of California. He is a nurturer of productive relationships with the business community and is passionate about research supervision and pastoral care. His research, in the area of agribusiness and sustainable supply chain management, has been published in *Acta Horticulturae* ranked by the USDA as a premier research journal in agricultural sustainability. His work has been presented at international practitioner conferences in the Asia-Pacific region. Dr. Veerapa has also conducted industry-funded research addressing the commercialization of new nanomaterials and sales in the Australian car industry. He has also lectured and taught a wide variety of business and marketing courses at a number of universities in Australia.

Nika Salvetti graduated in Economics with cum laude, whereby she left Italy and engaged in development work and field research for 15 years in war-affected countries. Currently, she is working on her Ph.D. at Nyenrode Business University on social responsible behaviours of local business leaders in the ready-made garment sector of Bangladesh. She spent 3 years in Bangladesh where she conducted her field research and taught at BRAC University/Governance Department, the American International University of Dhaka (AIUB). She is currently living in Vietnam where she is actively engaged in teaching on social responsibility and CSR as well as topics related to sustainability and peace at the UN Mandated University for Peace in Costa Rica, at the University of Economics of Ho Chi Minh/Institute of Business Studies and at the University of Technology/MSM Maastricht. She is the co-founder of Rethink Plastic Vietnam and the Advanced Leadership Programme for Sustainability.

Omer Nazir is currently pursuing his doctoral degree at Massey Business School, Massey University, New Zealand. Broadly, his research challenges the penchant for underpinning debt bondage as individualized relations between the debtor and the creditor to unpack the systemic economic, political and symbolic relations that help it to sustain. In particular, his Ph.D. research, via ethnographic study in Indian brick kilns, explores the structural factors that lead to bondage in a bid to reconceptualize modern slavery.

Rahizah Sulaiman has recently completed her doctoral degree from the School of Management, Massey University, New Zealand. Her research interest includes the subjects of organizational behaviour, human resource development, business ethics and sustainability.

René Schmidpeter, Ph.D., holds the Dr. Juergen Meyer Endowed Chair of International Business Ethics and Corporate Social Responsibility at Cologne Business School (CBS). He is the director of the Center for Advanced Sustainable Management (CASM) at CBS, General Secretary of the World Institute for Ethics and Sustainability (WISE) as well as Vice President of the Global Corporate Governance Institute and Ethics in Rising Economies (WISE). He is the series editor for Springer's *CSR, Sustainability, Ethics and Governance* books, section editor of the *Encyclopedia of Corporate Social Responsibility* (ECSR) and an editor of the *Dictionary of Corporate Social Responsibility* (DCSR) as well as editor-in-chief of the *International Journal of CSR* (IJCSR). His research and teaching activities focus on the management of corporate social responsibility, international perspectives on sustainability, social innovation and sustainable entrepreneurship as well as the relationship between business and society. He is also the Founder of the www.M3TRIX.de sustainability consultancy.

Sumona Ghosh, Ph.D., has been associated with St. Xavier's College, Kolkata, India, since 2002. Presently, she is the Head of Business Regulatory Framework in the Department of Commerce. After completing her postgraduation in commerce with rare distinction, Prof. Ghosh has been conferred with the Ph.D. in Business Management by the University of Calcutta on 31st of July 2014. Her area of research was on corporate social responsibility (CSR). The title of her doctoral dissertation was "Pattern of participation of public and private sector companies in corporate social responsibility activities". She has published in journals of national and international repute. Dr. Ghosh has been highly acclaimed for her guest lectures on CSR in premier institutes of higher learning including the Indian Institute of Management (Calcutta) and Indian Institute of Management (Shillong). She has taken sessions in Management Development Programmes conducted by premier institutes on CSR. She has presented papers on CSR at various national and international conferences.

Ülane Vilumets is a serial entrepreneur in the travel field, having founded among other companies a niche travel site Like A Local, which has won several startup awards and design prizes. Her background is from human resources and after obtaining a BA and an MBA from the Estonian Business School, she has taught human resource planning (since 2011) and entrepreneurship and market validation (since 2015) in Estonian Entrepreneurship University of Applied Sciences. Her interest in contemporary HR concepts and startup ecosystems initiated the study on meaningfulness of work among the participants of startup events. Ülane has been committed to bring more women into business through numerous speeches at business conferences in the Baltics.

Umashankar Venkatesh, Ph.D., is a Professor of Marketing and the Director of the Post Graduate Program in Management at the Great Lakes Institute of Management, Gurgaon, India. With a Ph.D. in Management, and graduate qualifications in management and agricultural economics, he has worked for more than 30 years in business education, research and industry. He is published nationally and internationally in the realm of—consumer behaviour, services, brands, ethical marketing and branding, etc. and is on the editorial board of various research journals. He has designed and conducted training programmes for senior executives from corporations; civil services, academic institutions and NGOs in the areas of marketing and service orientation; customer centricity; and organizational design, ethics, institution building, etc.

Waqar Ahmad is currently pursuing his doctoral degree at Kunming University of Science and Technology, China. Broadly, his research focuses on how leaning organization disciplines are perceived by the faculty members at the university level, and further how this concept can be developed in higher education institutions in developing countries context. Further, his Ph.D. research investigates how trust climate plays a significant role in employees' performance in an organization.

About the Editors

Nayan Mitra comes with a rich mix of diverse professional experience, in which she straddles seamlessly between academics, social and corporate sectors. She has many years of experience in coaching undergraduate, postgraduate students and corporate members in the areas of CSR and corporate governance and editing and publishing over 35 peer-reviewed research publications in international journals and books, and she is Academic Council member and Science Board member in International Conferences. Dr. Mitra is the editor of the books *Corporate Social Responsibility in India: Cases and Development after the Legal Mandate* in India (2017) and *Mandated Corporate Social Responsibility: Evidence from India* (2019) with co-editor, Dr. René Schmidpeter. She spearheads the India CSR Leadership Interview Series by India CSR, where she brings together the collective thoughts, ideas and practices of distinguished leaders. She works closely with some of the eminent corporations and civil societies of India and is a pro-bono member of the Advisory Council and Board of some of the eminent NGOs in India, whose work has received global recognition. Dr. Mitra was a finalist of the prestigious Chevening Gurukul Scholarship for Leadership and Excellence (2013), by the FCO, British Deputy High Commission; recipient of the prestigious Author Award at the Indian CSR Leadership Summit three years in a row: 2017, 2018 and 2019; and adjudged as one of the 25 most impactful CSR Leaders in India 2019 and many other international awards for her contribution to CSR. She was recognized as an Exceptional Woman of Excellence at the Women Economic Forum, 2019 (New Delhi, India). Her startup, Sustainable Advancements, broadly aims to promote the 5Ps of the Sustainable Development Goals (SDGs) or the Global Goals, viz. people, planet, prosperity, peace and partnerships (as laid down by the United Nations) through advocacy and implementation (www.sustainableadvancements.com).

René Schmidpeter holds the Dr. Juergen Meyer Endowed Chair of International Business Ethics and Corporate Social Responsibility at Cologne Business School (CBS). General Secretary of the World Institute for Ethics and Sustainability (WISE) as well as Vice President of the Global Corporate Governance Institute. He is the series editor for Springer's *CSR, Sustainability, Ethics and Governance* books, section editor of the *Encyclopedia of Corporate Social Responsibility* (ECSR) and an editor of the *Dictionary of Corporate Social Responsibility* (DCSR) as well as editor-in-chief of the *International Journal of CSR* (IJCSR). His research and teaching activities focus on the management of corporate social responsibility, international perspectives on sustainability, social innovation and sustainable entrepreneurship as well as the relationship between business and society. He is also the Founder of the www.M3TRIX.de sustainability consultancy.

Contributors

Waqar Ahmad Kunming University of Science and Technology, Kunming, China

Arabinda Bhattacharya University of Calcutta, Kolkata, India

C. Eller School of Business, Innovation and Entrepreneurship, Melbourne Polytechnic, Melbourne, Australia

Sumona Ghosh St. Xavier's College, Kolkata, India

J. Jacob-John La Trobe University, Melbourne, Australia

Ameeta Jain Deakin University, Melbourne, VIC, Australia

Akanksha Jumde Deakin University, Melbourne, VIC, Australia

Majid Khan Massey University, Palmerston North, New Zealand

Martin Tobias Knopp German Graduate School of Management and Law gGmbH, Heilbronn, Germany

Mari Kooskora Estonian Business School, Tallinn, Estonia

Bonnie Lewtas TurtlCo, Amsterdam, Netherlands

Nayan Mitra Sustainable Advancements (OPC) Private Limited, Kolkata, India

Omer Nazir Massey Business School, Massey University, Palmerston North, New Zealand

André Nijhof Nyenrode Business Universiteit, Breukelen, Netherlands

Nika Salvetti Nyenrode Business Universiteit, Netherlands

René Schmidpeter World Institute of Sustainability and Ethics (WISE), Cologne, Germany

Meeta Sengupta Centre for Education Strategy, New Delhi, India

Maia Shekriladze German Graduate School of Management and Law (GGS), Heilbronn, Germany

Christopher Stehr German Graduate School of Management and Law, Heilbronn, Germany

Rahizah Sulaiman Massey Business School, Massey University, Palmerston North, New Zealand

Florian Urbański Hewlett Packard Enterprise, Wrocław, Poland

N. K. Veerapa St. Marys College of California, Moraga, CA, USA

Umashankar Venkatesh Great Lakes Institute of Management, Gurgaon, India

Ülane Vilumets Estonian Entrepreneurship University of Applied Sciences, Tallinn, Estonia

Abbreviations

AA	Association Agreement
ACCA	Association of Chartered Certified Accountants
ACCESS	Advancing CSO Capacities and Engaging Society for Sustainability
ACCORD	Action for Community Organisation, Rehabilitation and Development
ALLIANCE	Alliance for Bangladesh Worker Safety
ASV	Adherence to standards and shared values
ATS	African Traditional Society
BGMEA	Bangladesh Garment Manufacturers and Exporters Association
BP	British Petroleum
BRICS	Brazil, Russia, India, China and South Africa
BRR	Business Responsibility Report
CEO	Chief executive officer
CIA	Central Intelligence Agency
CiDA	Civil Development Agency
CMWS	Comprehensive Meaningful Work scale
CPEC	China-Pakistan Economic Corridor
CPI	Corruption Perceptions Index
CPSE	Central Public Sector Enterprises
CR	Corporate reporting
CSI	Corporate social investment
CSO	Civil society organizations
CSR	Corporate social responsibility
CSRDI	Centre for Strategic Research and Development
DSDG	Division for Sustainable Development Goals
EAS	Enterprise Estonia
EC	European Commission
EDA	Entrepreneurship Development Agency
e.g.	exempli gratia, for example
EM	Emerging market
EMAS	Environmental Management and Audit Scheme

EU	European Union
EWMI	East West Management Institute
f.	and the following one
FAO	Food and Agriculture Organization of the United Nations
FCPA	Foreign Corrupt Practices Act
ff	following pages
FIFA	Federation Internationale de Football Association
FMCG	Fast-moving consumer goods
FOP	Forum Odpowiedzalnego Biznesu
FY	Financial year
GDP	Gross domestic product
GHG	Greenhouse Gas
GRI	Global Reporting Initiative
GPN	Global Production Networks
GSP	Generalised Scheme of Preferences
GUS	Główny Urząd Statystyczny
HRD	Human resource development
H1N1	Swine flu
H7N9	Bird flu
i.a.	inter alia, among others
IBGE	Instituto Brasileiro de Geografia e Estatística
ICT	Information and communications technology
i.e.	id est, that is
IFC	International Finance Corporation
ILO	International Labour Organization
IMF	International Monetary Fund
INR	Indian Rupee
IPCC	Intergovernmental Panel on Climate Change
IR	Integrated reporting
IIR	Internal integrated report
IIRC	International Integrated Reporting Council
IRI	Integrated Reporting Index
ISBUSJ	International Black Sea University Scientific Journal
ISO	The International Organization for Standardization
IT	Information technology
JDS	Job Diagnostic Survey
JIT	Just in time
KMBL	Kotak Mahindra Bank Limited
MCA	Ministry of Corporate Affairs
MFA	Multi Fibre Arrangement
MNC	Multinational companies/corporation
MNE	Multinational enterprise
MOU	Memorandum of understanding
MS	Microsoft

MUFG	Mitsubishi UFJ Financial Group
MWI	Meaningful Work Inventory
NGO	Non-governmental organization
NIMBY	Not in my backyard
NPO	Non-profit organization
NTPA	National Tripartite Agreement
NVGs	National voluntary guidelines
OECD	Organisation for Economic Co-operation and Development
OHS	Occupational health and safety
PKR	Pakistan Rupee
plc.	Public limited company
PROLoG	Promoting Rule of Law in Georgia
RCS	Responsible confined sourcing
RFSCM	Responsible food supply chain management
RSC	Responsible supply chain
RSCM	Responsible supply chain management
S.A.	Sociedade Anônima
SBI	State Bank of India
SBSR	Small business social responsibility
SDGs	Sustainable Development Goals
SEBI	Securities and Exchange Board of India
SMEs	Small and medium enterprises
SMEDA	Small and Medium Enterprise Development Authority
SP	Sustainable practices
SRB	Social responsibility of business
SSA	Sub-Saharan Africa
SSCM	Sustainable supply chain management
Tk	Taka
TSR	Traditional sustainability reporting
T& C	Transparent and collaborative
UK	United Kingdom
UN	United Nations
UNDESA	United Nations Department of Economic and Social Affairs
UNDP	United Nations Development Programme
UNESCO	United Nations Educational, Scientific and Cultural Organization
UNGC	United Nations Global Compact
UNICEF	United Nations International Children's Emergency Fund
UNIDO	United Nations Industrial Development Organization
UNI Global	Union Network International Global
UN-SDGs	United Nations Sustainable Development Goals
UNWMO	United Nations World Meteorological Organization
US	United States
USA	United States of America
USAID	United States Agency for International Development

USD	United States Dollar
USSR	Union of Soviet Socialist Republics
USTDA	United States Trade and Development Act
WAMI	Work as Meaning Inventory
WB	World Bank
WBCSD	World Business Council for Sustainable Development
WTO	World Trade Organization
WWF	World Wildlife Fund

List of Figures

List of Tables

The Future of the UN Sustainable Development Goals: Business Perspectives for Global Development in 2030

René Schmidpeter, Nayan Mitra, and Bonnie Lewtas

1 Introduction

In the midst of writing this article, a force invisible to the human eye is sweeping across the planet; forcing the world to come to a grinding halt. It stops not at borders, cares not about intentions, plans or laws, and for the first time in history, has forced every global citizen to come together; by staying apart. Of course, we are talking about the corona virus: COVID-19.

With the news about the state of the pandemic evolving on an hourly basis and grim reports from hospitals as exponential as the spread itself, it is difficult to write with any degree of certainty what the impact will be on life as we know it in the coming days, months, and even years.

Buried within the widespread loss of life, pleas from healthcare workers on the front lines, economic turmoil and fear for the future, we see glimmers of hope. From physicians coming out of retirement to serve their communities, to balcony choirs keeping spirits high, businesses shutting their doors before being sanctioned to do so, and student's leaving notes in apartment buildings offering to get groceries for the elderly.

We have seen experts sharing top-research and science with each other, governments working tirelessly to arrange financial support to SME's, online global

R. Schmidpeter (✉)
World Institute of Sustainability and Ethics (WISE), Cologne, Germany
e-mail: schmidpeter@m3trix.de

N. Mitra
Sustainable Advancements (OPC) Private Limited, Kolkata, India

B. Lewtas
TurtlCo, Amsterdam, Netherlands
e-mail: bonnie@turtlco.com

N. Mitra, R. Schmidpeter (eds.), *Corporate Social Responsibility in Rising Economies*, CSR, Sustainability, Ethics & Governance,
https://doi.org/10.1007/978-3-030-53775-3_1

isolation parties, viral hand-washing dance-off videos, and people risking their lives to check on other people's stranded pets. Most importantly, we are seeing targeted collaboration between individuals, business, science, and politics on a global level that most of us never thought possible.

However easy it is to be consumed by negative reports, a fear of the unknown, and criticism of certain political, corporate, or individual responses, we must notice the undeniable trend of compassion, camaraderie, and most importantly, a united global response to a borderless issue; exactly what is required for the United Nations Sustainable Development Goals (UN-SDGs). From the smallest island to the biggest city, local action with international coordination is leading to global results.

2 A Lesson from the Virus

Environmental advocates and climate scientists have long since pleaded for a united front to reduce global greenhouse gas (GHG) emissions. Nothing has yet to force it upon us quite like the corona virus. Industry came to a halt, planes grounded by the thousands, and cruise ships stayed in their ports. Reports are emerging that we are in the midst of the largest drop in GHG since World War II. These impacts are likely to be short-lived and therefore, not have a direct significant impact on climate change. However, in cities such as New Delhi, we can already see a clear reduction in smog and pollution.

In a virtual press conference, Lars Peter Riishojgaard of the Geneva based United Nations World Meteorological Organization (UNWMO) stated that, we can see this as an experiment and that "It will lead some people, and perhaps also some governments to rethink." He compared it to the 2008 Beijing Olympics during which China scaled down environmental production, "They demonstrated very clearly that you can absolutely, if you have enough control over the situation, you can turn off the air pollution." Although we should not claim much of a "climate victory" yet, this should empower us. It demonstrates that when the sense of urgency is there, we can coordinate globally.

From different countries, backgrounds and writing on various topics, every author in this book represents a piece of the puzzle. Not only do we encourage you to read their insights, but we hope they inspire you to act. Only together can we turn this "experiment" into a lesson on how to tackle international issues quicker and more efficiently than ever before.

3 Analyze, Restructure, Relaunch

This series has never been about simply halting economic activity to save the environment. Rather it is about redesigning the business paradigm to work for us. It is about targeted economic activity that in its DNA is socially beneficial and environmentally regenerative. It is about taking a hard and honest look at our economies and asking ourselves, what do we really need to thrive on the long-term? What do we need to truly be happy? How can authentic progress be measured? And, what does sustainable development really mean?

As tough as the current crisis may be, it has forced us to do just that; to take off our rose-colored glasses and make the hard distinction between essential and non-essential goods and services. It is highlighting the weaknesses but also the strengths in our social and economic systems and showing us exactly where our vulnerabilities lie.

For years, this series has been calling for a dismantling of "business as usual" and now we would like to drive that message home: As entrepreneurs, politicians, and citizens, the coming months will largely determine the fate of our future. Never before have we had a better opportunity to analyze and most importantly strategically restructure the way our societies and businesses operate.

An abrupt scale-down of global economic activity of this magnitude does not come by often, and we have to use it to our advantage. We have to reevaluate the way we do business and we have to do it now.

In 2015, during an interview about sustainable development, the chief engineer of a prominent resort in the British Virgin Islands told us: "Every engineers dream would be to shut down and build everything from scratch. However, because of the high level of occupancy, that will never happen. (Our resort) is such an expensive property to run that it is not possible to shut down." While this was many years ago, this quotation is relevant to today's situation. All these years, sustainable development specialists around the world have been fantasizing about how much easier it would be if we could just hit pause on the economy, restructure it to be more sustainable, and then press start again.

At this time, the most significant threat to our survival and the systems that support us is not the virus itself, but rather wasting this time of near "economic standstill", and once it passes, continuing with business as usual. If we allow that to happen, the one thing we can say for certain is that this will not be the last time, and next time it is likely to hit much harder.

The current situation can be compared to a hurricane, but on a global level. An island can get hit hard by a hurricane once and bounce back. Some can get hit twice and bounce back. But get hit a third time within a couple of years, without having put the systems in place to mitigate the effects, and what you are left with is such utter devastation that you are not even sure if it's worth trying to put the pieces back together. Let's not be that island. Let's learn from our mistakes and use the framework of the United Nations Sustainable Development Goals to guide the fundamental restructuring of the way we live, eat, work, and play. Let's create dynamic businesses that are prepared, at the drop of a hat, to adapt from supplying things we want to things we need.

3.1 *Expecting the Unexpected vs. Neglecting the Predicted*

Sustainable development is about future proofing our economies and "expecting the unexpected." It is about getting real with ourselves about why we are so complacent about future risks and so focused on immediate gratification. Let us be honest, the threat of a global pandemic was not a surprise, hurricanes in the Caribbean were not a surprise, the wildfires in Australia were not a surprise. All of this was not only predictable, it was predicted. We did not know exactly when it was going to happen, or how bad it would be, but we knew the risk was there and we chose not to be prepared. We must agree once and for all that it is simpler and cheaper to act and not react.

3.2 *True Cost*

The current pandemic is pointing a spotlight on the industries which have been unsustainable all along. They have been disguised by an unrelenting demand for their products at an unsubstantiated low cost. While there are many industries which need to be completely reformed if we are to achieve the SDGs, three come to mind: transportation (airlines), tourism (cruises) and agriculture; specifically, animal agriculture. What do these industries have in common? They are excessively environmentally degrading as well as sold far cheaper than they should be. When the price of a product does not represent the true cost of that product, with regards to environmental and social costs, it is inherently unsustainable. In fact, investment banks around the world are finally starting to take notice of this and calculate it into their risk management strategies.

That being said, we are not proposing mere price increases. We are proposing a deep analysis into why these industries are so "cheap" and who is really footing the bill. Then we should ask ourselves, for each individual case: At the "true cost", can we justify this product? And if yes, how should it be? Here, we take a look into each of these industries and examine why they are being highlighted in the face of COVID-19, what we can learn from their mistakes, and what impact they are having on the SDGs.

3.2.1 Airlines

Virtually everyone living in Europe who cares even remotely about sustainability has run into this common situation: You want to get from point A to point B in a sustainable but also cost-effective and time-efficient way. You search for trains, for example, from Cologne to Berlin and find that, for the date you want, the direct train is being sold for 90 €, meanwhile there is a flight for 15. Determined to find another way, you check coach busses and are happy to find one for 10 €, until you realize it takes an absurd 9 h to reach the destination. The fact is that it is not the train that is overpriced, or the bus that takes too many stops along the way, the flight is simply being offered at a an unrealistically low price.

Flights have become so cheap that many businesses fly their employees all over the world on a daily basis for meetings, which we now know can take place from home. Price undercutting is rampant among the airline industries and in order to stay competitive, profit margins are cut so close that they are left dependent on government bailouts. Even though aviation is one of the leading sources of greenhouse gas emissions, and climate change is costing economies billions each year, aviation fuel is exempt from tax in most countries, while other fuel is not.

This mismatch between the true cost of flights and the actual cost, leads to some very noteworthy and unsustainable behavior by the industry, which the COVID-19 pandemic has put to light. For example, airlines have been called out by media channels for flying "ghost flights", virtually empty from airport to airport in a sort of high-stakes poker game. The price: protecting slots on their most profitable routes.

The global scientific consensus for years has been that climate change is the most existential threat to not only our economies, but our very existence as a species. Yet in the name of competitive advantage, airlines did not hesitate to spew unnecessary GHG emissions into the atmosphere. This is a clear example of placing short-term profits above Corporate Social Responsibility (CSR) and demonstrates a complete disregard for people and the planet. Meanwhile, after a week or two of reduced operation, airlines which have been around for nearly a century threatened bankruptcy, and to lay off all of their employees if the government does not bail them out with taxpayer money. Still think that train is looking too expensive?

We would like to draw attention to the absurdity of that scenario by proposing an analogy: Imagine you have been working for 100 years and you do not even have enough money set aside to support your family for several weeks or months in the event that you stop receiving a paycheck. While this might seem like an unreasonable comparison, the fact is that at this very moment many people are being forced to rely on their savings; and it is highly unlikely that they have had 100 years to prepare.

Why are the airlines in such a situation that they cannot afford a short period of reduced income without going under? With a basic analysis of the risks, it would not have been hard to predict that at some point there would be a situation like COVID-19. We can certainly already predict that it will not be the last.

So why are businesses not managing their risks? Why do we not hold industry to the same standards (or even higher) than we hold ourselves? Why is industry permitted to pollute, play with money, and make few people extremely wealthy, while someone else foots the bill? These are all questions that we must ask ourselves if we are to redesign our economies in a way that is compatible with the achievement of the UNSDGs. We must finally start looking at the entire puzzle, as only then can we understand the intricacies of each piece and how they relate to each other.

Update: In the midst of editing this article, airlines in the US were awarded the 58-billion-dollar bailout package they requested.

Why are we so dependent on a paycheck from a company that we bend over backwards to keep it afloat at any cost? Will companies ever learn to manage their risks if someone else foots the bill? Could their downfall have led to sustainable innovation and leave room for something better? These are fundamental questions we need to start asking. We are not necessarily against subsidies in the face of unprecedented and unpredictable catastrophes, but the ends have to justify the means. Humanity is in the midst of a losing battle against climate change. We can no longer afford to cater to the unsustainable behavior of companies, which could have done better, but chose not to. Perhaps that $58 billion could have been better spent furthering the development of emission free high-speed transportation, creating thousands of jobs; rather than putting a Band-Aid on an industry that was unsustainable all along.

"Jobs vs. the environment is a false choice—there are millions of jobs to be had fighting climate change and protecting the environment. Addressing the environmental crisis offers up the largest job creation project since WW2."

3.2.2 Cruise Ships

During the initial stages of the virus spreading across international borders, something rather peculiar was a common sight on official disease reports: Amongst the list of number of confirmed cases per country, was the Diamond Princess cruise ship. Quarantine efforts on a ship that initially began with a handful of cases, ended up a breeding ground for COVID-19. It ultimately resulted in over 700 infected patients, 8 of whom died. The situation was extremely unfortunate, and there is no doubt that mistakes were made. However, we will focus on the behavior of the industry in the days and weeks which followed; once cruise companies undeniably understood the risks.

On March 14, 2020, over a month after the Diamond Princess tragedy, reports began to emerge of large cruise companies bullying Caribbean islands to loosen their health regulations; pushing to allow thousands of passengers, many of which could be carrying COVID-19 to debark at their ports. Caribbean islands have already fragile economies, which are extremely vulnerable to external risks. This however did not sway the industry from doing what they often do: threatening to pull their business if the islands do not cater to their demands.

While this behavior might come as a shock for those not involved in the case of the cruise industry in the Caribbean, it is actually very "in character" and representative of the relationship between large cruise companies and small islands. Basically, "Do what we say, or we will go somewhere that will." Cruise ships have been pushing their way into island economies for so long now that many islands became dependent on them as one of the only sources of income.

But how sustainable are the effects? Do cruise ships really provide a long-lasting benefit for the islands which they visit? Do they stimulate highly qualified jobs in the marketplace? Do they demonstrate environmental stewardship? Is sustainability in the DNA of the industry?

If we examine the DNA of the tourism industry, although it is not always conducted this way, there is an argument that can be made for environmental and social benefits going hand in hand with profitability. Tourists do not want to go to a polluted destination with low safety and social standards. Therefore, the "stationary" operators like hotels and restaurants are bound by a basic principal that is in line with the SDGs: Keep the environment beautiful and the product high-quality, or no one will want to visit anymore.

Unfortunately, this is not a model that the cruise industry must adhere to. That is because they are mobile. If their activities destroy a certain bay or even entire destination, they will simply go somewhere else. If the price is too high, or the health and safety regulations too strict, they will simply go somewhere else. Now for the first time, cruise ships are finding themselves with "nowhere else to go" and the results for the people aboard are disastrous.

Passengers often have such a limited time to explore the destinations and such an unauthentic view, they will likely not even have time to notice the destruction left behind. This is all part of the model and it represents the kind of "throw away" mentality that is not compatible with the SDGs.

While the case can be made for the economic interest of hotels protecting their host countries, can it be made for large cruise ships? Is there really a place for an industry, which is inherently programed to this type of behavior? If yes, how can we design it differently? Businesses of the future are ones that profit from win-win-win situations; protecting the planet and people and therefore their prosperity—not vice versa. The cruise ship challenges with COVID-19 may seem like isolated events during unprecedented times. In reality however, they shine a light on the inadequate regard for social responsibility of an industry responsible for the vacations of 30 million people annually.

3.2.3 Our Relationship with Other Species

There is still some debate as to the exact origins of COVID-19, however it is widely considered to be zoonotic in nature. Regardless of whether it was passed on through a bat, or a pangolin, or another species, pandemic after pandemic has demonstrated that there is something wrong with the way humans interact with animals. Ebola, SARS, MERS, Influenza A and even HIV migrated to humans through animals. It is not only exotic animals that pose a risk to human health, H1N1 (Swine Flu) was transmitted through pigs and H7N9 (bird flu) was transmitted through chickens. Around the world, it is estimated that 60% of all known infectious diseases can be transmitted from animals; and that 75% of new infectious diseases come from animals.

Are animals the enemy? Pandemics rarely spread from harmonious coexistence with animals, but rather systematic exploitation of animals and their ecosystems; whether for food or other use. Until we stop viewing animals as products, to use and exploit as we please, we will continue to suffer the consequences. COVID-19 pales in comparison to other risks associated with animal exploitation. Animal agriculture is a major contributor to global greenhouse gas emissions, but also the leading cause of species extinction, habitat destruction, water pollution and ocean dead zones.

Oceans and forests are the lungs of our planet. We survive when they survive. We thrive when they thrive. How we treat other species has a direct impact on our health and well-being, from a social, environmental and economic standpoint. How are we doing on maintaining our life-support systems? It is estimated that more than 150 billion terrestrial and marine animals are slaughtered every year. At the time of writing this paper (beginning of April, 2020), in the US (United States of America) alone, 14 billion 385 thousand animals have already been killed for food since the start of 2020 (animalclock.org).

In 2018, a first-of-its-kind study was conducted by Bar-On, Phillips, and Milo on the composition of the earth's biomass. The researchers found that livestock accounts for 50% more biomass than humans, and exceeds wild animals and birds collectively tenfold. The study found that a shocking 70% of all birds on the planet are farmed poultry. And if that isn't scary enough, with regards to mammals, 60% are livestock (mainly cattle and pigs), 36% are humans, and a mere 4% are wild animals.

Aside from the obvious loss of biodiversity and ethical arguments, what does this have to do with business and the UNSDGs? Resources. All of these animals need to eat, they need to drink, and they produce exuberant amounts of waste. In **June 2018, the Journal of Science published a report by Poore and Nemecek** on the impacts of global food production. It is arguably the most comprehensive study ever conducted on the topic and examined 38,700 farms, 1600 processors, packaging types, and retailers spanning 119 countries. The study assessed the full impact of the most popular 40 foods eaten (which make up 90% of the global diet) and examined the entire life cycle including land use, GHG emissions, freshwater use, water pollution, and air pollution. The findings are that while livestock produces only 18% of calories and 37% of protein, it accounts for 83% of farmland and 60% of agriculture based GHG emissions.

It is important to look at the true cost of these products. Aside from the associated environmental and social costs, the cost of resource inputs is also not reflective of the price. In **September 2019, The Global Consultation Report of the Food and Land Use Coalition** found that only 1% of the $700 billion taxpayer subsidies goes to sustainable forms of agriculture, while the rest supports cattle production, deforestation and pollution from the overuse of fertilizers. In the US, it is estimated taxpayers subsidize the animal food system with $38 billion annually. This may represent as much as $2 for every $1 of product sold **(Meatonomics, 2017).**

Considering the massive impact of animal agriculture on the environment, the question arises if it is necessary, or even beneficial for human health? In 2016, the Academy of Nutrition and Dietetics, which is comprised of 100,000 dietetics professionals holding undergraduate and advanced degrees in nutrition and dietetics, released a peer-reviewed statement on the topic: "It is the position of the Academy of Nutrition and Dietetics that appropriately planned vegetarian, including vegan, diets are healthful, nutritionally adequate, and may provide health benefits for the prevention and treatment of certain diseases." Plant-based businesses around the world are booming and demonstrating the health, economic, and environmental benefits of a more compassionate way of relating to animals.

4 Businesses of the Future

The silver lining is that as citizens, as governments, and as businesses we have the power to change. The science is clear about what we have to do to mitigate climate change and the UNSDGs help us as guiding principles to design business differently. There are already examples of this around the world. Whether that be in food, transport, or tourism, or any of the other topics which will follow in this book; innovative minds are finding entrepreneurial solutions to the world's biggest challenges.

In the coming chapters, you will find a wealth of knowledge by change-makers from around the world. Jubin Jacob John presents the topic of responsible food supply chain management. Mari Kooskora takes a dive into the role of meaningful work with regards to entrepreneurial activities and start-up events. Meeta Sengupta discusses CSR in the education sector in rising economies.

After establishing the fundamentals and approaches, we take a dive into country-specific studies, starting with Majid Kahn, who takes us to Pakistan with a look into the attitudes of SMEs (Small and Medium Enterprises) on CSR and how even with their small size, they can lead to big impacts. **Nika** uncovers the topic of CSR within the garment Sectors of Bangladesh by reflecting on the challenges of sustainability. Ameeta Jain presents a study of Indian and Asia Pacific Banks under the lens of CSR regulation, ethical obligation, and legitimacy. Christopher Stehr, Maia Schkriladze, Florian Urbanski, and Martin Knopp then bring us to Georgia, Poland, and Brazil for deep dives into the state of CSR in these three very different emerging economies. The section is concluded with a chapter by Sumona Ghosh and Arabinda Bhattacharya on understanding integrated reporting through a study of a selection of Indian companies. In the final section of this book you will find a review by Uma Shankar Venkatesh about CSR in India with cases and developments after the legal mandate.

Just as the role of government is to serve the people, so is the role of business. With an ever-increasing complexity of the global supply chains, it is ever more important that we can make informed decisions about the true costs of products and services. Environmental degradation and societal health risks (like the current pandemic) mean we have to also be able to predict the future costs and manage risks accordingly. The current crisis again reiterates what we have been calling for a long time: simplified, as much as possible localized, and most importantly transparent supply chains that create benefits along the way rather than destruction, risks and shortcuts.

Let us not be fooled. When a company takes a shortcut and sells a product at a low price to gain a competitive advantage, that price will be paid. And it will be paid with interest, whether that is by a developing country, a poor community, or even globally through environmental devastation or a health pandemic. Someone is going to pay. We must realize that when the majority of an economy operates in such a way, we are heading for unprecedented disaster. COVID-19 can be considered a soft warning compared to where we are headed if we do not restructure our entire global economic system to accurately reflect the true cost of goods and services. Emerging economies have a valuable role to play, which is demonstrated in this book.

5 Final Words

Climate change, biodiversity loss, mass migration, social injustice, economic obstacles, trade-wars, and even pandemics are a reality. Looking at the current global social and economic challenges, we need to think about the future of our Businesses as consistently as we did after World War II. The United Nations Sustainable Development Goals represent one of the most powerful political visions in history of our civilization. The SDGs have been signed by almost 200 countries around the world. Addressing critical issues surrounding social, economic and environmental progress, governments and sectors have committed themselves to working towards achieving their ambitious targets.

Business leaders start to see the opportunities, challenges and material topics surrounding the achievement of the UNSDGs in different industries. This broad discourse of sustainable management addresses all kinds of topics—from green financing to energy transition, from responsible supply chain management to innovative sustainable business models and even leadership development and education are seen from a completely new perspective. More and more public debate such as social innovation and the role of entrepreneurs, as well as the establishment of legal sustainability investment frameworks connect to the global SDGs. Thereby the SDGs are fostering a new management paradigm by providing new goals for business besides mere profit maximization.

More and more executives of the world's largest companies are fundamentally questioning the former 'corporate value/shareholder value' business paradigm, which lead to short-term profit orientation as well as to an unacceptable trade-off thinking in management. At the World Economic Forum in Davos as well as all over the world, business leaders are beginning to change their mindset and start implementing the SDGs. For the emerging new leadership, it is obvious that creating sustainable values and having a positive impact on society are just as important—if not more so—than profitability.

The example of the airline, cruise, and agriculture industries show that companies need to realign their business models, minimizing any negative effects and keeping the positive effects for society as high as possible. Most recent academic studies show that, the more positive the impact of a company towards society, the higher the entrepreneurial return. More and more top executives are realizing that the current far-reaching environmental and social changes are leading to unpredictable risks but, at the same time, are also creating unforeseen business opportunities. The SDGs are leading business in this sustainable transformation process of our societies.

How can companies foster sustainable development goals? Europe has invented the idea of the social market economy which provides a good basis for resolving paradoxes, such as the incommensurability of profit and sustainability, thus creating an "eco-social" market economy. But besides the political frameworks we also need to integrate the SDGs systematically in all areas of the business organizations. Instead of an isolated add-on Sustainability Management approach—companies need a holistic sustainable management approach which is purpose driven and creates positive impact for society in all dimensions of the SDGs.

Innovative Companies no longer discuss what 'ought' to be done—but rather strategically increase their sustainable business potential and thus, the "ability" to do more. Thus, they change from a moral oriented sustainability to an action and solution-oriented approach by implementing the SDGs. This leads to a more positive and value-added idea of sustainability. The new mindset of sustainability is no longer a mere matter of avoiding damage, rather the systematic generation of positive impact and achieving the SDGs. Thus, ecological and social topics are not seen from a defensive but from a more proactive perspective—which gives companies new opportunities rather than limitations. This leads to a much more focused idea of sustainable management. Companies identify the real challenges and material issues and do not waste time and resources for unessential questions or mere PR (Public Relation) issues without real impact. The new value-driven management approach targets the Sustainability Sweet Spot—in which the corporate strategy and its derived measures promote social, ecological and economic added- value at the same time. The SDGs will be an entrepreneurial answer to the public discussion about sustainability and become an economic necessity for business survival!

There is no stopping globalization and nor should we. If we want going to live in a globalized society then we have to start dealing with issues like the SDGs on a global level. As the corona virus has taught us so abruptly, sometimes that means simply "staying home." While this was the literal way to deal with the pandemic, with response to other global challenges we can understand it in a metaphorical sense with regards to self-sufficiency, and resource security. We need to at the very least be able to produce and distribute necessary goods and services at a local level. Through global partnerships and borderless cooperation, we can achieve this and so much more. It is what will make the difference between just being able to survive and being able to thrive.

Part I
Fundamentals and Approaches

Responsible Food Supply Chain Management: Cases of Irresponsible Behaviour and Food Fraud

J. Jacob-John, N. K. Veerapa, and C. Eller

Abstract Responsibility is a critical element of today's business. This responsibility transcends the fiscal element of sustainability and encompasses societal and environmental elements. However, through several ethical fiascos in the modern-day supply chain, the impact of irresponsible behaviour has been evidenced many a time. This chapter focuses on the relevance of responsible supply chain management by using stakeholder theory as a theoretical lens. To show the relevance of responsibility in the food supply chain, this chapter evidences two major cases of irresponsible behaviour within the supply chain context; slavery in modern food supply chains and food fraud. A conceptual solution using a four-pronged RSC (Responsible Supply Chain) approach which involves responsible sourcing, greater transparency, sustainable practices, and adherence to shared standards and values is proposed here. The effective implementation of this conceptual solution could mitigate irresponsible supply chain activity and as an extension, improve the responsibility orientation of the entire supply chain.

Keywords CSR · India · Supply chain · Sustainable supply chain management · Responsibility · Triple bottom line · Ethics · Social responsibility · Food fraud · Slavery

J. Jacob-John (✉)
La Trobe University, Melbourne, Australia
e-mail: J.JacobJohn@latrobe.edu.au

N. K. Veerapa
St. Marys College of California, Moraga, CA, USA

C. Eller
School of Business, Innovation and Entrepreneurship, Melbourne Polytechnic, Melbourne, Australia

N. Mitra, R. Schmidpeter (eds.), *Corporate Social Responsibility in Rising Economies*, CSR, Sustainability, Ethics & Governance,
https://doi.org/10.1007/978-3-030-53775-3_2

1 Introduction

Food is central to life. Even in an apocalyptic era, there are only four aspects that are mandatory for the sustenance of human life; air, food, water, and security. In this regard, irrespective of all of life's innovations and advancements, these four aspects are the most pivotal factors.

However, the 'eating' habits of human life have changed, significantly. Hummus, a chickpea-based thick sauce which was consumed within the Middle Eastern world since the last millennia has the Australian palate to such an extent that today, it is not uncommon to glimpse a hummus relish at an Aussie barbeque. Therefore, hummus, a spread which had been confined to a specific region of the world (Middle East) has today become a common relish within another continent. This is like the case of Indian Tikka Masala, an Indian dish of roasted chicken in a spiced curry sauce becoming one of UK's most popular dishes. A study by Beharrell and Crockett (1992) relate this to the changes in consumption habits of man since the 60s which in turn, could be attributed to the "breakdown of mass consumerism". They explain this as a factor of the change from a mono-dimensional order-oriented culture to a multi-dimensional culture wherein there are several sub cultures in which food becomes a source of expression of an individual's or a group's values and beliefs. This change in the consumption habits of man could not have been possible without the coordinative efforts of several players within the food industry; an industry which transcends the traditional boundaries of operations and nations. Therein lies the importance of global food supply chains.

Traditional food industry players were confined predominantly to their geographical locations and operations which were limited to the food industry and included the likes of cultivation, minimal processing and distribution within a locality. This change could not have been possible without an intricately linked network of different supply chain actors ranging from the wheat farmer in India to the processor in Australia, which was transported by a European logistics provider. This is more pertinent today with the globalisation of 'ethnic food', resulting in the globalisation of the food supply chain. Thus, it is not surprising that India today is a global hub for exporting processed, powdered, and value-added spices.

However, such complexities involving different supply chain actors (farmers, traders, wholesalers, importers, exporters, etc.) along the globe has also resulted in health and quality related issues. In recent times, there is an increase in the number of food-quality and safety-related scandals that has affected consumers around the world. When the 'Chinese fake eggs' scandal erupted in 2011, it further destroyed the trust that consumers have towards the food companies. Food adulteration, however, is not a new concept. Artificial eggs sold as chicken eggs can be manufactured by a chemist using materials like sodium alginate, benzoates, water, gelatine, etc. in 24 h, at a quarter of the cost of having a real chicken produce it naturally. Adding water to bulk up ham or milk, mixing cheap canola oil with extra virgin olive oil and marketing farmed salmon as 'wild salmon' has been a common practice within the industry for a long time. On closer scrutiny, these issues are more of a supply chain-related issue and not specific to one organization's unethical activity. This is very evident in India too as illustrated by a study on adulterants in the Indian milk sector which found the rampant use of Urea, neutralizers, salt, formalin, detergents and hydrogen peroxide (Singuluri & Sukumaran, 2014). In most cases, such acts are committed by non-visible actors like contracted producers, agents, etc. and not the brand company thereby illustrating the importance of responsibility in the food supply chain. Thus, stakeholders called for greater supply chain transparency, labelling and stricter regulations that could mitigate the risks associated with global food supply chains.

Such food safety scandals are not new; as evidenced by the 1900 English beer poisoning wherein arsenic entered the beer supply chain as a result of the use of impure sugar. Fast forward a century later, with the globalization of food manufacturing, such cases are beginning to be less uncommon in global food supply chains. Within the Australian context too, the frozen berry scandal of 2015 and 2017 is a stark reminder of the importance of responsible supply chain behaviour. Creative Gourmet, the Australian company in the centre of the Hepatitis A food scare had sourced their berries from China and subsequent tests detected a strain of hepatitis A, forcing the company to recall their 300-g packs of mixed berries. In short, the reason for the hospitalisation of several Australians could be attributed to ineffective and irresponsible behaviour by supply chain actors in a different country—in this case, China. Since global sourcing is focusing more on procuring products from emerging economies including the BRICS (Brazil, Russia, India, China, and South Africa) countries, the relevance of responsible behaviour is more pronounced today than ever before.

The importance of implementing socially responsible strategies within an organization is increasing in an exponential manner owing to greater stakeholder awareness. As Amaeshi, Osuji, and Nnodim (2008) illustrate, much of the pressure to employ a socially responsible operation is "channelled through the supply chain". As a result of such issues associated with irresponsible behaviour by the suppliers, organizations have illustrated an increasing trend on the implementation of responsibility centric policies (using CSR or other instruments) towards the supplier segment. Bjorner (2004) illustrates that the adoption of socially responsible strategies need not necessarily be driven only by the market power of the end customer but could be a result of market power of supply chain intermediaries. This could be evinced from Starbucks, the American coffee chain company's responsible procurement strategy. Starbucks mandates a higher level of sustainability in their supply chain by implementing responsible purchasing practices and investing in farming communities. Thus, with greater stakeholder awareness (and often consumer awareness), the supply chain actors are pressurised to act responsibly. However, the extent to which responsibility is engrained in the food supply chain is questionable and food safety scandals that are not uncommon today are an exemplification of this. This book chapter analyses responsibility from a food supply chain perspective and creates a conceptual framework of Responsible Food Supply Chain Management (RFSCM).

2 Responsible Supply Chain Management

Setthasakko (2007) illustrates that, even though the components of the food supply chain can be divided into four: the primary producers, manufacturers, processes, and traders, owing to the complex roles that they play, today's food supply chain is extremely complex which involves an intricate network of several actors. Roth, Tsay, Pullman, and Gray (2008) illustrate six supply chain actors including farm suppliers, farmers, marketers, processors, wholesalers, and retailers. Figure 1 illustrates, in a very brief manner, the supply chain actors who are involved in the production, processing, and the transportation of the food products to the consumer.

The increasing pressures for ethical behaviour within the supply chain resulted in proportional interest in academia and this is exemplified by the increasing number of articles and papers published in this spectrum of research (Ageron, Gunasekaran, & Spalanzani, 2012; Carter & Rogers, 2008; Zimmer, Fröhling, & Schultmann, 2015). Research within the field of responsibility and supply chain management defines responsible behaviour in supply chains in several definitions which include the like of Green Supply Chain Management, Sustainable Supply Chain Management (SSCM), and Responsible Supply Chain Management (RSCM). However, a majority of the studies define responsibility in a myopic sense; by accounting only the environmental sustainability concept and, it is imperative that responsibility accounts for more than one dimension (Ashby, Leat, & Hudson-Smith, 2012; Carter & Easton, 2011; Zimmer et al., 2015). Thus, this chapter defines responsible supply chain management by accounting for the three dimensions of responsibility; environmental, social, and financial. To illustrate the concept of RSCM, Carter and Rogers (2008) illustrate the amalgamation of the social and environmental concepts into the holistic perspective of the triple bottom line strategy in a supply chain context. According to Carter and Rogers (2008), SSCM should involve a balance between the fiscal, environmental and the social dimension of the organization. Carter and Rogers (2008) opine that the focus on just two factors i.e. Profits and

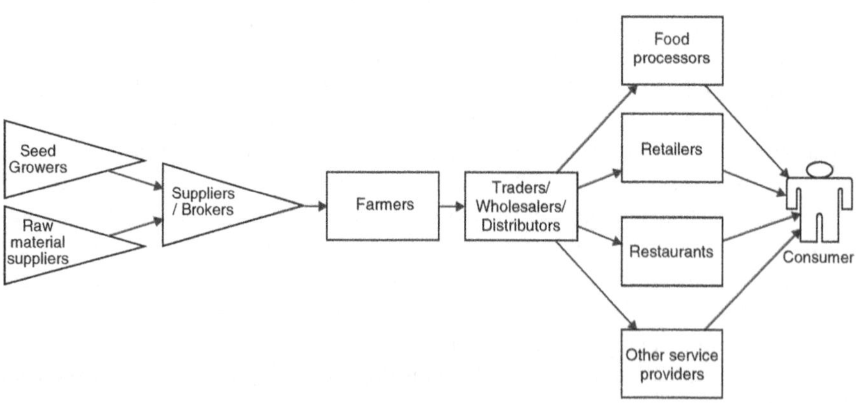

Fig. 1 A simplified food supply chain. Source: Authors' own

Planet, or Profits and People would be inefficient when compared to the focus on the triple bottom line. Since Carter and Roger's (2008) definition encapsulates all the three dimensions, Responsible Supply Chain Management is defined here as "the strategic, transparent integration and achievement of an organisation's social, environmental and economic goals in the systemic coordination of key inter-organisational business processes for improving the long term economic performance of the individual company and its supply chains" (Carter & Rogers, 2008). To implement RSCM, along with the cooperative nature of the supply chain and a triple bottom line perspective, having a voluntary commitment to responsible sourcing is mandatory (Opijnen & Oldenziel, 2011). Leire and Mont (2010) define such responsible purchasing by illustrating the need to account for the consequences of organizational purchasing and account for the social repercussions of such an activity.

Linnenluecke and Griffiths (2015) illustrate that climate change is a major problem that businesses have to account for and anthropogenic activities resulting in an emission of greenhouse gases is to blame for climate change. Non-sustainable farming activities will result in an exacerbation of this issue and such a trend will have a major impact on the agriculture due to potential changes in agricultural yields, damages to crops and land degradation (Linnenluecke & Griffiths, 2015). A sustainable mode of farming and distribution of food is imperative to minimise climate change through minimising of Green House Gas (GHG) emissions. Rimmington, Smith, and Hawkins (2006) illustrate several components pertaining to food sustainability which includes being local, healthy for consumption, accessible to consumers, and final products that are farmed sustainably and by being socially inclusive. In terms of comparing the benefit to the product with the environmental impact of the product, the organization has its greatest environmental impact during the sourcing of the resources needed to create the product. In a multi-tiered supply chain with several elements involved in the production process, the resource extraction supply chain partner might not necessarily be within the radar of the stakeholders of the brand company. For example, labour conditions fraught with violence, bondage, and coercion are particularly acute in several rising economies within the African continent and some brand companies might not account for this when they source minerals or metals extracted from such countries. However, in cases wherein the stakeholders of the product company also account for these extended supply chain partners, the sustainability orientation of the resource extraction supply chain partner could also have an influence on the overall sustainability orientation of the brand company. Apart from the mining sector, this is pertinent in the food supply chain too as for several countries; agriculture is still the main source of livelihood for its citizens. Coffee can be exemplified here as the World's largest coffee producing countries includes mainly Brazil, Vietnam, Columbia, Indonesia, etc.—all rising economies.

The concept of business ethics is a well-studied area in business literature and words like Corporate Social Responsibility (CSR), Business Ethics, Responsible Business, and corporate self-regulation has been used to define this. Within the CSR domain, as Branco and Rodrigues (2006), there are two contrasting cases that are stated to be the motivation for business to act responsibly. The normative case, as

Branco and Rodrigues (2006) define is "to be, and to do good." The business case, according to them, is based on the organizational assumption of 'enlightened self-interest'. Defining further, the normative component of CSR would be a motivational factor for CSR since the organizational elements believe that 'this is the morally appropriate way of operating.' The business case perspective would account for growth: fiscal or non-fiscal by implementing a CSR strategy. Smith (2003) points out that the implementation of CSR within an organization would be motivated by both the business case and the normative case of CSR. MacGregor (2008), cites five rationales for an organization to implement a CSR strategy and these include risk mitigation, competitive advantage from a marketing perspective, inter and intra organizational demands, political-social factors and conviction. Within the supply chain context, Eastham and Sharples (2012) notes that only a fraction of the cost that the final business customer spends in procurement, is the 'actual' cost of the product and a majority of the monies is pocketed by the supply chain actors and not the producers. The avaricious activities of the stronger supply chain members negatively affect the weaker supply chain actors and within the food supply chain, this means the farmers.

3 A Theoretical Lens: The Stakeholder Theory

Carroll and Buchholtz (2009) opine that the stakeholder theory is one of the most dominant theoretical perspectives for business responsibility today. The origins of the stakeholder theory have been attributed to Freeman (1984) in his book titled "Strategic Management: A Stakeholder Approach." As Fassin (2009) illustrates, the stakeholder theory proposes that every party that is associated with an organization associates with the organization to obtain benefits from this association. The stakeholder theory transgresses the shareholder theory ideology by proposing that it is not only the shareholder that the organization has a duty towards, but all the parties that are related to the organization which includes non-governmental organisations (NGOs), unions, employees, suppliers, etc. This is more important today due to the growth in global procurement and especially procurement from companies in rising economies where the systems to protect the stakeholders are either weak or ineffective in their implementation. For example, the farmer in India, being a weaker actor within the global spice supply chain can be taken advantage of by a stronger actor; a trader. Thus, the stakeholder theory proposes that the weaker actor is also a significant stakeholder, and as an extension, must benefit equally in the process. Fassin (2009) suggests that today there is an increasing interrelation between this theory, CSR and business ethics. Although the stakeholder theory is one of the most widely accepted theoretical models involving CSR, this theory is not without its critics. One of the major critiques for stakeholder theory is that the definition of a stakeholder is unclear thereby lacking in normative foundations (Phillips, Freeman, & Wicks, 2003; Waxenberger & Spence, 2003). Hall and Vredenburg (2005) define two types of stakeholders: primary and secondary stakeholders in different practical management scenarios. Primary stakeholders, as implied by Hall and Vredenburg (2005) include directly related parties like that of customers, suppliers, and shareholders and secondary stakeholders might include non-governmental organisations (NGOs), media; thereby rendering it extremely content specific.

Morali and Searcy (2012) use Freeman, Harrison and Wicks' (2010) elaboration of the different aspects of the stakeholder theory which holds that the normative aspect to be the core base of this theory since all the agents of the organization "recognizes all stakeholders' interests with 'intrinsic' moral values. "Equating this to the concept of supply chain management, Morali and Searcy (2012) opine that from such a perspective, i.e. companies have to account for the stakeholders, the organization would have to account for the suppliers and the supply chain partners' pressures and thereby adopt sustainable and socially responsible practices. This might, as Sarkis, Zhu, and Lai (2011) put it, could be fiscally non-viable (at least in the initial stages). On the other hand, Paloviita and Luoma-aho (2010) analysed the stakeholders from a supply chain perspective using a case study analysis of organizations, and thus, illustrated that the supplier organization could potentially be a "definitive stakeholder owing to mutual relationships in the complex stakeholder networks". Thus, since the supplier possesses legitimacy through its relationships within the network, and through their associations with other stakeholders, they could be perceived as a definitive stakeholder.

4 Why RSCM?

From a marketing perspective, Ganesan, George, Jap, Palmatier, and Weitz (2009) opine that in recent times there has been an increasing trend in terms of customers' expectation about "product assortments," regulatory pressures for accurate data and improved products. As a result, the brand organizations look beyond the organizational boundaries to analyse avenues which would create a competitive advantage for the brand and its product. Sarbutts (2003) suggests that reputation is a source of competitive advantage within organizations and since reputation is directly affected by implementing socially responsible activities, there is a need for CSR within the supply chain context. Processes aimed at increasing operational efficiency like that of Just In Time (JIT) manufacturing might be, as Benjaafar, Li, and Daskin (2013) state 'an extremely beneficial factor for achieving competitiveness'. However, from a sustainability perspective, this could have serious repercussions owing to more frequent deliveries of containers and truck-load shipments which are less than full capacity, smaller production runs and such factors could eventually lead to a negative influence on overall sustainability. This implies that there are major issues during the implementation of a sustainable and socially responsible supply chain.

Pedersen and Andersen (2006) suggest that reputation is the primary rationale for organizational CSR strategy. However, such a view is "usually not shared by other supply chain actor" and since the reputation of an organization could be directly related to the reputation of the supplier, it is usually in the interest of the purchasing company that the supplier company be ethical and sustainable in operations. Fabian (2000) implied that a poor CSR performance by any of the supply chain partners would be detrimental to the organization's most valuable asset, the reputation of the brand and therefore organizations have to account for socially responsible practices along all levels of the supply chain. From an operations perspective too, Cruz (2013) points out that there are several benefits associated with a sustainable supply chain which includes risk mitigation, avoidance of costly unreliable business relationships with supply chain partners, minimal operational disruptions and so on.

5 Responsibility Within the Food Supply Chain

Sustainability within the food industry, due to its global nature is rather difficult to define. For example, in a specific country A, there might not be any strict environmental and social control set up to define the sustainability orientation of food but in another country B, there might be such mechanisms set up to control the sustainability orientation of the food products. Under such logic, from a customer perspective, to be a sustainable consumer, the customer could opt for purchasing the product from the country B rather than country A even in the case wherein the customer is from country A. Though this seems to be a lucid decision, such a decision could be considered to be seriously flawed when taken into consideration the hidden factor of food miles wherein the food miles account for the distance the food travels from the point of production to the point of consumption. Similarly, the definition of sustainable food is fraught with several problematic aspects of the processing and preservation of food. The adding of chemical ingredients to food products aimed at increasing the longevity of the food product could be perceived as unhealthy by some consumers but accounting for the fact that the longevity of the product is enhanced, thereby reducing wastage—this could be positively perceived by some consumers.

Smith (2008) illustrates the different perspectives of sustainable food supply chain and notes several characteristics that are mandatory for sustainable food supply chains. This includes food safety, factors supporting the viability and diversity of the stakeholder economics and communities by accounting for fairness in remuneration account for the ecological impacts of operating in this industry. According to Smith (2008), accounting for the ecological and social aspects of food would involve the reduction of energy consumption, minimisation of water; and social aspects would involve creation and maintenance of a safe and socially appropriate working condition for all the employees, not only within a single organization but across the entire supply chain. Other characteristics of a sustainable food supply chain would include the consistent achievement of a high level of animal welfare and also in sustaining the environment for future generations. Food safety is a pivotal issue within the food supply chain since stakeholders including the suppliers and business customers must account for the activities such that the safety of the food product that they deal in is not affected adversely owing to their operations (Manning & Soon, 2013). Similarly, from a supply chain perspective, Roth et al. (2008) opines that the six Ts of food quality management could be critical to the public welfare and these include: traceability, transparency, testability, time, trust and training. Enhancing the six Ts could result in a higher degree of responsibility within the supply chain. Likewise, Carter and Easton (2011) define four facilitators of Sustainable Supply Chain Management; a sustainability centric strategy, efficient risk management, a values-based culture and transparency.

5.1 A Conceptual Solution

Taking all the previous conceptualisations of responsible food supply chain management into consideration, there are four factors that contribute to responsible food supply chain management and these are discussed below and illustrated in Fig. 2.

5.1.1 Responsible Confined Sourcing (RCS)

The first aspect of the Responsible Food Supply Chain Management must account for local sourcing which implies that responsible procurement must account for local suppliers in an ethical fashion. This ensures that the point of production and consumption is closer to each other and if raw materials are available in a satisfactory quality, quantity, and pricing, the customer must prioritise local procurement. This would ensure better traceability due to lowering the supply chain complexity and also minimise transit time thereby improving the quality of produce from a freshness perspective. Moreover, the ethical nature of purchasing will be socially and environmentally responsible in nature.

Fig. 2 A framework for responsible food supply chain management. Source: Author's own

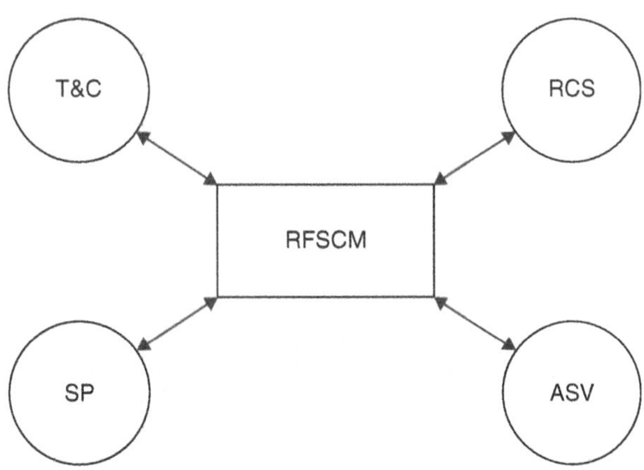

5.1.2 Transparent and Collaborative Supply Chain Management (T&C)

A transparent supply chain is imperative for effective collaboration since providing clear and truthful information about the products is important for the customers to make choices based on the source and sustainability orientation of the product. Wognum, Bremmers, Trienekens, Van Der Vorst, and Bloemhof (2011) defines transparency within the context of a supply chain as the "degree of shared understanding of and access to product-related information as requested by a supply chain's stakeholders without loss, noise, delay, or distortion". Wognum et al. (2011) state that transparency is pivotal for sustainable operations within supply chains especially, 'within the food supply chains'. This is so, since as Wognum et al. (2011) note that "there is an increasing trend in terms of consumers wishing to be informed about the safety of their food, its origin, and the sustainability of the processes that have produced and delivered it".

In asymmetric supply chains where there is a difference in power between supply chain actors, the smaller/weaker producers might be taken advantage of by the more powerful actor. A critical component of RFSCM is that the larger organizations must include such procurement systems that include the smaller producers, if it is healthy and safe for procurement. Increased collaboration will result in better traceability of the product since the information pertaining to the product is communicated effectively.

The horsemeat scandal in Europe of 2013 is a stark reminder of the need for better traceability and transparency within supply chains. Retailing giants like that of Tesco had been purchasing their frozen lasagnas from Findus, a major European frozen food brand which had outsourced its production to a subsidiary. The supply chain partners were scattered around Europe and since the transparency was minimal due to a lack of visibility and the lack of direct influence within this supply chain network, Findus' beef frozen lasagnas were found to be containing up to 100% of horsemeat.

5.1.3 Sustainable Practices Through Efficient Resource Utilisation (SP)

Effective resource utilisation during the production and transportation process is imperative to ensure reduced consumption of energy and the minimisation of wastage produced during the production. This is important even in the farming processes for example, as Rasul and Thapa (2004) cite, the increasing and incessant use of chemicals during the farming processes by using fertilizers, insecticides and pesticides that affect the environment negatively. Such practices also led to negative impacts on the society since the contamination of water bodies due to artificial cultivation methods resulted in the spread of diseases in the vicinity of the farm which adversely affected aquatic life, livestock and people's health. Similarly, during the manufacturing/processing stage too, responsible production methods are important. For example, although additives could prolong the life of the product, it might have a negative correlation with safety and quality. Within the transporting stage too, it is mandatory to have a fuel and energy efficient system involved in the redistribution and transportation of the food product from the production locality to the place of consumption.

5.1.4 Adherence to Standards and Shared Values (ASV)

Barnard (1938) defines shared values as a common set of values that ensures the minimisation of diverging interests and thereby, effectively augment a perception of interdependence within the organization, thereby bolstering competence. Equating this to the supply chain context, sharing of responsibility centric values will result in bettering the competence of the supply chain and thereby aligning each supply chain actor with the shared goal of the supply chain (Jacob-John, 2018). This involves drafting of better policies and standards that ensure responsibility within the supply chain and mandate the adherence to such standards.

6 Cases of Irresponsible Behaviour in the Food Supply Chain

6.1 Food Fraud: The Case of Manuka Honey and Adulterated Milk

With the lengthening, complication, and acceleration of the modern food supply chain, the risk of food fraud has reached its zenith today. Spink and Moyer (2011) define food fraud as a collective term that encompasses all intentional acts that involve the deliberate and intentional substitution, addition, tampering, misrepresentation or false/misleading statements that are performed with an intent to gain economically. This poses three types of risks- direct, indirect, and technical risks. Direct risks are posed when there is an immediate danger to the consumer; indirect risks, when the consumer is at risk due to the long-term exposure to the fraudulent food product; and technical risks are of nonmaterial nature and includes fraud in documentation including a deliberate misinterpretation of country-or-origin (Spink & Moyer, 2011).

In addition, food fraud is a major issue within the food industry wherein there is rampant mislabelling and fraud. This can be exemplified using the case of New Zealand Manuka honey. Manuka honey, commonly sold as an alternative medicine is perceived to be a premium product due to the perceived benefits of antibacterial properties. Recent research by industry pundits point out that there is large scale deception and food fraud within this product segment (Akkoc, 2014; Leak, 2013). When analysing branded products in the United Kingdom (UK), Europe and Far-East, it was found that a majority did not have any Manuka component and a majority of the products were mixed with cheaper substitutes like sugar syrup to bulk the honey.

Adulterating involving the adding of unwanted ingredients in milk has always been a problem in India with the milk producer adding water to increase the volume and as an extension, profit. However, consumers can easily understand the presence of water through differences in look, viscosity, boiling point, and the formation of cream between adulterated and unadulterated milk. This resulted in the rampant use of other adulterants including formalin, urea, starch, neutralizers, detergents, sodium chloride, skim milk powder, sucrose, glucose/dextrose, and hydrogen peroxide (Singuluri & Sukumaran, 2014). Though producers profiteer with this, it is at the expense of the health of the consumer (Bhaskaran, 2015).

Additionally, the food supply chain is an important driver of job and wealth creation; especially within the emerging economies. Such safety scandals will not only adversely affect human health, but also impede the social-economic development due to a sick populace—something very detrimental to a rising economy.

According to Fassam, Dani, and Hills (2015), there are four supply chain drivers for food fraud and these include; lack of trust between supply chain actors, opportunistic behaviour by supply chain partners, inadequate governance of the supply chain and complexity of the supply chain. This can be reduced through the employment of effective legislative tools, innovative technological systems and a novel framework to mitigate the drivers of supply chain fraud. As the RFSCM model encapsulates these, the implementation of these four facets of RFSCM will ensure the mitigation of irresponsible behaviour in the food supply chain. For example, the first component of the model, RCS mandates sourcing locally and in an ethical manner. This ensures procurement within the supply chain is performed as local as possible, thereby minimising procurement from unethical suppliers, for example—suppliers who adulterate products. Moreover, greater transparency of the supply chain ensures visibility in the operations of the supply chain actors along the entire supply chain. This would ensure that such unethical activities (adulterating food products) could be minimised.

6.2 Slavery in Food Supply Chains

Throughout the history of mankind, the elite had the notion of obtaining labour from the lower classes within the society and thus, profiting through this. Although slavery was abolished in the Western world since the introduction of constitutional forms of Government in the nineteenth century, freedom, or at least the illusion of freedom through elected governments was considered the norm, in all parts of the world (Global Slavery Index, 2018). However, even today, the notion of slave labour is not a thing of the bygone era and in fact; slave trading is considered a profitable and lucrative industry in several countries. This is more prevalent in the Asia-Pacific region, with the highest number in India; a rising economy.

Slavery can be defined as the condition in which there is severe exploitation of humans such that workers are not able of the leave their workplace in their free will. Slavery persists today through the ‘owning systems’ that ensure that the workers are controlled against their free will through means including recruitment debts, threats of harm, and such.

Modern slavery, as it is defined today, has manifested itself in several domains; within global supply chains, prostitution, and tied visas of migrant workers. Within the global supply chains, slavery thrived due to the complexity within the supply chains that minimises transparency and traceability thereby resulting in global brands unwittingly involving exploitative labour within the supply chain. Apart from legal sanctions that corporations could face due to their supplier’s use of exploitative labour, this can also result in loss of market share and reputational damage.

A study by Gallup on slavery in India illustrates more than 18 million people or 1.4% of the total population in India is currently living in conditions of modern slavery (Abrams & Nauman, 2016). The industries implicated where they are employed include domestic work, the construction and sex industries, agriculture, fishing, manufacturing, manual labour, and forced begging. Though this has been outlawed by the Indian constitution and legislations being very progressive, the regulatory systems and enforcement of such laws are still considered very weak; ergo slavery is still rampant in India (Domínguez, 2013).

A recent report by the International Labour Organisation (ILO) illustrates that the forced labour, in 2014, generated annual profits to the tune of 150 billion US dollars and the number of people in forced labour, modern slavery, and trafficking is around 21 million. The breakdown of profits, according to the ILO illustrate that a profit of 9 billion United States Dollar (USD) was generated through the forced economic exploitation of agriculture workers (which included forestry and fishing) (ILO, 2014). Big businesses, particularly the big retailers have a major influence in this industry according to an investigation by the Associated Press which investigated the 7 billion-dollar Thai shrimp industry and exposed the slave labour rampant in this sector. Though the initial finger pointing was towards the retailers including the likes of Wholefood, Krogher, Walmart, the brand producers were also a stakeholder in this practice (Booth, 2016). Nestle announced, after self-policing its supply chain, that their products were not exempt from slave labour. This included the cat food brand Fancy Feast which had seafood sourced in Thailand, a sector wherein there is rampant slave labour (Chantavanich, Laodumrongchai, & Stringer, 2016). Though Nestle mandates ethical procurement of raw materials, an independent assessment by Fair Labour Association of farms producing cocoa for Nestlé’s products illustrate that Child and slave labour, apart from Occupational Health and Safety (OHS) and discrimination related issues were present in the supply chain of Nestlé’s chocolate bars (FairLabor, 2014).

7 A Note to the Manager

The implementation of these four facets of RFSCM will ensure the mitigation of irresponsible behaviour in the food supply chain through the percolation of responsibility along the supply chain. For example, the responsible and confined sourcing would ensure that stakeholders within the industry will no longer have a not in my backyard (NIMBY) attitude towards slavery, food fraud, and other irresponsible behaviour in the food industry. This account for the compliance of standards set by industry bodies regarding ethical procurement, adherence to governmental regulations, drafting of better legislation to regulate industry, downgrading suppliers and countries that do not adhere to stricter regulatory standards. Increasing transparency along the supply chain will ensure that the retailers and brand companies get the source of the product and therefore, abstain from purchasing products that are produced through forced labour.

References

Abrams, C. & Nauman, Q. (2016). India has the most people living in modern slavery. *Wall Street Journal*. Accessed July 19, 2018, from https://blogs.wsj.com/indiarealtime/2016/06/02/india-has-the-most-people-living-in-modern-slavery/

Ageron, B., Gunasekaran, A., & Spalanzani, A. (2012). Sustainable supply management: An empirical study. *International Journal of Production Economics, 140*, 168–182.

Akkoc, R. (2014). Popular with celebrities but could that manuka honey in your cupboard be fake? *Telgraph*.

Amaeshi, K. M., Osuji, O. K., & Nnodim, P. (2008). Corporate social responsibility in supply chains of global brands: A boundaryless responsibility? "Clarifications, exceptions and implications". *Journal of Business Ethics, 81*, 223–234.

Ashby, A., Leat, M., & Hudson-Smith, M. (2012). Making connections: A review of supply chain management and sustainability literature. *Supply Chain Management: An International Journal, 17*, 497–516.

Barnard, C. (1938). *The functions of the executive*. Cambridge, MA: Harvard University Press.

Beharrell, B., & Crockett, A. (1992). New age food! New age consumers! With or without technology fix please. *British Food Journal, 94*, 5–13.

Benjaafar, S., Li, Y. Z., & Daskin, M. (2013). Carbon footprint and the management of supply chains: Insights from simple models. *IEEE Transactions on Automation Science and Engineering, 10*, 99–116.

Bhaskaran, M. (2015). *White poison: Why drinking milk could prove fatal for you*. Accessed July 19, 2018, from https://indianexpress.com/article/lifestyle/health/white-poison-why-drinking-milk-could-prove-fatal-for-this-generation/

Bjorner, T. (2004). Environmental labeling and consumers? Choice? An empirical analysis of the effect of the Nordic Swan. *Journal of Environmental Economics and Management, 47*, 411–434.

Booth, B. (2016). The victims of the 21st-century slave trade. *CNBC*.

Branco, M., & Rodrigues, L. (2006). Corporate social responsibility and resource-based perspectives. *Journal of Business Ethics, 69*, 111–132.

Carroll, A. B., & Buchholtz, A. K. (2009). *Business and society: Ethics and stakeholder management*. Mason, OH: South-Western Cengage Learning.

Carter, C. R., & Easton, P. L. (2011). Sustainable supply chain management: evolution and future directions. *International Journal of Physical Distribution and Logistics Management, 41*, 46–62.

Carter, C., & Rogers, D. (2008). A framework of sustainable supply chain management: Moving toward new theory. *International Journal of Physical Distribution and Logistics Management, 38*, 360–387.

Chantavanich, S., Laodumrongchai, S., & Stringer, C. (2016). Under the shadow: Forced labour among sea fishers in Thailand. *Marine Policy, 68*, 1–7.

Cruz, J. M. (2013). Mitigating global supply chain risks through corporate social responsibility. *International Journal of Production Research*, 1–16.

Domínguez, G. (2013). *Slavery in India – 'an uncomfortable truth'*. Accessed July 19, 2018, from https://www.dw.com/en/slavery-in-india-an-uncomfortable-truth/a-17182856

Eastham, J., & Sharples, L. (2012). *Food supply chain management*. Hoboken: Taylor & Francis.

Fabian, T. (2000). Supply chain management in an era of social and environment accountability. *Sustainable Development International, 2*, 27–30.

Fairlabor. (2014). *Independent external monitoring of nestlé's cocoa supply chain in ivory coast*. Accessed 2/4/2016, from http://www.fairlabor.org/sites/default/files/documents/reports/august-2014-nestle-executive-summary_0.pdf

Fassam, L., Dani, S. & Hills, M. (2015). Supply chain food crime & fraud: a systematic literature review of food criminality.

Fassin, Y. (2009). The stakeholder model refined. *Journal of Business Ethics, 84*, 113–135.

Freeman, R. E. (1984). *Strategic management: A stakeholder approach*. New York: Cambridge University Press.

Freeman, R. E., Harrison, J. S., & Wicks, A. C. (2010). *Stakeholder theory: The state of the art*. Cambridge: Cambridge University Press.

Ganesan, S., George, M., Jap, S., Palmatier, R. W., & Weitz, B. (2009). Supply chain management and retailer performance: Emerging trends, issues, and implications for research and practice. *Journal of Retailing, 85*, 84–94.

Global Slavery Index. (2018). *Global slavery index*. Accessed July 19, 2018, from https://www.globalslaveryindex.org/country/india/

Hall, J., & Vredenburg, H. (2005). Managing stakeholder ambiguity. *MIT Sloan Management Review, 47*, 11–13.

ILO. (2014). *ILO says forced labour generates annual profits of US$ 150 billion*. Washington, DC: ILO. Accessed 1/2/2016, from http://www.ilo.org/global/about-the-ilo/newsroom/news/WCMS_243201/lang%2D%2Den/index.htm

Jacob-John, J. (2018). Adherence to responsibility in organic dry food supply chains. *European Business Review, 30*, 26–37.

Leak, J. (2013). Food fraud buzz over fake manuka honey. *The Australian*.

Leire, C., & Mont, O. (2010). The implementation of socially responsible purchasing. *Corporate Social Responsibility and Environmental Management, 17*, 27–39.

Linnenluecke, M., & Griffiths, M. (2015). Chapter 2: The threat of climate change. In M. K. Linnenluecke & A. Griffiths (Eds.), *The climate resilient organization: Adaptation and resilience to climate change and weather extremes*. Cheltenham: Edward Elgar Publishing.

Macgregor, S. F. J. (2008). *Exploring the fit between CSR and innovation*.

Manning, L., & Soon, J. M. (2013). GAP framework for fresh produce supply. *British Food Journal, 115*, 796–820.

Morali, O., & Searcy, C. (2012). A review of sustainable supply chain management practices in Canada. *Journal of Business Ethics*, 1–24.

Opijnen, M. & Oldenziel, J. 2011. Responsible supply chain management. *Potential success factors and challenges for addressing prevailing human rights and Other CSR issues in supply chains of Eu-based companies*. Accessed August 13, 2013, from http://ec.europa.eu/social/main.jsp?langId=en&catId=331&newsId=1014&furtherNews=yes

Paloviita, A., & Luoma-Aho, V. (2010). Recognizing definitive stakeholders in corporate environmental management. *Management Research Review, 33*, 306–316.
Pedersen, E. R., & Andersen, M. (2006). Safeguarding corporate social responsibility (CSR) in global supply chains: How codes of conduct are managed in buyer-supplier relationships. *Journal of Public Affairs, 6*, 228–240.
Phillips, R., Freeman, R. E., & Wicks, A. C. (2003). What stakeholder theory is not. *Business Ethics Quarterly, 13*, 479–502.
Rasul, G., & Thapa, G. B. (2004). Sustainability of ecological and conventional agricultural systems in Bangladesh: An assessment based on environmental, economic and social perspectives. *Agricultural Systems, 79*, 327–351.
Rimmington, M., Smith, J., & Hawkins, R. (2006). Corporate social responsibility and sustainable food procurement. *British Food Journal, 108*, 824–837.
Roth, A. V., Tsay, A. A., Pullman, M. E., & Gray, J. V. (2008). Unraveling the food supply chain: Strategic insights from china and the 2007 recalls. *Journal of Supply Chain Management, 44*, 22–39.
Sarbutts, N. (2003). Can SMEs "do" CSR? A practitioner's view of the ways small- and medium-sized enterprises are able to manage reputation through corporate social responsibility. *Journal of Communication Management, 7*, 340–347.
Sarkis, J., Zhu, Q., & Lai, K.-H. (2011). An organizational theoretic review of green supply chain management literature. *International Journal of Production Economics, 130*, 1–15.
Setthasakko, W. (2007). Determinants of corporate sustainability: Thai frozen seafood processors. *British Food Journal, 109*, 155–168.
Singuluri, H., & Sukumaran, M. (2014). Milk adulteration in Hyderabad, India-a comparative study on the levels of different adulterants present in milk. *Journal of Chromatography and Separation Techniques, 5*, 1.
Smith, N. C. (2003). Corporate social responsibility: Whether or how? *California Management Review, 45*, 52–76.
Smith, B. G. (2008). Developing sustainable food supply chains. *Philosophical Transactions of the Royal Society B: Biological Sciences, 363*, 849–861.
Spink, J., & Moyer, D. C. (2011). Defining the public health threat of food fraud. *Journal of Food Science, 76*, R157–R163.
Waxenberger, B., & Spence, L. (2003). Reinterpretation of a metaphor: From stakes to claims. *Strategic Change, 5*, 239–249.
Wognum, P. M., Bremmers, H., Trienekens, J. H., Van Der Vorst, J. G. A. J., & Bloemhof, J. M. (2011). Systems for sustainability and transparency of food supply chains – Current status and challenges. *Advanced Engineering Informatics, 25*, 65–76.
Zimmer, K., Fröhling, M. & Schultmann, F. (2015). Sustainable supplier management–a review of models supporting sustainable supplier selection, monitoring and development. *International Journal of Production Research*, 1–31.

The Role of Meaningful Work in the Context of Startup Events and Entrepreneurial Activities

Mari Kooskora and Ülane Vilumets

Abstract Research on meaningful work has gained more popularity in the recent years and there is plenty of evidence on how meaning is positively related to work motivation. However, various events on the Baltic startup scene have made it possible to become an entrepreneur in a safe environment and launch a service or a product quickly and with very little investment. This has created a circle of people participating in different entrepreneurship-related events and working on startup ideas as hobby projects whilst also being employed. The aim of this paper is to discover the connection between different dimensions of meaningful work and the probability of leaving one's work and founding a company. To examine these links, a web-based survey was conducted involving Estonians, as well as some Latvians, Lithuanians and residents of other countries (n = 198) who were connected to the Baltic startup scene. Meaningful work was measured with the help of two scales—the Comprehensive Meaningful Work Scale (CMWS) developed in 2012 by Lips-Wiersma and Wright as well as the shorter and more general Work as Meaning Inventory (WAMI) developed in 2012 by Steger. The study revealed that meaningful work appeared to have negative correlation to the predicted likeliness of quitting one's job; however, relationship between meaning and attending various entrepreneurship- related events or being more likely to start a business was not identified.

Keywords Meaning · Meaningful work · Job characteristics · Work values · Startups · Business idea contents · Entrepreneurship

---

M. Kooskora (✉)
Estonian Business School, Tallinn, Estonia
e-mail: mari.kooskora@ebs.ee

Ü. Vilumets
Estonian Entrepreneurship University of Applied Sciences, Tallinn, Estonia
e-mail: ylane@likealocalguide.com

N. Mitra, R. Schmidpeter (eds.), *Corporate Social Responsibility in Rising Economies*, CSR, Sustainability, Ethics & Governance,
https://doi.org/10.1007/978-3-030-53775-3_3

1 Introduction

Meaningful work has become an increasingly popular research topic in the recent decades since it plays a significant role in important employee outcomes (Fairlie, 2011a). On a personal level studies of meaning, and meaningful work might shed some light on what best facilitates the realization of fundamental needs, goals, and values. According to May, Gilson, and Harter (2004) knowing the sources of meaningful work are important from management's point of view because "the restoration of meaning in work is seen as a method to foster an employee's motivation and attachment to work."

Startup boom in the Baltics is a reality and in Estonia, which is often portrayed in the international media as the country with the highest concentration of start-ups in the world, several questions have arisen. We may ask should the HRD (Human Resource Development) departments be worried about the participation in startup events? Are lower levels in certain dimensions of meaning more connected to the tendency of being interested in entrepreneurship events and startups? Can attending one of those events predict that employee leaving in the near future? In any case, with that many people being interested in founding startups, it is relevant for top management to discover the reasons behind professionals earning an above-average salary, leaving their jobs and investing their time and money into a high-risk tech companies which have a very low chance of succeeding.

To find answers to these questions, we first review the literature on the construct of meaning, meaningful work, its measures, connection to other employee outcomes and previous empirical research concerning work meaningfulness and compare the perceived work meaningfulness among different groups of people connected to the Estonian start-up community; as well as examine the links between meaningful work and quitting one's job to become an entrepreneur. In the end, useful implications for both managers and HRD will be proposed on work meaningfulness.

2 Job Motivation and Meaningful Work

We can argue that meaning of work in general is not a novel concept, as it has been indirectly present in numerous studies on job motivation. Meaning is commonly associated with the "self" and expressing or actualizing one's "self" and as early as 1960, McGregor described desired work as something that allows the expression of imagination, ingenuity and creativity. Accordingly, McGregor (1960) listed realizing one's potential, continued self-development and being creative as the self-fulfillment needs which he considered the capstone on the hierarchy of needs.

Although being criticized for lacking empirical support, one of the most influential theories on the matter has been the Herzberg's two-factor theory of satisfaction and motivation (Herzberg, 1966, 1968; Herzberg, Mausner, Peterson, & Capwell, 1957; Herzberg, Mausner, & Snyderman, 1959). According to Hackman and

Oldham (1976), Herzberg's theory has prompted a great deal of research and inspired several successful change projects in the field involving the redesign of work. Next, Maslow (1965) and Alderfer (1972) proposed self-actualization as an important aspect of work. According to Maslow, self-actualization through commitment to an important job and to worthwhile work could be the path to human happiness. Moreover, Locke (1976) argued that job satisfaction basically means doing what is personally valued. Even though meaning as such is not directly defined or mentioned, it is clear that the roots of this discussion lie in attempts to experience higher motivational levels in work.

2.1 *Meaning as a Construct*

We may say that attempts to define meaning itself as a construct activated in the 1990s and 2000s. According to Ryff (2000) meaning often accompanies issues of "life meaning, purpose, and coherence". Meaning is also present in constructs related to personal strivings (Emmons, 1991; Siwek, Oleszkowicz, & Słowińska, 2017), current concerns (Klinger, 1998), personal projects (Little, 1983), life longings (Kotter-Grühn, Wiest, Zurek, & Scheibe, 2009), and self-determination (Allan, Autin, & Duffy, 2016; Ryan & Deci, 2000). Moreover, research suggests that attaining meaning is very important to individuals (Berg, 2015; King & Napa, 1998) whereas Baumeister (1991) identified four main needs for experiencing meaning: (1) propose—perceiving one's current activities as having an effect on future outcomes; (2) values—being morally good and correct; (3) efficacy—a sense of having control over one's outcomes; and (4) self-worth—feeling one is a good, admirable, worthy individual with desirable traits.

Meaning seems to be a multidimensional construct and several researchers have developed multidimensional models of meaning (Emmons, 1999; Ryff & Keyes, 1995; Wong, 1998). However interestingly enough, happiness doesn't appear on any of these models. Therefore, we can ask, whether happiness is not an integral part of meaning? Nevertheless, it has been argued that realization of one's goals and purposes require effort and discipline and that may be contradicting short-term happiness (Waterman, 1984). Furthermore, several other authors have emphasized the distinction between meaning and happiness. King and Napa (1998) argued that the two are more likely to have moderate positive association, rather than demonstrating complete independence.

Further, McGregor and Little (1998) and Stillman and Baumeister (2009) explained that "doing well" which is associated with happiness and "being yourself" which is associated with meaning, are two different measures of personal well-being. Examining people's personal projects has played a significant role in the research of meaning. Their main intent is to legitimize integrity by showing its empirical research to well-being and they manage to do so by associating efficacy to happiness and integrity to meaning. Additionally, Emmons (2005) and several other authors (Krok, 2015) emphasize the role of religion as a goal- based meaning system. For

Fairlie (2011a) development is central to the concept of meaning; moreover, despite the fact that different researchers define meaning and the route to it slightly differently, they all agree that meaning *is* crucial and humans are characterised by an innate drive to find meaning and significance in their lives, and that failure to achieve meaning results in psychological distress (Steger, Frazier, Oishi, & Kaler, 2006). The roots of meaning lie, however, in the humanities rather than management theory and the deeper existential layer of meaningfulness may be the human need to grow and develop (Lips-Wiersma & Wright, 2012).

2.2 Meaningfulness in Work

According to Lips-Wiersma and Morris (2009) the interest in meaningful work has significantly increased since 1990s through developing theories of transformational leadership, organizational culture and, more recently, employee engagement. Most of the researchers of meaningful work agree that the field lacks structure and overall integration (Rosso, Dekas, & Wrzesniewski, 2010; Steger, Pickering, Shin, & Dik, 2009; Wrzesnieswski, Dutton, & Debebe, 2003). However, growing interest in the topic is evident. According to Fairlie (2011b) the research on work meaningfulness has increased and several bestsellers in popular business press have dissected the topics of meaningful work.

It can be argued that although meaningful work has previously been integrated into several models of work characteristics, it has rarely been the main focus of research. For example, Hackman and Oldham (1975) developed a Job Diagnostics Survey (JDS) that among other scales measures the experienced meaningfulness of one's work and suggested the use of such instrument to diagnose the motivational properties of a job. According to Hackman and Oldham (1976) and Oldham and Hackman (2010), when meaningfulness is achieved in combination with experienced responsibility and knowledge of the actual results of the work activities, it results in several positive outcomes, such as high internal work motivation, quality of work performance, job satisfaction (especially satisfaction with opportunities for personal growth and development on the job) and low absenteeism and turnover.

Roberson (1990) identified three categories of work meaning: work centrality, work values, and work orientation. Following Roberson's theory Shea-Van Fossen and Vredenburgh (2011) showed how individual's work orientations—job, career and calling orientation—are differentiated by preference for challenging work, rather than work enjoyment, concern for others, or income. According to Steger et al. (2006) meaningfulness is defined in career literature as "the sense made of, and significance felt regarding the nature of one's being and existence". Its absence, however, is associated with existential burnout, apathy and detachment from one's work (May et al. 2004).

Based on two previous qualitative research projects, Lips-Wiersma and Wright (2012) proposed four dimensions of meaningful work: (1) developing the inner self—moral development, personal growth, being true to self; (2) unity with others—working together, sharing values, belonging; (3) service to others—making a difference, meeting the needs of humanity; and (4) expressing full potential—creating, achieving, influencing. In Fairlie's research (2011b) meaningful work is defined as aspects of one's job or work environment that facilitate the attainment or maintenance of one or more dimensions of meaning that enable individuals to become self-actualized, realise their life purpose, values, and goals, have positive social impacts, experience feelings of accomplishment, and achieve their highest career advancement within an organization. He shows that work meaningfulness has strongest positive correlation with work engagement, job satisfaction, organizational commitment and (low) turnover cognitions. It also shows the strongest negative correlation with disengagement, exhaustion (i.e. burnout), depression and stress symptoms.

2.3 *Measuring Meaningful Work*

Several researchers have come up with their own measures for meaningful work. One of them is the MWI (Meaningful Work Inventory) developed by Fairlie (2010). This 64-item measure has 8 sub-scales which measure work characteristics that are aligned with models of meaning: intrinsic rewards, extrinsic rewards, leadership and organizational features, supervisory relationships, co-worker relationships, organizational support, work demands and balance, and finally—meaningful work itself. The last sub-scale is most aligned with models of meaning and according to Fairlie's (2011b) paper accounted for unique variance in work engagement, disengagement, and work adjustment. Lips-Wiersma and Wright (2012) also developed and validated a comprehensive scale measuring meaningful work (CMWS—Comprehensive Meaningful Work Scale). Since it was previously identified that meaningful work is likely to be a multidimensional construct, a list of 91 items were generated representing each of the previously identified dimensions and through several studies narrowed down to a 28-item scale.

Next, Steger, Dik, and Duffy (2012) presented a measure of the core dimensions of the experience of meaningful work—the Work and Meaning Inventory (WAMI) and demonstrated the relevance of meaningful work for important work-related and well- being variables. According to Steger et al. (2012) meaningful work consists of the following three primary facets such as: Positive meaning in work—the subjective experience that what one is doing has personal significance; Meaning making through work—linked to the ways in which people's meaning in life benefits from meaningful work; and Greater good motivations—the desire to make a positive impact on the greater good.

In the context of the current study, WAMI and CMWS were found to be the most relevant measures because Fairlie's inventory consists of more than 60 items and includes other work characteristics that are not relevant to this paper. While it does have a separate sub-scale specifically for meaningful work, the other measures seemed more appropriate because they focussed on models of meaning and are easier to collect responses to.

2.4 Finding Meaning Outside of Work

Even though the basis for understanding the construct of meaning lies largely in analyzing personal projects (Little, 1983) the research on how meaningful work is associated with various "extracurricular" activities or hobbies and how the search of meaning outside the workplace relates to employee outcomes is relatively modest.

One of the few attempts is done by Rodell (2013) who aims to show how an individual's job and its meaning is connected to volunteering. In her study she tries to capture the conflicting speculations about job meaningfulness–volunteering relationship through compensation and enhancement perspectives (Burke & Greenglass, 1987). The results of Rodell's (2013) research suggested that volunteering was associated with both volunteer and job meaningfulness, and that the pull of meaningful volunteer work was even stronger when employees experienced less meaning in their jobs. However, the results also revealed the benefits of volunteering for employers, as volunteering was related to job absorption but not job interference, thus being associated with better job performance.

Similarly, the recent startup boom has facilitated a range of events that can raise similar questions in employers as volunteers (Startups in Estonia, 2012). Business idea contests, workshops, "hackathons" and other startup-related events are often sponsored and supported by big companies, despite the fact that they are essentially promoting an entrepreneur and building a (startup) business.

Interviews with business founders and the general narrative around becoming an entrepreneur often emphasize similar dimensions that researchers of meaningful work have identified as key aspects of work meaning, such as doing something that "makes a difference", serving others with their product, feeling inspired, realizing one's full potential etc. It can be assumed that someone working on their own business i.e. something they believe solves a bigger problem (i.e. a startup idea) and will have higher levels of work meaning.

According to a data analysis conducted by the biggest professional network LinkedIn (Rao, 2011) a first-time startup founder is not someone recently out of university, but typically 30–39 years old and has been in their previous position for roughly 2.5 years, most likely having worked for a big Information Technology (IT) corporation like Yahoo, Ebay, Google, Apple or Microsoft. Although these numbers are based on startup founders in the United States, the results are not radically different in the Baltics. Similarly, the organizers of Ajujaht, Estonia's biggest business idea contest initiated by Enterprise Estonia, have noticed an increase in the age of its participants over the last few years and point out that most of them do not have previous business experience—only a reported 15% of them are entrepreneurs when entering the contest (Ajujahi statistika, 2007–2013).

This average profile allows us to believe that most of them have already acquired some professional credibility along with the respective financial stability. Thus, the pay gap between the first years of starting a business and their previous job may be substantial. However, as argued by King and Napa (1998), wealth compared to meaning and happiness is only a marginal predictor of how valuable or desirable a life is perceived. Why else would well-paid professionals quit a full-time job and start working on a startup business?

The reason why this paper focuses on people connected to tech startups and the startup community as a sample lies in the specifics of the tech industry. According to Investopedia (2014), a startup is a company that is in the first stage of its operations. These companies are often initially bank rolled by their entrepreneurial founders as they attempt to capitalize on developing a product or service for which they believe there is a demand. So due to limited revenue or high costs, most of these small-scale operations are not sustainable in the long term without additional funding from venture capitalists and are considered a high-risk investment because of their high failure rate.

Moreover, the founders of an early stage company are usually working a lot harder than they used to at their previous job and due to limited resources common to startups, the perceived levels of happiness may be quite low, yet it could be expected that the meaningfulness is perceived higher than at their previous job. The difference between efficacy and integrity shown by McGregor and Little (1998) explains this phenomenon quite well. In the context of this paper it is interesting to know whether there is anything lacking in those people's career in terms of meaning that makes them long for a more meaningful experience in the form of entrepreneurship.

3 Background of Empirical Study

We can argue that Estonia has promoted itself in the recent years as a bustling startup hub with a great ecosystem for new scalable businesses to be founded. This has sparked series of different events organized by various private companies, non-profit and governmental organizations to bring the ideas of entrepreneurship and building tech startups to people who have no previous business experience. Within this paper our intent is to find links between different dimensions of meaningful work and participating in different startup-related and entrepreneurial events and activities. Specifically, can looking around with the aim of finding a new business idea to start executing or joining a startup team be associated with lower perceived levels of meaning in one or more dimensions of meaningful work?

Since meaning is a multidimensional construct we aim to compare the scores of employees, entrepreneurs and potential entrepreneurs (those interested in the events and activities explained below) and hope to provide some interesting data on how the components of meaningful work are perceived differently and what could be done by the employers in terms of job design to achieve higher levels of meaning and thus keeping high performers in the company.

Mobley (1977) developed a model to explain the process by which a dissatisfied employee arrives at a decision to leave the organization. Thoughts of quitting were predicted to directly affect intention to search, which, in turn, was predicted to directly affect intention to quit. Furthermore, the probability of finding an acceptable alternative was proposed to affect intentions to search and to quit. Since turnover cognitions are negatively associated to meaning and based on this theory as well as the fact that entrepreneurship and startup events provide plenty of networking opportunities as well as numerous business and job offers, the following hypotheses will receive attention in our paper.

H1: Entrepreneurs, startup founders and self-employed freelancers experience greater meaning in their work than employees.

H2: The estimated levels of meaningfulness in one's work are negatively correlated to the estimated likeliness of quitting one's job and starting a business.

H3: People who work (i.e. are employed by somebody else), but have higher attendance and interest in entrepreneurship events, score lower on the meaningful work scales than those with less connection and interest to entrepreneurship events.

4 Study Methodology

To find connections between meaningfulness and entrepreneurial activities and to test the above-mentioned hypotheses, an online survey was conducted in April 2014 and data collected through SurveyMonkey survey software. The study was mainly quantitative, including some elements of qualitative research, such as open-ended questions.

Since the startup community is generally very well connected with each other and tech-savvy, social media was used to get responses. Several active members and opinion leaders were approached to share the survey in their social networks or distribute it via various e-mail lists to achieve snowball sampling (referral sampling).

In the first part of the survey, demographic data were collected about the respondents to make sure the sample did not differ too much from the typical potential business or startup founder. Each respondent was asked to determine their current career status which then led them to additional questions on their work, business, startup or freelancing. Each person was then asked to evaluate different dimensions of meaning in their main work-related activity.

To measure the meaningfulness of work, two different scales were chosen. Comprehensive Meaningful Work Scale (CMWS) by Lips-Wiersma and Wright (2012) was chosen as it helps to understand different aspects of meaningfulness in work and also sheds some light on how the individual or the organization can contribute to crafting and fostering those aspects. Respondents were asked to evaluate each of the 28 items on a Likert- type frequency scale of 1 to 5 (answer choices ranging from never to always).

In addition to the CMWS a simpler and shorter measure for meaningful work, the WAMI (Work As Meaning Inventory) was added for comparable results, where the

Likert-type scale was used as well. Those two meaningfulness scales supported each other producing nearly identical results and the decision to use both of them was made to be able to go back to the more detailed dimensions of meaning.

The last part of the questionnaire focused on connection to and interest in entrepreneurship. Data were collected on the participants' general interest in entrepreneurship, connection to entrepreneurial activities, events such as business idea contests and various startup-related events which may refer to the participant's wish to potentially become an entrepreneur. Data were collected about the respondent's experience in attending a selection of entrepreneurship and startup events as well as expected probability to participate in various events in the next 12 months. For previous participation, a 4-score scale was used to understand respondent's experience ranging from 1 (no, never) to 4 (yes, several times). The probability of participating in various events in the next 12 months and starting a business or founding a startup was also evaluated on a Likert- style scale with answer choices ranging from 1 (extremely unlikely) to 5 (extremely likely). Arithmetic means for the scores were used to find correlation with meaningfulness. As a control question, the last section listed several ways of becoming an entrepreneur, both full-time and part-time, joining a startup team and becoming a co- founder that also had to be evaluated on a likeliness scale of 1 to 5.

4.1 Sample Characteristics

The aimed sample size of participants was determined by the confidence level required for significant data results and allowable confidence interval. It is difficult to estimate the size of the total population interested in startups and entrepreneurship in Estonia. According to the biggest online start-up network, AngelList Estonia currently has 148 start-up companies listed, followed by 108 from Latvia, 88 from Lithuania and 44 from Belarus (as of March 5, 2014). The most well-known and popular startup event Garage48 is followed by more than 9000 people and the business idea contest Ajujaht by more than 6600 people on social network Facebook.

Considering the above, the authors aimed to find 200 respondents to adequately draw conclusions. The questionnaire reached various networks of entrepreneurial-minded people, such as e-mail lists of different events, Enterprise Estonia's mentorship program attendees, startups in Ülemiste Tehnopol. More specifically, the following networks and communities were approached to collect responses:

Garage48 Participants Garage48 is a 48-h hackathon-style event that promotes turning an idea into a working service or a prototype in one weekend and starting new web and mobile projects with a very lean budget. More generally it promotes entrepreneurship and startup culture in Estonia, Northern Europe and Africa. From the beginning of 2013 to the time of writing this paper Garage48 had organised

6 events in Estonia, 5 events in Latvia and numerous others in Russia, Belarus and other countries each producing a selection of startup ideas and teams.

Ajujaht Participants Ajujaht is a business idea contest brought to life by Enterprise Estonia (EAS) in 2007. In 2012–2013 as many as 409 participants took part in the contest, only 14% of whom had previously been entrepreneurs. The average age of participants has risen in the recent years, being the highest in 2013 when the average participant was 29 years old at the time of joining the program.

Different Business Incubators and Support Institutions The survey was sent to the main contact of those institutions with a request to forward it to the residents of Tallinn Business Incubators, including the Loov Eesti Centre for Creative Industries, as well as to Tartu Science Park, Tehnopol, representatives of Enterprise Estonia, Estonian Development Fund and Kredex.

Survey was initially started by 300 people and completed by 206, showing a completion rate of 69%. Out of the participants, 8 respondents were neither employed, nor working on a business or a volunteer project, so for the data analysis they were discarded due to the fact that they could not provide any answers on perceived meaningfulness.

The final sample of the current study consisted of 198 respondents between ages of 20 and 54 who are in various ways connected to the startup community of Estonia. One age response was not taken into consideration due to an obvious mistake. The average age of participants was 30.69 years which is quite similar to the figures provided by Enterprise Estonia on Ajujaht participants and also LinkedIn's analysis on startup founders.

Out of the respondents, 70% resided in Estonia. It is important to note that the sample was not restricted geographically, including people from Estonia, as well as from Latvia, Lithuania and other European countries. Atypically to most surveys, men were more likely to complete this one, even though more women clicked on the link. Even though 54% of the respondents were men, taking into consideration the gender breakdown of any entrepreneurship contest, event or tech conference, the proportion of male respondents should have been a lot higher to accurately represent the population.

Participants of the survey identified whether they consider themselves employees (61%), entrepreneurs (25%) or freelancers in order to answer the following questions about meaningful work. The majority of respondents had higher education, 17.17% of them were still in university and 13.13% had no higher education. Out of those with university degrees, 30.3% reported to have a degree in business or economics and 20.7% an engineering or IT-related degree.

Out of the participants 67% worked for the private sector, 27% for the public sector and the remaining 6% for the non-governmental organization (NGO) and non-profit sector. As far as the size of the employer was concerned, 41% worked for a company with 50–249 employees. None of the respondents mentioned their employer being bigger than 250 people which was predictable for Estonia.

Out of the respondents 34.34% said they were making a monthly net income of less than 1000 €, while the remaining 65.66% made more than 1000 €, which allows us to believe that the majority of the sample makes more than the average Estonian monthly gross salary (986 € before taxes, IV quarter of 2013). The number of people in each of the salary intervals also deviated from a typical population with an unproportionally big percentage earning more than 2000 € a month after taxes. This may be explained by high salaries in the respective areas of life (30.3% business/economics, 20.7% engineering/IT) or including a rather large proportion of entrepreneurs.

The channels used for collecting data lead authors to believe that more startup founders would end up among the participants, however the proportion of people working full time on their startup ended up being too small in the sample to draw any significant conclusions and entrepreneurs in general were grouped together with freelancers and startup founders. The sample comprised of 127 employees and 68 entrepreneurs respectively.

The answers collected through an online survey were analyzed by the authors and regression analysis was performed on several sets of data. The sample questions of the survey can be seen in Annexure 1.

5 Results

5.1 Differences in Perceived Meaning

Hypothesis 1 predicted that entrepreneurs, startup founders and self-employed freelancers experience greater levels of meaning in their work than employees (i.e. people employed by someone other than themselves). To compare the scores of perceived meaningfulness the respondents were divided into two groups according to the answer to Question No. 26—whether they evaluated the meaningfulness of their job or business (including startups and freelancing work). Among the participants there was also a small number of people who defined their current career status differently in Question No. 6.

Average scores were calculated for each dimension of meaningful work developed by Lips-Wiersma and Wright (2012), using reverse coding for all three items in "developing the inner self" dimension. On an average, entrepreneurs scored higher than employees in all the dimensions. Three people who answered the meaning questions about their unpaid internship, academic research or voluntary work were left out of this comparison.

The biggest difference between the two groups occurred in two dimensions: expressing full potential and inspiration. In those two dimensions entrepreneurs scored 29.8% and 43.7% higher than employees respectively (minimum score being 1 and maximum score 5). It was revealed that inspiration is a central part to meaningful work and since starting a business is often referred to as "doing what you love" and "realizing your full potential" the results were rather predictable.

The scores of WAMI, the measure validated by Steger confirmed and supported the previous results with entrepreneurs scoring 4.18 and employees 3.56 on the

9-item Work as Meaning Scale. So it is safe to conclude that founding a business is personally important and meaningful to most entrepreneurs not just an opportunity to make profit.

5.2 *Leaving Work and Starting a Business*

Hypothesis 2 predicted that perceived levels of meaningful work are negatively correlated to the estimated likeliness of quitting one's job. Those that marked in the survey that they are employed, either full-time or part-time, were asked to answer additional questions about their job, including how likely they consider quitting their job and how likely are they to start a business in the next 12 months.

Regression analysis was run on this data with the help of Microsoft Excel's data analysis toolbox. The self-reported likeliness of quitting one's job in the next 12 months and the likeliness of starting a business in the next 12 months were both tested to correlate with the results of WAMI as well as CMWS.

The sample in this case was 116 because there were 11 respondents who did not give a rating to how likely they thought quitting their job was. As the likeliness of quitting one's job and starting a business as well as meaningfulness scores were all evaluated on a 5-score Likert scale, we decided to use mean ratings rather than median which is not recommended when the dispersion of the results is very high and there are a few extreme values.

The prediction made in hypothesis 2 that levels of meaning are associated negatively with the likeliness of quitting one's job was supported. Regression analysis showed that the perceived likeliness of quitting one's job in the next 12 months had significant negative correlation with perceived meaningfulness. This was true in the case of WAMI meaningfulness scores ($r = -.32$, $p < 0.001$) as well as averages of CMWS ($r = -.48$, $p < 0.001$).

Regression analysis also showed that the correlation between starting a business and perceived meaningfulness was not significant in the case of either one of the meaningfulness scores. This shows that becoming an entrepreneur cannot be explained by simply feeling less meaning in one's work and there is a variety of additional motives behind that decision. Looking more specifically at the scores of different dimensions of CMWS provides some useful data on what exactly makes someone think about leaving their well-paid job. Regression analysis was performed on the average scores of the seven dimensions of CMWS testing in which one of them would predict the chance of someone quitting most accurately.

Regression analysis of the dimensions of CMWS showed that each of the dimension scores separately also have a significant negative correlation with the predicted likeliness of quitting one's job. The strongest negative relation occurred with the dimensions of unity with others, developing inner self and inspiration, which means that in the case of one of these are absent from the work place, employees are most likely to consider quitting.

Inspiration is an important predictor of quitting a job as this dimension is the one that employees of our sample scored the lowest in. Also, the average inspiration score had the biggest difference when comparing employees to entrepreneurs. Another interesting finding is that even though employees also perceived a big difference from entrepreneurs in expressing full potential, that dimension had a modest correlation with leaving one's work.

Finding no connection between starting a business and meaningfulness was supported by the answers of the open-ended Question No. 12 in the survey, where only 8 people mentioned that starting their own business could be the reason they would consider quitting their job (including the ones that said they are already working on a startup that may require their full-time attention) and 1 participant mentioned possibly joining friends if they start a business.

The majority of respondents mentioned finding a better job or getting a better offer without specifying what a better offer means for them as the reason to consider quitting their job. Salary or higher pay was mentioned on the most occasions, which contradicts previous findings that financial success is only a minor predictor of the value of a life (King & Napa, 1998).

Due to these answers, the relation between salary and meaningfulness was also tested with regression analysis. Salary intervals were converted into numbers from 1 (less than 500 € a month) to 5 (more than 2000 € a month). Regression analysis showed no significant relation between salary and levels of meaning in the case of either WAMI or CMWS score.

5.3 Interest in Entrepreneurship Events

Hypothesis 3 predicted that those frequently attending various entrepreneurship-themed and startup-related events are experiencing lower levels of meaningfulness in their work and thus may be out on a search for a new job or new business opportunities (Mobley, 1977).

In the last part of the survey, the respondents had been asked to evaluate their interest in different entrepreneurship-related topics as well as provide info on their previous participation (last 12 months) and predicted participation (next 12 months) in different entrepreneurship and startup-related events. The scale of previous participation was a 4-score Likert scale ranging from 1 (no, never) to 4 (yes, several times). The likeliness of attending one of the listed events was evaluated on a 5-score Likert scale from 1 (extremely unlikely) to 5 (extremely likely). Regression analysis was performed on the data, first for the whole sample, later separately for the respondents whose meaningfulness score was about their job i.e. they are employed by someone else.

Hypothesis 3 was not supported by the results of the survey. What the authors expected to find a negative correlation appeared to be a weak positive link instead. The respondents covered in this analysis ($N = 198$) included also entrepreneurs, startup founders and freelancers. The positive correlation was significant in the case of both WAMI and CMWS scores, however the relationship is rather modest. After extracting the employees from entrepreneurs, startup founders and freelancers the picture was not very different. The findings of this analysis correspond to Rodell's (2013) research on volunteering. It appears that interest in entrepreneurship and startup events is not negatively correlated to meaning and may, in fact, be useful to different employee outcomes.

The respondents were also asked to list the main reasons for participating in the mentioned entrepreneurship events. The answers lead us to believe that in most cases participating in events related to entrepreneurship is more related to self-development and networking rather than serious attempts to find a business idea, new job or a co-founder for your business. These findings are parallel to Rodell's (2013) findings about volunteering and meaningful work where volunteering appeared to be related to job absorption but not job interference, thus being associated with better job performance. Similarly we can conclude that since meaningfulness is not negatively correlated to being interested in entrepreneurship and attending different events, it is more likely to have a positive effect on one's work and can be not only allowed, but also encouraged by employers. This is especially relevant in the IT sector where ideas of products or services may be developed into new business opportunities benefitting the employer or its customers.

6 Discussion and Limitations

Being an entrepreneur proved to have clear advantages in terms of perceived meaningfulness when compared to employees; so, the rhetoric around promoting entrepreneurship is indeed based on the assumption that entrepreneurs are able to realize their full potential by growth and development. Meaningfulness has previously been associated with work engagement, job satisfaction, organizational commitment and (low) turnover cognitions (Fairlie, 2011a; George & Jones, 1996). Testing hypothesis 2 confirmed the latter, as the self-reported intention or probability of quitting had a negative relationship with scores of meaningful works, being most influenced by the dimensions of unity with others, developing inner self and inspiration.

Limited research on different after-work activities and their relation to meaningful work suggests that the influence of having a meaningful job on other areas of life is underestimated. Meaningful work may have other spillover effects (Burke & Greenglass, 1987) and it could also be connected to having more energy for hobbies and other projects, to higher quality relationships with friends and family as well as generally higher performance in more than one area of life.

The results of this paper may be of interest to HRD practitioners and top management as by testing hypothesis 3, the findings suggest that employees can be encouraged to participate in entrepreneurship events with no reasoned fear of them quitting.

Even though management literature since 1980s has emphasized the role of leadership in identifying for subordinates what is important and giving them direction, it appears that with or without direction – employees tend to evaluate the meaning of work constantly and independently in relation to their inner compass. This may suggest that focusing on creating meaning in the workplace through different programs is not effective because the inner value systems of an individual are in place and that far from needing to be provided with meaning, employees already have their own meaning, so it is more important to engage with the existing value systems rather than creating new ones (Lips-Wiersma & Morris, 2009).

Although the sample characteristics, like age, education level and salary were quite representative of a typical startup founder portrayed by Ajujaht organizers as well as LinkedIn's study, the sample should have also been demographically aligned with the audience of entrepreneurship events, startup hackathons and tech conferences. Discarding the online survey and using the corresponding events as a place to collect data would have achieved better representativeness. Another potential limitation of this research is the common method bias due to using self-reported data. However, there seems to be no other effective way to measure meaningful work other than using the evaluation of the individuals themselves. We acknowledge that the results may have been different if only people who work full-time while participating in an entrepreneurship event or a contest with a business idea were included in this study. As a future development, a longitudinal study could be conducted among the participants of business idea contest winners to identify whether those with lower levels of meaningful work will indeed quit their jobs to at least temporarily work on a startup.

7 Conclusions

With the help of the current study, the authors aimed to answer questions like how do employees, entrepreneurs and freelancers differ in terms of perceiving their work meaningful, what dimensions contribute most to the entrepreneurial experience, how does meaningful work relate to the likeliness of quitting one's job and starting a business and is attending entrepreneurship-related events connected to lower levels of meaning in one's work.

Since meaning is a multidimensional construct, several researchers have developed corresponding measures. Two measures of meaningful work were chosen to evaluate the meaningful—the WAMI (Work as Meaning Inventory) developed by Steger and CMWS (Comprehensive Meaningful Work Scale) validated by Lips-Wiersma and Wright. An online survey was conducted among 198 people connected to the Estonian startup and entrepreneurship ecosystem. Collected data was analysed and correlations found between different variables with the help of Microsoft Excel.

Results showed that compared to employees, entrepreneurs experience higher levels of meaning in all dimensions of the CMWS, with remarkable differences in the inspiration and expressing full potential scores. The hypothesis that lower meaningfulness in one's work can predict the intention to quit one's job was supported, however significant relation to founding a business was not identified.

Even though we predicted negative connections between the perceived meaningfulness and frequent attending to entrepreneurial and startup-related events, this hypothesis was not supported by research data. Instead, the connection between interest in entrepreneurship, following business idea and startup news, and participating in various startup events appeared to have a modest positive relation with meaningful work. Meaningful work was not associated to becoming a startup founder, full-time or part-time, working in a startup team or becoming a co-founder on a statistically significant level.

This leads us to believe that entrepreneurship interest as well as volunteering may have positive spillover effect and employees might enhance their work absorption rather than interfering with work. It is also important to note that if the perceived meaningfulness is low, an individual is anyway likely to quit, having a business idea or participating in a startup contest will not have an impact on that. Thus it is important to find ways to engage with employees' existing value systems as it is inherently human to constantly search for meaning and compare it to one's inner compass.

Annexure 1

Sample Questions from the Questionnaire

11. Please evaluate how likely do you consider the following to happen within the next 12 months

Being promoted

❒ Very likely ❒ Somewhat likely ❒ I don't know ❒ Quite unlikely ❒ Almost impossible

Getting a pay raise

❒ Very likely ❒ Somewhat likely ❒ I don't know ❒ Quite unlikely ❒ Almost impossible

Having more responsibility

❒ Very likely ❒ Somewhat likely ❒ I don't know ❒ Quite unlikely ❒ Almost impossible

Having a bigger workload

❒ Very likely ❒ Somewhat likely ❒ I don't know ❒ Quite unlikely ❒ Almost impossible

Becoming a partner in the company

❒ Very likely ❒ Somewhat likely ❒ I don't know ❒ Quite unlikely ❒ Almost impossible.

Finding a better job

❒ Very likely ❒ Somewhat likely ❒ I don't know ❒ Quite unlikely ❒ Almost impossible.

Quitting my job

❒ Very likely ❒ Somewhat likely ❒ I don't know ❒ Quite unlikely ❒ Almost impossible.

Starting my own business instead

❒ Very likely ❒ Somewhat likely ❒ I don't know ❒ Quite unlikely ❒ Almost impossible.

12. What would be the factors or events that would make you consider quitting your current job?

____.

20. Five years from now I see myself

❒ running the same business

❒ running a different business

❒ doing something different ______________________

How interested are you in the following topics?

Entrepreneurship in general

❒ not at all ❒ not very ❒ neutral ❒ somewhat ❒ very

New business ideas

❒ not at all ❒ not very ❒ neutral ❒ somewhat ❒ very

Startup ideas

❒ not at all ❒ not very ❒ neutral ❒ somewhat ❒ very

Events promoting entrepreneurship

❒ not at all ❒ not very ❒ neutral ❒ somewhat ❒ very

Business idea contests

❒ not at all ❒ not very ❒ neutral ❒ somewhat ❒ very.

36. How likely do you consider attending one of the following in the next months?

any business idea contest

❒ Extremely unlikely ❒ Somewhat unlikely ❒ Undecided ❒ Somewhat likely ❒ Extremely likely

a startup or a tech conference

❒ Extremely unlikely ❒ Somewhat unlikely ❒ Undecided ❒ Somewhat likely ❒ Extremely likely

a hackathon-style event

❒ Extremely unlikely ❒ Somewhat unlikely ❒ Undecided ❒ Somewhat likely ❒ Extremely likely

a pitching contest

❒ Extremely unlikely ❒ Somewhat unlikely ❒ Undecided ❒ Somewhat likely ❒ Extremely likely

a startup networking event

❒ Extremely unlikely ❒ Somewhat unlikely ❒ Undecided ❒ Somewhat likely ❒ Extremely likely

a fireside chat with an entrepreneur/startup founder

❒ Extremely unlikely ❒ Somewhat unlikely ❒ Undecided ❒ Somewhat likely ❒ Extremely likely

a coding/programming workshop

❒ Extremely unlikely ❒ Somewhat unlikely ❒ Undecided ❒ Somewhat likely ❒ Extremely likely

investor event

❒ Extremely unlikely ❒ Somewhat unlikely ❒ Undecided ❒ Somewhat likely ❒ Extremely likely

applied to an accelerator program

❒ Extremely unlikely ❒ Somewhat unlikely ❒ Undecided ❒ Somewhat likely ❒ Extremely likely

some other startup-related event

❒ Extremely unlikely ❒ Somewhat unlikely ❒ Undecided ❒ Somewhat likely ❒ Extremely likely

some other entrepreneurship event

❒ Extremely unlikely ❒ Somewhat unlikely ❒ Undecided ❒ Somewhat likely ❒ Extremely likely

References

Ajujahi statistika 2007–2013. Ettevõtluse Arendamise Sihtasutus. 2014.

Alderfer, C. P. (1972). *Existence, relatedness, and growth: Human needs in organizational settings*. New York, NY: Free Press.

Allan, B. A., Autin, K. L., & Duffy, R. D. (2016). Self-determination and meaningful work: Exploring socioeconomic constraints. *Frontiers in Psychology, 7*, 71. https://doi.org/10.3389/fpsyg.2016.00071.

Baumeister, R. (1991). *Meanings of life*. New York: Guilford Press.

Berg, J. L. (2015). The role of personal purpose and personal goals in symbiotic visions. *Frontiers in Psychology, 6*, 443. https://doi.org/10.3389/fpsyg.2015.00443.

Burke, R. J., & Greenglass, E. (1987). Work and family. In C. L. Cooper & I. T. Robertson (Eds.), *International review of industrial and organizational psychology* (pp. 273–320). New York: Wiley.

Emmons, R. A. (1991). Personal strivings, daily life events, and psychological and physical well-being. *Journal of Personality, 59*, 453–472.

Emmons, R. A. (1999). *The psychology of ultimate concerns: Motivation and spirituality in personality*. New York: Guilford Press.

Emmons, R. A. (2005). Striving for the sacred: Personal goals, life meaning, and religion. *Journal of Social Issues, 61*(4), 731–745.

Fairlie, P. (2010). The meaningful work inventory: Development and initial validation. In *Paper presented at the 118th Annual Convention of the American Psychological Association*. San Diego: CA.

Fairlie, P. (2011a). Meaningful work, employee engagement, and other key employee outcomes: Implications for human resource development. *Advances in Developing Human Resources, 13* (4), 508–525.

Fairlie, P. (2011b). *Meaningful work: A sleeping giant in the context of other work characteristics, work engagement, and other employee outcomes*. Department of Psychology: York University.

George, J. M., & Jones, G. R. (1996). The experience of work and turnover intentions: Interactive effects of value attainment, job satisfaction, and positive mood. *Journal of Applied Psychology, 81*(3), 318–325.

Hackman, J. R., & Oldham, G. R. (1975). Development of the job diagnostic survey. *Journal of Applied Psychology, 60*(2), 159–170.

Hackman, J. R., & Oldham, G. R. (1976). Motivation through the design of work: Test of a theory. *Organizational Behaviour and Human Performance, 16*, 250–279.
Herzberg, F. (1966). *Work and the nature of man*. Cleveland, OH: Holland.
Herzberg, F. (1968). One more time: How do you motivate employees? *Harvard Business Review, 46*(1), 53–62.
Herzberg, F., Mausner, B., Peterson, R. D., & Capwell, D. F. (1957). *Job attitudes: Review of research and opinions*. Pittsburgh: Psychological Service of Pittsburgh.
Herzberg, F., Mausner, B., & Snyderman, B. B. (1959). *The motivation to work*. New York: Wiley.
Investopedia. http://www.investopedia.com/terms/s/startup.asp (March 5, 2014).
King, L. A., & Napa, C. K. (1998). What makes a life good? *Journal of Personality and Social Psychology, 75*, 156–165.
Klinger, E. (1998). The search for meaning in evolutionary perspective and its clinical implications. In P. T. P. Wong & P. S. Fry (Eds.), *The human quest for meaning: A handbook of psychological research and clinical applications* (pp. 27–50). Mahwah, NJ: Lawrence Erlbaum Associates Publishers.
Kotter-Grühn, D., Wiest, M., Zurek, P. P., & Scheibe, S. (2009). What is it we are longing for? Psychological and demographic factors influencing the contents of Sehnsucht (life longings). *Journal of Research in Personality, 43*(3), 428–437. https://doi.org/10.1016/j.jrp.2009.01.012.
Krok, D. (2015). The role of meaning in life within the relations of religious coping and psychological well-being. *Journal of Religion and Health, 54*(6), 2292–2308. https://doi.org/10.1007/s10943-014-9983-3.
Lips-Wiersma, M., & Morris, L. (2009). Discriminating between 'meaningful work' and the 'management of meaning'. *Journal of Business Ethics, 88*, 491–511.
Lips-Wiersma, M., & Wright, S. (2012). Measuring the meaning of meaningful work: Development and validation of the comprehensive meaningful work scale (CMWS). *Group & Organization Management, 37*(5), 655–685.
Little, B. R. (1983). Personal projects: A rationale and method for investigation. *Environment and Behavior, 15*, 273–309.
Locke, E. A. (1976). The nature and causes of job satisfaction. In M. D. Dunnette (Ed.), *Handbook of industrial and organizational psychology* (pp. 1297–1343). Rand McNally: Chicago, IL.
Maslow, A. H. (1965). *Eupsychian management*. Chicago, IL: Irwin-Dorsey.
May, D. R., Gilson, R. L., & Harter, L. M. (2004). The psychological conditions of meaningfulness, safety and availability and the engagement of the human spirit at work. *Journal of Occupational and Organizational Psychology, 77*, 11–37.
McGregor, D. (1960). *The human side of enterprise*. New York, NY: McGraw-Hill.
McGregor, I., & Little, B. R. (1998). Personal projects, happiness, and meaning: On doing well and being yourself. *Journal of Personality and Social Psychology, 74*, 494–512.
Mobley, W. (1977). Intermediate linkages in the relationship between job satisfaction and employee turnover. *Journal of Applied Psychology, 62*, 237–240.
Oldham, G. R., & Hackman, J. R. (2010). Not what it was and not what it will be: The future of job design research. *Journal of Organizational Behavior, 31*, 463–479.
Rao, L. (2011). LinkedIn takes a deep data dive on startup founder profiles. TechCrunch http://techcrunch.com/2011/09/01/linkedin-takes-a-deep-data-dive-on-startup-founder-profiles/
Roberson, L. (1990). Functions of work meanings in organizations: Work meaning and work motivation. In A. P. Brief & W. R. Nord (Eds.), *Meanings of occupational work: A collection of essays* (pp. 107–134). Lexington, MA: Lexington Books.
Rodell, J. B. (2013). Finding meaning through volunteering: Why do employees volunteer and what does it mean for their jobs? *Academy of Management Journal, 56*(5), 1274–1294.
Rosso, B. D., Dekas, K. H., & Wrzesniewski, A. (2010). On the meaning of work: A theoretical integration and review. *Research in Organizational Behavior, 30*, 91–127.
Ryan, R. M., & Deci, E. L. (2000). Intrinsic and extrinsic motivations: Classic definitions and new directions. *Contemporary Educational Psychology, 25*, 54–67.

Ryff, C. D. (2000). Meaning of life. In A. E. Kazdin (Ed.), *Encyclopedia of psychology*. Oxford: Oxford University Press.

Ryff, C. D., & Keyes, C. L. M. (1995). The structure of psychological well-being revisited. *Journal of Personality and Social Psychology, 69*, 719–727.

Shea-Van Fossen, R. J., & Vredenburgh, D. J. (2011). *Exploring differences in work's meaning: An investigation of individual attributes associated with work orientations*. Institute of Behavioral and Applied Management.

Siwek, Z., Oleszkowicz, A., & Słowińska, A. (2017). Values realized in personal strivings and motivation, and meaning in life in polish university students. *Journal of Happiness Studies, 18*, 549. https://doi.org/10.1007/s10902-016-9737-x.

Startups in Estonia: Baltic Green Shoots. (2012) Schumpeter blog, *The Economist*. http://www.economist.com/blogs/schumpeter/2012/01/start-ups-estonia (Jan 6, 2018).

Steger, M. F., Dik, B. J., & Duffy, R. D. (2012). Measuring meaningful work: The work and meaning inventory (WAMI). *Journal of Career Assessment, 20*(3), 322–337.

Steger, M. F., Frazier, P., Oishi, S., & Kaler, M. (2006). The meaning in life questionnaire: Assessing the presence and search for meaning in life. *Journal of Counselling Psychology, 53* (1), 80–93.

Steger, M. F., Pickering, N. K., Shin, J. Y., & Dik, B. J. (2009). Calling in work: Secular or sacred? *Journal of Career Assessment, 18*(1), 82–96.

Stillman, T. F., & Baumeister, R. F. (2009). Uncertainty, belongingness, and four needs for meaning. *Psychological Inquiry, 20*(4), 249–251.

Waterman, A. S. (1984). *The psychology of individualism*. New York: Praeger.

Wong, P. T. P. (1998). Implicit theories of meaningful life and the development of the Personal Meaning Profile. In P. T. P. Wong & P. S. Fry (Eds.), *The human quest for meaning: A handbook of psychological research and clinical applications* (pp. 111–140). Mahwah, NJ: Erlbaum.

Wrzesnieswski, A., Dutton, J. E., & Debebe, G. (2003). Interpersonal sensemaking and the meaning of work. *Research in Organizational Behavior, 25*, 93–135.

Corporate Social Responsibility in the Education Sector in Rising Economies

Meeta Sengupta

Abstract Education is often the easiest and first of the various community development initiatives that receives support and funding from corporates, but is not necessarily the most dominant Corporate Social Responsibility investment. While the nature of CSR interventions in all economies remains similar, the sequence of investments is seen to follow a pattern across rising economies, both for local as well as transnational corporates. While all CSR has moved from philosophy to philanthropy to more modern stakeholder approaches, the requirements remain community driven. EduCSR (Education in CSR) is an understudied area with inadequate datasets, so the paper gathers key data and illustrations to connect the dots and build insights into the workings of EduCSR in rising economies. The paper identifies an EduCSR Progression Pathway for rising economies that typifies the sequence of investments in communities. This progression also raises the game for value add and impact, and the paper maps the maturity of the EduCSR sector in rising economies by identifying an EduCSR Value Chain. Combining the two, it finally creates a positioning map for economies to enable policy decisions to leapfrog to higher impact EduCSR interventions even in rising economies where CSR is yet to mature. We note that EduCSR is a bellwether investment in CSR, and plot the positioning map as a nudge tool to enable EduCSR to continue to play this role and build for higher impact interventions.

Keywords Education · Rising · Economies · School · India · Vietnam · Kenya · Uganda · Thailand · Malaysia · Bangladesh · Sustainability · EduCSR · CSR impact · Value chain

---

M. Sengupta (✉)
FRSA, New Delhi, India

Centre for Education Strategy, New Delhi, India

N. Mitra, R. Schmidpeter (eds.), *Corporate Social Responsibility in Rising Economies*, CSR, Sustainability, Ethics & Governance,
https://doi.org/10.1007/978-3-030-53775-3_4

1 Introduction

As the process of Corporate Social Responsibility (CSR) begins to find new form across the world, sometimes via legislation, and at other times via a process of consolidation of norms and best practices, the landscape across rising economies continues to shift. While some rising economies such as India have found themselves legislated into a more organized approach to CSR, other economies such as Uganda find themselves in a place where intellectual consensus does not necessarily translate to a normative praxis for corporations down the line. It is a mixed bag if one seeks a shared strand through the rising economies, yet, some interesting phenomena can be observed from the developments in CSR across a range of rising economies.

This paper seeks to consolidate observations and studies on the evolution of CSR as an investment into education in order to achieve two things. (1) An understanding of the impact of CSR on overall education efforts in countries where they will have a higher impact, and (2) An understanding of the overall cycle of CSR investment in education across rising economies. In this study, while one is constrained by the lack of organized data, this lack of data is also recognized as part of the CSR investment and impact cycle that is observed in rising economies.

In taking a sectoral view of the life cycle of CSR praxis, we note that is not always in line with the standard models and growth cycles of CSR overall. There are elements that are specific to the education sector that will clearly see replication across rising economies, and are thus useful to forecasters and policy makers. By focusing on education, one is able to observe and illustrate the life cycle of CSR investments. In laying the EduCSR activities in a simple sequence, we observe a pattern across countries and this leads to the first Finding of this paper—the Edu-CSR Progression Pathway.

The second finding of the paper is the Edu-CSR Value Chain that evolved by observing the impact and value add of the CSR activities in education, in line with maturity, requirements, funds available and indeed the risk-taking capacity of the CSR units. As Edu-CSR matures, the investments tend to diversify and support innovation rather than confine themselves to the basics. This is observed across countries.

The third finding of this study combines the two findings across countries to create an Edu-CSR positioning map. The three findings together are guide to policy makers. These are useful milestones to track progress, or even better, to design policies to leapfrog certain milestones and build a forward-looking approach to CSR goals.

2 Methodology

Most of the process is via secondary study of existing datasets and information available publicly. Datasets on CSR are not easy to build or find across the world, and the problem becomes even more difficult in rising and developing economies. This is both due to the nascence and nature of the CSR sector. It gets compounded by the fact that till very recently philanthropy by company ownership and CSR funding were often combined. Education financing too has had serious gaps in understanding the problem, so much so that as recently as 2016 UNESCO (United Nations Educational, Scientific and Cultural Organization) created a roadmap to better data that acknowledged that "data on spending by households, corporations, NGOs (Non-governmental Organisations) and off-budget donor funding is often either unavailable or available in a format which requires significant manipulation and estimations to be useable in the context of education policymaking" (UNESCO, 2016). The lack of quality datasets affects any comparative or evolutionary study including this one.

This approach is to align with the lens of a corporate or policy maker in any of the rising economies and to understand the level of information and insights that they might be able to capture. Gaps in this study are highlighted in the conclusion and lead us to the path forward both in seeking better quality data that guides impactful investment via CSR, and also in seeking to guide the capacity building that is required as a consultative and co-operative effort across these economies.

3 Developments in EDU-CSR

3.1 Global Overview

While Education competes with Health for the lead position in CSR investments, it remains prime for the CSR conversation. According to The Brookings Institution (Brookings), as reported in the UNESCO Business Backs Education Report (2015), corporate giving to global health is 16 times the figure for global education. As an example, the two largest corporate foundations in the USA (United States of America) are those of Novartis and Sanofi, the global healthcare and pharmaceutical providers. Data for the top 10 corporate foundations in the Republic of Korea (Korea) show that healthcare made up an average 89% of spending in the period 2007–12, with education the fourth most popular recipient at around 3%. The same report also quotes a study done by the (United Nations) UN System Task Team on the Post-2015 UN Development Agenda thus "The process included a Global Survey covering 850,000 participants across 194 countries; 77% of participants were from low- or medium-income countries and 64% were under 30 years of age. A majority of the participants (584,329) chose Good Education as the top priority for the Post-2015 Development Agenda."

3.2 CSR Traditions

CSR often follows traditions of philanthropy in rising economies even though the traditional literature currently tracks its Greek origins and is only now beginning to recognize it's connect with African, Buddhist, Hindu and social and historical value systems. "It is strongly believed that CSR in many developing countries takes its root from the ancient practices of religions such as Hinduism, Buddhism, Islam and Christianity, which promote and encourage philanthropic and community embedded activities (Visser, 2008). Vives (2006) stated in his survey of more than 1,300 Small and Medium Enterprises (SMEs) in the Latin America region that religious beliefs played an important role in motivating the application of CSR (Tran, 2017). For example, in Kenya "Corporate Social Responsibility (CSR) is a very old concept and practice in Uganda. Literature roots it in the African culture and values, which are well described by the African Traditional Society (ATS)" (Katamba & Nkiko, 2016).

Global investors contributing across countries to CSR also found that corporations are continually expected to work with the host government and communities to better the quality of life, educational, economic and social welfare of the natives through provision of training opportunities and employment especially for those from disadvantaged backgrounds as noted by Hufbauer and Schott (2013). Some community work was part of the traditional CSR of large local businesses since the fifties. Babirye (2014) notes that "CSR activities in Uganda can be traced back to the 1950s when the communal values of the African traditional societies were being upheld. Communities engaged in developmental activities such as building schools, hospitals and roads." Moreover, Visser and Tolhurst (2010), noted that by the 70s, this had moved on to stakeholder engagement-based CSR. Thus, most of these have a tradition of contributing to education, among other community requirements and the modern construct of CSR funding continues to follow this lead.

3.2.1 Primacy of Education in CSR Traditions

Where there is little quantitative data, it is remarkable to note that almost no conversation, conference or discussion on CSR is reported without a reference to education, across countries. Most CSR efforts across the globe, but even more particularly when the destination is a rising economy, include or lead with investments in education. While most significant CSR reporting will almost invariably include the word education, other segments may or may not find mention. Education seems to rise above all conflicts and discourse as a worthy recipient of CSR funds. An example from South Africa, "A large number of NGO practitioners reported that they found it hard to gain funding for activities that were not concerned with welfare or education" (Hirth, 2016).

Even in countries such as Laos, Cambodia and Vietnam where CSR is seen as an import, or countries such as South Africa, Kenya, Uganda with very different political histories and approaches to CSR, each report on CSR includes mention of education along with other issues. Not just that, where there is a listing of issues for CSR impact, the list is almost invariably led by education. For example, in the case of Uganda, a study lists the top 5 CSR activities thus: "The top 5 CSR activities are education, sponsorship of events related to the company's marketing strategy, health, HIV/AIDS related issues, and employee volunteerism" (CSR in Uganda, 2008). Similarly, in South Africa, the largest share of Corporate Social Investment (CSI) spend is allocated to education, with 89% of the leading corporations supporting this sector through an average 43% of their budgets (ibid.). Next in importance are social and community development causes (15%) and health (11%). Advocacy and human rights activities are less readily funded (Hirth, 2016).

Where partial data exists, education continues to rule the count. In rising economies where data collection for the largest companies is fairly standardized now, education proves to be the lead investment for CSR. Indeed, when a corporate starts off its CSR journey, one of the most obvious first investments is in education.

4 Bellwether Effect of EduCSR

By tracking the evolution of education in CSR, one can even begin to form an understanding of the state of CSR in a particular economy. Our model charts the journey of education investments through its phases, but stops short of using it as a predictive model for CSR capacity while recognising the potential. Further work between the correlation between CSR maturity and the divergence between CSR-Education spend as compared to total CSR spend will yield interesting results as increased CSR spending leads to creating more sophisticated portfolios of impact that are likely to take share of total funds away from the education sector. As long as CSR spend on education is rising for an economy and region, we can say that CSR capacity is still learning and growing, as we evidence through the case studies and references in this study. CSR in Education can therefore be used as a functional rule of thumb or almost like a bellwether for overall CSR capacity.

Corporate Social Responsibility efforts often find their first expression by investing in education, especially in rising economies or in unfamiliar terrain. Yet, they form a negligible part of the global narrative on filling the education gap both in terms of funding and in terms of solutions. Not just that, when it comes to global CSR spend, education does not necessarily remain a top spending priority as was revealed by a UNESCO report of Fortune 500 companies spend on Education conducted by the Varkey Foundation. While firms at the top of the donors list give most to education, overall the "2013 Fortune Global 500 companies only spend \$2.6bn (13%) of their combined CSR budget of \$19.9bn on education related activities. Interestingly, according to the World Bank, in 2016, the government spend on education across the world averaged around 13% of total government expenditure (World Bank, 2016).

5 Global Leadership in EduCSR

The report also finds that less than half of the Fortune Global 500 provide any spending on education-related CSR." The top donors are Santander, at 79% of its CSR budget with (United States Dollar) USD 197 m (million), IBM at 72% with USD144m and Toyota at 41% of its total CSR spend to education. The Business Backs Education Report also stated that (United Kingdom) UK firms were the largest spender on Education with the top 500 UK firms averaging USD102m. It adds, "Although US companies, with more firms in the top 500, give the biggest overall amount. There are 26 UK companies in this group of global giants, contributing about $331m (£218m) of their corporate social responsibility budgets to education projects. This is much more than the donations of 89 Chinese companies, which between them were identified as giving $47m (£31m) to education, almost all of which was spent within China. While UK top 500 firms have an average $102m (£67m) annual spend on corporate social responsibility, in China the average is $5m (£3.3m)" (UNESCO, 2019). Many of these global CSR funds are directed at rising and developed economies, though not necessarily in order of need, but more likely to be around communities where they operate.

The report finds the majority of education related CSR spending is through a handful of large companies. In order, the top ten spenders on education-related CSR in the Fortune Global 500 are: Banco Santander ($197 m), IBM ($144 m), Telefonica ($130 m), Exxon Mobil ($116), Target ($95 m), GlaxoSmithKline ($87 m), Microsoft ($87 m), Toyota Motor ($84 m), Rio Tinto Group ($82 m), Wells Fargo ($82 m) (Figures are an average of the 3 years 2011–2013). The top ten companies contribute 42% and the top 20 contribute 62% of the total education related CSR spend. The most popular area of spending for education related CSR activities is higher education (33%), while only 16% goes to primary education and 14% to secondary education.

6 Global Gaps in EduCSR

Education-related CSR spending is not concentrated on where it is needed most. In total, the CSR spend on UNESCO-designated education priorities, including Africa, Asia Pacific and Latin America, together with all global spending on primary and secondary education, only amounts to $1bn or 42% of the total Fortune Global 500 Education CSR spend. Australia (62%) and Germany (60%) are the developed countries that devote the greatest percentage of their education related CSR spend to these UNESCO priority areas. The US spends 40% and the UK spends 24% of their education related CSR spend in priority areas; France spends only 4% of its education related CSR spend on priority areas.

The global funding gap in education is significantly larger than the combined total of these large contributors to education. According to a Brookings report, after taking account of available domestic and donor resources, it was estimated that an additional $26 billion would be needed per year to make sure all children receive a basic education by 2015 (Rose & Steer, 2013). This gap grew to USD 38 billion for the Sustainable Development Goals (SDGs) post 2015 (UNESCO Media Services, 2015). This has, infact, been validated by the more recent policy paper on the funding gap confirming that an annual funding gap of at least US$39 billion per year would persist in 2015–2030 as per the estimate of the Global Education Monitoring Report of 2015 (UNESDOC, 2018).

7 The EDU-CSR Challenge

7.1 The Case of Kenya

Education leads CSR but CSR barely makes a dent in the need/or investment bucket of education. For example, let us take the example of a typical CSR project in Kenya (Ndonye, 2014), that references the Wings to Fly program which is a scholarship program that is 'Kenya's largest secondary education and leadership program". "This scholarship program is a partnership between Equity Group Foundation and The MasterCard Foundation, supported by USAID, UK-Aid and KFW." The size of the fund is not small either. "According to Equity Bank Group and the Mastercard Foundation (2013), the fund has grown from USD 50m in 2010 to USD 75.6m in 2013; benefiting nearly 8700 secondary scholars as part of a 10,000 scholarship target annually. The program anticipates enabling 5600 academically gifted, but financially disadvantaged Kenyan students to complete secondary school at the end of their circle each year." This was an excellent investment for a CSR project since it was part of the dramatic improvement in secondary school achievement rates that went up to over 80% by 2016 (Global partnership for Education—Kenya, 2019). The numbers of out of school children in the country have gone down from two million in 2002 to 771,000 by 2007 (GIZ, 2013). The CSR program's target group of secondary students in the nation had only 0.03 million out of school in 2010 (Education for all Global Monitoring Report, 2012), and this is excellent progress. But contrast this with the target set for the program which is the second largest in the country at 10,000 students.

Clearly CSR projects cannot ever be the whole of the solution to education gaps and can only support at the margins. This is a missed opportunity for CSR to get a seat at the policy table and build its impact and access. Of course, Kenya has invested heavily in solving for its education gaps, spending around 5.3% of its GDP on education (Trading Economics—Kenya, 2019), thus narrowing the gap. But the story of CSR impact remains the same across countries if one views them through the lens of the impact of individual CSR efforts, however well-intentioned and designed.

7.2 The Case of Uganda

Recent trends in Education CSR can be evidenced by a sampling of announcements made by large corporates in Uganda. As recently as 2017, three large companies, MTN, NTV and National Oil made separate statements where 60% of CSR funds were committed to education by one, another noted that the CSR investment by Banks alone in Uganda exceeded USD 2.5 Billion Ugandan Shilling and the third handed over twin staff houses and an ablution block to a local secondary school.

Once the aggregate is parsed, we can see a few trends highlighted here. One, that there is clearly a commitment to education via CSR in rising economies. Second, the commitment is reflected in promises of significant investments in the aggregate, both in terms of share of CSR funds and in terms of absolute value invested. Third, CSR investment in education is a matter of pride and gives credibility to the corporate that is making the investment. Fourth, while CSR investments are called upon to strengthen the corporate image, it is not necessarily significant enough for the CEOs (Chief Executive Officers) to directly lend their name or time to these efforts. Fifth, even as the investments and announcements are grand, the reality of CSR in education often is that the contributions are a slow and steady drip feed that support the sector, rather than high impact catalysts for progress. This remains a missed opportunity for CSR in rising economies and we catalogue it in our model below to allow for policy makers to address.

The impact of CSR to the education sector in Uganda can be illustrated with a series of examples and data. Take the case of the multinational oil company Tullow, that calls itself Africa's largest independent oil company. In the Hoima district, where it has operations, "Tullow is constructing two health centers and two primary schools at an estimated cost of 2.6 million dollars. This brings the total investment by one company into the community to at least 5 million dollars." Tullow's partner, "CNOOC launched a $ 50,000 one-year basic skills training programme at Nile Vocational Institute in Hoima, sponsoring 70 youths to train in metal fabrication, wielding and other vocational skills. The company also supports a primary school and health center in Buhukya (Hoima), where the Kingfisher discoveries are located" (Oil in Uganda, 2018). Schools are an essential investment in a country where primary school completion rates are around 57% (2014) and secondary school completion hovers around 30% (Global partnership for Education—Uganda, 2019) and the CSR efforts will benefit the local community, but the scale of the problem requires investments larger than are currently being offered via CSR projects.

Uganda specifically does quite well when it comes to the quality CSR engagement, even if the quantity remains limited. The regulatory mechanisms too are supportive even though it does not have specific CSR legislation at the time of writing, yet. Education, as we have seen via surveys and case studies remains the leading target for CSR funding, though amongst other community services as evidenced by a survey study of Ugandan corporates conducted by UCCSRI/DED" (Katamba et al., 2014) that revealed that "Companies are to a great extent involved in communities, but the range of their activities vary widely in scope. The top 5 CSR activities are education, sponsorship of events related to the company's marketing strategy, health, HIV/AIDS related issues, and employee volunteerism."

Even as Education remain very high on the list for CSR, CSR does not form a significant part of the education discourse in Uganda. CSR needs to either accept that it will remain on the sidelines when solving for education and progress, or the CSR engagement needs to be increased both in terms of funds and care. The problem in Ugandan schools is one of drop outs, since in the Hoima district (National Population and Housing Census, 2014), one in ten have never attended school. Thus 90%, on average, do start off, but due to structural issues impacting quality delivery, achievement and attainment rates are very low. Current CSR efforts are often geared towards more basic needs such as infrastructure directly around their areas of interest whereas few have moved on to owning the question of quality and relevance. The 'CSR-Edu' model proposed will then place Uganda somewhere in the left quadrants, while the overall CSR discourse in the country is quite mature and investments in education projects tend to focus on physical infrastructure, education technology investments and similar basic development needs. These are important support structures to the host country and district, but will never create high impact change to catalyze growth unless CSR projects include contextual design elements with clearly stated goals. For example, the CAMFED model creates high impact leadership and community training via girl education and beyond but does not operate in Uganda. This is reflective of the pressures on education in the Ugandan system with severe capacity constraints—and CSR funding is reacting to the present rather than creating a strategic pathway for the future of education in the country. CSR for Education has the opportunity and the freedom to go above and beyond in ways that national and multilateral funds cannot, and if CSR strategists do not design their investments along long term goals, they are missing a clear opportunity for leadership.

7.3 *The Case of India: The Missed Opportunity*

In India, the CSR discourse is quite mature and it is one of the only countries to have mandated CSR investments via legislation. The legislation is fairly recent and has triggered professionalization of the sector amongst the larger players, where it applies. These corporates already had strong CSR programs but now the law asks them to align them to specific strategies while allowing them to engage with national development schemes for a minimum of 2% of their average net profits. A KPMG report on CSR spend assesses that "A total of 1019 listed Indian companies have spent an amount to the tune of INR 9034 crore in the financial year (FY)17 to fund their CSR projects and activities." and that "nearly 37% of these funds were used for education and vocational skill building activities" (KPMG, 2018).

Even so, this was a drop in the ocean. Corporate CSR spending on education worked out to about INR 4000 crores at best. According to the Asian Venture Philanthropy Network, "India's total financial requirement to reach SDG4 by 2030 is USD 2258 billion, which works out to an average USD of 173 billion per year from 2017 to 2030, far exceeding the current government budget of USD 51.5 billion a year for education.". They also report that Education has been one of the most invested causes where "the sector received USD 419 million through CSR just in 2016, which makes it one of the most invested causes across the spectrum in 2016 (IDR, 2017). CSR spending is significant, and skewed towards education in this fast-growing economy, and yet it is merely a decimal fraction of both governments spend, and of the funding gap (IDR, 2017).

7.4 The Case of Vietnam

In countries like Vietnam with its specific socio-political history, the impact of CSR on education is very selective. In our model, it stands with early stage CSR but the education impact is not on infrastructure or the basics. Most CSR is nascent and directed by the requirements of the home countries of MNCs that operate here or source their goods from Vietnamese manufacturers, thus most CSR is about the environment and clean supply chains. Vietnam has invested about 20% of its GNP (Gross National Product) in education each year, primary education is compulsory and completion rates are near 100%, and have exceeded them in past years (Global Partnership for Education—Vietnam, 2019). Under such circumstances, the potential for CSR to impact the education sector is in the gap areas—quality, innovation, entrepreneurship and IT training. For example, Aeon of Japan funds CSR projects in Vietnam that include scholarships, teen ambassadors, student exchanges, school construction support and tree planting (AEON, 2019). Also, "Vietnamese firms are found to actively participate in community investment to help alleviate various social ills, such as a lack of sufficient funding for educational institutions, national poverty, social inequality, and illiteracy (C. L. Hoang, 2015)" (Nguyen et al., 2018). Vietnamese firms do engage in projects in education, but clearly play only a supportive role as part of community development initiatives and not direct education interventions. "Vietnamese firms are found to actively participate in community investment to help alleviate various social ills, such as a lack of sufficient funding for educational institutions, national poverty, social inequality, and illiteracy (C. L. Hoang, 2015)" (Nguyen et al., 2018).

The irrelevance of CSR funding to the education funding gap discourse cannot be demonstrated more starkly than by referring to the UNESCO's roadmap to better data on Education financing published by the UNESCO's Institute for Statistics as recently as 2016 which does not include either the words 'corporate' or 'business'. Even worse, the term CSR does not refer to Corporate Social Responsibility at all but to Education Country Status Reports (UNESCO, 2016). It is an interesting feature of data and discourse in education that neither direct investment in the sector, nor the CSR (corporate social responsibility this time) funding of projects is included. This is both ideological and biased towards the global north. Most of the theories of education as a public good, as well as the better-quality data come from these countries where the private sector has a very small share of the market. This is in contrast to many rising economies such as Nigeria and India where private sector education establishments, while being smaller than the public sector, are a significant provider both in terms of quality as well as volume. Other rising economies with stronger socialist and communist history tend to have a very small private sector. Across rising economies though, when it comes to CSR funding, the influence remains small enough to be, at best, marginal, as evidenced above.

8 Impact of CSR Funding in Education: Catalysing the Value Chain

CSR funding of education might be small in rising economies but it does have the potential to create significant impact on the education conversation. CSR, while operating at the margins may not be able to impact for volume and scale, but it does have the ability to make a difference to education. For example, in India, while CSR funds in education do follow the pattern identified in the model but have also ascended the value chain to enable innovation and robust pilots of concepts that can be adopted in scaled solutions. CSR funded education pilots could be pioneers in various south—south solutions since there is a high degree of contextual similarity that can be found in specific parts of rising economies. For example, the CSR efforts of Aeon Japan replicates the success of their travel and educational programs across Laos, Vietnam, Thailand among other countries. A transnational corporation is uniquely placed to replicate its methodology and learnings across the various countries in which it does business and thus enable rising economies to leapfrog the learning curve in delivering quality solutions to education.

Replication gains in Education can extend across countries via direct CSR programs such as Aeon, or via funding interventions in education that scale across countries. An example of this is via STIR Education, a UK based intervention that operates in India, and now Uganda. According to their website (Stir Education, 2019) they have impacted 200,000 teachers and six million children in India and Uganda. While honing their model in India to meet the needs of both funding agencies and the needs of students, teachers and partner governments, they have been able to create whole system of teacher enablement programs that can now be rendered at an average cost per student (and falling) of as little as $0.40 USD per year. Their numbers say that, "Every $1 USD invested can yield our partner governments $7 USD in improved short- & mid-term efficiencies. And up to $100 USD in measurable long-term economic growth.". Here is a classic opportunity that is typically available to corporates to invest in scaleable, replicable, and, rigorous solutions that have evidenced impact. Yet organizations such as these find that traditional government and grant funding from bilateral and multilateral agencies are way ahead of corporate funding. Indeed, family funds run by owners of corporates seem to invest as much or more in education than CSR funding to education.

The Stir Education website lists its funding partners (STIR Education, 2019) and we find that only 'innovative' corporates have engaged in this solution.

This highlights a third trend in CSR funding for education across rising economies. The CSR conversation has not reached the C Suite and decisions are delegated to either corporate communications departments or similar. These staffers have limited degrees of freedom and high accountability for funds. This becomes even more tight in countries that bring in more regulation and order to CSR, such as India, where laws and internal policies restrict the range of investments in which the department can invest (Sengupta, 2017). Creating a CSR strategy often restricts the degree of freedom that was otherwise available to officials in charge of CSR. Some tend to pull their CSR efforts in house, while others create a portfolio of partnerships, in order to manage the branding and the positioning better. As the system begins to become more effective towards improving the corporate brand image, the engagement with the Owner/CEO also begins to rise, leading to stronger accountability systems. While this brings a better understanding of impact, and consequently more efficiency in deploying CSR, it also brings with it a certain risk aversion, which in turn has an adverse impact on funding innovative interventions. When seen from a sectoral lens, this transition is often a missed chance for innovations—an area where CSR could have created deep impact and demonstrated leadership.

8.1 *Identifying the Elements of the Progression Pathway and Value Chain*

As CSR systems become more professional, we see that the nature of projects funded via CSR moves up the value chain in rising economies. As the CSR ecosystem becomes more sophisticated, so does the CSR investment portfolio in education. This is well illustrated by the example of the SRF Foundation from India, the CSR arm of the large transnational firm that operates in chemicals. Its key focus has been education, though it does work in Health and Environment too. It started by founding schools, both elite and accessible and continues to strengthen the sector by supporting government schools to improve the quality of education available to all. This is topped up with work on vocational skills and livelihood training. Over the years SRF Foundation (2019) has built on the credibility of its founders and has gone on to create a professional approach to both brand building and consolidating its contribution to education. This portfolio of CSR-Edu is a high-level investment of not just funds, but also senior management time. The SRF fund, while attached to the corporate and managed by senior CSR professionals is also overseen by the family that has majority shareholding in the corporation.

Similarly, an example from Japan, where Aeon invests heavily in education in many rising and developing Asian economies including (China), Indonesia, Malaysia, Thailand, Vietnam, Laos, Cambodia, Myanmar and Laos. The CSR-Edu portfolio has five main products, but each is not applied to every country. All of them have School Construction, except for Indonesia and Myanmar. The Scholarship applies to most, as does Tree Planting. The Student Ambassador program is engaged in more countries than the Leadership program. These reflect on the sophistication with which this Edu-CSR portfolio has been designed and places it high on the Value Chain in our model.

Finding 1: Identifying the Edu-CSR Progression Pathway
Often Edu-CSR is much simpler than these, starting with donations, and possibly scholarships. This is how most companies start their journey, but are cautioned thus, (Magdalene, 2014) "despite the call for corporations to fully engage in the promotion of education, Rong (2010) cautions companies to avoid "low level involvement" where they just make donations without bothering to track and support the implementation of the educational projects. He claims that this habit has led to wastage of resources with little or no direct impact." Our model then recognizes the next stage of investment, which involves building and maintaining infrastructure, and in current times has extended itself to providing digital infrastructure—funding a computer lab, electricity, a generator, clean water supply and more.

The next stage is where it begins to get interesting for educators and where we begin to see some impact. This requires schools to partner in the journey towards quality solutions. "Porter and Soper (2003) argue that schools must exhaustively identify their strengths, weaknesses as well as needs and formulate strategies to curb them in order to benefit from sustainable improvement through CSR activities. Likewise, the firms availing these activities should design CSR plans that; (1) Incorporates all aspects of the school especially management (2) Programs that motivate and enable children to meet their daily academic goals and challenges (3) A plan to use research to drive the move towards a unified plan with a sole focus. Importantly, a good CSR strategy considers both the implementation of a CSR plan and sustainability" (Magdalene, 2014).

Solutions for improving outcomes are the third phase, chronologically, of Edu-CSR intervention design, and are the most interesting part of the sector today. Impact assessment reports keep the school and the intervention partners on their toes, and conversely, we see stronger investments in areas that can bring better impact metrics to the investors. For example, from South Africa we see, "maths and science continue to be the most popular subject areas for investment in education, attracting 38% of education spend. Infrastructure, facilities and equipment (23%), and bursaries and scholarships (22%), were the most popular types of intervention in 2013 in the corporations surveyed by Trialogue (ibid.)" (Mueller-Hirth, 2016).

The hierarchy of investments too follows a familiar pattern—simple infrastructure investments take the lead, followed by scholarships and it is only much later that investments in soft infrastructure, innovation or even technology is funded by CSR efforts. All of these findings can be observed via the CSR-Education Progression model proposed below (Fig. 1). The pathway outlines the impact on education via CSR as countries traverse the increased consolidation of CSR principles and practices on one hand, and the value chain of education initiatives on the other hand. The

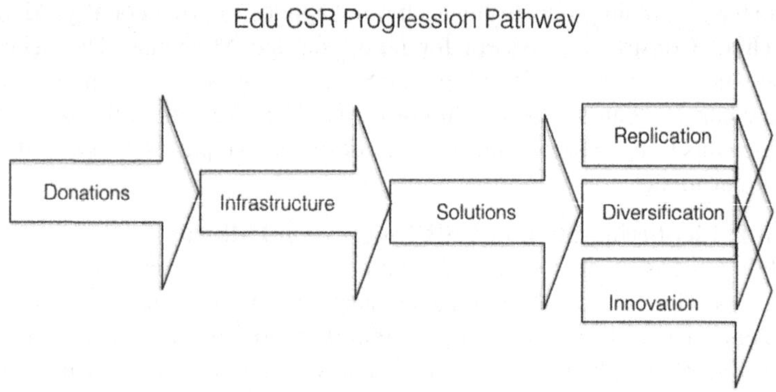

Fig. 1 Finding 1: EduCSR progression pathway by time/phase. Source: Author contribution

progression model finally leads to a portfolio of investments in CSR, not necessarily just EduCSR. This "Eg in India, KPMG's report, 'India CSR Reporting Survey' showed that while education and healthcare have been in focus for the past 3 years, organizations have slowly begun diversifying their area and geography of development in the last one year."

Finding 2: The EduCSR value chain progression pathway

When we layer this with the variables impact and investment, we begin to perceive the value chain linkages of these components. Following chronology, the simplest progression pathway is along the four stages, starting with donations and moving on towards a portfolio. Donations, scholarships, building infrastructure etc. fall at the low involvement end of the spectrum. They take limited management time and there are no follow up or care issues. It reflects a one-time investment, or a limited involvement. Schools built by corporations can then be donated to governments to run, and a computer lab, once set up and running needs no more attention. Building specific solutions, and proving their impact is a higher order ask from Edu-CSR and then further along the spectrum, we as Edu-CSR to take on some risk as well, by either replicating their successful model or by diversifying their education interventions since they have now honed management capacity.

The value chain works not just along the line of chronology, as comfort levels with the target sector rise, but also works along the investment, impact and risk spectrum with the goal of achieving higher impact. In order to do that, we can lay these components in a matrix with risk-reward axes, such as impact and investment. *Low impact, Low investment interventions include donations etc*. But now we realize that once solutions have been honed and are ready to scale, the returns to investment are not equivalent to the three pathways. Replication is a high impact option with lower costs than innovation and diversification which will have to bear the extra investment of understanding new terrain and recontextualizing the solution. This modelling exercise (Fig. 2) outlines an EduCSR tool that can help decision making within the corporate both for choosing initial education CSR investments, and also for choosing a path forward for growth.

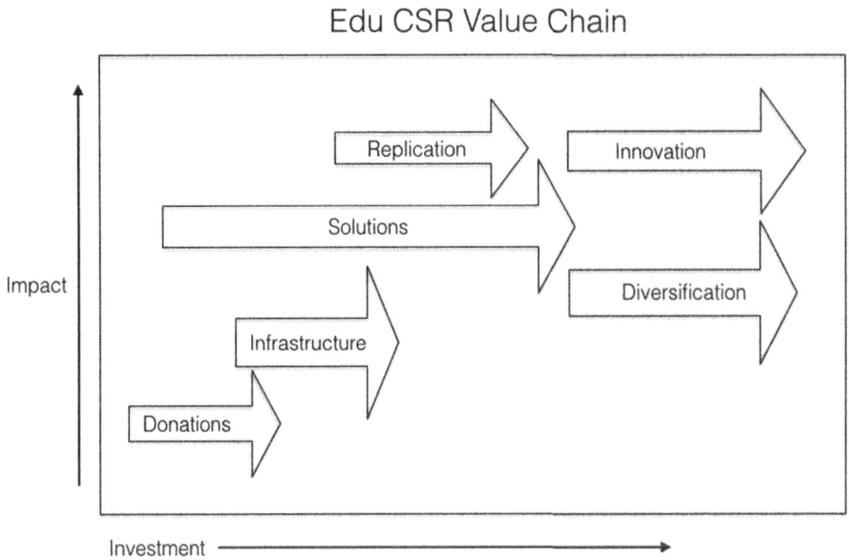

Fig. 2 Finding 2: EduCSR value chain by impact of CSR investment

Finding 3: CSR Positioning Model

Building on the broad understanding of the EduCSR progression pathway and mapping it to a general CSR maturity axis, we broadly plot the progress made by countries according to their CSR ecosystem and allocation priorities. This is a conceptual model that seeks to understand a country's positioning along CSR Maturity as measured in EduCSR, since EduCSR is often a bellwether CSR investment. We broadly plot the rising economies that we have studied in this paper along the axis as defined by the model to reveal opportunities for growth and making directional choices in policy formulation.

Further empirical studies could establish more precise understanding of the relative positioning of countries—but that is out of the scope of this current analysis, partially due to the paucity of data. The lack of data is compensated with a comprehensive study of secondary sources of contemporary reporting and evidence presented here is restricted to representative illustrations of the trends observed. Mature systems themselves do not have strong and consistent reporting systems even in advanced economies. As recently as 2003 only 48% of the top 100 firms in the world produced public reports on social or environmental issues, (O'Rourke, 2014), according to a World Bank report on obstacles in CSR Reporting in Developing countries. To find little credible and consolidated data in countries that are evolving their CSR journeys could be considered evidence of their stage of evolution. An investment in data and studies about CSR is also indicative of the energy and possibilities identified by market forces and helps set expectations from CSR funding for social impact.

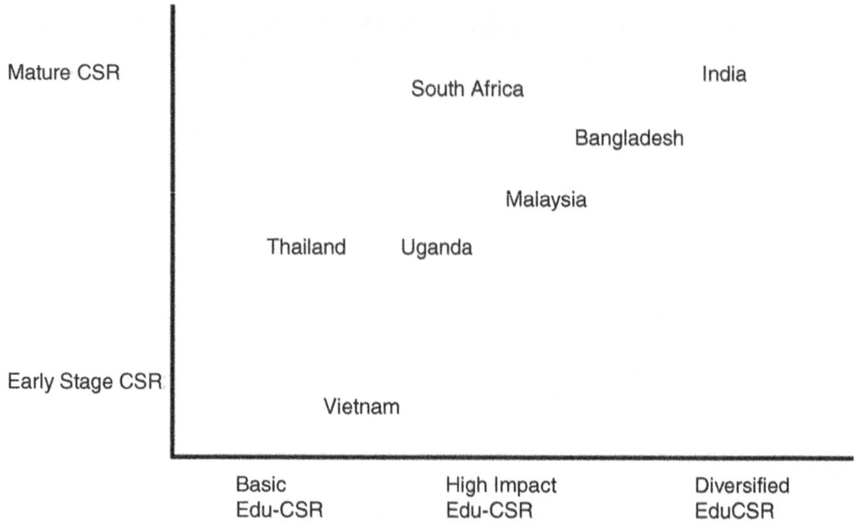

Fig. 3 Finding 3: EduCSR positioning model. Source: Author contribution

On one axis, we rely on our Value Chain Progression Pathway that already defines the spectrum of EduCSR and can be further simplified into Basic-EduCSR, High Impact EduCSR and Diversified EduCSR. Thus, countries with only basic Edu-CSR such as scholarships, donations or school building exercises get placed accordingly, whereas countries with strong Edu-CSR strategies that include a portfolio of CSR products implemented in different locations are placed at the higher end of the scale.

On the other axis we place countries according to the maturity of their CSR sector. While various theoretical models offer great sophistication, for our purpose we merely section them along the spectrum of Early stage CSR and Mature CSR. For the purposes of this model (Fig. 3) we will merely classify them as Early Stage and Mature CSR systems. Early stage CSR systems are typified as those where there is (1) low awareness of CSR, (2) CSR and philanthropy are often conflated, (3) CSR funding is for basic local development projects, and (4) low engagement of the C-Suite. Mature CSR systems are economies where (1) CSR impacts the business discourse, (2) Strategic CSR is a senior management concern, (3) CSR communities build self-improvement pathways such as forums, consulting services, awards and best practice records in addition to studies and data gathering. Entry Stage CSR systems often do not have data available, and this is clearly a limitation of this study but does not affect the robustness of the model.

8.2 The Mapping

The mapping of EduCSR to CSR Maturity gives us very interesting insights and guidelines to further action. The model places countries on this continuum observed and evidenced in this study with the objective of creating a framework that will enable rising economies to create policies that can leapfrog the lower levels of the value chain in education projects even if they are at the early stage in their CSR journey. While we see that it is possible to look at Edu-CSR mapped as a predictor of CSR capacity, thus giving us a rule of thumb or bellwether measure of overall CSR, there is more to this mapping. Creating a positioning map for countries is a **wakeup call to policy makers** by identifying the potential to leapfrog traditional patterns. So a rising economy with nascent or early stage CSR does not necessarily need to allow EduCSR to wallow in low impact areas such as building schools, which can easily be done by the government or local philanthropy. It is a nudge to create policies that enable Edu-CSR to work their management capacity harder along with their funds and create high impact interventions and a diversified portfolio of education solutions that can catalyse learning outcomes and national progress.

9 Conclusions

We note that CSR in Education is an important part of the CSR investments but given the scale of the global education gaps, CSR has not been able to create much impact so far. This is an opportunity for Education CSR to take a look at its interventions and move up the value chain towards interventions that are difficult for governments to undertake but will make a high impact change to the current problems. To this end, this paper has proposed a framework for the Value chain of CSR in Education and used it to create a decision framework for managements and for countries. Further work is required to refine both the models and populate them, and this is expected as the models are used to guide policy and decision making for education CSR investments.

References

AEON. (2019). *CSR activities in Asian countries*. Accessed on December 17, 2019, from http://aeon1p.or.jp/1p/en/others/vietnam/

Babirye, M. (2014). *Corporate social responsibility in Uganda's oil and gas industry. What can Uganda learn from The Norwegian policies and practices?* Accessed November 16, 2019, from http://www.wgei.org/wp-content/uploads/2018/01/Magdalene-DISSERTATION.pdf

CSR in Uganda. (2008). *CSR in Uganda: Perceptions, approaches and needs of companies*. Final Draft. Conducted by: UCCSRI: David Katamba DED Uganda: Sabine Gisch-Boie, Aleksander Slowinski Funded by: DED Kampala, December 17th, 2008.

Education for all Global Monitoring Report. (2012). *Education in Kenya*. Accessed November 3, 2019, from https://en.unesco.org/gem-report/sites/gem-report/files/EDUCATION_IN_KENYA_A_FACT_SHEET.pdf

GIZ. (2013). *Shaping corporate social responsibility in sub-Saharan Africa guidance notes from a mapping survey*. GIZ.

Global Partnership for Education – Kenya. (2019). *Education in Kenya*. Accessed December 23, 2019, from https://www.globalpartnership.org/country/kenya

Global Partnership for Education – Uganda. (2019). *Education in Uganda*. Accessed December 22, 2019, from https://www.globalpartnership.org/country/uganda

Global Partnership for Education – Vietnam. (2019). *Education in Vietnam*. Accessed December 29, 2019, from https://www.globalpartnership.org/country/vietnam

Hirth, N. M. (2016). *Corporate social responsibility and development in South Africa: Socio-economic contexts and contemporary issues*. Accessed December 15, 2019, from https://www.researchgate.net/publication/300123472_Corporate_Social_Responsibility_and_Development_in_South_Africa_Socio-economic_Contexts_and_Contemporary_Issues

Hufbauer, G. & Schott, J. (2013). *Report to the ICC Research Foundation*, Institute. World Trade Agenda. Accessed November 27, 2019, from https://www.piie.com/sites/default/files/publications/papers/hufbauerschott20130422.pdf

IDR. (2017). *Funding education with impact*. Accessed December 3, 2019, from https://idronline.org/funding-education-with-impact/

Katamba, D., & Nkiko, C. M. (2016). The landscape of corporate social responsibility in Uganda: Its past, present and future. In S. Vertigans, S. Idowu, & R. Schmidpeter (Eds.), *Corporate social responsibility in Sub-Saharan Africa. CSR, sustainability, ethics and governance*. Cham: Springer.

Katamba, D., Tushabomwe-Kazooba, C., Babiiha, S., Nkiko, C., Nabatanzi-Muy, A. K. & Hensley, K. J. (2014). *CSR in Uganda – Perceptions approaches and needs of companies*. Accessed December 19, 2019, from https://www.researchgate.net/publication/265087442_CSR_in_Uganda_-_Perceptions_Approaches_and_needs_of_companies/citation/download

KPMG. (2018). *India's CSR reporting survey 2017*. Accessed December 16, 2019, from https://assets.kpmg.com/content/dam/kpmg/in/pdf/2018/02/CSR-Survey-Report.pdf

Magdalene, B. (2014). *Corporate social responsibility in Uganda's oil and gas industry. What can Uganda learn from the Norwegian policies and practices?* The Robert Gordon University, Aberdeen, UK Aberdeen Business School. Accessed December 4, 2019, from http://www.wgei.org/wp-content/uploads/2018/01/Magdalene-DISSERTATION.pdf

Mueller-Hirth, N. (2016). Corporate social responsibility and development in South Africa: Socio-economic contexts and contemporary issues. In S. Vertigans, S. Idowu, & R. Schmidpeter (Eds.), *Corporate social responsibility in Sub-Saharan Africa. CSR, sustainability, ethics and governance*. Cham: Springer.

National Population and Housing Census. (2014). *Hoima District*. Accessed December 4, 2019, from https://www.ubos.org/onlinefiles/uploads/ubos/2014CensusProfiles/HOIMA.pdf

Ndonye, M. M. (2014). *Introduction to corporate social responsibility and community relations in Kenya*. Egerton University, Nioro. Accessed November 26, 2019, from https://www.academia.edu/8497022

Nguyen, M., Bensemann, J. & Kelly, S. (2018). Corporate social responsibility (CSR) in Vietnam: a conceptual framework. *International Journal of Corporate Social Responsibility, 3*, 9. https://doi.org/10.1186/s40991-018-0032-5. Accessed December 16, 2019, from https://link.springer.com/article/10.1186/s40991-018-0032-5

O'Rourke, D. (2014). *Opportunities and obstacles for corporate social responsibility reporting in developing countries*. Berkeley: University of California.

Oil in Uganda. (2018). Accessed on August 14, 2018, now closed, from http://www.oilinuganda.org/features/infrastructure/3281.html

Rong, G. (2010). *Education and corporate social responsibility*. Paris: Social Business/Enterprise & Poverty Certificate Project.

Rose, P. & Steer, L. (2013). *Financing for global education. Opportunities for multilateral action*. Accessed December 3, 2019, from https://www.brookings.edu/wp-content/uploads/2016/06/Basic-Education-Financing-Final-webv2.pdf

Sengupta, M. (2017). Impact of CSR on education sector. In N. Mitra & R. Schmidpeter (Eds.), *Corporate social responsibility in India. CSR, sustainability, ethics and governance*. Cham: Springer.

SRF Foundation. (2019). Accessed December 29, 2019, from http://www.srf.com/srf-foundation/foundation.html#education

STIR Education. (2019). Accessed December 29, 2019, from https://stireducation.org/partners.html

Trading Economics – Kenya. (2019). https://tradingeconomics.com/kenya/public-spending-on-education-total-percent-of-gdp-wb-data.html. Accessed December 29, 2019.

Tran, T. T. (2017). *Corporate Social Responsibility (CSR) Situation in Vietnam*. Saimaa University of Applied Sciences, Faculty of Business Administration Lappeenranta, Degree Programme in International Business, Thesis.

UNESCO. (2016). *A roadmap to better data on education financing*. UNESCO Institute for Statistics. Accessed on November 26, 2019, from http://uis.unesco.org/sites/default/files/documents/a-roadmap-to-better-data-on-education-financing-2016-en.pdf

UNESCO. (2019). *New report finds Fortune 500 companies commit a fraction of CSR spend on education*. Accessed November 25, 2019, from https://en.unesco.org/news/new-report-finds-fortune-500-companies-spend-fraction-csr-spend-education

UNESCO Business Backs Education Report. (2015). Accessed on November 26, 2019, from www.unesco.org/education/BBE-EPG-Report2015.pdf

UNESCO Media Services. (2015). *Funding gap for education growing, according to new figures released by UNESCO*. Accessed November 25, 2019, from http://www.unesco.org/new/typo3temp/pics/6c74086bb4.jpg) (http://www.unesco.org/new/en/media-services/in-focus-articles/funding-gap-for-education-growing-according-to-new-figures-released-by-unesco-study-also-proposes-ways-to-close-it/

UNESDOC. (2018). *Aid to education: a return to growth?* Accessed November 23, 2019, from http://unesdoc.unesco.org/images/0026/002636/263616e.pdf

Visser, W. (2008). Corporate social responsibility in developing countries. In A. Crane, A. McWilliams, D. Matten, J. Moon, & D. Siegel (Eds.), *The Oxford handbook of corporate social responsibility* (pp. 473–479). Oxford: Oxford University Press.

Visser, W., & Tolhurst, N. (2010). *The world guide to CSR: A country-by-country analysis of corporate sustainability and responsibility* (pp. 296–304). Greenleaf: Sheefield.

Vives, A. (2006). Social and environmental responsibility in small and medium enterprises in Latin America. *Journal of Corporate Citizenship, 2006*. https://doi.org/10.9774/GLEAF.4700.2006.sp.00006.

World Bank. (2016). Accessed December 16, 2019, from https://data.worldbank.org/indicator/SE.XPD.TOTL.GB.ZS?view=chart

Part II
Country-Specific Studies

Small Size, Bigger Impact: Do SMEs Care About Social Responsibility In Pakistan?

Majid Khan, Rahizah Sulaiman, Omer Nazir, and Waqar Ahmad

Abstract Drawing upon the literature, this chapter highlights the socially responsible activities of Small and medium enterprises (SMEs) in the developing country context i.e. Pakistan. SMEs are considered to be at a better position to create jobs and alleviate poverty in the developing countries given their proximities to the local community and other stakeholders. Therefore, we examine the contextual factors of SMEs—including potential contribution and specificities with respect to social responsibility. By doing so, we start with discussing the working conditions in developing countries. We also highlight the impediments of Pakistani SMEs in relation to social responsibility. The chapter concludes with a brief summary of prospects and recommendations for both SMEs and policy makers.

Keywords Social responsibility · Small and medium enterprises (SMEs) · Sustainable development · Contextual factors of developing countries · Pakistan

1 Background

Recently there has been a surge of academic interest in social responsibility in emerging countries, articulated through research articles, books and chapters written on the topic (Jamali, Lund-Thomsen, & Jeppesen, 2017). However, this uptake in research on Corporate Social Responsibility (CSR) is mainly focussed on larger organisations; and Small and Medium Enterprises (SMEs) have received less

M. Khan (✉)
Massey University, Palmerston North, New Zealand
e-mail: m.khan@massey.ac.nz

R. Sulaiman · O. Nazir
Massey Business School, Massey University, Palmerston North, New Zealand

W. Ahmad
Kunming University of Science and Technology, Kunming, China

N. Mitra, R. Schmidpeter (eds.), *Corporate Social Responsibility in Rising Economies*, CSR, Sustainability, Ethics & Governance,
https://doi.org/10.1007/978-3-030-53775-3_5

attention in emerging countries. SMEs are significantly different from the larger organisations, and the findings from larger organisations cannot be applicable to SMEs when it comes to social responsibility (Spence, 2007). Due to the resource deficiency, lack of formal structure and consistent struggle for survival, SMEs are less likely to be involved in socially responsible activities. Consequently, there has been less academic inquiries on social responsibility of SMEs in developing countries.

This is surprising, considering the role SMEs play in developing economies in terms of job creation and their cumulative impacts on environment and society (Fox, 2004). For example, in Pakistan SMEs constitute 90% of all the businesses, contributing over 40% to Gross Domestic Product (GDP) and a proportion of 30% to the overall country's exports (Zafar & Mustafa, 2017). Additionally, SMEs are considered to be closer to the society and community in which they operate (Azmat & Samaratunge, 2009). Despite this considerable contribution of SMEs to national exchequer, SMEs in Pakistan have been involved in irresponsible behaviour such as child labour, appalling work conditions and below minimum wage rate payment to employees (Bhutta, 2006). Moreover, the foreign buyers expect Pakistani enterprises to adopt international CSR standards for fair labour practice, social and environmental issues (Sajjad & Eweje, 2014). Noting these issues, SMEs in Pakistan are expected to respond to the social and environmental concerns with their operations by international affiliates, government and the civil society. This is one of the areas that has received relatively less attention in developing countries in general and Pakistan in particular considering the contribution of SMEs in the country.

SMEs are an overwhelmingly important segment of the Pakistani economy. They spread across the country including the remote towns and villages. This proximity of SMEs gives them exposure to local problems and local resources as well. Therefore, they are more suited to consider socially responsible behaviour. Currently, at the institutional level, Small and Medium Enterprise Development Authority (SMEDA) provides support for SMEs by creating networks among the relevant constituents and directly initiating development projects. However, more efforts from the policy makers are required to acknowledge what many SMEs are already doing with regard to job creation and poverty alleviation.

SMEs are expected to grow under the recent China-Pakistan Economic Corridor (CPEC). CPEC is a United States dollar ($) 62 billion connectivity project envisioned to connect the western city of China Kashgar to Arabian sea port of Gawadar, Pakistan, located near the Persian Gulf shipping lanes. This mega project offers enormous opportunities to flourish ("*SMEs to benefit the most from CPEC*," 2018). CPEC has the potential to transform the SMEs in the country and could lead to the birth of new enterprises in sectors such as transport, telecommunication, travel and finance, among others (Javed, 2017). This can also happen through joint ventures by the provision of technologies by the Chinese enterprises. Given this importance of SMEs in the region, we believe that socially responsible behaviour would further enhance their chances to flourish and will minimise their environmental impacts.

2 SMEs' Workings Conditions in Developing Countries

An increasing attention has been paid to small businesses by the policy makers in developing countries to consider their multifaceted role in economic development (Singh, Garg, & Deshmukh, 2009). Nevertheless, the working conditions of these enterprises, particularly when they are part of global production networks, are below standards (Munir, Ayaz, Levy, & Willmott, 2018); i.e., the working conditions in these SMEs are poor and unsafe comprising of low-skilled and low-quality jobs. Moreover, SMEs often fall short in terms of market share, competitiveness and productivity.

As SMEs account for creating majority of employment, their transition to sustainable and socially responsible business practices will be significant in both developed and developing countries (ILO, 2015). According to Soundararajan, Spence, and Rees (2018), there are still instances of industrial accidents in SMEs in India, Pakistan, Bangladesh and some regions of South America. These involve notorious cases such as Child labour in soccer ball manufacturing in Pakistan (Khan, Munir, & Willmott, 2007), exploitation of workers in Jalandhar football manufacturing industry India (Jamali, Lund-Thomsen, & Khara, 2017) and the industrial disasters in garment factory of Bangladesh (Haque & Azmat, 2015), to name few.

Moreover, the regulatory measures, self-regulatory initiatives and international standards are not improving working conditions. This is because the attitudes of governments towards SMEs have varied within and between the countries over time (Zhu & Sarkis, 2007). Soundararajan et al. (2018) provided three reasons for the failure of regulation to solve these problems of SMEs in developing countries. Firstly, majority of the SMEs have resource scarcity and they focus on day to day survival rather than taking care of the environmental and social problems. Secondly, SMEs in many developing countries are immune to environmental and labour laws on the plea that legal compliance hinders their growth and entrepreneurship. For instance, some of these countries include, India, Pakistan, Chile, South Africa, Vietnam and Kenya. Finally, SMEs in developing countries, especially those that are part of the global production networks (GPN) (Jamali, Lund-Thomsen, & Jeppesen, 2017), face the paradox in the form of pressures to enhance efficiency by reducing the cost and improving quality of the product on one hand and standardised management tools in the form of codes and measures that sometimes go beyond the regulation on the other hand. These standards rarely represent the perspective of SME or the developing country in which it operates (Soundararajan et al., 2018).

Therefore, there remains a lack of proper research on working conditions and other social responsibility practices in SMEs in developing countries. This is due to the fact that major social responsibility models are emerging from the West and are incapable of dealing with the realities of developing countries in terms of cultural values and religious beliefs (Fox, 2004). This is because developing countries are facing challenges that are not prevalent in the developed world such are poverty alleviation, fight against corruption and employment generation. Therefore, this milieu requires academic attention to understand the social responsibility practices of SMEs working in developing country conditions.

3 Challenges for SMEs and Where Does Pakistan Stand?

SMEs generally are started by a single entrepreneur or a small group of people with a flat organisational structure (Saini & Budhwar, 2008). The term SME was initiated by European Commission in 1969 and was referred to as organisations employing less than 250 people (Burns, 2001). However, in Pakistan SMEs are defined primarily by Small and Medium Enterprises Development Authority (SMEDA) and other relevant organisations. A categorisation in provided in the following Table 1.

Pakistan has a huge population with a workforce of 65 million (Farid, 2016). However, when it comes to economic outputs, the country is placed at the lowest end of middle-income countries. With the population advantage, SMEs in Pakistan have the potential to contribute more towards GDP. Currently, SME sector contributes 40% to GDP, contribute substantively to creation of jobs and is still marred with problems which are primarily due to lack of attention from the government (Rana, May 02, 2018). There has been a rise in Pakistan's overall exports in the last year as the country exported goods worth Pakistani Rupee (PKR) 21.88 billion in 2017 compared to PKR 20.53 billion in 2016, which is an increase of 6.6%, notwithstanding, the trade deficit has increased due to a surge in imports from PKR 47 billion in 2016 to PKR 57.44 billion in 2017 (International Trade Centre, 2018). However, the share of SMEs in total exports has been estimated to be 24.8% in the year 2016 (SMEDA, 2017). Thus, the share of SME exports in the overall exports of the country is low which suggests that SMEs in Pakistan are underrepresented in the global trade. This is a common observation as SME exports are fewer relative to the larger businesses, and mostly target the neighbouring countries (OECD, 2017). Therefore, in order to realise the potential of SMEs to bolster export, generate

Table 1 Defining SMEs in Pakistan

Institution	Employment size	Paid up capital	Annual sales	Fixed assets
SMEDA	Up to 250	Up to 25 Million	Up to 250 Million	N/A
SME Bank	Not over 250	N/A	N/A	100 million
Federal Bureau of Statistics	Not less than 10	N/A	N/A	N/A
State Bank of Pakistan	Not over 250	N/A	Up to 300 million	100 million

Note: All amounts in Pakistani Rupee (Source: www.smeda.org.pk)

employment and bring flexibility in the economy, close attention is needed from the policy makers.

SMEs are a very heterogeneous group in term of product/service, location, number of employees, size and customer profile. SMEs include a wide range of businesses such as agriculture and food processing, construction, dairy, food and beverages, furniture, leather and footwear, livestock, plastic, services and textile, among others. SMEs are becoming backbone of economy and playing an active role in sustainable development of Pakistan. However, Pakistan is far behind when it comes to comparison with the neighbouring countries such as China and India. In India SMEs constitute of 95% of the overall registered units, whereas in China SMEs account for 99% of overall registered firms (Singh et al., 2009). This highlights that the SMEs in Pakistan are facing a plethora of challenges because of which benefit of SMEs in Pakistan has not been transferred to people in true sense (Zafar & Mustafa, 2017). Some of the challenges faced by SMEs to their growth are labour, taxation, productivity enhancement, trade finance and access to capital. Sherazi, Iqbal, Asif, Rehman, and Shah (2013) argued that internal issues such as finance, management and training coupled with external issues such as corruption, infrastructure and economic and technological issues will continue to persist unless and until the new revolutionary policies are introduced by the government.

There are enough groups of clustered SMEs (agriculture, dairy, furniture, livestock, surgical instruments, among others) with the potential to transform the economy. All it needs is a concerted effort to resolve the internal and external issues faced by SMEs so that they can participate in international trade either as a direct or indirect exporter. It is therefore, important to focus on the policies that help SMEs to achieve success of this sort.

Majority of the studies on social responsibility of SMEs focus on developed countries such as United Kingdom (e.g. Spence, 2007) and United States (Burton & Goldsby, 2009). There is a scarcity of research in the developing countries on small business social responsibility (Jamali, Lund-Thomsen, & Jeppesen, 2017). Especially, there is dearth of knowledge in how SMEs are embedded in global production networks (Munir et al., 2018), and institutional demands for improving working conditions in the form of coercive regulation or self-regulatory approach (Egels-Zandén, 2017). The research on social responsibility of businesses in South Asian countries has received the least attention. Moreover, within South Asia the research on social responsibility is primarily focused on Bangladesh and India, and in Pakistan it remains moot in general (Khan, Lockhart, & Bathurst, 2018). According to a report by International Labour Organisation, in labour intensive countries like India, Pakistan and Bangladesh, SMEs employ at least half of the industrial workforce who normally work under substandard working condition (ILO, 2015). There have been major industrial accidents in small businesses in Pakistan and other developing countries, which reflects the debilitating working conditions. As majority of the population lives in rural areas of Pakistan (70% approximately) and most of the SMEs are closely connected to this population, SMEs have the potential of initiating rural development, protection of environment, health care, ensuring transparency, promoting education and development of community through their socially responsible initiatives.

With the rise of global competition and trade liberalisation, SMEs face challenges from the bigger organisations that are penetrating the local markets in developing countries (Singh et al., 2009). In such environment, it is important for SMEs to improve manufacturing and business processes in order to survive in the long run. Moreover, SMEs face the challenge of narrow specialisations and serve local niches. These enterprises also have the issues of flat organisational structure, scarcity of resources, a lack of technical expertise and intellectual capital and a paucity of innovation (Saini & Budhwar, 2008; Singh et al., 2009). Therefore, such work settings may hamper the sustainability goals of SMEs.

3.1 Contextual Factors

It is rudimental to point out that the management tools promoting social responsibility among developing countries must be considered in relation to the institutional context within which SMEs operate (Lund-Thomsen, Jamali, & Vives, 2014). Institutional theory provides an appropriate lens to look at the factors that propel enterprises to embark on social responsibility in seeking legitimacy from the internal and external actors. This is due to the fact that voices of local actors in the developing world have been largely overlooked and a strong Western managerial orientation in the mainstream literature on CSR exists (Khan & Lund-Thomsen, 2011). Moreover, institutional theory also provides an important perspective on why and how businesses go about social responsibility in an institutional field (Risi, 2016).

Early institutionalist (DiMaggio & Powell, 1991; Meyer & Rowan, 1977) ascribed institutions as an agency rather than an individual (Pache & Santos, 2013). However, the contemporary institutional work presented individuals with powers that can change and influence institutions (Battilana, 2006). Recently, the term institutional work has emerged as an alternative to these two positions (Lawrence, Leca, & Zilber, 2013). The concept of institutional work helps to explain how institutional pressures determine actions of individuals within a field (Soundararajan et al., 2018). Therefore, it is important to understand how small and medium enterprises respond to institutional pressures with respect to social responsibility within a field. There has been a growing recognition that social responsibility practices are determined by the context in which they operate (Doh, Husted, & Yang, 2016; Ioannou & Serafeim, 2012) especially in SMEs (Nguyen, Bensemann, & Kelly, 2018). Context is very important to organisations as "in a fundamental sense, this privileging of context is incontestable. Just as children are born into a world of already socialized adults, similarly organisations are established in societies that are already institutionalised (Schneiberg & Clemens 2006, p. 217)". Context has been considered in CSR research extensively but the focus primarily remained on multinational organisations. However, Mair and Marti (2009) contended that there are two limitations with respect to context and the actors covered. Firstly, most attention has been given to the resourceful and powerful actors within a context, and less powerful people, who are located at the periphery of society, have normally been ignored (Lawrence, Suddaby, & Leca, 2009). That is to say, process of production of commodities, or of knowledge, has been dominated by those who occupy the position of privilege. Secondly, the level of analysis has mostly been the professional organisations in developed countries (Mair & Marti, 2009), and there is a lack of research on more marginalised groups in the developing world.

However, there have been attempts to explore the marginalised actors in the developing world such as India, Bangladesh and Egypt (Mair & Marti, 2009) and Middle East (Karam & Jamali, 2013). These studies are a welcome contribution to a still small, but now rapidly growing concerns on understanding the institutional realities of SMEs in developing countries with relation to social responsibility. Following the increase in call for more research globally with appropriate consideration of context, it is immensely important for SMEs in Pakistan to engage in socially responsible activities. With the recent accountability and green and clean drive launched by the government in Pakistan, SMEs are increasingly expected to respond to these pressures by government, non-governmental organisations (NGOs), public and the larger organisations.

3.2 *Social Responsibility and SMEs*

This section will focus on the social responsibility practised among SMEs in Pakistan. Before discussion on the specific context of Pakistan, it is worth reviewing the benefits and comparison between developed and other developing countries, where literature shows convergence and divergence of these practices.

Corporate social responsibility (CSR) is generally used as an "umbrella term to describe the complex and multi-faceted relationships between business and society and to account for the economic, social, and environmental impacts of business activity in the developing world" (Jamali, Lund-Thomsen, & Jeppesen, 2017, p. 11). However, according to Lenssen, Perrini, Tencati, Lacy, and Sweeney (2007), due to the difference in the nature of large firms and SMEs, the concept of corporate social responsibility cannot be applied equally to SMEs. One of the major reason is because the ownership and management of SMEs usually belong to the same person, which enable the owners to make personal choices of resource allocation (Spence, 1999). Therefore, the leader needs to understand the purpose of social responsibility and the benefits of being part of the community. Nejati and Amran (2013) state alternate terminologies for CSR among SMEs that include, "responsible business practice", "social/societal engagement" and "environmental involvement". Recently, Soundararajan et al. (2018) used the term 'small-business social responsibility' (SBSR) for SMEs. The subsequent paragraphs will demonstrate how these different terms would be fitting in the study of socially responsible practices of SMEs.

Social responsibility can bring various benefits for small and medium enterprises. Herrera Madueño, Larrán Jorge, Martínez Conesa, and Martínez-Martínez (2016) found that small businesses can reap the advantages of high competitiveness by embarking on social responsibility. Various other studies support the claim that stakeholder management results in performance outcomes. For instance, the study by Martinez-Conesa, Soto-Acosta, and Palacios-Manzano (2017) in Spain also support this notion, and attribute this to association between social responsibility and innovation performance. Moreover, Bohlin and Wiebe (2016) find that the social and the environmental performance of SMEs positively influences financial performance. SMEs can also develop an effective organisational culture by incorporating social responsibility within their activities. Enhanced organisational culture means attracting and maintaining the best employees (Pastrana & Sriramesh, 2014). For SMEs, social responsibility is seen as a two-way process. Brunton, Eweje, and Taskin (2017) report that the communication of CSR strategies and initiatives for employees would increase awareness and create positive organisational culture to enhance involvement in CSR programmes targeted within the organisation (activities such as recycling, carpooling, staff development and social activities) and outside the organisation (examples include volunteering, fundraising and charitable donations). Employees would have increased identification with the organisation, to lead to promoting of better organisation and a more ethical business environment (Brunton et al., 2017). As mentioned, the SMEs do not have the necessary resources to invest in a social responsibility policy or hiring a social responsibility manager and complying with the codes or regulation. One way of approaching social responsibility can be getting together in cooperatives and coalitions to tackle the social responsibility agenda more formally. Another way of approaching can be to get benefits from training, that is, SMEs can improve their social responsibility performance and continue to grow. Finally, SMEs need to look at whether they are a part of global supply chain (e.g. hand stitched soccer ball manufacturer are working for companies like Adidas). Such SMEs have to comply with codes and standards such as SustainaAbility (SA) 8000 (labour) or International Standards Organisation (ISO) 14,000 (environmental issues). Visser and Chiloane-Tsoka (2014) argued that sometimes SMEs practice implicit social responsibility rather than explicit responsibility. In other words, social responsibility of SMEs does not have to be formalised. It is more about living the principles of social responsibility in its true essence, and not necessarily as a formalised practice.

4 A Review of Social Responsibility Practices Among SMEs: From Developed to Developing Countries

The study by Lenssen et al. (2007) among SMEs in Ireland found that social responsibility practices in SMEs is best described as an *ad hoc* activity and the volume of those activities positively correlated with firm size. Involvement and support of senior management is important for the successful implementation of socially responsible activities. For SME, no person or department is especially appointed to manage social responsibility. The same was observed by Coppa and Sriramesh (2013) in Italy. This correlates with one of the major barriers of social responsibility among SMEs, which include financial, human and time constraint. Moreover, Lee, Herold, and Yu (2016) reported that the case studies conducted among Swedish SMEs show that social responsibility communication is done through website homepages and social media, which is seen to have little impact in gaining the public's attention. The authors suggested that this points to the limitation in communicating their social responsibility activities due to lack of resources and management skills.

SMEs tend to mention the community as an important stakeholder. Common activities included working free of charge for charities, making charitable donations and recycling initiatives (Lenssen et al., 2007). This resonates with the study of SMEs in Pakistan, where Raza and Majid (2016) noted that besides the employees, the community have strong influence on social responsibility practices in the country. For them, the notion that SMEs are better placed to respond to the changing needs of society compared to large corporations (Sweeney, 2007). Interestingly, the study by Coppa and Sriramesh (2013) in Italy found that the community is considered as the secondary stakeholder that is not placed as important as the primary stakeholders (which include customers, employees and suppliers).

Cassells and Lewis (2011) examined the environmental practices of SMEs in the manufacturing sector in New Zealand. The majority of owner-managers showed awareness of the risk their business activities posed to the environment, and were of the opinion that regulation alone was insufficient to address business-environment issues. In addition, two-third of respondents also indicated that they would not wait until required by law to improve the environmental performance of their firm. A qualitative study conducted by Battisti and Perry (2011) highlighted that SMEs would limit environmental action to regulatory compliance without adversely affecting their financial performance. As a developed country, environmental action is increasingly accessible for business owners, for example, switching to energy-saving options or recycling. This is consistent with previous literature that suggests that personal values of SME owners influence the uptake of responsible business practices (Murillo & Lozano, 2006; Sajjad & Eweje, 2014; Vives, 2006). This is supported by Azmat and Samaratunge (2009), who highlight the similarity between developed and developing countries with regards to the strong link between the socially responsible activities and orientation of SMEs and the ethical and cultural values of the leader. Overall, the governments have solved many problems for SMEs in the developed countries such as the access to finance and check on compliance with labour and environmental regulations. This, unfortunately, is still not the case in developing countries, glimpse of which is provided in the following section.

Norbit, Nawawi, and Salin (2017) studied SMEs in Malaysia and reported that SMEs are more involved in social responsibility practices if they receive financial support and established policies by the government. This highlights that the role of governments is incontestable in developing countries. Similarly, in Nigeria and Tanzania, SMEs have developed different coping strategies (or institutional works) to manage the challenges presented by their weak institutional environment (Amaeshi et al., 2016). Examples of institutional works include gender diversity at the workplace and work-life balance (most SMEs would have less than 45 h of working every week). Furthermore, the role of government goes beyond supporting the initiatives, policies and financial assistance of SMEs. According to Baughn, Bodie, and McIntosh (2007), there is an evidence of positive relationship between social responsibility and 'clean' government. The corruption by government officials was considered to be the strongest predictor of social responsibility. In the same vein, cultural aspect is deemed significant in the Colombian context as SMEs' social responsibility is influenced by cultural and contextual aspects of the country's contextual factors (Pastrana & Sriramesh, 2014). Further, these practices among the SMEs are mostly limited to ethical and religious factors, concern for employees, and the desire to improve profits.

In general, the distinctive elements of social responsibility practices of SMEs in developing countries are more sunken, less formalised and philanthropic in nature (Nguyen et al., 2018). Due to these reasons there is a paucity of socially responsible practices among SMEs in developing countries. In the same vein Hamann, Smith, Tashman, and Marshall (2017) contended that SMEs in developing countries are socially and environmentally risk prone firms. Consequently, in academic discourse their environmental and socially responsible activities are often misinterpreted (Jamali, Lund-Thomsen, & Jeppesen, 2017). This scepticism regarding socially responsible practices of SMEs is often equated with symbolism and lip service (Hamann et al., 2017). Therefore, more attention is required to understand responsible business practices of SMEs and their unique contribution in the developing world.

5 Social Responsibility Among SMEs in Pakistan

Some of the aspects that have been discussed in developing nations in the previous section have a lot in common with the situation in Pakistan. The discussion is based on the adoption of social responsibility in Pakistan, motivators and challenges with some examples from previous research.

While there are claims that SMEs in Pakistan are largely unaware of the idea of socially responsible behaviour (Ahmed & Ahmed, 2011). Lund-Thomsen et al. (2014) suggest that the current social responsibility management tools are generic, while these practices cannot be universalised. Khan and Lund-Thomsen (2011) went further and contended that the idea of best practices of social responsibility is embedded in Western imperialism and is not relevant to the situation in Pakistan. Furthermore, they found that local business perceptions regarding Western-based social responsibility practised by soccer ball industry in Pakistan are seen merely as a tool to keep their Western customers. The interviews were conducted with large, medium and small size business owners, NGO workers, and triangulation made with secondary sources such as newspapers and NGO reports. They concluded that the practice of social responsibility brings additional costs to the local manufacturers while being inappropriate to the cultural sensitivities and social structures. There was no significant input from local manufacturers and workers in formulating the social responsibility practice; and the local values and tradition were marginalised. The standardised practice adopted from Western countries may not only overlook important social issues, but also result in unintended consequences for local stakeholders. Jamali (2014) also cautioned to consider local culture prior to interpreting business practices in the developing world. For instance, the Islamic religion, based on the Quran, requires that every free and financially able Muslim make charitable donations to the needy people; this is called "zakat" or obligatory charity. Social responsibility in many instances is confused with Zakat to charity to NGOs and social welfare institutions (Qasim & Ramaswamy, as cited in Jamali, 2014).

Sajjad, Jillani, and Raziq (2018) conducted interviews among managers from six hotels around Pakistan and found that some hotel managers were not aware of the term 'sustainability'. However, efforts of sustainability were practised especially in energy efficiency, workforce diversity and employee welfare. Energy efficiency was considered a key focus of almost all sample hotels in order to reduce electricity consumption due to the country's power outage issue. Employee welfare is addressed through staff training and providing employee benefits such as healthcare, insurance and retirement benefit. Sajjad et al. (2018) found that the hotels have no structured sustainability strategy and well-established frameworks in the business models. This could be due to unawareness of the benefits and practical implications of sustainability practices. Further, the hotels are seen to lack in capacity, resources, and knowledge to respond to sustainability issues, other than the ones that affect them directly.

Personal values is generally assumed to be the driver behind socially responsible conduct (Vives, 2006). In Pakistan, cultural and moral values as well as religious beliefs have considerable influence that direct owners and managers to participate in philanthropic and ethical responsibilities (Sajjad & Eweje, 2014). In line with this, the relationship between religiosity and social responsibility is starting to get attention from scholars, where importance is sought for spiritual insight with relations to social responsibility (Palakshappa & Chatterji, 2018). A study by Zaman, Roudaki, and Nadeem (2018) highlighted that religion plays an important role in moral conduct and complement legal institutions for effective governance in society. As discussed, the institutions are weak in Pakistan and Islamic religiosity plays a key role in social responsibility related issues. Thus, social responsibility in a developing country context is significantly driven by informal institutional mechanisms such as religiosity that lies beyond a firm's management control. The same was noted by Khan et al. (2018).

However, interviews conducted by Wahga, Blundel, and Schaefer (2015, November) among owner-managers and senior managers in the leather industry found that the environmental and societal engagement largely depend on the awareness of the owner of the business. Only the SME owners who had prior informal training/learning of environmental knowledge (five out of eight SMEs) would engage in green initiatives. Informal learning includes seminars and workshops arranged by the local Chamber of Commerce, environment-specific educational interventions by the Government of Pakistan, discussions with experienced entrepreneurs, learning through observing the shop floor activities and discussion with employees. Another source of informal learning was described as self-development (through books and access to internet-based information).

Skills and knowledge is another area that is considered to be crucial for SMEs in Pakistan. While studying the intellectual capital in the electronics manufacturing companies, Khalique, Bontis, Shaari, and Md. Isa (2015) concluded that being under-developed in the knowledge economy affect intellectual capital to drive organisational performance. Another area that is affected by the challenge in skills and knowledge is the absence of sustainability reporting. Mahmood, Kouser, and Iqbal (2017) lamented that despite establishment of local institutions in Pakistan, (for instance Corporate Social Responsibility Centre Pakistan, CSR Association of Pakistan, and Sustainable Development Policy Institute), SMEs in the country did not publish any sustainability report. This is opposed to the 190 sustainability reports following the Global Reporting Initiative (GRI) guidelines published by SMEs world-wide. This is consistent with the findings by Raza and Majid (2016), where they found that SMEs in Pakistan mainly communicate socially responsible activities through meetings, lip service, newsletters and campaigns. The two main reasons suggested by Mahmood et al. (2017) on why Pakistani SMEs are not reporting on sustainability practices are lack of awareness about sustainability reporting and lack of training and skills.

Overall, multinationals in Pakistan take the lead when it comes to social responsibility. They regularly publish CSR reports (Khan et al., 2018) and have specialised CSR departments. SMEs on the other hand, are mostly unaware of the concept of social responsibility and its reporting. Moreover, there is a lack of knowledge among the general public of basic human rights, labour laws, consumers rights and lack of courage to speaking up against any sort of injustice.

6 Conclusions

General public in Pakistan needs to be educated regarding the benefits of social responsibility. With the accountability drive by the new government, the SMEs also need to take appropriate measures by engaging in social responsible activities. This can be initiated at the grass root level by SMEDA and other institution in associations with the SMEs. This will help aligning the social responsibility goals of SMEs and the policy makers in a way that is inclusive for all the stakeholders. Additionally, the government of Pakistan needs to impart social responsibility among SMEs through regulatory policies. Dar, Ahmed, and Raziq (2017) suggested that if Government of Pakistan has consistent and encouraging policies on SMEs, this could create a favourable environment for the growth of SMEs. Lund-Thomsen et al. (2014) recommended that the Pakistani government should arrange mass training program through SMEDA for SME owners/managers so that they would better manage their organisations, especially training in technical and human resource management. Strong linkages between SMEs and government agencies are also required in making sure that skilled labour are compensated and rewarded sufficiently (Fayyaz, Mian, & Khan, 2009). Lund-Thomsen et al. (2014) also observed that the government needs to take concrete steps in implementing the environmental laws. The developing countries have environmental laws in place, however, there is lack of capacity in implementation. The law enforcement in the country could be improved through regulatory inspections to keep an eye on the compliance with existing regulations such as health & safety, minimum wages, environmental issues.

SMEs have the potential to create a difference in the country through their social responsibility initiatives in the areas such as community development, development of rural areas, environmental protection, education, women empowerment, health care and infrastructure development. Apart from the government, civil society and other local institutions need to play an active role in order to promote social responsibility.

References

Ahmed, A., & Ahmed, I. (2011). *Corporate conscience: CSR in Pakistan - A study*. Retrieved from https://www.sdpi.org/research_programme/uploads/Corporate percent20Conscience percent20CSR percent20in percent20Pakistan.pdf

Amaeshi, K., Adegbite, E., Ogbechie, C., Idemudia, U., Kan, K. A. S., Issa, M., & Anakwue, O. I. J. (2016). Corporate social responsibility in SMEs: A shift from philanthropy to institutional works? *Journal of Business Ethics, 138*(2), 385–400. https://doi.org/10.1007/s10551-015-2633-1.

Azmat, F., & Samaratunge, R. (2009). Responsible entrepreneurship in developing countries: Understanding the realities and complexities. *Journal of Business Ethics, 90*(3), 437–452. https://doi.org/10.1007/s10551-009-0054-8.

Battilana, J. (2006). Agency and institutions: The enabling role of individuals' social position. *Organization, 13*(5), 653–676. https://doi.org/10.1177/1350508406067008.

Battisti, M., & Perry, M. (2011). Walking the talk? Environmental responsibility from the perspective of small-business owners. *Corporate Social Responsibility and Environmental Management, 18*, 172–185. https://doi.org/10.1002/csr.266.

Baughn, C. C., Bodie, N. L., & McIntosh, J. C. (2007). Corporate social and environmental responsibility in Asian countries and other geographical regions. *Corporate Social Responsibility and Environmental Management, 14*(4), 189–205. https://doi.org/10.1002/csr.160.

Bhutta, M. F. (2006). Fair trade for surgical instruments. *British Medical Journal, 333*(7562), 297–299.

Bohlin, I., & Wiebe, J. (2016). *Does it pay for SMEs to be good and green? Evidence on the impact of CSR on financial performance in the contextual setting of European and Asian SMEs.* (Masters Thesis), Uppsala University, Uppsala, Sweden. Retrieved from http://urn.kb.se/resolve?urn=urn:nbn:se:uu:diva-297462

Brunton, M., Eweje, G., & Taskin, N. (2017). Communicating corporate social responsibility to internal stakeholders: Walking the walk or just talking the talk? *Business Strategy and The Environment, 26*(1), 31–48. https://doi.org/10.1002/bse.1889.

Burns, P. (2001). *Entrepreneurship and small business*. New York, NY: Palgrave.

Burton, B. K., & Goldsby, M. (2009). Corporate social responsibility orientation, goals, and behavior: A study of small business owners. *Business and Society, 48*(1), 88–104.

Cassells, S., & Lewis, K. (2011). SMEs and environmental responsibility: Do actions reflect attitudes? *Corporate Social Responsibility and Environmental Management, 18*(3), 186–199. https://doi.org/10.1002/csr.269.

Coppa, M., & Sriramesh, K. (2013). Corporate social responsibility among SMEs in Italy. *Public Relations Review, 39*(1), 30–39. https://doi.org/10.1016/j.pubrev.2012.09.009.

Dar, M. S., Ahmed, S., & Raziq, A. (2017). Small and medium-size enterprises in Pakistan: Definition and critical issues. *Pakistan Business Review, 19*(1), 46–70.

DiMaggio, P. J., & Powell, W. W. (1991). *The new institutionalism in organizational analysis* (Vol. 17). Chicago, IL: University of Chicago Press Chicago.

Doh, J., Husted, B. W., & Yang, X. (2016). Guest editors' introduction: Ethics, corporate social responsibility, and developing country multinationals. *Business Ethics Quarterly, 26*(3), 301–315. https://doi.org/10.1017/beq.2016.40.

Egels-Zandén, N. (2017). The role of SMEs in global production networks: A Swedish SME's payment of living wages at its indian supplier. *Business and Society, 56*(1), 92–129. https://doi.org/10.1177/0007650315575107.

Farid, F. (2016). *SME sector backbone of economy*. Retrieved from https://pakobserver.net/sme-sector-backbone-of-economy/

Fayyaz, A., Mian, S., & Khan, J. (2009). State of entrepreneurship and globalisation in Pakistan. *International Journal of Business and Globalization, 3*(3), 271–287.

Fox, T. (2004). Corporate social responsibility and development: In quest of an agenda. *Development, 47*(3), 29–36. https://doi.org/10.1057/palgrave.development.1100064.

Hamann, R., Smith, J., Tashman, P., & Marshall, R. S. (2017). Why do SMEs go green? An analysis of wine firms in South Africa. *Business and Society, 56*(1), 23–56. https://doi.org/10.1177/0007650315575106.

Haque, M. Z., & Azmat, F. (2015). Corporate social responsibility, economic globalization and developing countries: A case study of the ready made garments industry in Bangladesh. *Sustainability Accounting, Management and Policy Journal, 6*(2), 166–189. https://doi.org/10.1108/SAMPJ-04-2014-0028.

Herrera Madueño, J., Larrán Jorge, M., Martínez Conesa, I., & Martínez-Martínez, D. (2016). Relationship between corporate social responsibility and competitive performance in Spanish SMEs: Empirical evidence from a stakeholders' perspective. *BRQ Business Research Quarterly, 19*(1), 55–72. https://doi.org/10.1016/j.brq.2015.06.002.

ILO. (2015). *Small and medium-sized enterprises and decent and productive employment creation*. Retrieved from https://www.ilo.org/wcmsp5/groups/public/%2D%2D-ed_norm/%2D%2D-relconf/documents/meetingdocument/wcms_358294.pdf

International Trade Centre. (2018). *Pakistan's trade indicators*. Retrieved from www.trademap.org/index

Ioannou, I., & Serafeim, G. (2012). What drives corporate social performance? The role of nation-level institutions. *Journal of International Business Studies, 43*(9), 834–864. https://doi.org/10.1057/jibs.2012.26.

Jamali, D. (2014). CSR in developing countries through an institutional lens. In G. Eweje (Ed.), *Corporate social responsibility and sustainability: Emerging trends in developing economies* (Vol. 8, pp. 21–44). Warrington: Emerald Group Publishing Limited.

Jamali, D., Lund-Thomsen, P., & Jeppesen, S. (2017). SMEs and CSR in developing countries. *Business and Society, 56*(1), 11–22.

Jamali, D., Lund-Thomsen, P., & Khara, N. (2017). CSR institutionalized myths in developing countries: An imminent threat of selective decoupling. *Business & Society, 56*(3), 454–486. https://doi.org/10.1177/0007650315584303.

Javed, A. (2017). *CPEC offers opportunities of growth for SMEs*. Retrieved from https://tribune.com.pk/story/1579442/6-cpec-offers-opportunities-growth-smes/

Karam, C. M., & Jamali, D. (2013). Gendering csr in the arab Middle East: An institutional perspective. *Business Ethics Quarterly, 23*(1), 31–68. https://doi.org/10.5840/beq20132312.

Khalique, M., Bontis, N., Shaari, J. A. N., & Md. Isa, A. H. (2015). Intellectual capital in small and medium enterprises in Pakistan. *Journal of Intellectual Capital, 16*(1), 224–238. https://doi.org/10.1108/JIC-01-2014-0014.

Khan, M., Lockhart, J. C., & Bathurst, R. J. (2018). Institutional impacts on corporate social responsibility: A comparative analysis of New Zealand and Pakistan. *International Journal of Corporate Social Responsibility, 3*(1), 1–13. https://doi.org/10.1186/s40991-018-0026-3.

Khan, F. R., & Lund-Thomsen, P. (2011). CSR as imperialism: Towards a phenomenological approach to CSR in the developing world. *Journal of Change Management, 11*(1), 73–90. https://doi.org/10.1080/14697017.2011.548943.

Khan, F. R., Munir, K. A., & Willmott, H. (2007). A dark side of institutional entrepreneurship: Soccer balls, child labour and postcolonial impoverishment. *Organization Studies, 28*(7), 1055–1077.

Lawrence, T. B., Leca, B., & Zilber, T. B. (2013). Institutional work: Current research, new directions and overlooked issues. *Organization Studies, 34*(8), 1023–1033. https://doi.org/10.1177/0170840613495305.

Lawrence, T., Suddaby, R., & Leca, B. (2009). *Institutional work: Actors and agency in institutional studies of organizations*. Cambridge: Cambridge University Press.

Lee, K.-H., Herold, D. M., & Yu, A.-L. (2016). Small and medium enterprises and corporate social responsibility practice: A Swedish perspective. *Corporate Social Responsibility and Environmental Management, 23*(2), 88–99. https://doi.org/10.1002/csr.1366.

Lenssen, G., Perrini, F., Tencati, A., Lacy, P., & Sweeney, L. (2007). Corporate social responsibility in Ireland: Barriers and opportunities experienced by SMEs when undertaking CSR. *Corporate Governance: The International Journal of Business in Society, 7*(4), 516–523.

Lund-Thomsen, P., Jamali, D., & Vives, A. (2014). CSR in SMEs: An analysis of donor-financed management tools. *Social Responsibility Journal, 10*(4), 602–619. https://doi.org/10.1108/SRJ-02-2013-0012.

Mahmood, Z., Kouser, R., & Iqbal, Z. (2017). Why Pakistani small and medium enterprises are not reporting on sustainability practices? *Pakistan Journal of Commerce and Social Sciences, 11*(1), 389–405.

Mair, J., & Marti, I. (2009). Entrepreneurship in and around institutional voids: A case study from Bangladesh. *Journal of Business Venturing, 24*(5), 419–435. https://doi.org/10.1016/j.jbusvent.2008.04.006.

Martinez-Conesa, I., Soto-Acosta, P., & Palacios-Manzano, M. (2017). Corporate social responsibility and its effect on innovation and firm performance: An empirical research in SMEs. *Journal of Cleaner Production, 142*(4), 2374–2383. https://doi.org/10.1016/j.jclepro.2016.11.038.

Meyer, J. W., & Rowan, B. (1977). Institutionalized organizations: Formal structure as myth and ceremony. *American Journal of Sociology, 83*(2), 340–363.

Munir, K., Ayaz, M., Levy, D. L., & Willmott, H. (2018). The role of intermediaries in governance of global production networks: Restructuring work relations in Pakistan's apparel industry. *Human Relations, 71*(4), 560–583. https://doi.org/10.1177/0018726717722395.

Murillo, D., & Lozano, J. M. (2006). SMEs and CSR: An approach to CSR in their own words. *Journal of Business Ethics, 67*(3), 227–240. https://doi.org/10.1007/s10551-006-9181-7.

Nejati, M., & Amran, A. (2013). Corporate social responsibility terminologies in small businesses: Insights from Malaysia. *Business Strategy Series, 14*(1), 11–14. https://doi.org/10.1108/17515631311295668.

Nguyen, M., Bensemann, J., & Kelly, S. (2018). Corporate social responsibility (CSR) in Vietnam: A conceptual framework. *International Journal of Corporate Social Responsibility, 3*(1), 1–12. https://doi.org/10.1186/s40991-018-0032-5.

Norbit, N., Nawawi, A., & Puteh Salin, A. S. A. (2017). Corporate social responsibility practices among the SMEs in Malaysia – A preliminary analysis. *Management and Accounting Review, 16*(2), 17–39.

OECD. (2017). *Entrepreneurship at a glance 2017*. Paris: OECD Publications.

Pache, A.-C., & Santos, F. (2013). Inside the hybrid organization: Selective coupling as a response to competing institutional logics. *Academy of Management Journal, 56*(4), 972–1001. https://doi.org/10.5465/amj.2011.0405.

Palakshappa, N., & Chatterji, M. (2018). Guest editorial: Exploring spirituality and social responsibility. *Social Responsibility Journal, 14*(2), 249–254. https://doi.org/10.1108/SRJ-04-2018-0087.

Pastrana, N., & Sriramesh, K. (2014). Corporate social responsibility: Perceptions and practices among SMEs in Colombia. *Public Relations Review, 40*(1), 14–24. https://doi.org/10.1016/j.pubrev.2013.10.002.

Rana, P. I. (May 02, 2018). *SME sector ignore in budged.* Retrieved from https://www.dawn.com/news/1405101/sme-sector-ignored-in-budget

Raza, J., & Majid, A. (2016). Perceptions and practices of corporate social responsibility among SMEs in Pakistan. *Quality and Quantity, 50*(6), 2625–2650. https://doi.org/10.1007/s11135-015-0281-2.

Risi, D. (2016). Longitudinal comparison between CSR implementation and CSR function's resource access. *Academy of Management Proceedings, 2016*(1), 1–5. https://doi.org/10.5465/ambpp.2016.69.

Saini, D. S., & Budhwar, P. S. (2008). Managing the human resource in Indian SMEs: The role of indigenous realities. *Journal of World Business, 43*(4), 417–434. https://doi.org/10.1016/j.jwb.2008.03.004.

Sajjad, A., & Eweje, G. (2014). Corporate social responsibility in Pakistan: Current trends and future directions. In W. Sun (Ed.), *Corporate social responsibility and sustainability: Emerging trends in developing economies* (pp. 163–187). Warrington: Emerald Group Publishing Limited.

Sajjad, A., Jillani, A., & Raziq, M. M. (2018). Sustainability in the Pakistani hotel industry: An empirical study. *Corporate Governance: The International Journal of Business in Society, 18* (4), 714–727.

Schneiberg, M., & Clemens, E. S. (2006). The typical tools for the job: Research strategies in institutional analysis. *Sociological Theory, 3*, 195–227. https://doi.org/10.1111/j.1467-9558.2006.00288.x.

Sherazi, S. K., Iqbal, M. Z., Asif, M., Rehman, K., & Shah, S. H. (2013). Obstacles to small and medium enterprises in pakistan. Principal component analysis approach. *Middle-East Journal of Scientific Research, 13*(10), 1325–1334.

Singh, R. K., Garg, S. K., & Deshmukh, S. G. (2009). The competitiveness of SMEs in a globalized economy: Observations from China and India. *Management Research Review, 33*(1), 54–65. https://doi.org/10.1108/01409171011011562.

SMEDA. (2017). *State of SMEs in Pakistan.* Retrieved from http://www.smeda.org/index.php?option=com_content&view=article&id=7:state-ofsmes-inpakistan&catid=15

SMEs to Benefit the Most from CPEC. (2018). Retrieved from http://www.cpecinfo.com/news/smes-to-benefit-the-most-from-cpec/NTIwNQ==.

Soundararajan, V., Spence, L. J., & Rees, C. (2018). Small business and social irresponsibility in developing countries: Working conditions and "evasion" institutional work. *Business & Society, 57*(7), 1301–1336. https://doi.org/10.1177/0007650316644261.

Spence, L. J. (1999). Does size matter? The state of the art in small business ethics. *Business Ethics: A European Review, 8*(3), 163–174. https://doi.org/10.1111/1467-8608.00144.

Spence, L. J. (2007). CSR and small business in a european policy context: The five "c"s of CSR and small business research agenda 2007. *Business and Society Review, 112*(4), 533–552. https://doi.org/10.1111/j.1467-8594.2007.00308.x.

Sweeney, L. (2007). Corporate social responsibility in Ireland: Barriers and opportunities experienced by SMEs when undertaking CSR. *Corporate Governance: The International Journal of Business in Society, 7*(4), 516–523.

Visser, T., & Chiloane-Tsoka, E. (2014). An exploration into family business and SMEs in South Africa. *Problems and Perspectives in Management, 12*(4), 427–432.

Vives, A. (2006). Social and environmental responsibility in small and medium enterprises in Latin America. *Journal of Corporate Citizenship, 21*, 39–50.

Wahga, A., Blundel, R., & Schaefer, A. (2015, November). Human capital and environmental engagement of SMEs in Pakistan: A comparative analysis of the leather industry. Paper presented at the *ISBE Annual Conference*, Glasgow.

Zafar, A., & Mustafa, S. (2017). SMEs and its role in economic and socio-economic development of Pakistan. *International Journal of Academic Research in Accounting, Finance and Management Sciences, 6*(4), 1–16.

Zaman, R., Roudaki, J., & Nadeem, M. (2018). Religiosity and corporate social responsibility practices: Evidence from an emerging economy. *Social Responsibility Journal, 14*(2), 368–395. https://doi.org/10.1108/SRJ-10-2017-0204.

Zhu, Q., & Sarkis, J. (2007). The moderating effects of institutional pressures on emergent green supply chain practices and performance. *International Journal of Production Research, 45* (18–19), 4333–4355.

CSR Evolution in the Garment Sector of Bangladesh: The Challenges of Sustainability

Nika Salvetti and André Nijhof

Abstract Many researchers believe that Bangladesh's garment sector is at a crossroads, with its sustainability depending on its adequate and collective response to addressing the structural causes that provoked fatal accidents at the Tanzeer Factory (December 2012) and Rana Plaza (April 2013). These tragedies have placed Bangladesh's garments industry under serious scrutiny by the international community as represented by institutional and nongovernmental organizations, buyers and consumers. Such additional pressure has led to the signing of multi-stakeholder agreements between buyers, United Nations (UN) agencies, local government and labour union organizations on the improvement of safety and fire conditions at work and the revision of the wage structure with an increase in the minimum wage. Besides and beyond such immediate actions, visionary garment industry leaders are taking the lead in ensuring an industrial transformation towards a more sustainable and responsible business environment. The garment sector of Bangladesh is the most significant revenues' contributor to the Bangladeshi economy and its remarkable economic growth. However its economic growth is not necessarily progressing along the sustainability and social responsibility paths. This study analyses the Corporate Social Responsibility's (CSR) evolution in the garment sector of Bangladesh by reviewing its institutional historical evolution and the gap in sustainability. It identifies relevant historical benchmarks that, according to primary and secondary sources of information, determined such evolution. At the same time it analyses the sustainability gaps from the demand and supply side. Even though the study is descriptive in nature, it uses qualitative research methods such as semi structured interviews with 25 experts and extensive review of secondary information of official documents, reports, and media articles. The findings reveal that there are still several structural problems that need to be solved to ensure progress in sustainability of the garment sector. And it is through concerted efforts of strategic alliances among several stakeholders along the supply chain, that such result can be achieved.

N. Salvetti (✉) · A. Nijhof
Nyenrode Business Universiteit, Breukelen, Netherlands
e-mail: n.salvetti@nyenrode.nl; a.nijhof@nyenrode.nl

N. Mitra, R. Schmidpeter (eds.), *Corporate Social Responsibility in Rising Economies*, CSR, Sustainability, Ethics & Governance,
https://doi.org/10.1007/978-3-030-53775-3_6

Keywords CSR · Bangladesh · Garment sector · Sustainability challenges

1 Introduction

It is broadly recognized that Bangladesh is a rising economy. During the last conference at the Harvard Kennedy School on "Bangladesh Rising" in May 2018, the economic success of Bangladesh which achieved a 7% growth over the past 2 years was applauded. Such results are also reported by the International Monetary Fund (IMF), World Bank (WB) and Governmental sources (BBS, 2018; IMF, 2018; World Bank, 2018a). In particular the garment sector has kept a steady growth, accounting for 82% of Bangladesh's exports. In the recent years it showed signs of deceleration but the financial year (FY)18 resulted again in exports' growth (World Bank, 2018b).

However a rising economy is often challenged by the need to align economic growth with sustainable and inclusive growth. This study aims at understanding what factors promote sustainable growth in the garment sector of Bangladesh, looking through the lenses of Corporate Social Responsibility (CSR). First, it describes how CSR has historically evolved in the garment sector of Bangladesh and what have been the benchmarks that have helped build its sustainable path. Second, it analyses the current sustainability gaps that hamper the ready-made garment sector from the demand and supply side of the local economy. In order to prepare for this study the authors conducted semi structured interviews with 25 local and foreign experts from the garment sector. These experts were selected based on snowball sampling. Furthermore an extensive review was conducted of official documents, reports, and media articles about sustainability in the garment sector.

The available literature of the Bangladesh garment sector provides several different interpretations of CSR since the birth of the sector in the 1970s. In fact, according to the most recent research on CSR in Bangladesh, CSR is still understood by most business leaders as a philanthropic charitable action, a voluntary contribution to society with no specific link to business purposes (CSR Center, 2012; Islam, Khan, & Islam, 2013; Reed Consulting, 2010, 2013). Such an approach can also be understood from the fact that most businesses in Bangladesh are family-owned and follow the Islamic religious principles of Zakat, which are interpreted as a responsibility to help the poor (Abeng, 1997; CSR Center, 2012).[1]

It is only recently that the term has been associated with 'compliance' as a consequence of the pressure on brands to satisfy international compliance standards aligned to both international and national regulations (Miyan, 2006; Mondol, 2009). The global exposure of the sector and its integration in global supply chains has helped to enhance CSR application in Bangladesh, due in part to the greater

[1]Information retrieved from a semi-structured interview with the director of Reed Consulting. Dhaka, 2013.

expectations of the international community on businesses to contribute to society. Moreover, attention is now paid to carrying out business responsibly along the entire supply chain, thus expanding the allocation of responsibilities from multinational headquarters to subcontractors in developing countries (European Commission, 2011). As predicted by Porter and Kramer (2006), CSR is becoming increasingly synonymous with competitive advantage and reputation. Nevertheless, it should also be noted that the shift from philanthropic action to compliant reaction has largely been triggered by the fatal accidents at the Tanzeer factory in December 2012 and Rana Plaza in April 2013, which can be seen as a result of the progressive, but not necessarily responsible, internationalization of the garment sector which started at the end of the 1990s and continues to grow exponentially ever since (CSR Center, 2014).

Bangladesh has committed itself to becoming a middle-income country by 2021. To achieve such a goal, the garment sector will have to achieve a total export value of approximately United States dollar (US$) 50 billion, from the current US$ 24.49 billion (BGMEA, 2014). Bangladesh's garment sector is the second largest exporter of garments in the world, and it is the most important sector of the Bangladesh economy in terms of export value and revenues with approximately 5400 factories and 4.4 million workers, of whom 80% are women.[2] However, to achieve the 2021 target, the sector will have to address structural challenges, from both the demand and supply sides, which are threatening its sustainable growth.

2 A Contextual Historical Analysis of the RMG Sector of Bangladesh from a CSR Perspective

Looking back, one can appreciate that Bangladesh, and before that East Bengal, has always been renowned for its textile traditions, characterized by thousands of artisans using hand spinning looms and weavers to produce magnificent products such as Jamdani, all sorts of muslin and silk, as well as other fabrics. When Britain started to mechanize its own textile production at the beginning of the eighteenth century, this inflicted a drastic brake on local Bengali textile production. When East Bengal became East Pakistan following secession in 1947, and thus independent from the British Empire, local mechanized textile factories started to rapidly emerge, thanks to the abundance of water supply, the dying process and the availability of a highly skilled and cheap labour force. Unfortunately, Pakistan soon shifted all resources and investments from the East to West Pakistan in order to promote and enhance textile production in the West, also leaving the factories in the eastern part under the control and ownership of West Pakistani businessmen. It was only after the war of independence in 1971 that the Bangladeshi textile sector had the opportunity to flourish. Given that there were only a few Bangladeshi businessmen who had set

[2]BGMEA presentation and database, Sept 2014.

up their own factories, the Government decided to expropriate all factories in order to avoid business and political interference from Pakistani owners. The overall nascent national industry became re-organized under the control of the Bangladesh Textile Mills Corporation (Islam et al., 2013).

Data from the Bangladesh Garment Manufacturers and Exporters Association—BGMEA (2014) indicate that the sector started with nine factories in 1979 and that this had risen to 5400 units at the time of their report. Initially, the sector's business pioneers were not only motivated by the promising business environment but also by strong patriotic enthusiasm and a sense of responsibility and eagerness to contribute to the construction of a new country. However, it was only during the mid-1980s that the sector boomed, thanks to important institutional changes and new policies. At the institutional level, Bangladesh was witnessing a gradual economic transformation from state control of the textile industry, which had been nationalized and organized under the Bangladesh Textile Mills Corporation since Independence, to privatization (Momen, 2007). Following a political change in 1975, the new government declared a revised industrial policy through which the public sector delegated the industrialization process to private-led investments, following the Declaration of Industrial Investment schedule of 1976 (Yunus & Yamagata, 2012).[3]

Placing Bangladesh under the Multi Fibre Agreement quota system in 1986 increased the garment sector's exposure to the changing globalization environment and to the increasing requirements of buyers to comply with standards and regulations established by foreign authorities (Mondol, 2009). Despite the restrictions imposed by the quota system, it seems that it actually favoured Bangladeshi factories by protecting them from international competition because they were granted a greater export quota than India and Sri Lanka (Mottaleb & Sonobe, 2011). Adaptation to the quota system also provoked a change in terms of ownership and control over local factories and a shift in the value chain focus: from producer-driven commodity chains to buyer-driven commodity chains. This also helped create a new form of global supply chain, known as Triangle Manufacturing, through which production was subcontracted by foreign multinationals to manufacturers in the Newly Industrialized Economies (Taiwan, South Korea and Hong Kong) who, in turn, subcontracted part or all of the production to local factories in low-wage countries such as China, Indonesia, Vietnam and later Bangladesh. Once the goods were ready, they would be shipped directly to foreign buyers under the United States of America (USA) quotas issued for exporting nations. The development of Triangle Manufacturing was also a reaction to the shift of manufacturing from the West to the East. Since the 1990s, Bangladesh, as well as Sri Lanka, Pakistan,

[3]The new policy introduced important amendments to promote the privatization of industrial processes: (1) elimination of a ceiling on private investment, (2) reduction in the reserve list of industries under the public sector and the creation of "free sectors", (3) relaxation of investment sanctioning procedures, (4) amendment of the Constitution to allow disinvestment and denationalization of both abandoned and taken-over industries, (5) establishment of a Disinvestment Board in 1975, (6) reopening of the stock market, (7) shift to a floating exchange rate and (8) introduction of various export promoting measures.

Vietnam and Cambodia, have been benefiting through their low-wage structures attracting and consolidating the production of ready-made garments in their countries (Ahamed, 2013). Still today, Bangladesh retains competitive advantages in both global and domestic markets thanks to the relatively low wages in the garment sector (in relation to other industries) and its reasonable quality.

Nevertheless, to the extent that CSR practices have gained international recognition and become integrated into international business practices, their adaptation helps local businesses access the global market. Moreover, as Bangladesh intensifies its trade relationships with the United States (US) and the European Union (EU), it becomes closely linked and interdependent on the increased importance attached to CSR by all stakeholders. Consequently, the sector becomes increasingly subservient to foreign resolutions or regulations in favour of CSR (Miyan, 2006). These external influences were quickly responded to by Bangladeshi society; in particular. Since the late 1990s, garment workers have started claiming their rights and demanding better labour conditions through violent strikes and the greater awareness generated of the deplorable conditions under which the labour force, with a high percentage of women, was forced to live. Since then, local civil society organizations, with technical and financial support from international organizations, have made joint efforts to promote the social and environmental betterment of the sector (Ahamed, 2012).

One example, which according to Farooq Sobhan[4] marked the birth of CSR in Bangladesh, was the Harkin Bill of 1994, which led to the formulation and approval by the US Senate of the "Child Labor Deterrence Act of 1999". Harkin was the lead sponsor in calling for a Bill that would prohibit the importation of manufactured and mined goods produced by children under the age of 15 into the US. The original wording of Senate Bill 706, in 1995, included the purpose of, "*prohibit[ing] the importation of goods produced abroad with child labor and for other purposes.*" It included civil and criminal punishments for anyone or any business defying the Act. Before the Harkin Bill was enacted in 1993, a large number of children were working in the garment factories. According to statistics published by Bhorer Kagoj (2012), at that time, approximately 30% of workers in the garment sector were children. With the enacting of the Harkin Bill, almost all child workers were removed from the garment factories for fear of US repercussions. At that time, the US was the single largest importer of garments from Bangladesh (Aktar & Abdullah, 2013).

As a result of such external pressure, the Bangladesh Government signed a Memorandum of Understanding (MOU) in 1995 with International Labour Organisation (ILO), United Nations International Children's Emergency Fund (UNICEF), and Bangladesh Garment Manufacturers and Exporters Association (BGMEA) one with the active participation of the Child Labour Coalition, to respond to the negative reactions of consumers and the threat of product boycotts in the US, on the issue of

[4]Semi-structured interview with the chairman of the Bangladesh Enterprise Institute (BEI), Mr. Farooq Sobhan, Dhaka, November 2013.

products being made by child labour. This MOU was the first significant step in tackling the issue of child labour in the garment sector, and stated that no children under 14 years old were allowed to work but had to be enrolled in school until that age when they could go back to the factories.

The rise of consciousness around child labour promoted the formulation of compliance standards, and the application of CSR principles was also triggered by the inclusion of social clauses introduced in the 1996 World Trade Organisation (WTO) charter. According to the clauses, restrictions would be imposed on imports of products from those countries not fulfilling the minimum standard, environment and employment rules (Sultana, Alam, Saha, Ashek, & Sarker, 2011). In addition, the sector felt threatened by the WTO decision to gradually abolish the quota system over a 10-year period from 1994 to 2004. The elimination of quotas was felt as an increased competitive pressure on suppliers, who initially believed that they would lose considerable market share (Rahman, Bhattacharya, & Moazzem, 2008).

Moreover, the introduction of the US Trade and Development Act, 2000 (USTDA), which gives duty and quota free access to the US (for exported textile and apparel products) to 72 countries of the Caribbean Basin (CBI) and Sub-Saharan Africa (SSA), excluded Bangladesh from the list of favoured suppliers. Bangladesh soon started to negotiate with the US for a free access quota to its market, but such a provision had not been granted by the time the Multi-Fibre Arrangement (MFA) agreement ceased in 2004. The garment sector recognized that to gain free access to the US market, it would have to improve its image and promote social responsible businesses.

On the European side, knitted garments from Bangladesh gained remarkable access to the European Union market during the period 1996–2005. Duty and quota-free access for garment products manufactured under "two-stage local transformation" (yarn to fabrics, and fabrics to garment) have accelerated the exports of knitted garment products from Bangladesh to the European Union. As the knitted textile subsector is relatively less capital intensive and requires relatively simple technologies, it has managed to undergo rapid expansion, benefiting from the European Union Generalized System of Preferences (Haider, 2007). In addition, the emphasis on quick delivery due to the intensification of international competition has given the knitwear producers a competitive advantage over the woven ones. This is because woven garment factories rely heavily on the import of raw materials (almost 60%) whereas knitwear producers can make use of a ready and quick supply of domestically produced yarns and fabrics (Mottaleb & Sonobe, 2011).

With the phasing out of the quota system, the export destination for garments gradually shifted from the US to the EU, to an extent also as a consequence of the USTDA 2000 and of Bangladesh being given access in 1996 to the European generalized scheme of preferences (GSP), which granted zero duty entry for garment products to the EU market (Haider, 2007). This also coincided with the new consciousness and attitude of the EU towards social responsibility, which matured in the elaboration of the 2001 Green Paper as the result of the appeal of the Lisbon Council to all companies to pursue social responsibility. This was followed by a CSR communication in 2002, the setting up of an EU Multi-Stakeholders Forum on

CSR in 2004 and the publishing of a new policy in 2006 which gave strong support to the business-led initiative known as the European Alliance for CSR. The Government of Bangladesh followed this example by raising a Government Act in 2008 that offered a 10% tax exemption to all companies that donated to charity. Despite the political commitment to CSR, such an act reinforced the philanthropic concept of CSR rather than promoting a more inclusive and social-led value approach.[5]

The reaction from European businesses to the European Commission (EC) policies indicates that there is now much more awareness with respect to CSR, especially with reference to United Nations Global Compact (UNGC) principles, Environmental Management and Audit Schemes (EMAS), labour standards, improving working conditions along the supply chain, and disclosure of information over sustainability (European Commission, 2011). The latest report by McKinsey (2013), who carried out a survey of 29 Chief Purchasing Officers of major brands operating in Bangladesh, confirms such a change of behaviour, with most of their interviewees stating that international brands are devoting much more attention to compliance issues in their sourcing allocation decisions.[6] Compliance is slowly becoming a determining factor that influences the competitive advantage of the sector. As Miyan (2006) stressed, if Bangladesh wants to retain its current competitive advantage, it will have to ensure good governance practices that enable CSR to flourish and thus promote responsible behaviours in the business sector.

Despite the strengths of the sector in offering a high production capacity, with productivity and supplier capabilities to meet deadlines and contractual requirements, the fatal accidents at the Tanzeer Factory (December 2012) and Rana Plaza (April 2013), have raised serious concerns over the sustainability and competitiveness of the garment industry in Bangladesh (World Bank, 2013). Following the tragedy of Rana Plaza, the US government suspended the Generalized System of Preferences (GSP) facility given Bangladesh's failure to abide by international standards for workers' rights and safety. While such actions might jeopardize the image of Bangladesh abroad, it did not have a major impact on the demand for its garments as these items were not included in the US GSP. From the European Union, there is no common position among the EU member states on using the EU GSP as a measure to pressure the Government of Bangladesh to enforce compliance. This is because some of the European member states believe that suspending the GSP would only inflict negative impacts on the living conditions of the workers.

In 2013, several initiatives took place to address the structural causes of the two fatal accidents. As a consequence of the Rana Plaza accident, two major trade unions organizations IndustriALL and UNI Global Union, international brands and many retailers (currently over 100) signed the Accord on Fire and Building Safety in

[5]In late 2008, the Government of Bangladesh approved the long-awaited proposal for a tax exemption facility at the rate of 10% on a part of the corporate income to be spent on complying with CSR practices.

[6]The survey was conducted with 29 chief purchasing officers (CPOs) in Europe and the US who are responsible for a combined annual sourcing value of USD 39 billion.

Bangladesh. This is a 5-year programme under which companies commit themselves to ensuring the implementation of health and safety measures. In July 2013, the European Union, the Bangladesh Government and ILO issued the Global Sustainability Compact to promote improved labour standards, the structural integrity of buildings, occupational safety and health, and responsible business conduct in Bangladesh's RMG and knitwear industries. The Compact builds upon the National Tripartite Agreement (NTPA) on fire safety and structural integrity adopted by the Ministry of Labour and Employment with the participation of tripartite committee (Policy agency, Lead executive agencies, Partner agencies) and the coordination support of ILO in March 2013 (Ministry of Labour and Employment, 2013). In July 2013, the "Northern American Alliance for Bangladesh Worker Safety" was launched by a number of North-American retailers and brands. This is a 5-year programme under which the companies commit to ensuring the implementation of health and safety measures.

Besides and beyond such immediate actions, visionary garment leaders are taking the lead in promoting a gradual industrial transformation built on a more sustainable and responsible business environment (GIZ, 2013). Concerted actions and joint efforts are seen as the answer to the structural challenges still present in Bangladesh's garment industry. Despite the fact that CSR interpretation and application is strongly affected by the local institutional and cultural environment, the global interconnectedness of the garment industry of Bangladesh has exposed it to international pressures demanding more responsible business behaviours and greater respect of international labour standards. There is a growing recognition among business leaders that, if new sustainable business models are not implemented, their competitive advantages as well as their financial performance will be at risk in a world that is increasingly looking for alternative strategies and approaches which can promote more conscious and responsible behaviours (Lacy, Cooper, Hayward, & Neuberger, 2010; Prahalad, Nidumolo, & Rangaswami, 2009). Such recognition is also reinforced by the increasing unrest among the garment workers since this might gradually erode the competitive advantage of the garment sector due to reduced labour productivity and the loss of favourable trade agreements if labour standards do not improve.[7]

This review of the historical evolution of CSR in Bangladesh contributes to a deeper understanding of the stages and challenges facing CSR and thus sustainability. From the above analysis, it would appear that CSR in Bangladesh is the result of pragmatism and opportunism in response to the strong pressures applied by international forces. Nevertheless, there is a great potential to advance CSR onto a more strategic level, which could help move the sector beyond compliance actions and address common social and environmental problems that affect the industry overall. In terms of Zadek's CSR stages analysis (Zadek, 2004), the CSR status in Bangladesh is moving from the defensive stage to a compliant stage, with only a

[7]Daily Stars article by R.U. Mirdha on Karel de Gucht (European Trade Commissioner) warning at BALI WTO conference. 5 Dec. 2013.

few companies achieving the management and strategic stages of CSR. International pressure, and hopefully consistent actions by the local government and civil society, might help promote an adequate environment for the civil stage of CSR, in which all of industry will actively practice CSR.

3 Main CSR Developments on the Demand Side

Despite a clear indication that demand of garment is steadily increasing due to the strength of the sector, characterized by its low production costs (i.e. labour costs), production capacity and timely delivery, its competitive advantage might be gradually undermined by an unsatisfactory response in addressing compliancy issues, particularly in relation to working conditions, leading to the global demand being redirected to other markets (Ahamed, 2013). European and American markets are the main absorbers of Bangladesh's garment manufacturing, taking 60% and 21% respectively of total production (BGMEA, 2014).

However, the Rana Plaza incident triggered a rapid reaction from the international community amounting to a **greater demand for responsible behaviours at the industrial level**, thereby putting pressure on local suppliers and authorities to improve working conditions, starting with the health and occupational safety of the workers. While the USA suspended the Generalized System of Preferences (GSP) (Majority of Staff, 2013) for all products imported from Bangladesh until the Government proved itself capable and effective in addressing social compliance, the European Union adapted a more cautious path, retaining the GSP on the condition that certain compliance criteria and targets would be met. This allowed the formulation and implementation of various agreements such as the National Tripartite Agreement (NTPA) as a consequence of the Tanzeer fire, the European-led "Accord on Fire and Building Safety" (ACCORD) and the related US-based initiative, the "Alliance for Bangladesh Worker Safety" (ALLIANCE) through which brands, civil society organizations, governments and international organizations have combined to design a plan to reform the garment sector. Such reforms include the inspection of all factories working for the major brands to ensure safety and occupational health by upgrading buildings and by equipping factories with all the necessary equipment to reduce the risk of fatal accidents. An outcome of these inspections is remediation plans through which non-compliant factories will have to upgrade their buildings within a defined timeframe or, if unable to do so, will be closed down or reallocated to a different location. Table 1 shows the outcome of the first round of inspections presented by the EU on July 2014.

Another factor influencing the global demand is the **potential increase in labour costs, and thus the unit price per garment,** as a consequence of better working conditions as well as an investment in environmentally friendly technology unless these are accompanied by targeted financial and fiscal incentives. In this respect, the Bangladesh Bank is promoting Green Banking and offering attractive loans to those companies investing in environmentally friendly technology (Bangladesh Bank,

Table 1 Technical progress report on sustainability

	NTPA	Accord	Alliance	Total
Total factories	1500	1400	608	3508
Completed factory inspections	282	834	604	1720
Referred to review panel	1	23	14	38
Partially closed	0	3	2	5
Closed	2	12	3	17
Decision pending	0	1	0	1
Allowed operation	0	6	9	15

Source: Compact-July 08, 2014, EU from Report on workers' safety and rights presented at the Dhaka Apparel Summit on 7–9 December 2014

2013). The Government of Bangladesh has decided to reduce the fiscal load on equipment that the inspectors deem necessary to upgrade the safety of buildings. International organizations are also implementing innovative projects that contribute to environmental sustainability. For example, the Netherlands-funded IFC-PACT project aims to reduce the water footprint of garment companies by coupling brands and retailers to the initial capital investments made by local companies.

On the social compliance side, the Government of Bangladesh reviewed the Labour Act in 2013 to set premises for an overall improvement in the working conditions of garment workers. Within this perspective, the ILO is striving to introduce living and fair wages on the industry level by engaging companies on a voluntary basis.

However, more is needed to sustain the demand in the medium term. The **sourcing practices of the brands** have to improve in order to provide rewarding mechanisms that support those suppliers that show financial and technical commitments in achieving compliance targets. As expressed by several business leaders, the role and responsibility of the brands is still unclear due to their contradictory behaviours which, on the one hand, put pressure on companies to become more compliant but, on the other, still negotiate for the lowest unit price per garment. Reflecting on the allocation of responsibility among the different stakeholders, the weak compliance in terms of labour standards as well as in meeting environmental requirements should be analysed from the perspective of shared responsibility and transparency along the supply chain. Since the financial crisis that hit Europe and the US, buyers have been focusing on getting quality products at much lower prices but also requesting local producers to upgrade their compliance standards. The pressure from buyers to keep prices low has forced local suppliers to address the loss of profit margins by reducing costs, thereby sacrificing any betterment of the working environment. Even worse, many manufacturers have felt the need to subcontract part of the production line to companies which are less monitored by auditing inspections. Further, the lack of, or weak, regulatory frameworks and enforcement of the rule of law by public authorities puts any initiatives to promote social responsibility at risk of failure.[8]

As a result of such processes, international efforts to improve working conditions in Bangladesh following the Rana Plaza collapse have focused on undertaking physical building inspections in an attempt to quickly respond to repeated failures in health and safety standards in the industry. Such actions are based on a multi-annual 5-year plan that aims to inspect all factories and develop a remediation process that includes substantial capital investments for either upgrading the existing facilities or reallocating to other premises. The costs of remediation are borne almost entirely by the local companies, which are pushed to undertake these repairs by the threat of losing reputation and trust and thus orders from the buyers. However, such unilateral efforts will be hard to sustain if there is insufficient contributions from the buyers and other stakeholders. Considerable amounts of financial and technical resources will be needed to transform the sector in terms of upgrading and reallocating the factories, and complying with environmental and labour standards. It can be argued that without contributions from all stakeholders in ensuring the availability and accessibility of low-cost financing to factory owners that it will be difficult to sustain the transformation. At the same time, the establishment of a better industrial relationship between buyers and suppliers would encourage a smoother and more sustainable process of change.

As buyers still hold the negotiation power when it comes to unit price, they should engage closely with those suppliers who are committed to improving labour and environmental standards. Among other aspects, there is a need to 'level the playing field', making a distinction between those factories that perform well in terms of compliance and those who are negligent. Here, buyers could play a crucial role in this process by selecting preferential first-tier suppliers, and applying more rigid control over second- and third-tier suppliers.[9]

In the long term, compliance should replace cheap labour costs as an indicator of competitive advantage. At the same time, a more transparent and direct business relationship between buyer and supplier might help simplify the supply chain and reduce the interference of intermediaries who are currently adding pressure in price negotiations and expanding the chain to unaudited tiers of suppliers. A better relationship might also strengthen cooperation through more open accountability and transparent procedures, which would help in explaining complex cost calculations and allocations which currently undermine attempts to improve labour conditions.[10] If the 'Made in Bangladesh' mark fails to re-establish its image and reputation, brands will gradually look to other markets and shift their attention to those countries which can guarantee a better and more responsible business environment.

[8]Based on the interviews with local business leaders.

[9]As defined by ACCORD, first-tier factories are primary suppliers, second tier factories are major or long-term suppliers and third-tier factories are minor suppliers.

[10]From the report on financial remediation presented at the Dhaka Apparel Summit in Dec 2014.

Table 2 Comparison of infrastructure quality 2014–2015

Country	Country ranking[a]	Overall infrastructure score	Electricity	Roads	Railroads	Ports
Bangladesh	109	2.8	2.5	2.9	2.4	3.7
India	71	3.7	3.4	3.8	4.2	4.0
China	28	4.4	5.2	4.6	4.8	4.6
Cambodia	95	3.4	3.0	3.4	1.6	3.6
Myanmar	134	2.3	2.8	2.4	1.8	2.6
Pakistan	129	3.3	2.1	3.8	2.5	4.4
Sri Lanka	73	5.0	4.8	5.1	3.7	4.2
Thailand	31	4.1	5.1	4.5	2.4	4.5

Source: The Global Competitiveness Report 2014–2015 (2014 World Economic Forum)
[a]Ranking among 144 countries. The rankings are in descending order with '1' as the best performer

4 Main CSR Developments on the Supply Side

Looking at the most recent competitiveness report (2014–2015) in Table 2, Bangladesh, despite its cheaper labour costs, ranks quite low (109th) in comparison to its neighbours. This suggests that if its infrastructural bottlenecks (electricity, roads, railroads, ports, energy and water) are not tackled through a timely and strategic response then its overall competitive advantage will be drastically eroded even if labour conditions are improved.

The main challenges facing the supply side and undermining sustainable growth can be summarised using the following categories[11,12]:

Inadequate Physical Infrastructure The capacity of the current infrastructure, in terms of roads, railways, harbours and airports, is inadequate to further increase logistical performance. A disruption in the transportation system can result in unnecessary delays causing a loss in orders and huge fines for the local suppliers. In response, the Government of Bangladesh has recently opened bidding procedures for the expansion and modernization of the harbours, roads and railways, here adopting public-private partnership modalities.

Insufficient Supply of Power and Energy The supply and cost of energy is erratic and vulnerable to international price fluctuations. Bangladesh is highly dependent on imported oil, gas and coal, and it has to rationalize distribution to fulfil wider industrial requirements of energy sources. Gas is the main source of energy for the garment industry, and demand has already overtaken domestic reserves due to the accelerated economic growth. To further boost industrial growth, the Government will have to provide more power from both domestic and international sources. Its current strategic plan envisions close partnerships with other stakeholders as it lacks the financial capacity to provide it alone. Further, most of the factories run their own

[11]BGMEA President Speech at the Dhaka Apparel Summit. Dhaka Dec 2014.

[12]Initial findings from semi-structured interviews with local experts and business leaders.

generators and power plants as the energy provided by the Government or through the Industrial Zones is often insufficient. It is becoming clear to most factories that, to reduce their vulnerability to energy shortages, they will have to find alternative technological solutions to reduce consumption, an approach that will ultimately make a positive contribution to environmental sustainability (Salvetti, 2013).

Poor Labour Conditions Despite the availability of an extensive workforce, the challenge lies with its low level of productivity. On one productivity index, Bangladesh scores 77% whereas India, Pakistan and Vietnam are already above 90%. Approximately 80% of the workforce is composed of women, who tend to have been recruited in poor areas and lack the basic skills required. Normally these women are employed in operational sections, with management and supervisory positions held by men or foreigners. The poor labour conditions, in terms of minimum wages, excessive working hours and unfriendly environment, affect their engagement and thus productivity. Despite regular training, skills development is still lagging, and does not satisfy the more demanding buyers' requirements. A huge consequence of the poor working conditions is the low level of retention, especially after workers, both men and women, receive specialized training. While company owners blame the poor retention on a lack of loyalty and professionalism, the workers emphasize delays in paying salaries and extra bonuses along with the physical and verbal abuse they receive as the main reasons for leaving (Ahmed, Raihan, & Islam, 2013; AMRF, AWAJ, CSI, 2013). Ensuring the dignity of workers as well as their safety would thus seem an imperative if one is to create a safe and sustainable industry. At the same time, linked to the pressure applied by civil society organizations and the irregular actions by labour unions, workers are finally recognizing and claiming their rights, often by making use of violent forms of unrest rather than by holding a constructive dialogue with company managers. As Hossan, Sarker, and Afroze (2013) noted, high workload, unreasonable behaviour by line managers, low skills and poor wages are the main reasons for the high turnover and social unrest. Fundamentally, there is a lack of mutual understanding, respect and communication between supervisors/managers and workers in the garment sector. Freedom of association and collective bargaining are still exceptions to the rule (ILO, 2013; US Dept State, 2012). Another consequence of the low level of skill in the labour force is the industry's dependence on foreign skilled workers to fill higher management positions, which frustrates any attempt by local employees to make a professional career shift. After the collapse of Rana Plaza, workers' rights and safety became high priorities for the Government following explicit demands from the EU sustainability compact and the US Action Plan. In this respect, the Government decided to increase the minimum monthly wage from Bangladesh Taka (Tk) 3000 to Tk 5300; to review the Labour Act in order to amend and integrate regulations that support workers' association and collective bargaining; ease the involvement and engagement of labour unions; provide fiscal incentives on the purchasing of safety equipment; and require compulsory health insurance for companies with more than 100 employees. Despite these initial attempts, the effectiveness of law enforcement in the longer term has to be proven.

Political Instability and Weak Governance In recent years, the antagonist and violent clashes between the governing party, the Awami League, and the opposition, Bangladesh National Party, have undermined business confidence and created major barriers to further investment. Political instability is frequently accompanied by general strikes that paralyze the entire country obstructing transportation and the flow of trade, and discouraging foreign as well as domestic investments. The on-going abuse of human rights, in terms of disappearances, kidnappings and violent reprisals against anti-government advocates, further increases uncertainty and thus business risks. At the same time, weak governance, characterized by high levels of corruption, inadequate policies to address industrial bottlenecks and weak technical and financial capacities are gradually harming the positive long-term prospects for growth. According to the World Bank (2013), policies and reforms need to focus on reinforcing regulations, tackling corruption, providing solutions to the infrastructural challenges and improving the working conditions of labourers if one is to restore confidence among investors and buyers. The main challenge will be to maintain a steady policy continuation through the political cycle and to enforce the regulatory framework and implement actions and agreements in the long term. The ambitious National Action Plan that addresses safety and occupational health in the garment sector has now been implemented with the support and guidance of international donors and organizations. However, the challenge will be to continue the advances when the international pressure and support runs out. Will the government of Bangladesh then be able to financially and technically sustain the improvement in labour conditions as well as grow the garment industry?

Macro-economic Factors The garment sector is highly dependent on the import of raw materials, especially from Pakistan, India and China. The volatile exchange rate, inflation and inadequate monetary policies can have a dramatic influence on production costs. The heavy dependency on raw materials, and the volatility in their prices, can undermine financial outcomes (McKinsey, 2011). At the same time, the difficulty in accessing the financial market at an acceptable interest rate undermine proposed investments in upgrading the industry and in promoting the application of technology that would improve environmental standards as well as the safety of buildings. However, recently, the Bangladesh Bank has started to issue easier loans for green investments and the Government of Bangladesh is relaxing import duties on equipment that can improve the health and safety of workers.

Complexity of the Supply Chain While subcontracting through the practice of indirect sourcing at different tiers helped the garment sector to flourish in the 1980s by creating a division of labour between manufacturers and traders and by the influx of knowledge from abroad (Mottaleb & Sonobe, 2011), today these practices reduce the transparency in the relationships between the different stakeholders along the supply chain and its overall sustainability. It is becoming much harder to identify all those intermediaries, agents and traders that are involved in the process, and thus to allocate responsibility fairly. While such practices boost profit margins, increase production capacity and reduce the costs of production, this is at the expense of compliance and responsible behaviour. Tracing third-tier suppliers is difficult but a necessary step is needed towards reforming the industry (Labowitz & Dorothée Baumann-Pauly, 2014). Despite its complexity and the interconnections between different stakeholders, the industry is still a buyer-driven one in which a small number of brands and retailers exercise control and negotiation power. Most buyers are multinational groups that control the production process in terms of location, timeframe and unit price. They can opt to either enter into a direct relationship with the suppliers or go through intermediaries.[13]

Temporary Agreements The Accord and Alliance agreements have been welcomed by Bangladesh society as they show the serious commitment of various stakeholders to addressing the major challenges that pressure the garment sector: the safety and occupational health of the workers. This is viewed as a first step towards major lasting reforms that would also address the poor overall working conditions. However, the 5-year plans target only those factories, approximately 2000, that are working directly with the main brands, the signatories of the agreements, and do not cover those factories and facilities which are beyond the scope of their intervention, including the second and third tier suppliers. Further, their interventions often overlap internal systems of monitoring and auditing, executed either by the factories or by the brands (Labowitz & Dorothée Baumann-Pauly, 2014). This creates considerable confusion as to the standards that should be respected and the actions that should be taken to address faults in the system, and adds to the financial and technical resources required. Even though inspectors report on the situation of each factory and publish a remediation plan, the final decision on the proposed remediation, in terms of upgrading the physical infrastructure, closure or reallocation, remains with BGMEA and the Government. It is also still not clear what will happen when the inspectors' work is completed and if they will succeed in implementing the plans and achieving all the objectives given the very expensive factories' inspections. Finally, most of the brands that are participating financially in the agreements are somewhat reluctant to contribute directly to the upgrading of the factories from which they source, and this undermines the establishment and enhancement of direct and more transparent industrial relationships between buyers and suppliers.[14] The expected outcome of ACCORD and ALLIANCE is to have a clearer idea of who are the most responsible and most compliant suppliers, and then to reward them through establishing preferential contractual agreements and ensuring long-run purchase orders at a better price. The question remains whether responsibility and compliance could replace low labour costs as competitiveness criteria.

Missing CSR Culture CSR has not evolved in Bangladesh beyond philanthropy and compliance. While philanthropic activities are mainly motivated by cultural and religious obligations to give back to society in the form of grants and donations for

[13]From an article by Peter van der Werf in Robecosam: Sustainable Investing. Can the textile industry prevent another Rana Plaza? December 2014.

[14]Findings from interviews with business leaders.

the most vulnerable, the recent pressure on compliance has led the private sector to focus on abiding by the law and meeting new regulations rather than applying strategic CSR interventions that would enhance their efficiency and competitiveness. As noted by the CSR centre and the Bangladesh Bank (2014), CSR activities remain technology- and welfare-driven. Lately, CSR has become a matter of repairing one's image and reputation to please buyers and retailers. The CSR climate in Bangladesh is intimately related to the context in which it operates and the weak regulatory framework and law enforcement enable business leaders and entrepreneurs to act irresponsibly and not to conform with a CSR culture. There is still a general misunderstanding of CSR due to the lack of policies and guidelines on its common definition and application.

Lack of Trust However, CSR engagement remains focussed on providing humanitarian relief and disaster response, supporting the most vulnerable with healthcare, education and training and stimulating green initiatives to arrest environmental degradation. Most of these activities are not directly related or mainstreamed within the companies' policies and strategies, and thus represent ad hoc and isolated interventions with limited impacts on society and the environment. In other words, they are temporary and unsustainable actions (Bangladesh Bank, 2008). The Government's decision to provide tax incentives for CSR activities has also had only a limited impact. First, the mistrust the private sector has of the Government, because of its corrupt behaviour, limits the private sector's willingness to take this opportunity. Second, the perceptions of what constitutes CSR activities still focus on donations and welfare, and not on strategic mainstreaming of CSR into business operations. Proper national guidelines and policies on CSR are still missing. Despite the efforts of local organizations and donor initiatives, there is a lack of concerted efforts at all levels to develop a CSR culture based on shared values and ethical codes of conduct at the industry level but the key issue remains the lack of a common understanding of CSR and its relevance.

Too Few Visionary Business Leaders It is only recently that CSR has got the attention of business leaders in the garment industry, and this is mainly due to opportunistic and reputational reasons linked to the negative impacts of the Rana Plaza and Tanzeer accidents on the garment sector. Most of the business leaders still apply short-term business strategies counting on the rapid growth of the sector and generally not planning beyond 10 years ahead.[15] Political instability, weak governance and the industry's vulnerability to irresponsible and unsustainable practices push leaders to take a 'wait and see' approach to their investments and future business decisions. The few leaders who do understand the added value of implementing CSR in the social and environmental arena are investing in innovation, technology; and research and development; and are deciding to either consolidate their conglomerates, expand into foreign countries or diversify their production to go beyond the garment sector. They have learnt that being responsible, compliant

[15]Common pattern among business leaders in the garment sector.

and investing in CSR makes business sense as it provides a higher return on investment and/or reduces production costs. These leaders have solid and strong motivation, derived from strong family and cultural values, their commitment towards society and high competency and knowledge of their business. Applying Maslow's pyramid (Maslow 1943) of needs, they can be seen as striving to achieve the self-actualization goal.[16] However, they also realize, that to be able to run their businesses sustainably, the market needs to demand CSR and differentiate between those leaders who run responsible businesses from those who pay lip service to compliance without any genuine interest or concern about the impacts of their decisions and actions on the wider society and the environment. Responsible leaders could set examples and become the reference for others to follow, but, for this to happen, they will have to be encouraged and supported by all stakeholders along the supply chain and be recognized and rewarded for their good practices (Salvetti, 2013).

5 Conclusions

This historical review of CSR evolution reveals that CSR has changed its meaning and relevance over time, and today it is at the centre of crucial debates about investments in the garment sector. There is a growing recognition among business leaders that if new sustainable business models are not implemented, their competitive advantages, as well as their financial performance, will be at risk in a world that is increasingly looking for alternative strategies that can promote more conscious and responsible behaviours. Although CSR interpretation and application is strongly affected by the institutional and cultural environments, the global interconnectedness of Bangladesh's garment industry has exposed it to international pressures that demand more responsible business behaviours and higher respect of international labour standards.

The garment sector of Bangladesh is at a crossroads as its sustainability and competitiveness is under scrutiny by the international community. If serious and consistent actions by all relevant stakeholders do not take place, failures in social and environmental compliance could put the sector at serious risk and might undermine its growth. From this perspective, and besides the current NTPA, ACC ORD and ALLIANCE initiatives, buyers should strategically review their supply chain and their sourcing strategies to support the efforts of those suppliers who are attempting to move beyond compliance. Strategic alliances should be built with those captains of the industry who can lead a process of change in favour of more responsible behaviours and innovative technological solutions contributing to efficiency, reliability and reputation. At the same time, the Bangladesh Government, with support from the international community, should strengthen the business

[16]Preliminary findings of my PhD research.

environment to sustain the industrial transformation with strategic interventions that enhance labour conditions and also address infrastructural as well as service-related bottlenecks, such as those in the banking sector, and reward those companies that are investing in positive change.

All these actions should be carried out in conjunction with a more resolute response from the international community. The EU should use the GSP in a more strategic way to ensure that new laws and regulations on compliance are enforced. At the same time, civil society, both national and international, should be mobilized to raise awareness and pressure with timely actions and interventions. Other important regional players, such as China, India and the Middle East, should be brought in to join the efforts in supporting the transformation of the sector through a common agenda. Finally, an independent judiciary system should be established to ensure the effectiveness and sustainability of all actions.

References

Abeng, T. (1997). Business ethics in Islamic context: Perspectives of a Muslim business leader. *Business Ethics Quarterly, 7*(3), 47–54. ISSN 1052-150X.

Ahamed, F. (2012). Can Trade Unions play an effective role in defending workers' rights in the Bangladesh Ready-made Garment industry? *Middle East Journal of Business, 7*(3), 12–16.

Ahamed, F. (2013). Background of history of Bangladesh and ready-made garment industry: Key challenges in the RMG industry. *Middle East Journal of Business, 8*(1).

Ahmed, S., Raihan, M. Z. & Islam, N. (2013). Labor unrest in the ready-made garment industry of Bangladesh. *International Journal of Business and Management, 8* (15), 6880. ISSN 1833-3850 E-ISSN 1833-8119.

Aktar, S., & Abdullah, A. S. M. (2013). Protecting Child Labour in Bangladesh: Domestic Laws versus international Instruments. *Bangladesh e-journal of Sociology, 10*, 153–172.

AMRF, AWAJ, CSI. 2013. *Workers' voice report 2013. Insight into life and livelihood of Bangladesh's RMG workers*. The Workers' Voice Report 2013 is part of the Workers' Voice Project, a collaboration of AWAJ Foundation, AMRF Society, and Consulting Service International Ltd. Dhaka, September 25, 2013.

Bangladesh Bank. (2008). Financial sector CSR engagements: indicative guidelines for expenditure allocations and end use oversight. *Dhaka, 2008*.

Bangladesh Bank. (2013). *Annual report 2012–2013*.

Bangladesh Bank. (2014). *Annual report 2013–2014*.

Bangladesh Bureau of Statistics (BBS). (2018). *GDP of Bangladesh. Report*, Agargaon, Dhaka.

Bangladesh Garment Manufacturer Export Association (BGMEA). (2014). *RMG: The outlook and trend. Bangladesh-update on production & sustainability. BGMEA Report*. Dhaka, 2014.

CSR Center. (2012). *Report on CSR in Bangladesh. Practicing Responsible Business for Mutual Benefits*. CSR Center, June 2012.

CSR Center. (2014). *Report on CSR in Bangladesh. Sustainability for a better future*. CSR Center, May 2014.

European Commission. (2011). *A renewed EU strategy 2011-14 for Corporate Social Responsibility*. Communication from the Commission to the European Parliament, The Council, The European Economic and Social Committee and the Committee of the Regions. Brussels, 25.10.2011 COM(2011) 681 final.

GIZ. (2013). *Social and environmental excellence award 2012. Giz and Bangladesh brand forum report*.

Haider, M. Z. (2007). Competitiveness of the Bangladesh ready-made garment industry in major international markets. *Asia-Pacific Trade and Investment Review, 3(1)*, 3–27.

Hossan, C. G., Sarker, A. R., & Afroze, R. (2013). Unrest in the RMG sector of Bangladesh: Is this an outcome of poor labour practices? *International Journal of Business and Management, 7*(3); February 2012. www.ccsenet.org/ijbm ISSN 1833-3850 E-ISSN 1833-8119.

ILO. (2013). *Growth with equity. Bangladesh seeking better employment conditions for better socio economic outcomes*. ILO studies, Dhaka 2013.

IMF. (2018). *Bangladesh Macro economy Update. Bangladesh Economic and financial indicators*. IMF Office in Bangladesh.

Islam, M., Khan, A. M. & Islam, M. (2013). Textile industries in Bangladesh and challenges of growth. International Science Congress Association. *Review Paper Research Journal of Engineering Sciences,* 2 (2), 31–37. ISSN 2278-9472.

Labowitz, S. & Dorothée Baumann-Pauly, D. (2014). *Business as usual is not an option. Supply chain and sourcing after Rana Plaza*. NYU, Stern. Center for Business and Human Rights.

Lacy, P., Cooper, T., Hayward, R. & Neuberger, L. (2010). *A new era of sustainability CEO reflections on progress to date, challenges ahead and the impact of the journey toward a sustainable economy*. Accenture and United Nations Global Compact.

Majority Staff Report. (2013). *Worker safety and labor rights in Bangladesh's garment sector*. Prepared for the use of the Committee on Foreign Relations US Senate. 113 Congress, First Session. November 22, 2013. Available via World Wide Web: http://www.gpoaccess.gov/congress/index.html

Maslow, A. H. (1943). A theory of human motivation. *Psychological Review, 50*(4), 370–396. Retrieved from http://psychclassics.yorku.ca/Maslow/motivation.htm.

McKinsey. (2011). *Background of history of Bangladesh and ready-made garment industry: Key challenges in the RMG industry*. Apparel, Fashion & Luxury Practice. November 2011. Designed by Visual Media Europe. Copyright McKinsey & Company,

McKinsey. (2013). *The global sourcing map – balancing cost, compliance, and capacity*. McKinsey's apparel CPO survey 2013. Apparel, Fashion & Luxury Group. September 2013. Designed by Visual Media Europe. Copyright McKinsey & Company,

Ministry of Labour and Employment. (2013). *National Tripartite Plan of Action on fire safety and structural integrity in the ready-made garment sector of Bangladesh*. Ministry of Labour and Employment, Government of the Republic of Bangladesh. Dhaka, 25th July 2013.

Miyan, A. M. (2006). *Dynamics of CSR- Bangladesh context*. Paper published by the International University of Business Agriculture and Technology. Dhaka, 2006.

Momen, N. (2007). *The Innovation Journal: The Public Sector Innovation Journal, 12*(2), Article 4. Rajshahi: University of Rajshahi.

Mondol, E. P. (2009). *Article published by the CSR Foundation Bangladesh*.

Mottaleb, K. A. & Sonobe, T. (2011). An inquiry into the rapid growth of the garment industry in Bangladesh. *GRIPS Policy Research Center Discussion Paper: 11–10.*

Porter, M. E., & Kramer, M. R. (2006). Strategy & society: The link between competitive advantage and corporate social responsibility. *Harvard Business Review, 84*(12), 1–14.

Prahalad, C. K., Nidumolo, R. & Rangaswami, M. R. (2009). Why sustainability is now the key driver of innovation? *Harvard Business Review*, September 2009.

Rahman, M., Bhattacharya, D. & Moazzem, K. G. (2008). *Bangladesh Apparel Sector in Post MFA era. A study on the ongoing restructuring process*. Center for Policy Dialogue and IFC SEDF Bangladesh.

Reed Consulting. (2010). *A CSR guide for entrepreneurs and factory managers. Internal Report.* Dhaka, 2010.

Reed Consulting. (2013). *International Standard Social Responsibility- Implementing ISO 26,000 in Bangladesh. Report supported by the Government of Canada. Internal Report*, Dhaka, 2013.

Salvetti, N. (2013). *Report on the II global social responsibility conference. Bangladesh-German Chamber of Commerce*. Dhaka, March 2013.

Sultana, S., Alam, A., Saha, A. K., Ashek, U. M., & Sarker, A. T. (2011). Likely impacts of quota policy on RMG export from Bangladesh: Prediction and the reality. *International Journal of Business and Management, 6*(11).
United States Department of State. (2012). *Country reports on human rights practices for 2012.* Bureau of Democracy, Human Rights and Labour, Washington, DC.
World Bank. (2013). *Poverty reduction and economic management, South Asia Region.* Bangladesh Development Update. # 81347. The World Bank Report.
World Bank. (2018a). *Bangladesh Country overview.* Report forecasts.
World Bank. (2018b). *Bangladesh policy notes: Enabling export diversification (English).* Washington, DC: World Bank Group. http://documents.worldbank.org/curated/en/235211537422879242/Bangladesh-Policy-Notes-Enabling-Export-Diversification
World Economic Forum. (2014). *Global competitiveness report 2014-2015. World Economic Forum Annual Meeting.* Davos, 2014.
Yunus, M. & Yamagata, T. (2012). The garment industry in Bangladesh. Chapter 6. Fukunishi ed. *Dynamics of the garment industry in low-income countries: Experiences of Asia and Africa (interim report).* Chousakenkyu Houkokusho IDE-JETRO.
Zadek, S. (2004). The path to corporate responsibility. *Harvard Business Review, 82*, 125–132.

CSR Regulation, Ethical Obligation, and Legitimacy: A Study of Indian and Other Asia Pacific Banks

Ameeta Jain and Akanksha Jumde

Abstract India's new Companies law (2013) introduced a unique provision mandating Corporate Social Responsibility (CSR) spending and disclosure of the CSR performance by Indian companies. This paper evaluates the before and after effects of CSR spending and disclosures by four major Indian banks from 2010 to 2018, compared with banks from Japan, Australia, and China, where CSR is largely voluntary. Using self-reported CSR disclosures, this study aims to understand whether the new law has affected the quality of the disclosures made by major banks in India and compares them with quality of the CSR disclosures by other Asia-Pacific Banks. This research finds that there is marginal change in CSR spending by Indian banks and minimal improvement in the reporting quality following change in legislation in 2013. Indian Banks tend to use consistently vague and generic language to describe their CSR performance. Therefore, while quantity (length of the CSR disclosures) has improved, the quality (the level of detail) of CSR disclosures has not improved substantially. We find that the quality of the CSR disclosures made by other Asian Pacific banks remains better than those made by Indian banks. Further, due to inadequate drafting of the law, and poor institutional context, Indian banks are resorting to high levels of auto-interpretation and creative compliance to suit mainly self-interests. In conclusion, the law in its current form is failing to promote ethically responsible behaviour and not generating an ethical obligation to obey the law in spirit. These findings are of value to policy makers—to reform the law, and to design appropriate enforcement mechanisms.

Keywords CSR · Law · Business ethics · CSR spend · Disclosure

A. Jain (✉) · A. Jumde
Deakin University, Melbourne, VIC, Australia
e-mail: ameeta.jain@deakin.edu.au; ajumde@deakin.edu.au

N. Mitra, R. Schmidpeter (eds.), *Corporate Social Responsibility in Rising Economies*, CSR, Sustainability, Ethics & Governance,
https://doi.org/10.1007/978-3-030-53775-3_7

1 Introduction

There is widespread agreement amongst Chief Executive Officers (CEOs), politicians, and international organisations such as the United Nations (UN), World Bank and the Organisation for Economic Cooperation and Development (OECD), that corporations have certain responsibilities towards society. The rise of Corporate Social Responsibility (CSR) spending and adoption of Global Reporting Initiative (GRI) (2012) are evidence of this. The global financial crisis provided further impetus to the uptake of CSR as firms sought to take advantage of the reputational risk management aspects of CSR reporting (Bebbington, Larringa, & Moneva, 2008; Jain, Keneley, & Thomson, 2014; Thomson & Jain, 2006, 2010). This coincided with a greater understanding of the relationship between CSR and sustainability and the management of risk (see for example Godfrey, Merrill, & Hansen, 2009). Coevally, bailouts for financial institutions, and public anger at poor corporate governance raised the pressure on governments to utilise legal rules to regulate corporate activities more strongly (Dunn, 2014). At the same time, Michelon and Rodrigue (2015) also shows that there is a growing demand for CSR through activist shareholder proposals.

Governments are responding with rules associated with CSR goals, albeit at differing prescriptive levels around the world. For instance, in the United States of America (USA), the Securities and Exchange Commission issued rules mandating disclosure of payments made by resource extraction companies, and products containing conflict minerals pursuant to a provision in the Dodd Frank Act in 2016 (United States Securities and Exchange Commission, 2016). In the European Union (EU), the Directive (2014/95/EU) on disclosure of non-financial and diversity information entered into force in 2014, and requires Member States to adopt implementing legislation by December 2016 (European Parliament and the Council of the European Union, 2014). In Australia, the ASX Principles require a company to "disclose whether it has any material exposure to economic, environmental and social sustainability risks and, if it does, how it manages or intends to manage those risks" (ASX Corporate Governance Council, 2014).

India, one of the few countries in the world to transition from *voluntary CSR disclosures* to *legally mandated* CSR disclosures, under the new Companies Act (The Government of India, 2013). Section 135 of the Indian Companies Act (read with Companies (CSR) Rules, 2014 and Schedule VII of the Act), mandates, a "CSR spending of 2 percent of average net profits ... during the three immediately preceding financial years" (Companies Amendment Act, The Government of India, 2013) for all companies meeting specified financial thresholds. Companies must also report the distribution of their CSR spending, for every financial year, according to the list of prescribed activities, under Schedule VII of the Act. In the event of default in this reporting, "the company shall be liable to a penalty of 25,000 rupees (approximately USD[1] 400) and every officer of the company who is in default

[1]United States Dollar.

shall be liable to a penalty of 5000 rupees" (approximately USD 80) (The Government of India, 2013: 81, Section 136(3)). Despite the low penalty, the mandatory rule has brought attention to the relationship between legal rules and CSR.

Whilst an emerging body of scholarship measures CSR spending and assesses its efficacy, there is a dearth of research at the intersection of CSR and law—analysing the role of legal rules, their optimal design, and limitations of existing rules. Despite theorising by Campbell (2007) there is virtually no academic review of whether companies' CSR activity is affected by specific legal rules, whether CSR can be changed from a voluntary activity to a legal obligation, whether legal rules affect corporations' and CEOs' ethical obligations, or whether legal rules and their enforcement is efficient. This study seeks to fill this gap through the natural experiment offered by section 135 of India's Companies Act. We analyse the Indian rules and their impact on the CSR activity of major banks before and after enactment. This is then compared with major banks in Australia, China and Japan subject to voluntary disclosures. Australia and India are common law countries and their company laws derive from similar sources, i.e. judicial pronouncements. China and Japan are civil law countries but their corporate laws have been influenced by common law developments in recent decades. Our study provides insights into legislated CSR and suggestions for law reform in India and elsewhere.

1.1 Importance of CSR for Banks

Banks play an important role in the financial system and the economy of any country. Banks are some of the largest companies in any country by total assets or market capitalization. Therefore, as corporations, they have enormous responsibility for social and ethical behaviour.

The international media is awash with tales of banking scandals ranging from money laundering and rogue trading to interest rate fixing and potential criminal indictment (McDonald, 2012). Coupled with the fallout from the global financial crisis, banks have experienced a loss of credibility (Bravo, Matute, & Pina, 2012). The intense media and public scrutiny focused on the banking industry means that banks are increasingly concentrating on protecting their reputational assets (Soana, 2011) and image (Bravo et al., 2012).

The above discussions permit us to answer the following research questions:

I. Has the CSR law in India led to any change in the quality of the language used in CSR disclosures made by Indian banks?
II. How do the disclosures made by Indian banks compare with the disclosures made by banks from selected voluntary regimes: China, Japan and Australia?

This paper proceeds as follows: the next sections describe the case for legislated CSR activity and reporting, research method, results and discussion, implications and finally a conclusion.

2 The Case for Legislation

Initially, CSR was regarded as a purely voluntary activity undertaken by corporations pursuing philanthropic aims. However, problems such as free-riding, fake CSR, and false disclosures have prompted governments to enact legal rules. Corporate disasters such as the Arthur Anderson/ Enron collapse (Asthana, Balsam, & Kim, 2009), the global financial crises (Avgouleas, 2009; Bennett & Kottasz, 2011; Crotty, 2009; Davis, 2011), infringement of human rights by the likes of Nike and environmental disasters such as Three Mile Island, Love Canal, Bhopal, Chernobyl, and the Exxon Valdez Oil Spill (Kahn, 2007) have highlighted that inadequate or soft regulation cannot facilitate companies to behave in socially and ethically responsible ways. This is aided by the perception that key areas for CSR such as environmental protection, worker safety, corruption, and health have weak national legislation in many countries (Anderson & Gumley, 2008). In a review of government involvement in CSR, Steurer (2010) describes the reasons for governments increasingly providing legislative oversight stating that soft regulation has been used thus far because it is the low political cost option.

Corporate law scholars reject such legislation as misguided because the role of corporate law is to provide default rules and broader legislative agendas. Further, such laws, despite being well-intentioned, impinge on autonomy and impose unnecessary costs (Kraakman & Hansmann, 2017). This 'contractarian' scholarship posits that companies would spend on CSR if such expenditure were to be good for business, that disclosures would be accurate if investors truly cared, and that the market would weed out inefficiency (Strine Jr, 2015). These scholars also claim that directors' sole obligation is to maximise shareholder welfare and that CSR spending can only be done as long as it advances this end. For example, in *Revlon (Del., 1986)*, where the court had to consider a clash between the interests of different stakeholders, it ruled that "A board may have regard for various constituencies in discharging its responsibilities, provided there are rationally related benefits accruing to the stockholders."

In contrast, other scholars such as McBarnet (2009) state "that only legal regulation can provide systematic impact. It would be fairer . . . have more legitimacy, based on and providing due process of law, and . . . be effective." There is a varied history of CSR legislation with European nations leading the way with respect to environmental policy and laws (Delbard, 2008), and other countries have laws pertaining to some aspects of CSR, such as the Green Securities Policy in China. Previous research shows poor compliance with the letter and spirit of such regulation (Wang & Bernell, 2013).

Against this backdrop of fierce resistance by traditional legal scholars to mandatory rules, other scholars and CEOs have publicly embraced CSR. If the debate has tilted in favour of legal rules, and governments are enacting more rules, it is necessary to gain a better understanding of how the rules work and what form they should take if they are to be deployed in an optimal manner.

3 The Evolution of CSR

Our study is contextualised by Carroll's (1991) four dimensional pyramid which includes corporate philanthropic, ethical, legal, and economic responsibilities; and legal responsibility for CSR is predicated on the effectiveness of the law. Similarly, Elkington's (1994) triple-bottom-line model of '*People, Planet and Profits*' advocates that businesses serve economic as well as social and environmental interests (Van Marrewijk, 2003).

Essentially, CSR comprises of five dimensions: environmental, social, economic, stakeholder and voluntariness (Van Marrewijk, 2003). Thus, scholars extend responsibility of businesses to *shareholders* and investors *as well as stakeholders* that includes their own employees, suppliers, communities, governments and the natural environment.

Given the challenges for proper implementation of voluntary nature of CSR, authors have advocated the need for externally-regulated CSR. When externally regulated, CSR may be understood as a form of regulation that may be imposed upon the companies through either *hard law* (legal obligation by governments, thus binding) or *soft law* approach (norms and regulations that may be non-binding) by either private (stock-exchanges or industrial and trade groups) or public authorities (governments or their bodies) (Garriga, 2004).

Mandatory CSR may facilitate the establishment of regulated CSR indicators, improve their CSR disclosures, leading to greater transparency and confirmation to globally accepted CSR norms, and the establishment of a system of checks and balances, where corporations will be compelled to remain accountable to civil society and governmental bodies for their actions towards the society.

Despite the challenges with externally-regulated CSR mechanisms, governments in numerous countries, both developed and developing, are increasingly moving towards regulating the responsibilities of the corporations towards their stakeholders.

CSR in India is rooted in religious, cultural and moral ethos, reinforced by the trusteeship model advocated by Mahatma Gandhi. In 2009, the Ministry of Corporate Affairs (MCA) introduced the National Voluntary Guidelines (NVGs) to direct the companies to engage in CSR activities and produce CSR disclosures (Ministry of Corporate Affairs, 2011). In order to provide uniformity in the mandatory CSR reporting by the companies, Securities and Exchange Board of India (SEBI), the largest securities exchange regulator in India, formulated a framework known as Business Responsibility Reporting (BRR), based on the Global Reporting Initiative (GRI) guidelines (SEBI, 2012). Subsequently, the Ministry of Heavy Industries and Public Enterprises also issued guidelines on CSR for Central Public Sector Enterprises (CPSEs) (Department of Public Enterprises, 2010).

In 2013, Government of India introduced mandatory CSR under The Companies Act, 2013. **Section 135, read with Companies Act Rules, 2014 and Schedule VII of the Act,** forms the base for CSR law in India.

4 Methodology

The four largest banks by market capitalisation from Australia, China, Japan, and India are evaluated (Annexure 1). The reporting media of these banks including their annual reports, CSR reports, and websites were used. This was supplemented by document analysis (Bowen, 2009) to obtain a deeper understanding of the actual CSR activity to distinguish between rhetoric and substantive activity.

This research uses an adaptation of a disclosure index previously developed by Islam, Jain, and Thomson (2016); and Jain, Keneley, and Thomson (2015) for the evaluation of CSR reports. This index was based on extant literature, GRI guidelines, and banks' existing CSR reporting practices. This index comprises six broad categories of assessment: ethical standards, CSR reporting, community involvement, environment, products, and employees; with the figures in parenthesis denoting the total number of assessment criteria in the category (Annexure 2). Content analysis was used to code these items from banks' reporting media. Content analysis is a popular method of codifying and evaluating text from a report or other similar media using well defined inclusion criteria (Parker, 2005).

A bank reporting on any activity meeting the criteria gets a maximum score of 1 and 0 in the absence of any reported activity. Thus two banks, one spending 0.5 percent and 0.01 percent of annual profit on sponsoring and charitable donations would both get an equal score of 1. The disclosure index score provides a raw score based on the presence or absence of reporting criteria in the report (adapted from Islam et al., 2016; Jain et al., 2015).

The CSR reports from the four largest banks of the four countries during 2010–2018 were analysed using NVivo™ software. Document analysis permits us to delve deeper into CSR reports and identify the actual differences between reporting quality across countries and intra-country over time. Deeper analysis sheds light on whether the banks are just paying lip service to CSR to manage their reputational risk and protect their legitimacy in society (Deegan, 2002).

Like any other research, based on qualitative evaluation of published company media, this research has shortcomings in terms of both the use of reporting media as the source of data and the method of analysis. One of the drawbacks of content analysis is that there is no consensus concerning which unit of analysis is most appropriate, words, sentences, paragraphs or pages when codifying the reporting media (Tilt, 2001). To reduce these shortcomings and to reduce bias, we used multiple coders (as per Tilt, 2001; Yongvanich & Guthrie, 2005). Similarly, Bowen (2009) states that document analysis can be hampered by insufficient detail, difficulty in retrieval, and biased selectivity (Bowen, 2009).

5 Results and Discussion

5.1 Disclosure Index Scores

The results of the calculated disclosure index based on content analysis are shown in Table 1. Each bank is scored against the disclosure items listed in Annexure 2 with a maximum annual achievable sustainability score of 50 in any given year. The disclosure index score for four major banks in all countries increased between 2010 and until 2015, after which it appears to have plateaued.

Chinese banks have consistently higher Disclosure Index scores than Indian Banks from 2010 onwards. The promulgation of the Indian CSR law in 2013 does not appear to have made much difference in 2014 or 2015 to this disparity. However,

Table 1 Disclosure index for four major banks in Australia, China India and Japan

	2010	2011	2012	2013	2014	2015	2016	2017	2018
Australia									
ANZ	43	44	45	44	44	45	46	43	46
CBA	30	30	36	37	40	42	43	44	43
NAB	39	39	40	41	41	42	42	45	44
WBC	42	42	43	42	42	44	43	44	46
Annual Total	**154**	**155**	**164**	**164**	**167**	**173**	**173**	**176**	**179**
Japan									
Mitsubishi UFJ financial group	37	40	37	38	39	37	36	34	42
Sumitomo Mitsui financial group	27	30	29	31	34	34	35	36	43
Mizuho financial group	31	32	32	31	32	33	34	35	38
Nomura holdings Inc	26	27	27	27	29	30	31	32	39
Annual Total	**121**	**130**	**125**	**127**	**134**	**134**	**136**	**137**	**162**
China									
Industrial & commercial bank of China (ICBC)	20	20	23	22	22	22	24	25	26
China construction bank corporation	21	21	21	22	22	21	22	23	25
Agricultural Bank of China	22	22	22	22	22	20	23	23	26
Bank of China	18	19	18	18	21	22	24	24	25
Annual Total	**79**	**82**	**84**	**82**	**87**	**85**	**93**	**95**	**102**
India									
State Bank of India	16	18	21	20	20	20	21	22	23
HDFC Bank	8	8	11	15	22	22	26	28	29
ICICI Bank ltd	15	14	14	16	16	16	17	19	29
Kotak Mahindra Bank	9	10	11	15	19	19	20	21	22
Annual Total	**48**	**50**	**57**	**66**	**77**	**77**	**84**	**90**	**103**

Note: Maximum total for a bank is 50 in any given year

we do see improvements and steady growth after 2016 to 2018, in the scores of the CSR disclosure indexes by Indian companies, albeit the disclosures continue to remain abysmally lower than the rest of the selected sample of countries. Australian banks have consistently the highest disclosure index in this period, followed by Japan. This is most likely due to the inherent difference in the compliance culture, stronger legal institutions and enforcement mechanisms of these nations in comparison to India and China.

5.2 CSR Spending in Pre-2013 and Post-2013 Period

The SEBI guidelines provide a list of nine broad principles (P1 to P9). These are to be taken in concert with Section 135 of the Companies Act (The Government of India, 2013). In conformity with the law, from 2013, all banks reported to have established a CSR committee comprising of board members formulating CSR policy, recommending and monitoring CSR spend (except KMBL).

All the Indian banks published their first CSR report in 2013, with the exception of Kotak Mahindra Bank Limited (KMBL) which started in 2012. In 2012, ICICI, State Bank of India (SBI) and HDFC reported a small section on CSR as a part of their annual reports. Additionally, the CSR reports were compliant with the Securities and Exchange Board of India (SEBI) framework (2012).

Of the four Indian Banks evaluated, only SBI disclosed their CSR spend prior to the promulgation of the new Companies Act (2013); all banks disclosed from 2013. SBI reported every year that they had spent 1 percent of their annual post-tax profits on philanthropic activities since 2012 (Table 2). From 2016 to 2018, despite the legal mandate to spend 2 percent of the average net profits on CSR, SBI continued to spend only 1 percent of the profits on CSR, as a matter of company policy.

Despite the new law mandating 2 percent of pre-tax profit for corporations of this size, only ICICI met this target in 2014 and fell to 1.8 percent in 2015 and 2016. In 2017 and 2018, ICICI was able to meet its target of spending of 2 percent of the average net profits on CSR activities. KMBL Bank reported a CSR spend of less than 0.64 percent of post-tax profits in 2015. From 2016–18, KMBL continued its earlier trend of spending less than 2 percent of the profits on CSR, as mandated by the law, and has not shown any increase from the past years. None of the banks reported any fines or proceedings for breach of the law. On a positive note, HDFC has shown a steady increase in the amount of spending over the years. In 2018, it spent well above the 2 percent mark (almost 3 percent) on CSR activities, suggesting not only compliance of the law, but also an attempt to "go beyond" the requirements of the legislation.

Table 2 Percentage of annual profits spent on CSR as declared in annual or sustainability reports

Bank	2012	2013	2014	2015	2016	2017	2018
Australia (pre-tax profits)							
ANZ	0.16%	0.72%	0.73%	0.71%	0.78%	0.67%	0.79%
NAB	0.89%	0.87%	0.87%	0.65%	0.70%	0.68%	1.80%
Westpac	1.41%	1.3%	1.99%	1.04%	1.35%	1.36%	1.56%
CBA	2.03%	ND	ND	1.92%	2.06%	1.98%	ND
China (post-tax profits)							
Bank of China	0.003%	0.003%	0.003%	ND	ND	ND	0.004%
Agricultural Bank of China	ND	ND	ND	ND	ND	ND	ND
ICBC	ND	ND	ND	ND	ND	ND	ND
CCB	ND	ND	ND	ND	ND	ND	ND
India (post tax profits)							
HDFC	ND	0.74%	1.8%	1.2%	1.67%	2.04%	2.67%
ICICI	ND	1.4%	2.0%	1.8%	1.6%	1.8%	2.01%
Kotak Mahindra	ND	0.3%	0.24%	0.64%	0.69%	0.63%	0.71%
SBI	1.0%	1.0%	1.37%	1.06%	1.67%	1.45%	1.43%
Japan							
Nomura	ND	ND	ND	ND	ND	ND	ND
Mizuho	ND	ND	ND	ND	ND	ND	ND
MUFJ	ND	ND	ND	ND	ND	ND	ND
SMFG	ND	ND	ND	ND	ND	ND	ND

ND not disclosed in annual or CSR report

5.3 Sector-Wise Spending by Indian Banks After 2013

Delving deeper, it becomes clear that Indian Banks are indeed spending money on CSR activities prescribed by section 135 (The Government of India, 2013). Perhaps in an attempt to draw political mileage from such activity, the banks concentrate on and describe their educational and health promotional activities in detail. All the banks invest in the community primarily by setting up their own foundations and centres, and promoting staff volunteering at high profile events—likely a public relations exercise.

The other categories of CSR spend are the promotion of gender equality, employee training, environmental sustainability, and contribution to government natural disaster relief funds. None of the banks have reported any involvement in the eradication of malaria or combating other major communicable diseases. Contribution to natural disaster relief funds and other national and state developmental funds can be seen to be currying favour with the political parties in power in the central and state governments. The efforts towards "greening" and environmental sustainability are not as significant as their counterparts in Australia. There are many small-ticket items listed in this category rather than the true targets, specific spend and achievement of goals or long term goals. Again, reduction of energy and other consumables is dealt with in a philosophical manner with little global activity for each bank across their own networks: for example, each bank invests in "sentinel sites" showcasing their aspirational but as yet not declared goals.

In contrast, despite no legislative requirement, Australian Banks have been following this path since 2010. CBA and Westpac spend more on CSR as a percentage of pre-tax profits than the other two Australian banks. Chinese and Japanese banks report on targets and achievements to meet their respective environmental laws, albeit not in as much detail as Australian Banks. As there is no legal requirement to report on their actual CSR spends, Japanese banks do not disclose this amount in their reporting media (Table 2). Only one of the four Chinese banks under study (Bank of China) disclosed its CSR spend. This was miniscule .003 percent with a slight increase to 0.004 percent in 2017, of post-tax profits.

5.4 *Quality of Reporting*

Japanese Banks

In Japan, Nomura and Mitsubishi UFJ Financial Group (MUFG) have issued separate CSR reports since 2010, Mizuho since 2011, and SMFG since 2012. These reports provide detailed descriptions of these banks' environmental impact, consumption data, targets and achievements towards reducing their energy consumption and carbon footprint in compliance with the Law of Promotion of Environmentally Conscious Business Activities (2001). The letter and spirit of the law is followed. Once again, local legislation has provided direction and focus to companies' CSR activity. Japanese banks do provide descriptors of their CSR activity including community participation, illustrating their reports with case studies, similar to banks in other countries.

Australian Banks

Detailed CSR reports, separate to the annual reports have become the norm for Australian banks over the last decade. Australian bank disclosures tend to be factual and presented in a tabular form for easy sequential comparison. Australian banks have tended not to promote aspirational goals in their reports without following such assertions with achievements (for example, see, Sustainabililty Report, NAB, 2012; Sustainability Report, Westpac, 2012). Each report describes the CSR targets in each measurable category and whether they were achieved or not. Further, despite no legislative requirements to do so, Australian banks have provided an itemised description of money spent on CSR activity. Also, in keeping with the Australian Corporations Act 2001, Australian banks report, in depth, their environmental targets and achievements.

Chinese Banks

The Agricultural Bank of China, China Construction Bank and Industrial and Commercial Bank of China have been publishing CSR reports since 2007 and the Bank of China since 2010. The reports from Chinese Banks provide broad general statements about their CSR activity but do not describe any CSR targets or achievements towards meeting such targets. Again, these reports are mindful of the Green Securities Policy of Shanghai 2008/Shanghai Stock Exchange guidelines, even though this policy is not mentioned in these reports. Chinese Banks do describe their community participation and support activities albeit with emphasis on case studies. With the exception of the Bank of China, they do not disclose CSR spend.

Indian Banks: Pre 2013 and Post 2013

Annexure 3 lists excerpts from annual reports of Indian Banks using four general themes of analysis: general statements, financial inclusion and sustainable livelihoods, environment, and community and stakeholders. Sequential evaluation of HDFC's reports clearly demonstrates a change in language from generic and aspirational to more specific about real CSR activity. In 2012, the language used in the report was about belief, recognising a goal and moving towards it in the future.

In 2013, the language again acknowledged the importance of CSR but included action statements like embedding beliefs into value systems and undertaking initiatives. The 2014 report changed to reiterating commitment and expressing the desire to continue improvements (first goal driven CSR report). Crucially, in 2015, the language is more direct indicating what is actually being done and less "flowery" in relation to CSR, with the focus moving to "digital" sustainability. From 2016 to 2018, the language used in the CSR reports continue to be more descriptive in terms of the work being done and what the Bank wishes to achieve from the activity.

This is similar to the reports from KMBL. In 2012, KMBL's reports included brief statements mainly about commitment/beliefs, with the language changing slightly in 2013. Until 2015, the language suggests that CSR is undertaken mainly in the context of business opportunity (e.g. "KMBL views FI as a potential market opportunity, beyond a mandatory obligation" 2014 BR). The number of comments regarding CSR increased over the 4 years, with 2015 showing an increased volume on CSR but also more values statements. The same trend seems to have continued from 2016 to 2018.

There are significant problems in the quality of reporting. For example, SBI (2015) reports its digital banking project, mobile services, SBIePay services for electronic paperless transactions, smart card based banking and bar code based smart payment systems for small businesses under P2: Providing Sustainable Products and Services. This is similar to the disclosures by KMBL from 2013 onwards. However, ICICI Bank states that in the nature of its business there are no such products, highlighting the difference in the interpretation of the generic SEBI guidelines. KMBL describes its foray into work health and safety with the introduction of staff training in fire safety and evacuation, road safety and emergency situation handling (Annual Report, Kotak Mahindra, 2013). Even though HDFC addresses all these principles in its report, it does not follow the SEBI format and refer to each of the "principles" of CSR. These examples illuminate a high degree of auto-interpretation. This might be caused by confusion at a definitional level or by the underlying weakness in the legal system. Section 135's poor drafting and the fact that concepts such as sustainability are over-determined enables companies to adopt self-serving interpretations and engage in creative compliance at a low cost. For e.g., staff training in fire safety should be regarded as part and parcel of a contemporary workplace and not as CSR activity.

Crucially, detailed document analysis of these banks' annual and CSR reports shows that there was minimal shift in the nature of disclosures. For example, in 2010, HDFC's reports complied with the National Voluntary Guidelines (NVGs), and subsequently changed to the SEBI framework (SEBI, 2012) in 2013 through 2018. Table 3 demonstrates the areas listed in section 135 of the Companies Act (The Government of India, 2013), which HDFC complies with. Of note is that in the 2015 CSR report, HDFC did not indicate any CSR activity in three of the nine listed categories of CSR activity under Schedule VII. Further, HDFC did not recognise the community and society in which they operated as a stakeholder, beyond aiming to promote "engagement of the community." Responding to societal expectations is the *sine qua non* of corporate legitimacy and CSR (Bebbington et al., 2008; Boulding, 1978; Chauvey, Giordano-Spring, Cho, & Patten, 2015), yet this is ignored. This suggests that the legal rules lack clarity about purpose, or that the purpose has not been adequately communicated. In other words, companies seem to be interpreting Section 135 as compelled charity rather than as a social responsibility towards stakeholders.

Despite these negatives, there were some positive consequences that are attributable to the legal rules. There is a greater sense of precision or aspiration to communicate with detailed precision in the language used for reporting. For example, generic statements such as "strives for community empowerment by partnering with NGOs" (Annual Report, HDFC Bank, 2010), and "keen to engage positively with local communities" (Annual Report, HDFC Bank, 2013) changed to actual descriptors of activity in 2015. ICICI maintains its difference to the other banks in that it clearly describes the involvement with the ICICI Centre for Education, and provides statistics of people helped by its various CSR activities, and monies raised from 2010. Thus, the CSR reports demonstrate a small qualitative change in the content for two of the four banks and while the other two banks (Kotak Mahindra and ICICI) continue to pay lip service to the concept.

5.5 Legislative Compliance and Society

The inherent difference in the institutional and legal framework of business ethics between economies across the entire spectrum has led to variations in societal expectations of CSR (Crane & Matten, 2016; Matten & Moon, 2008). For example, causes espoused by American companies as CSR activity such as worker's rights, social and medical care, and environmental issues are most often dealt with by legislative requirements in Europe (Crane & Matten, 2016) leading to enforced ethical activity by businesses. Societies in poorer economies might have different expectations from their corporations in comparison to developed economies (Carroll, 1979; Sethi, 1975). In the developing world, a combination of poor legislative oversight, deficits in the rule of law even where legislation exists, and cultural

Table 3 Section 135 compliance of Indian Banks

Bank	(i) eradicating extreme hunger and poverty	(ii) promotion of education	(iii) promoting gender equality and empowering women	(iv) reducing child mortality and improving maternal health;	(v) combating human immunodeficiency virus, acquired immune deficiency syndrome, malaria and other diseases	(vi) ensuring environmental sustainability	(vii) employment enhancing vocational skills;	(viii) social business projects	(ix) contribution to the Prime Minister's National Relief Fund or others (armed forces war widows etc)
HDFC									
2010	–	Y	Y	–	–	Y	Y	–	–
2011	–	Y	Y	–	–	Y	Y	–	–
2012	–	Y	Y	–	–	Y	Y	–	–
2013	–	Y	Y	–	–	Y	Y	–	Y
2014	Y	Y	Y	–	–	Y	Y	–	Y
2015	Y	Y	Y	Y	–	Y	Y	–	Y
2016	Y	Y	Y	–	–	Y	Y	–	–
2017	Y	Y	Y	–	–	Y	Y	–	Y
2018	Y	Y	Y	–	–	Y	Y	–	–
ICICI									
2010	Y	Y	–	Y	–	Y	–	–	Y
2011	Y	Y	–	Y	Y	Y	Y	–	–
2012	Y	Y	–	Y	–	Y	Y	–	–
2013	Y	Y	–	Y	–	Y	Y	–	Y
2014	Y	Y	–	Y	–	Y	Y	–	Y
2015	Y	Y	–	Y	–	Y	Y	–	Y
2016	Y	Y	–	Y	–	Y	Y	–	–
2017	Y	–	Y	Y	–	Y	Y	–	Y
2018	Y	Y	–	–	Y	Y	Y	–	–

(continued)

Table 3 (continued)

Bank	(i) eradicating extreme hunger and poverty	(ii) promotion of education	(iii) promoting gender equality and empowering women	(iv) reducing child mortality and improving maternal health;	(v) combating human immunodeficiency virus, acquired immune deficiency syndrome, malaria and other diseases	(vi) ensuring environmental sustainability	(vii) employment enhancing vocational skills;	(viii) social business projects	(ix) contribution to the Prime Minister's National Relief Fund or others (armed forces war widows etc)
SBI									
2010	Y	Y	Y	–	–	Y	Y	–	Y
2011	Y	Y	Y	–	–	Y	Y	–	Y
2012	Y	Y	–	–	–	Y	Y	–	Y
2013	Y	Y	Y	Y	–	Y	Y	Y	Y
2014	Y	Y	–	–	–	Y	Y	–	Y
2015	Y	Y	Y	–	–	Y	Y	Y	Y
2016	Y	Y	Y	–	–	Y	Y	–	–
2017	Y	Y	Y	–	Y	Y	–	–	–
2018	Y	Y	Y	–	Y	Y	Y	–	–
KM									
2010	–	Y	Y	–	–	Y	–	–	–
2011	–	Y	–	–	–	Y	Y	–	–
2012	–	Y	–	–	–	Y	Y	–	–
2013	–	Y	Y	–	–	Y	Y	–	–
2014	–	Y	Y	–	–	Y	Y	–	–
2015	–	Y	Y	–	–	Y	Y	–	–
2016	–	Y	Y	–	–	Y	Y	–	–
2017	–	Y	Y	–	–	Y	Y	–	–
2018	–	Y	Y	–	–	Y	Y	–	–

differences in the ways of doing business prove a potential quagmire not just to businesses and ethicists but also to governments.

Specific to the Indian situation, the legal rule is a "comply or explain provision." Recent Developments have attempted to change the "comply-or-explain" provision to "comply-only" provision. In particular, the Companies (Amendment) Act, 2019, attempted criminalise the mandatory CSR provisions under the Companies Act, 2013. However, these provisions have been notified, but not yet effected. For instance, in its 2015 CSR report, HDFC reported that their annual CSR spend was of 1.2 percent of their post-tax profits. Section 135 of the Act specifies that if the company fails to spend 2 percent, the Board needs to provide an explanation for not doing so in the report. Whilst detailed accounts of CSR spend are provided; and since there is a "reasonable explanation" for the shortfall in CSR spend, no enforcement action has been taken against HDFC and its Board. Even if they were to be fined, the penalty provided is miniscule Indian Rupee (INR) 25,000 which represents less than 0.00125 percent of the prescribed CSR spend. In this instance, the bank does not have a financial imperative to spend 2 percent of post-tax profits on CSR spend to save 0.00125 percent of post-tax profits as penalty. Similarly, in 2017, ICICI Bank fell short of spending 2 percent of its average net profits on CSR by 0.40 billion INR, and "lower capital expenditure by ICICI Foundation" was cited as the reason for the deficit in CSR spending. On the other hand, Kotak Mahindra, which consistently underspent from 2013 to 2018, did not provide any explanation at all for the deficit in its CSR spending, and there are no records to show whether any penalty, howsoever miniscule it may be, was imposed on it.

This same theme echoes across the countries reviewed with banks complying with local legislation where the cost of compliance is less than the legislative penalty, reputational risk or both. Certainly in the case of Australia, reputational risk seems to be the driver for CSR spend and associated detailed reporting (Jain et al., 2014, 2015). CSR and annual reports are media used for communication by banks with their stakeholders and therefore respond to stakeholder expectations and legal context which differs across the Asia Pacific. In other words, the legal context signifies a reinforcing relationship between legal rules and ethical obligations, and triggers independent obligations to obey the law. Certainly, in Australia and elsewhere in the OECD, there seems to be rapid change in voluntary standards of CSR reporting following social contagion and isomorphism (Jain & Islam, 2016).

6 Implications

Clearly, legal rules and institutions matter. Scholars such as Cooter (1998) theorise that legal rules can change the preferences of rational individuals through its communicative function by expressing values. He writes that by creating opportunities for Pareto self-improvements, law induces rational people to change their preferences. Legal rules express social values and facilitate ethical behaviour by actors by setting a baseline for acceptable conduct. They reduce over-determination and confusion as to what might be ethical because the legal rules clarify and establish the boundaries of what is not acceptable.

In the CSR context, Section 135 could be described as a piece of expressive law. The text and drafting history suggests that the legislators intended the section to be expressive because it is framed as a comply-or-explain rule with minimal penalties. However, because the law is poorly worded, actors do not know precisely what they are obligated to do by the rule, and there is no attendant ethical activity above the baseline set by the law. A general ethical obligation to obey law might also be absent or poorly developed in India due to factors such as high corruption, low levels of public confidence, weak institutions, low development, and education. Further, there is little possibility of Pareto self-improvement because of weak drafting. In addition, the lack of clarity is also not generating an independent ethical obligation to obey the particular CSR law. In such circumstances, we posit that creative compliance of the sort described by our evidence is natural. This is not to say that the rules are doomed or that law should stay out of CSR debates. We posit the contrary—there is considerable indeterminacy in legal approaches to CSR and the very process of compliance will clarify and reinforce community expectations and harden them into more precise legal obligations (Picciotto, 2007). Our results show this trend—over time, in two of the four Indian banks, we see a shift toward more legalized language.

7 Conclusion

As governments increasingly resort to legal rules to promote ethical behaviour by businesses and enhance their CSR activity, it is necessary to understand the role of legal rules, their form and substance, monitoring mechanisms, and enforcement regime. The Indian Companies Act's attempt at mandating CSR spending offers a rich mine of data to understand these questions. This Act appears to be formulated based on the traditional understanding that top management is solely responsible for ethical behaviour and CSR activity without making the connection between the company and its stakeholders.

Based on our examination of the CSR disclosures by Indian Banks, we find that there is little material change in CSR spending by Indian Banks, even in the post-legislation period. CSR disclosures by Indian Banks, as a representative sample of Indian companies, over the period of examination (2010–2018), lack in substantive quality. We find that the quality of the CSR disclosures made by other Asia-Pacific banks remains better than those made by Indian banks. Due to these primary findings, we wish to readily question the efficacy of the new law.

The study offers important insights. First, merely stipulating specific legal rules mandating CSR is unlikely to be effective in achieving policy goals as corporate ethical behaviour is a reflection of the overall institutional framework. Second, at a qualitative level, there is small improvement in the precision of data reported in the CSR reports. Third, there is a high degree of auto-interpretation and self-interested actions in complying with CSR legal rules in India. Fourth, CSR reports in countries with poorer levels of governance and institutional frameworks tend to contain more generic and vague language. Fifth, higher quality of the CSR disclosures might indicate a higher degree of internalisation of CSR norms and more ethical behaviour reinforcing legal rules. Sixth, countries with poorer enforcement mechanisms enacting specific CSR rules should provide bright line rules with monitoring mechanisms and significant sanctions to increase the prospects of successful implementation. Such rules are also likely to generate ethical obligations of obedience and promote pro-social activities above the legal baseline.

We posit that positive change is unlikely to be achieved in corporate ethical behaviour in the form of either CSR spending or quality of disclosure unless Section 135 is reformed substantially. Further evaluation using a larger sample will likely confirm marginal improvements in quality of disclosure. This underscores the futility of mandatory CSR as an end in itself. In other words, mandatory rules are only effective if they are precise, backed up with robust enforcement, and generate ethical obligations of obedience. In absence of these conditions, voluntary CSR might be preferable because it saves the costs imposed by a futile law.

Annexure 1: Sample Bank Characteristics as at April 2019

	Reuters	Market Cap
Australia	**Code**	**AU$M**
Commonwealth Bank of Australia	CBA	139,556.97
Westpac Banking Group	WBC	107,313.69
Australia and New Zealand Banking Group	ANZ	80,064.56
National Australia Bank	NAB	74,109.97
China		
Industrial and Commercial Bank of China (ICBC)	1398.HK	345,214.69
China Construction Bank Corporation	0939.HK	275,399.05
Agricultural Bank of China	1288.HK	203,244.30
Bank of China	3988.HK	181,469.14
Japan		
Mitsubishi UFJ Financial Group	8306.T	111,660.30
Sumitomo Mitsui Financial Group	8316.T	67,328.06
Mizuho Financial Group	8411.T	50,018.44
Nomura Holdings Inc	8604.T	33,758.94
India		
HDFC Bank	HDBK.BO	88,435.07
State Bank of India	SBI.BO	40,562.90
ICICI Bank Ltd	ICBK.NS	37,473.79
Kotak Mahindra Bank	KTKM.BO	26,895.23

Annexure 2: CSR Disclosure Assessment Framework: Disclosure Indicators in Each Main Grouping

Ethical Standards (6)
Signatory to ICCC Business Charter for Sustainable Development
Signatory to UNEP Finance Initiative
Signatory to UN Principals for Responsible Investment
Signatory to Equator Principles
Signatory to UN Global Compact
OECD Guidelines for Multinational Enterprises
CSR Reporting (7)
Annual CSR Report
Interim CSR Report
Other Regular CSR Updates
Global Reporting Initiative G3 (Financial Services)
AA1000AS Assurance Standard
External Assurance of CSR Reporting
Community Investment Reporting Audit
Environment (5)
Certified Environmental Management System (ISO 14001)
Environmental Policy
Quantitative Environmental Management Targets
Transparency of Environmental Performance
Environmental Risk Management in Lending Policy
Products (12)
Socially Responsible Investment Products
Disclose of SRI Funds as % Total FUM
Socially Responsible Savings Products
Sustainable Financing
Microcredit
Environmental Advice Services
Climate Products
Participation in Environmental Markets
Socially Responsible Lending
Socially Responsible Lending Charter
Exclusion of Specific Sectors
Position Statements for Specific Sectors
Community (9)
Sponsoring & Charitable Donations
Target for $ Community Investment
Community Involvement
Community Consultation
Sustainability Advocacy
Paid Employee Volunteering

(continued)

Financial Literacy Programs
Financial Inclusion Programs
Independent financial counselling
Employees (11)
Training and Education
Leadership Training Programs
Women as % Management Target
Women as % Management Target Achieved
EOWA Employer of Choice
Disability Anti-Discrimination Programs
Mature Age Employment Plan
Work/Life Balance Policies
Employee Health Programs
Diversity Programs
Feedback from Employees

Adapted from Jain et al. (2015) and Islam et al. (2016)

Annexure 3: Change of Language in Reporting Media Over Time in Indian Banks (Changes Are Underlined)

	2012	2013	2014	2015	2016	2017	2018
HDFC							
General Statements (CSR Policy)	Your Bank has a defined guiding principle for all its social initiatives: 'Changing Lives by empowering individuals through Finance, Education and Training'... because, we believe that success in banking is . . .about making a difference and empowering lives.	We envision that Sustainability will become an integral part of our business....we stand committed to bringing about a sustainable change in the organisation in line with our strategy.... This year ..The belief was hard-wired into our value system....embarked on the journey towards becoming a truly sustainable organisation.	We want to give back to society by creating long-term solutions. We hope we are able to set higher benchmarks in our sustainability performance each year.	We are committed to embedding elements of. . .services. . . . acknowledge our responsibility in building sustainable communities. . . sustainability as the core, we are committed to contribute to a future that is 'Digitally Sustainable'.	We aim to make meaningful impact on the lives of the economically, physically and socially challenged communities. We promote initiatives that preserve, restore, and enhance environment, ecological balance, and natural resources. Our CSR Philosophy and motto is based on sustainable development.	'Creating Sustainable Communities' is the underlying philosophy that drives your Bank's CSR initiatives. . . The objective is to . . .growth, development and empowerment without disturbing the ecological balance.	HDFC Bank, has worked towards the vision of "Creating Sustainable Communities" through its CSR Programmes. The Bank's guiding force is the belief that businesses cannot prosper if the communities. . .your Bank has chosen to bring a holistic change in the lives of the people.
Financial Inclusion & Sustainable Livelihoods	Community initiatives which aim at empowering individuals at the bottom of the pyramid through developmental initiatives such as education and livelihood support....We have a	We believe in empowering the community . . .we understand that our journey towards empowering lives starts from within. . . .we are committed to improving financial literacy. . . .	We are committed to improving financial literacy. . . .committed to reaching out to the unbanked and under banked people at the bottom of the pyramid. . . .hope that we can empower more lives. . .	We have always taken an inclusive, empowering and responsible approach towards the marginalised sections of the society. . . .have gone beyond the regulatory mandate. . . .we aim	We have undertaken various rural financial literacy initiatives across the country . . .	. . . .the Bank conducts financial literacy workshops for communities to enable them to make smart financial decisions and sustain themselves. HDFC Bank's Sustainable Livelihood Initiative (SLI)	The guiding force for HDFC Bank is the belief that real development of the country is possible only when its communities are empowered. . . The Bank has undertaken various

	board approved program . . .			to support the weaker sections of the society.		epitomises the vision of 'Creating Sustainable Communities'.	initiatives to support inclusive growth. . . .
Environment	Your Bank believes in taking responsibility for the effects of its operations on society. . .	We are aware of our responsibility towards the environment and are undertaking various initiatives to reduce the environmental impact of our operations.	We intend to minimise the risks owing to the growing effects of climate change. . . .we are conscious of our usage of resources . . .We also hope to create a greater positive impact on the environment as we move forward as a responsible corporate citizen.	We aim to drive positive change towards environment through the projects we invest in.	The Bank constantly aims to reduce the impact on the environment. . . To ensure minimal carbon footprint, we have incorporated environmental friendly installations. . .	As a conscientious Bank, we understand our responsibility to operate in an environmentally sustainable way. . . We have incorporated environment friendly features in our infrastructure.	HDFC Bank is an environmentally and socially responsible organization. The Bank has rolled out various initiatives. . . The Bank has also undertaken initiatives. . . The Bank encourages the use of. . . to promote environment-friendly practices.
Community & Stakeholders	The Bank believes in empowering its employees and constantly takes various measures to achieve this objective.	We are keen to engage positively with the communities. . . . we aim to provide a gender-inclusive environment. . .	Our short term strategy is to bring about behavioural change in our employees as well as customers and to increase sensitivity towards environmental and social issues.	We have made significant efforts to create a work- place conducive for women and maintain a diverse workforce.	We believe that building a strong relationship with our stakeholders . . . We acknowledge their contribution in building our reputation and helping us attain a leadership position in the Banking industry.	The Bank believes, being responsible is a result of creating strong coalitions and trusted partnerships among different stakeholders. It recognises the value of its stakeholders. . .	Regular and planned engagements are conducted with all identified stakeholder groups. The Bank has identified its key stakeholders. . .. The Bank engages with them. . .

(continued)

	2012	2013	2014	2015	2016	2017	2018
ICICI							
General Statements (CSR Policy)	Through such efforts, we carry forward our ethos of being an institution that supports the realisation of our country's potential in a manner that takes the benefits of growth to every Indian.	We also continued to play a proactive role in nation building. The ICICI Group's current activities in this regard range from financial inclusion to working in the areas of education, healthcare and sustainable livelihoods.	The ICICI Group continues to focus on increasing shareholder value in a responsible and conscientious manner. . .	The ICICI Group set up ICICI Foundation for Inclusive Growth in early 2008 to build upon the Group's legacy of promoting development and inclusive growth.	Corporate Social Responsibility (CSR) has been a long-standing commitment at ICICI Bank.	The Bank established the ICICI Foundation for Inclusive Growth (ICICI Foundation) in 2008 with a view to significantly expand the activities in the area of CSR.	. . .The CSR Policy of the Bank sets the framework guiding the Bank's CSR activities.
Financial Inclusion & Sustainable Livelihoods	Promoting inclusive growth has been a priority area for the Group from both a business and social perspective.	. . .enhancing access to financial services is an important pillar of inclusive growth. . . .ICICI Bank's initiative on Financial Inclusion aims to provide banking services.	We have continued to focus on the areas of elementary education, healthcare, sustainable livelihood through skill development and financial inclusion.	ICICI Bank's commitment towards promoting inclusive growth spans several years....The ICICI Group's commitment towards promoting inclusive growth was further strengthened during fiscal 2015.	ICICI Foundation undertakes a number of initiatives for the under-privileged. . .	We believe that comprehensive socio-economic development of villages. . .	Community development forms the core for all initiatives undertaken by the Bank. The programmes of ICICI Foundation are designed to . . .encourage the active engagement of key stakeholders. . .while ensuring the sustainability of the programmes.

Environment	ICICI Bank believes that business practices that are environment friendly are key to sustainable growth. It seeks to create awareness of this among employees and customers.	The Bank complies with applicable environmental regulations in respect of its premises and operations...	Same as last year.	Same statements as last year.	As an environmentally responsible corporate, ICICI Bank has been striving towards. . .processes, policies and practices. '. The Bank complies with applicable environmental regulations in respect of its premises and operations. . . . .the Bank assists projects that promote bio-diversity and environmental sustainability and projects that reduce greenhouse gas emissions.	Same as last year. No new statements made.	The Bank has endeavoured to reach out to customers and seek their collaboration in the 'Go Green' movement. . . The Bank also adopted corporate objectives for environment conservation activities. . .
Community & Stakeholders	We strive to make a difference to our customers, to society and to the nation's development . . .	Our employees are our core resource and the Bank has continuously evolved policies to strengthen its employee value proposition.	Employee health and safety is of prime importance to ICICI Bank.	Same statements were made as last year.	We believe that comprehensive socio-economic development of villages will be a key driver of growth in India going forward.	Community development forms the core for all initiatives undertaken by the Bank. ICICI Foundation undertakes a number of initiatives for the under-privileged. . . .	Same statements repeated from 2016.

(continued)

	2012	2013	2014	2015	2016	2017	2018
SBI							
General Statements	CSR has always been a part of the State Bank of India covering various social, environmental and welfare activities.	SBI is committed to making a sustainable social change . . .	For decades it has practiced responsible banking and a consistent commitment to productive economic activity.	SBI believes that an organization will be able to achieve sustainable economic growth...the Bank takes its social responsibility seriously....	We believe that we owe a solemn duty to the less fortunate and underprivileged members of the society to make sustainable social change in their lives. Social Responsibility is an integral part of its business. . . . . .its CSR initiatives have made a true difference in the lives of millions from underserved communities.	Our commitment to business sustainability is demonstrated. . .by number of initiatives. . . .we are committed to the sustainable future of India. We believe in "Integrated Sustainability". . .	Your Bank believes that it owes a solemn duty to the less fortunate and underprivileged members of the society.
Financial Inclusion & Sustainable Livelihoods	In SBI, we believe that we owe a solemn duty to the less fortunate and underprivileged members of the society to make a sustainable social change in their development.	State Bank of India realizes the role it has to play as the largest Indian Bank in practicing and promoting Financial Inclusion. . .	. . . .rooted in the Bank's belief that it owes a solemn duty to the less fortunate and underprivileged . . . .To achieve the twin objectives of ensuring greater financial inclusion and increasing the outreach of the Bank. . .	State Bank of India tries to ensure that financial resources are made available in an easy and accessible manner to all sections of society. . . .testimony of the Banks commitment to serve residents across all geographies of the country.	. The Bank is the pioneer in the Business Correspondent (BC) model, an alternative mode for,. . . The Bank has successfully leveraged technology for propagating	It has pioneered the Business Correspondent (BC) model. . . . . .SBI has established 246 Financial Literacy Centres (FLCs) so far.	The spread of digital banking channels and expansion of Business Correspondents (BC) networks are giving your Bank the impetus to further grow its financial inclusion activities. Thus, to achieve inclusive development and growth, your Bank has worked out several strategies. . .to expand financial services to the door steps of people...

Environment	We will continue with our multi-pronged efforts to meaningfully contribute towards more sustainable development of the society and Green Planet. . . .We effectively propagate and implement sustainable usage of resources including renewable energy.	...the Bank is committed to keep its environmental footprint as small as possible. . . .The Bank strives to utilize optimally the resources for its operations.	The Bank takes proactive steps to reduce the direct impact of its operations on the environment. . . .the Bank is working to reduce its operational footprints on the environment.	The Bank is committed to keeping its environmental footprint as small as possible and has taken proactive steps to reduce the direct impact of its operations on the environment. . . . State Bank of India, in its constant endeavour to enhance the sustainability. . .	Your Bank continues to remain committed to issues pertaining to global warming and renewable energy. To this end, your Bank has made significant contribution. . .to environmental concerns and energy conservation.	Same statements repeated from last year.	Your Bank is committed to environment protection and contributes positively to reduce the carbon footprint.
Community & Stakeholders	The focus of the Bank has been to help provide the basic infrastructure support to ameliorate the condition of the common man.	The Bank prefers to support largely with community assets as the benefits of those are shared by all. . . . the Bank extends special support to the disadvantaged, vulnerable and marginalized ones.	The vision of the Bank for its human resources is to create an enabling environment to enhance the efficiency of the organization.	...efforts towards creating long lasting value for all its stakeholders in a responsible manner.	We sincerely attempt to engage and provide support to all socio-economic strata and contribute to an inclusive economy.	By engaging with them (stakeholders) on a regular basis, SBI looks to build strong . . .relationships	With our new internal budgeting processes, we're making sure that every aspect of our business. . .to our stakeholders. With this result orientated discipline, we can play a pivotal role in catalysing India's transformation. For SBI, engaging with stakeholders in an effective manner is crucial for improving decision making and maintaining accountability. A structured process has been developed. . .

(continued)

	2012	2013	2014	2015	2016	2017	2018
Kotak Mahindra							
General Statements	None	Business responsibility is ingrained in Kotak Mahindra Group …commitment towards business responsibility…	The Bank continually strives to intertwine Environmental, Social and Governance aspects with all facets of business…	Sustainability forms an integral part of the Bank's business functions and has established mechanisms for environmental and social compliance in its operations.	…environment, social and governance (ESG) practices are integral components of its business functions and are embedded in its systems and processes. …, Kotak not only ensures compliance with statutory requirements but also showcases its efforts to go beyond the requirements.	No change in the language of the general statements from last year.	Environment, Social and Governance (ESG) practices in its business operations and strategy. While doing so, it considers the impact of a wide range of sustainability issues, Kotak follows sustainable development practices… …the Bank also steps into the role of extending its banking services available to marginalised customers.
Financial Inclusion & Sustainable Livelihoods	We believe that one of the ways to change this is to work on removing poverty through education.	Inclusive growth and community development through financial inclusion products is one of the Bank's key initiatives for fostering development and improving quality of life of the people, especially those below the poverty line.	KMBL shares the vision of Reserve Bank of India (RBI) for Financial Inclusion (FI) and actively participates in the national FI agenda….The Bank also believes that it is equally important to make people employable and financially independent.	The Bank believes that in order to build a more sustainable future, it needs to develop products and provide services that enable a positive economic and social change.	Kotak Mahindra Bank believes in positively contributing to the economic, environmental and social well-being of communities through Corporate Social Responsibility (CSR) agenda.	Kotak's financial inclusion initiatives provide the Bank with an opportunity to reach out and make an impact on the large un-banked and un-served sectors of the society.	The Bank regularly conducts stakeholder engagements to take their feedback. It is the Bank's constant endeavour to create a positive impact on the society…

Environment	It is our constant endeavour to conduct operations in an environment friendly manner. We are making conscious efforts to migrate from traditional banking practices to more environment friendly solutions. . . .	. . . .continually strives to reduce its direct environmental impact.	...efforts towards creating enduring value for all stakeholders. . .KMBL takes continual measures to mitigate and reduce environmental impact of its operations.	KMBL. . .constantly works ..It aims to integrate its environmental policies and practices into everyday business operations. And by doing so, it ensures responsible decision making....	Kotak Mahindra Bank's environmental management practices focus on. . .encouraging the use of energy-efficient technology.	Kotak is well aware of its responsibility . . .more positive impact on the environment.	At Kotak, responsible Environmental Social Governance (ESG) practices have been embedded into existing systems and processes. . . It actively works to develop solutions and minimise its impact on environmental. . . The Bank has undertaken several initiatives towards energy conservation. . .
Community & Stakeholders	We nurture relationships across stakeholders. . . .It is the relationship based on trust and commitment to stakeholder interest that makes Kotak Mahindra group's operations robust, resilient and sustainable. . .	The Bank's 'people' policies and practices are aimed to provide a non-discriminatory and harassment-free workplace. . . .	Employee well-being and holistic development are cornerstones of the Bank's people agenda. . . .Gender diversity is one of the focus areas for the Bank.	KMBL has made considerable progress in its journey towards mainstreaming diversity and inclusion across the Bank. KMBL has developed initiatives that focus on improving diversity and inclusiveness within the Bank.	The Bank believes in adopting and adhering to the best standards of corporate governance to all the stakeholders.	Through value-creating dialogues and discussions, Kotak engages with its key internal and external stakeholders. . .	In line with its commitment for an inclusive growth, Kotak endeavours to provide services that are accessible to every segment of the society.

References

Anderson, H., & Gumley, W. (2008). Corporate social responsibility: Legislative options for protecting employees and the environment. *Adelaide Law Review, 29*, 29.

Asthana, S., Balsam, S., & Kim, S. (2009). The effect of Enron, Andersen, and Sarbanes-Oxley on the US market for audit services. *Accounting Research Journal, 22*(1), 4–26.

ASX Corporate Governance Council. (2014). *Principles of good corporate governance and best practice recommendations*. Sydney: Australian Stock Exchange Limited.

Avgouleas, E. (2009). The global financial crisis, behavioural finance and financial regulation: In search of a new orthodoxy. *Journal of Corporate Law Studies, 9*(1), 23–59.

Bebbington, J., Larringa, C., & Moneva, J. M. (2008). Corporate social reporting and reputation risk management. *Accounting, Auditing & Accountability Journal, 21*(3), 337–361.

Bennett, R., & Kottasz, R. (2011). Public attitudes towards the UK banking industry following the global financial crisis. *International Journal of Bank Marketing, 30*(2), 128–147.

Boulding, K. E. (1978). The legitimacy of the business institution. In E. M. Epstein & D. Votaw (Eds.), *Rationality, legitimacy, responsibility: Search for new directions in business and society* (pp. 83–97). Santa Monica, CA: Goodyear.

Bowen, G. A. (2009). Document analysis as a qualitative research method. *Qualitative Research Journal, 9*(2), 27–40.

Bravo, R., Matute, J., & Pina, J. M. (2012). Corporate social responsibility as a vehicle to reveal the corporate identity: A study focused on the websites of Spanish financial entities. *Journal of Business Ethics, 107*(2), 129–146.

Campbell, J. L. (2007). Why would corporations behave in socially responsible ways? An institutional theory of corporate social responsibility. *Academy of Management Review, 32*(3), 946–967.

Carroll, A. B. (1979). A three-dimensional conceptual model of corporate performance. *The Academy of Management Review, 4*(4), 497–497.

Carroll, A. B. (1991). The pyramid of corporate social responsibility: Toward the moral management of organizational stakeholders - balancing economic, legal, and social responsibilities. *Business Horizons, 34*(4), 39–48.

Chauvey, J.-N., Giordano-Spring, S., Cho, C. H., & Patten, D. M. (2015). The normativity and legitimacy of CSR disclosure: Evidence from France. *Journal of Business Ethics, 130*(4), 789–803.

Cooter, R. (1998). Expressive law and economics. *The Journal of Legal Studies, 27*(S2), 585–607.

Crane, A., & Matten, D. (2016). *Business ethics: Managing corporate citizenship and sustainability in the age of globalization*. Oxford: Oxford University Press.

Crotty, J. (2009). Structural causes of the global financial crisis: A critical assessment of the 'new financial architecture'. *Cambridge Journal of Economics, 33*(4), 563–580.

Davis, K. (2011). The Australian financial system in the 2000s: Dodging the bullet. *The Australian Economy in the 2000s, 2011*, 313–314.

Deegan, C. (2002). Introduction: The legitimising effect of social and environmental disclosures – A theoretical foundation. *Accounting, Auditing & Accountability Journal, 15*(3), 282–311.

Delbard, O. (2008). CSR legislation in France and the European regulatory paradox: An analysis of EU CSR policy and sustainability reporting practice. *Corporate Governance, 8*(4), 397–405.

Department of Public Enterprises (DPE). (2010). *The CSR Guidelines for CSPEs*. New Delhi: The Ministry of Heavy Industries and Public Enterprises.

Dunn, G. (2014). *Shareholder proposal developments during the 2014 proxy season*. Retrieved from http://www.gibsondunn.com/publications/pages/Shareholder-Proposal-Developments-During-the-2014-Proxy-Season.aspx

Elkington, J. (1994). Towards the sustainable corporation: Win-win-win business strategies for sustainable development. *California Management Review, 36*(2), 90–100.

European Parliament and the Council of the European Union. (2014). *Directive 2014/95/EU amending directive 2013/34/EU as regards disclosure of non-financial and diversity information by certain large undertakings and groups*, Brussels.

Garriga, E. M. D. (2004). Corporate social responsibility theories: Mapping the territory. *Journal of Business Ethics, 53*(1/2), 51–71.

Godfrey, P. C., Merrill, C. B., & Hansen, J. M. (2009). The relationship between corporate social responsibility and shareholder value: An empirical test of the risk management hypothesis. *Strategic Management Journal, 30*(4), 425–445.

GRI. (2012). *About GRI*. Retrieved from https://www.globalreporting.org/Information/about-gri/Pages/default.aspx

HDFC Bank. (2010). *Annual Report 2009–10*. Retrieved from https://www.hdfcbank.com/assets/pdf/AR-2010-11.pdf

HDFC Bank. (2013). *Annual report 2012–2013*. Retrieved from https://www.hdfcbank.com/htdocs/common/pdf/corporate/HDFC-Bank-AnnualReport-2012-13.pdf

Islam, M. A., Jain, A., & Thomson, D. (2016). Does GRI influence sustainability disclosures in Asia-Pacific banks? *Australasian Journal of Environmental Management, 23*(3), 298–313.

Jain, A., & Islam, M. A. (2016). The rise of GRI: A social contagion epidemic. In *Proceedings of the Ninth Asia-Pacific conference on global business, economics, finance and banking* (pp. Paper-ID).

Jain, A., Keneley, M., & Thomson, D. (2014). Bank reputation in Australia: A view from the inside. *JASSA: The Finsia Journal of Applied Finance, 2*, 29–34.

Jain, A., Keneley, M., & Thomson, D. (2015). Voluntary CSR disclosure works! Evidence from Asia-Pacific banks. *Social Responsibility Journal, 11*(1), 2–18.

Kahn, M. E. (2007). Environmental disasters as risk regulation catalysts? The role of Bhopal, Chernobyl, Exxon Valdez, Love Canal, and three Mile Island in shaping US environmental law. *Journal of Risk and Uncertainty, 35*(1), 17–43.

Kotak Mahindra. (2013). *Business reponsibility report*. Retrieved from https://www.kotak.com/content/dam/Kotak/about-us/csr-policy/Business-Responsibility-Report-(BRR)-FY-13-14.pdf

Kraakman, R., & Hansmann, H. (2017). The end of history for corporate law. In *Corporate governance* (pp. 49–78). London: Gower.

Matten, D., & Moon, J. (2008). "Implicit" and "explicit" CSR: A conceptual framework for a comparative understanding of corporate social responsibility. *Academy of Management Review, 33*(2), 404–424.

McBarnet, D. (2009). *Corporate social responsibility beyond law, through law, for law*. University of Edinburgh School of Law Working Paper.

McDonald, C. (2012). Banks behaving badly. *CFO Magazine*. Retrieved from http://www.cfo.com/risk-management/2012/09/banks-behaving-badly/

Michelon, G., & Rodrigue, M. (2015). Demand for CSR: Insights from shareholder proposals. *Social and Environmental Accountability Journal, 35*(3), 157–175.

Ministry of Corporate Affairs. (2011). *Government of India, national voluntry guidelines*. http://www.mca.gov.in/Ministry/latestnews/National_Voluntary_Guidelines_2011_12jul2011.pdf

NAB. (2012). *Annual Report 2012–2013*. Retrived from https://www.nab.com.au/content/dam/nabrwd/documents/reports/corporate/2012-annual-review.pdf

Parker, L. D. (2005). Social and environmental accountability research: A view from the commentary box. *Accounting, Auditing and Accountability Journal, 18*(6), 842–860.

Picciotto, S. (2007). Constructing compliance: Game playing, tax law, and the regulatory state. *Law & Policy, 29*(1), 11–30.

SBI. (2015). *Annual Report 2014–15: Bankers to digital India*. Retrieved from https://www.sbi.co.in/AR1516/

SEBI. (2012). *Business responsibility reports, (CIR/CFD/DIL/8/2012)*. Retrieved April 10, 2015, from https://www.sebi.gov.in/sebi_data/attachdocs/1344915990072.pdf

Sethi, S. P. (1975). Dimensions of corporate social performance: An analytical framework. *California Management Review, 17*(3), 58–64.
Soana, M. G. (2011). The relationship between corporate social performance and corporate financial performance in the banking sector. *Journal of Business Ethics, 104*(1), 133.
Steurer, R. (2010). The role of governments in corporate social responsibility: Characterising public policies on CSR in Europe. *Policy Sciences, 43*(1), 49–72.
Strine, L. E., Jr. (2015). The dangers of denial: The need for a clear-eyed understanding of the power and accountability structure established by the Delaware general corporation law. *Wake Forest Law Review, 50*, 761.
The Government of India. (2013). *The Companies Act 2013*.
Thomson, D., & Jain, A. (2006). Corporate governance failure and its impact on National Australia Bank's performance. *Journal of Business Case Studies, 2*(1), 41–55.
Thomson, D., & Jain, A. (2010). Corporate social responsibility reporting: A business strategy by Australian banks? *Corporate Ownership & Control, 7*(4), 213–227.
Tilt, C. A. (2001). The content and disclosure of Australian corporate environmental policies. *Accounting, Auditing & Accountability Journal, 14*(2), 190–212.
United States Securities and Exchange Commission. (2016). *Disclosure of Payments by Resource Extraction Issuers: 17 CFR Parts 240 and 249b Release No. 34–78167; File No. S7–25-15 RIN 3235-AL53*. Washington, DC. Retrieved from www.sec.gov/rules/final/2016/34-78167.pdf
Van Marrewijk, M. (2003). Concepts and definitions of CSR and corporate sustainability: Between agency and communion. *Journal of Business Ethics, 44*(2/3), 95–108.
Wang, H., & Bernell, D. (2013). Environmental disclosure in China: An examination of the green securities policy. *The Journal of Environment & Development, 22*(4), 339–369.
Westpac. (2012). *Annual Report 2012–2013*. Retrieved from https://www.westpac.com.au/docs/pdf/aw/ic/2012_Annual_Report.pdf
Yongvanich, K., & Guthrie, J. (2005). Extended performance reporting: An examination of the Australian mining industry. *Accounting Forum, 29*(1), 103–119.

Corporate Social Responsibility in Rising Economies: Georgia

Maia Shekriladze and Christopher Stehr

Abstract Economies over the world are undergoing similar processes but handle them, depending of the context they are situated in, in various ways. Georgia ranks sixth in ease of doing business and is second in starting a business worldwide. The country's recent economic reforms have moved it from a near-failed state in 2003 to a relatively well-functioning market economy. Still the results of the first Corporate Social Responsibility survey back in 2000 showed an unattractive picture of the Georgian enterprises, which were at the initial stage of entrepreneurship development. The basic form of Social responsibility of Business (SRB) in the country was charity. The strong traditions of the private charitable actions from the Georgian entrepreneurs were conditioned by the norms of the Orthodox Christianity, as well as the opportunities of improvement in their social status. Today many international Organizations support Georgian government and civil society to create the needed frameworks and raise awareness for CSR. Having analyzed these challenges, we compared them to cultural characteristics according to the GLOBE project and suggest that many of the CSR challenges of Georgia be explained within the content of the country's cultural characteristics.

Keywords CSR in Georgia · CSR in Caucasus · CSR in emerging economy · Sustainable business · Sustainable development

---

M. Shekriladze (✉)
Diploma in International Business – Intercultural Studies, Heilbronn Technical University, Heilbronn, Germany

C. Stehr
German Graduate School of Management and Law, Heilbronn, Germany
e-mail: welcome@polymundo.de

N. Mitra, R. Schmidpeter (eds.), *Corporate Social Responsibility in Rising Economies*, CSR, Sustainability, Ethics & Governance,
https://doi.org/10.1007/978-3-030-53775-3_8

1 Introduction

1.1 The Concept of Emerging Economies and CSR

Emerging or rising economies are low-income, rapid-growth countries using economic liberalization as their primary engine of growth. They fall into two groups: developing countries in Asia, Latin America, Africa, and the Middle East and transition economies in the former Soviet Union and China. Private and public enterprises have had to develop unique strategies to cope with the broad scope and rapidity of economic and political change in emerging economies (Hoskisson, Eden, Lau, & Wright, 2000).

The 2030 Agenda for Sustainable Development, adopted by all United Nations Member States in 2015, provides a shared blueprint for peace and prosperity for people and the planet, now and into the future. At its heart are the 17 Sustainable Development Goals (SDGs), which are an urgent call for action by all countries—developed and developing—in a global partnership. They recognize that ending poverty and other deprivations must go hand-in-hand with strategies that improve health and education, reduce inequality, and spur economic growth—all while tackling climate change and working to preserve our oceans and forests (UN, 2019a). Today, the Division for Sustainable Development Goals (DSDG) in the United Nations Department of Economic and Social Affairs (UNDESA) provides substantive support and capacity-building for the SDGs and their related thematic issues. In order to make the 2030 Agenda a reality, broad ownership of the SDGs must translate into a strong commitment by all stakeholders to implement the global goals. DSDG aims to help facilitate this engagement (UN, 2019b).

1.2 Significance and Perspectives of CSR in the Context of Emerging Economies

Arnold and Quelch reported back in 1998 that emerging markets (EMs) constitute the major growth opportunity in the evolving world economic order. Their potential has already affected a shift in multinational corporations (MNCs), which now customarily highlight EM investments when communicating with shareholders (Arnold & Quelch, 1998). They state that investments made in these countries are widely interpreted as heralds of a major restructuring of the global economy.

According to Charaia (2017), the best possible scenario is that Multinational Enterprises (MNEs) can significantly contribute to sustainable and inclusive economic development of the host country. Especially in developing countries it is their role to build a healthy business environment through responsible business practices (which is not a reality for every case). For the past decades international business environment has significantly modernized and faced real structural changes. Countries in all continents started to open their markets, businesses embraced new opportunities, and Foreign Direct Investments (FDIs) are welcomed and supported (Charaia, 2017). Georgia is one of the post-communist countries where FDIs played tremendous role in the transformation of the local economy in the last two decades, however, there are still a lot of questions regarding the quality of these investments and the answers are not on the horizon. What are the MNE motivations and their influence on the Georgian economy; how much it is assisting development and modernization of different economic sectors in Georgia and how deep MNEs are integrated into the different fields of Georgian Economy? To answer these questions Charaia (2017) offers a classification of FDI into resource based, market seeking, efficiency seeking, and strategic asset seeking; and argues that the goal for the host economy is to get as much benefits as possible, from the MNE created assets. However, it is very much dependent on the governmental policy and motivations of foreign investors (Charaia, 2017).

Charaia (2017) offers an overview of different MNEs' motivations for investing in Georgia within different sectors. Service sector, consisting of financial energy sectors, transport, communications, trade and tourism sectors, is one of the dominant sectors in terms of FDI attractiveness. However, this Market oriented investments in Georgian service sector are less efficient in terms of economic growth and exports, they are characterized with limited capabilities. Resource-seeking FDIs are most often concentrated in the enclave formations, with weak ties to local commodity and labor markets. Also, one of the negative side effects could be the corruption promotion on macro level by the local elite. Further he states, that despite the fact that Georgian Gross Domestic Product (GDP) per capita parameter does not seem to be the world's top performing one, still it is attracting a big portion of efficiency seeking investments, however the leader is the Local Market seeking investments of: energy sector, construction, hotels and restaurants, health and social work, real estate and financial sector. He further emphasizes the urgency of enabling efficiency seeking sectors like agriculture, manufacturing and communications invest in Georgia (Charaia, 2017).

1.3 Scope and Goals of this Research Paper

This paper is concerned with the current situation in one of the fastest rising economies in the world—Georgia (The World Bank, 2019). Furthermore, we will report on the government's involvement in supporting Corporate Social Responsibility (CSR) by means of legislative frameworks and voluntary measures for businesses, as CSR is the commitment of business to contribute to sustainable economic development, working with employees, their families, the local community and society at large to improve their quality of life (WBCSD, 2000). However, studies show a huge gap in the target and current situations on both, the country and local levels. Georgia's State Audit Office (SAI Georgia, 2018) found that the composition, roles and responsibilities of public entities for SDG implementation were not clearly defined. The SDGs have not been integrated at the local level, and little attention has been paid to policy synergies and trade-offs. While a national SDG strategy exists, agencies continue to work in silos. Also, the leading entities responsible for producing data for 32 indicators of the SDG global framework have not been identified and there are problems of articulation between human resources, budget processes, and the capacities required to produce reliable statistical data (Montero & Le Blanc, 2019). The FINANCIAL carried out a survey in recognition of the increasing importance of CSR to business. Out of over 300 companies only 30 responded. There were some examples of good practice, but majority of them misunderstood the idea of CSR. The survey results showed that Georgian businesses are contributing to environment protection on a minimal level. Most of them, especially those, who pollute the environment, are not involved in the greening of the areas where they operate (The FINANCIAL, 2016). We will discuss the results of this survey in the chapter below, when we describe the challenges of CSR in Georgia.

In order to understand the current situation and challenges Georgia deals with while implementing CSR and thus fulfilling the SDGs, we suggest the following research question:

- *What role does culture play in implementing corporate social responsibility practices in Georgia?*

In order to answer this main question, we expanded it into following sub questions:

- *What are the main challenges Georgia is facing while implementing CSR?*
- *What are main driving forces for CSR implementation in Georgia?*
- *What legal and voluntary Frameworks does the country offer for companies operating in Georgia?*
- *How can Georgia increase awareness on CSR?*

A growing number of scholars are examining culture's influence on sustainability and related concepts such as CSR and firms' CSR commitment, as well as corporate social and environmental performance (Miska, Szőcs, & Schiffinger, 2018).

Hofstede's cultural dimensions have been being extensively used in many cross-cultural studies predicting business ethics and CSR practice. For instance, there exist the differences in the general perception of CSR between people in European and North American countries. Palazzo (2002), Matten and Moon (2004) believe that the North American concept of CSR represent the original context of the phenomenon by emphasizing its philanthropic aspects, and the companies from these countries typically attach issues of social responsibility explicitly in their mission, policies and strategy. In Europe, however, the concept of CSR is more focused on actual company orientation and the responsibility for such issue is more implicit in the formal or informal institution business environment (Matten & Moon, 2004). Recognizing the role of cultural factor, during the last two decades, a number of social and business scholars have applied the cultural dimensions proposed by Hofstede in their cross-cultural studies in order to effectively evaluate and have a deeper understanding about the impact of national culture on individual as well as organizational perception of CSR. In general, these studies provide a strong agreement about the close linkage between national cultural dimensions with the managers' perceptions of CSR (Nguyen & Truong, 2016).

2 Georgia: Background and Current Situation

2.1 Current Political and Economic Framework

Georgia ranks sixth in ease of doing business and is second in starting a business worldwide (The World Bank, 2019). Considered to be an attractive market due to rich natural resources (mainly hydropower, timber, manganese, iron ore, copper, minor coal and oil deposits), as well as its unique strategic location and proximity to international markets, Georgian government actively promotes the country's potential to be a regional transit and logistic hub for trade (OECD, 2016).

Being a small country of over three and a half million habitants, Georgia looks back over a long history of surviving wars and invaders. After dissolution of the USSR it became the first republic to announce its independency in 1991, although its rapid political and economic development did not initiate simultaneously. Georgia has experienced a rapid transition of political, economic and social institutions since the 2003 Rose Revolution. Reforms since 2003 introduced free trade principles, deregulation of the economy and creation of a simplified and effective administration. The World Bank praised Georgia as one of the fastest reforming economies worldwide. According to the U.S. State Department (2015), Georgia's sweeping economic reforms have moved it from a near-failed state in 2003 to a relatively well-functioning market economy (OECD, 2016).

Georgia 2020, the socio-economic strategy adopted in 2014, prioritizes measures for ensuring rapid and more inclusive economic growth. These measures include increasing the competitiveness of the private sector, developing human capital, facilitating access to finance, and focusing on increasing the efficiency of public administration. A dedicated agency, Entrepreneurship Development Agency (EDA), has also been established in order to facilitate private sector development. A specific program *Produce in Georgia* was launched in 2015 with the aim to support domestic production capacity. Additionally, Private Sector Development Advisory Council on Private Sector Facilitation was established in 2016 within the Ministry of Economy and Sustainable Development (OECD, 2016).

The EU-Georgia Association Agreement (AA), a bilateral framework for cooperation on political, security, economic, and social issues, was signed on 27 June 2014. Notably, Article 231 of the AA states:

(e) *The Parties agree to promote corporate social responsibility, including through exchange of information and best practices* (OECD, 2016).

Charaia (2017) argues in his paper, that due to the current territorial problems, not all trade, transport and communication related projects can benefit Georgia, neither financially, nor politically, including the railway project through its breakaway region. He further states that, financial loses based on the Georgian Territorial problems are huge and are hindering possible future development of the whole country (Charaia, 2017).

Besides the above-mentioned facts, we introduce here an evaluation of Thomas Kolster, international marketing and sustainability adviser about the current situation in Georgia:

> A country that's experienced the first European war in recent time and continually is being bullied by Russia while the international community in many cases turns a blind eye as Georgia's territory is annexed. It's also a country that's still trying to cope with a challenging economic situation (Kolster, 2019).

2.2 *CSR Development in Georgia*

The social responsibility of business (SRB) became the indivisible part of discussions in the society of the post-soviet area almost immediately after the Union of Soviet Socialist Republics (USSR) disintegration. In 1999–2000 the first study on the corporations' participation in the life of the local community was carried out. The results showed an unattractive picture of the Georgian enterprises, which were at the initial stage of entrepreneurship development—poorly developed business ethics, weak awareness, lack of confidence in the State authorities, tax evasion and ignoring of the law enforcement bodies. The basic form of SRB in the country was charity and its awareness in the other forms of the social responsibility was rather poor. The strong traditions of the private charitable actions from the Georgian entrepreneurs were conditioned by the norms of the Orthodox Christianity, as well, as the opportunities of improvement in their social status (Takalandze, 2013).

After this modest beginning, over 40 companies signed the Georgian Code of Business Conduct in 2004 as a mechanism of self-assessment and self-regulation:

> The Georgian Business Code of Conduct encourages best business practices in the Georgian Business Community. The growth of corporate social responsibility, establishment of new values, and improvement of organizational culture on the part of business, will have a positive impact on the Georgian business climate and improve the image of Georgian businesses among investors and partners

The Georgian Business Code of Conduct is based on the following values: (1) Accountability—the ability to answer for our actions. (2) Caring—caring for our stakeholders. (3) Fairness—fairness in our relationships. (4) Integrity—wholeness of the team, fulfilling our commitments, (5) Transparency—sharing information and acting in an open manner (6) Trust—building confidence and a reputation for reliance through our actions (Georgian Code of Business Conduct, 2004).

In December 2006, the United Nations Global Compact was launched in Georgia, and under its support, the network of socially oriented Georgian companies was created. Global Compact impels the business circles to follow the fundamental principles of human rights, labor relations, environment protection and combating corruption in their activities. The first companies to join, were foreign companies related to international corporations, followed by larger Georgian companies, like *Nikora, Magticom* and *Bank Republic* (Takalandze, 2013).

In July 2009 the first national conference on the issue of the corporate social responsibility was held in Tbilisi. In the same year the Centre for Strategic Research and Development of Georgia and The Eurasian Cooperation Foundation in Tbilisi organized a workshop on CSR, where the representatives of business were introduced the Global Reporting Initiative (GRI) according to which the world's leading companies prepare and issue the social reports (Takalandze, 2013).

The next important step in the development process for CSR in Georgia was in April 2012, when the Centre for Strategic Research and Development of Georgia, with the support of Friedrich Ebert Foundation developed a Manual for the universities about the CSR and its further integration into educational programs of the faculties of economics (Takalandze, 2013).

2.3 CSR Challenges in Georgia

Takalandze reports back in 2013 that one of the most important limiting factors of CSR development in Georgia was the lack of understanding of CSR significance and criticizes the government failure to support companies by means of creating attractive tax system for implementing CSR. On the other hand, the survey held by the FINANCIAL in 2016 found out that most of the companies misunderstood the idea of CSR. In a very rare cases they could find a CSR Manager's position at the companies in Tbilisi. They argue this confirms CSR is not a part of long-term strategy of businesses in Georgia (The Financial, 2016).

Numerous good practices could be discovered: like *Natali Group*, spending 25 percent of its total revenue for education and professional development purposes. *IDS Borjomi Georgia* invested in education and employment. *Alliance Group Holding* spent more than 200,000 United States Dollar (USD) on CSR projects in Georgia. *TBSC Consulting* contributed to the recycling of paper and plastic materials; to name just some companies, mentioned in the survey. Unfortunately, most respondents pointed to differences between large and small business and noted this hat implications for how CSR is practiced. (The Financial, 2016) Having introduced the above results and studies makes it easier to comprehend the imperfections of civil society visible in social, political and economic characters, as listed by Natsvlishvili (2018) based on Balarjishvili (2017) in her research paper:

- Submissive role of society in the triad "state-business-civil-society"
- Negligible amount of relational goods supply caused by concentration of civil society organizations in the capital city
- Their closed, elite-corporate character
- Low level of investment in social capital by citizens
- Society dominated by participants and not by servants

- Nonexistence of middle class, which represents a life-style rather than a social group
- Free-rider problem
- Elite character of institutional transformation and passive role of society, which caused transformation of institutions into club goods.

Natsvlishvili (2018) further argues that, activities of CSR take place in societies where the individuals have certain entrepreneurial attitudes. According to the data from the "Global Entrepreneurship Monitor—2014 Georgia Report," Georgians consider successful entrepreneurs to have a high status in society (75.9 percent of adult population), and 66 percent of adults think that entrepreneurship is a good career choice. However, only 7.2 percent of Georgians are planning to open or are already running a new venture. Motivation to engage in entrepreneurial activities shows up almost equally between **necessity-driven** (48.6 percent) and **opportunity-driven** (50.6 percent) entrepreneurship. Compared with efficiency-driven European Union (EU) and non-EU economies, early-stage entrepreneurship activities in Georgia are mainly necessity-driven rather than opportunity-driven. The motivational index, i.e., a ratio between **improvement-driven opportunity** and **necessity-driven** entrepreneurs, indicates the entrepreneurial capacity within a country. A high motivational index indicates a high share of improvement-driven entrepreneurs, which ensures more long-term and ambitious expectations from the creation of a venture. The lowest motivation index is visible in non-EU countries, including Georgia. Moreover, Georgia has one of **the lowest motivational indexes** (0.6) among efficiency-driven European countries. Average score for European Union countries is 2.1 and average score for non-European Union countries is 1.4. The motivation index in the benchmark country (i.e., Estonia) is 2.7 (Bzhalava, Lezhava, Brekashvili, & Melua, 2017; Natsvlishvili, 2018).

Entrepreneurship is considered as a certain form of employability. Not all groups in society have equal access to employability and entrepreneurial opportunities. The majority in Georgia formally shares the idea of gender equality. A certain percentage of the population is in favor of traditional distribution of the gender roles. The gender hierarchy is still a top issue in Georgian families, in political as well as in business space. Women's entrepreneurship is affected by existing stereotypes, as entrepreneurship is largely a product of the environment. Thus, it can be concluded that the above-mentioned situation might be a basis of social entrepreneurship. (Guruli, 2018; Natsvlishvili, 2018).

Based on these findings we raise a hypothesis that the slow process of CSR implementation in the country is due to the cultural characteristics of the civil society and will discuss cultural specifications of Georgia in the following chapter.

2.4 Cultural Specifications of Georgia

The former soviet republic of Georgia in the Caucasus is sandwiched between the Caucasus Mountains to the north, the Black Sea to the west and dry deserts to the south. This small country, which borders Russia, Azerbaijan, Armenia and Turkey, is not only a crossroad of cultures, but has a wealth of spectacular landscapes (GNTA, 2016). Finding academic research describing Georgian cultural characteristics is very difficult, as there are very few reliable sources. We based our evaluation on the International Black Sea University Scientific Journal (ISBUSJ) article from 2010 by a PhD candidate Nino Tkeshelashvili "The Effects of Culture on the Leadership Style in Georgia" (Tkeshelashvili, 2010). Based on the general agreement among researchers, that national culture refers to cognitive systems and behavioral repertoires that are shaped as a result of individuals' common experiences (Hofstede, 1980, 2001), she analyzes Georgian culture and applies GLOBE nine culture dimensions' variables to measure culture dimensions in Georgia (House, Hanges, Javidan, Dorfman, & Gupta, 2004). Due to poor empiric results in this field, we will use the ISBUSJ study as a reference for Georgian cultural dimensions. The GLOBE studies, used by Tkeshelashvili (2010) had as a primary purpose to increase the understanding ISBUSJ, 2010 of cross-cultural interactions. As a part of their study of culture and leadership, GLOBE researchers developed their own classifications of cultural dimensions, she states (Tkeshelashvili, 2010). Table 1 visualizes all cultural dimensions according to the GLOBE project with respective definitions and scores for Georgia and average values for the global overall.

Table 1 Globe cultural dimensions and scoring Georgia

Dimension	Explanation	Globe overall	Score Georgia
Power distance	The degree to which members of a collective expect power to be distributed equally	5.17	5.03
Uncertainty avoidance	The extent to which a society, organization, or group relies on social norms, rules, and procedures to alleviate unpredictability of future events	4.16	3. 00
Humane orientation	The degree to which a collective encourages and rewards individuals for being fair, altruistic, generous, caring, and kind to others	4.09	3.25
Collectivism (institutional)	The degree to which organizational and societal institutional practices encourage and reward collective distribution of resources and collective action	4.25	3.31
Collectivism (In.-group)	The degree to which individuals express pride, loyalty, and cohesiveness in their organizations or families.	5.13	5.11
Assertiveness	The degree to which individuals are assertive, confrontational, and aggressive in their relationships with others.	4.14	5.04
Gender Egalitarianism	The degree to which a collective minimizes gender inequality.	3.37	2.77
Future orientation	The extent to which individuals engage in future-oriented behaviors such as delaying gratification, planning, and investing in the future.	3.85	3.08
Performance orientation	The degree to which a collective encourages and rewards group members for performance improvement and excellence	4.10	3.33

Source: Own illustration based on House et al. (2004) and Tkeshelashvili (2010)

Tkeshelashvili's evaluation of Georgian culture is as follows: "Georgia's culture dimensions high-score categories are In-Group Collectivism, Assertiveness and Power Distance. The low-score categories are Gender Egalitarianism, Uncertainty Avoidance, and Future Orientation. Human Orientation, Performance Orientation, and Institutional Collectivism are medium-score categories" (Tkeshelashvili, 2010).

Above findings can be considered as the explanation for all the mentioned challenges for CSR. The Table 2 below visualizes the high and low score characteristics of respective dimensions. We colored the corresponding boxes in grey whereas the scores under three and a half are low and over three and a half are high. This research paper does not offer enough space for a detailed analysis of each grey box and corresponding challenges. The link between the challenges and the characteristics is still evident.

In the following chapter we will introduce a detailed framework of CSR in Georgia and different stakeholders dealing with our previously found challenges and implementing CSR incorporations.

3 CSR in Georgia

3.1 Legal Framework for CSR

Government of Georgia submitted in 2016 its first Voluntary National Report on implementation of the SDGs that countries agreed upon during Sustainable Development Summit in September 2015. Although the governments created solid structures and legal framework for CSR Implementation in Georgia, Mghebrishvili argues the state structures should be more active in this respect. For further development of social and environmental thinking it would be reasonable to stimulate the scientists to conduct studies and introduce the obtained results to the wider society (Mghebrishvili, 2019).

CSR is a company's responsibility for the impact of its activities on society and the environment, and its CSR management, so that the use of appropriate procedures, and the implementation of projects allow the company and its activities to avoid or minimize the negative impact on individuals, society and the environment, respect applicable law, adequately consider the interests of stakeholders, and contribute to a sustainable development (Loew & Rohde, 2013). Integration of the economic, social and environmental directions of sustainable development has been the key challenge for Georgia's development in the past decades, further exacerbated by the need to create a new efficient, effective, lean and transparent system of governance (Sustainable development UN, GEO, 2016). In the following chapters we will discuss all CSR stakeholders in the country and present cases for each one of the stakeholders.

Table 2 Globe characteristics of societies according to cultural dimensions

Dimension	High score	Low score
Power distance Georgia 5.03	**– Society is differentiated into classes.** **– Power seen as providing social order.** **– Upward social mobility is limited.** **– Resources available to only a few.** **– Information is localized and hoarded.**	– Society has a large middle class. – Power linked to corruption and coercion. – Upward social mobility is common. – Resources are available to almost all. – Information is widely shared.
Uncertainty avoidance Georgia 3.0	– Use formality in interactions with others. – Are orderly and keep meticulous records. – Rely on formalized policies and procedures. – Take moderate, carefully calculated risks. – Show strong resistance to change.	**– Use informality in interactions with others.** **– Are less orderly and keep fewer records.** **– Rely on informal norms for most matters.** **– Are less calculating when taking risks.** **– Show only moderate resistance to change.**
Humane orientation Georgia 3.25	– The interests of others are important. – People are motivated primarily by a need for belonging and affiliation. – Members of society are responsible for promoting the well-being of others. – Child labor is limited by public sanctions. – People are urged to be sensitive to all forms of racial discrimination.	**– One's own self-interest is important.** **– `People are motivated primarily by a need for power and material possessions.** **– The state provides social and economic support for individuals' well-being.** **– Child labor is an issue of low importance.** **– People are not sensitive to all forms of racial discrimination.**
Collectivism (institutional) Georgia 3.31	– Members assume that they are highly interdependent with the organization. – Group loyalty is encouraged, even if this undermines the pursuit of individual goals. – The society's economic system tends to maximize the interests of collectives. – Rewards are driven by seniority, personal needs, and/or within-group equity. – Critical decisions are made by groups.	**– Members assume that they are largely independent of the organization.** **– Pursuit of individual goals is encouraged, even at the expense of group loyalty.** **– The society's economic system tends to maximize the interests of individuals.** **– Rewards are driven very largely by an individual's contribution to task success.** **– Critical decisions are made by individuals.**
Collectivism (In.-group) Georgia 5.11	**– Duties and obligations are important determinants of social behavior.** **– A strong distinction is made between in-groups and out-groups.**	– Personal needs and attitudes are important determinants of social behavior. – Little distinction is made between in-groups and out-groups.

(continued)

Table 2 (continued)

Dimension	High score	Low score
	– People emphasize relatedness with groups. **– The pace of life is slower.** **– Love is assigned little weight in marriage.**	– People emphasize rationality in behavior. – The pace of life is faster. – Love is assigned great weight in marriage.
Assertiveness Georgia 5.04	**– Value competition, success, and progress.** **– Communicate directly and unambiguously.** **– Try to have control over the environment.** **– Expect subordinates to take initiative.** **– Build trust on basis of calculation.**	– Value cooperation and warm relationships. – Communicate indirectly; try to "save face." – Try to be in harmony with the environment. – Expect subordinates to be loyal. – Build trust on basis of predictability.
Gender Egalitarianism Georgia 2.77	– More women in positions of authority. – Less occupational sex segregation. – Similar levels of educational attainment for males and females. – Assign women a greater decision-making role in community affairs.	**– Fewer women in positions of authority.** **– More occupational sex segregation.** **– A lower level of female educational attainment compared to that of males.** **– Assign women little or no decision-making role in community affairs.**
Future orientation Georgia 3.08	– Propensity to save now for the future. – Emphasize working for long-term success. – Organizations tend to be flexible and adaptive. – View material success and spiritual fulfillment as an integrated whole.	**– Propensity to spend now, rather than save.** **– Prefer gratification as soon as possible.** **– Organizations tend to be inflexible and maladaptive.** **– View material success and spiritual fulfillment as separate, requiring trade-offs.**
Performance orientation Georgia 3.33	– Value training and development. – Value competitiveness and materialism. – View formal feedback as necessary for performance improvement. – Value what one does more than who one is. – Expect direct, explicit communication.	**– Value societal and family relationships.** **– Value harmony with the environment.** **– View formal feedback as judgmental and discomfiting.** **– Value who one is more than what one does.** **– Expect indirect, subtle communication.**

Source: Own illustration based on House et al. (2004)

3.2 Society and NGOs

Non-Governmental Organizations (NGO) in developing countries help to solve many social problems, but, due to the limited organizational capacity and low organizational maturity, their efforts are not always sufficient. On the one hand, the recent situation of civil society development in Georgia is not satisfactory, which is reflected in economic indicators via social and political implications. The government considers the civil society as a competitor, and the agreed division of labor between the government and civil society does not exist (Natsvlishvili, 2018).

Sadzaglishvili and Kartvelishvili (2018) also report that civil sector in Georgia is not well developed. They cite the survey carried out by the East West Management Institute (EWMI) showed a considerable amount of progress across various aspects of the civil society in Georgia, the general public's awareness and understanding of NGOs is still rather low. Only 29 percent of the population reported to have high levels of trust in NGOs, while 40 percent were neutral, and 15 percent reported distrust. Furthermore, 21 percent of the respondents thought that NGOs were mainly motivated by securing funding and employment prospects for their members and staff, and 20 percent reported no knowledge of NGO purposes. Sadzaglishvili and Kartvelishvili (2018) further argue that a possible reason for the relatively low levels of public trust and awareness of NGOs is that the majority receive funding from international donors and tend to focus on fulfilling donor interests. They further emphasize the importance of shifting NGOs' focus from international toward local donors and argue that one way to do so is to recognize the role of the private sector in solving social problems through the development and implementation of CSR initiatives (Sadzaglishvili & Kartvelishvili, 2018). EWMI initiated two projects in recent years:

2014–2019: Advancing CSO Capacities and Engaging Society for Sustainability (ACCESS)

ACCESS is funded by the US Agency for International Development (USAID). This project works to strengthen the civil society organizations (CSOs) throughout Georgia. ACCESS will enable Georgian non-profit organizations to improve their financial sustainability, organizational management, policy influence, and civic engagement. The goal is to empower CSOs to become respected community representatives capable of leading public debate and collaborating with government to create more transparent and accountable governance. EWMI is implementing ACC ESS in partnership with local organizations: the Centre for Training and Consultancy (CTC) and the Civil Development Agency (CiDA). The Project will build on the progress achieved under EWMI's USAID-funded Policy, Advocacy, and Civil Society Development in Georgia (G-PAC) project, which bolstered the advocacy capabilities of CSOs and increased their policy influence on priority public issues (EWMI, 2019a).

2015–2020: Promoting Rule of Law in Georgia (PROLoG)
The purpose of PROLoG is to strengthen the justice system in Georgia to ensure due process, judicial independence, and the protection of human rights. The activity is designed to address key challenges in the rule of law sector and capitalize on opportunities for accelerated rule of law and justice sector reforms where there is political will and/or interest from civil society. PROLoG works to strengthen the legal environment for the application of due process rights and improve their implementation. PROLoG is structured around four sub-purposes:

(A) Strengthen the legal framework relating to human rights and due process protections.
(B) Further improve the management of essential justice system institutions, such as the High Council of Justice (HCOJ), the High School of Justice (HSOJ), the courts, the Georgian Bar Association (GBA), and Legal Aid Services (LAS).
(C) Enhance the capacity of Georgian legal professionals by further strengthening legal education at the university level.
(D) Improve access to justice for marginalized citizens, in particular women and ethnic and sexual minorities. This component will expend significant effort on regions beyond Tbilisi (EWMI, 2019b).

Positive development is reflected in the society and although CSR does not have a long history in Georgia, on May 27th, 2015, within the ACCESS project CSO CiDA and the Public Relations (PR) and Marketing Communications Company Gepra founded a CSR Club. The Club is a non-registered union and has a general mission to contribute to the sustainable development through promoting the corporate social responsibility. Specific missions are listed on the site and are as follows: (a) Raise awareness about international standards of the corporate social responsibility among business and the general public and promote or encourage sustainable business practices; (b) Influence national policies on corporate social responsibility; (c) Encourage business to undertake partnerships with the civil society in implementing sustainable social projects; (d) Mobilize business in support of the Sustainable Development Goals (SDGs). CSR Club awards best CSR practices in different categories since 2018. Three different categories and companies were selected out of 23 applied projects.

Although financed from USAID, CSR Club aims to gain contributors within the country and addresses target companies and corporations offering them a transparent application process on their website (CSR Club, 2019).

Besides, the Centre for Strategic Research and Development of Georgia (CSRDG) organizes Georgia's Responsible Business Award—MELIORA since 2018. The Contest is organized within the framework of the project "Georgian Civil Society Sustainability Initiative" (2017–2020). The project was developed and is implemented by the consortium led by the Konrad-Adenauer-Stiftung. The project is co-funded by the European Union. The project aims to improve the environment for the civil society in Georgia, by empowering civil society organizations and actors, and increasing their accountability towards citizens (Meliora, 2019).

3.3 Multinational Enterprises (MNES)

Charaia (2017) in his Fig. 1 offers an overview of MNE development since 2007 and concludes that Foreign Direct Investments (FDIs) in Georgia for the last 3 years are becoming more efficiency oriented, which he assumes, can be explained by the country's progress and its deeper inclusion to the regional and global economic projects, transit corridors and export-oriented manufacturing industry development. We will not introduce all MNEs operating in Georgia, rather we would like to share the case of British Petroleum (BP) and its impact on Georgian economy and CSR in Georgia.

British Petroleum (BP) is strategically one of the most important MNEs not only for Georgia, but also for the whole region. According to their own CSR report in 2013, BP Georgia is one of the companies who pioneered Corporate Social Responsibility projects in Georgia. It spent around 1 million USD on CSR in 2015. Development of the local population is one of the most important projects to be implemented by BP in 2015. A project which was started in 2013 brings many benefits to the population who live close to the pipeline. 322 infrastructure rehabilitation projects are implemented with an average of 50 percent community contribution. 20 Social Enterprises were created by the Community Based Organizations (CSOs) generated income and extended the provision of social services to their constituent communities; 2050 farmers established individual and group demonstration farms using new technologies and increased their harvest. The increased yields resulted in an increase of the target households' incomes by an average of 20–22 percent.

BP's objective is to create value for shareholders and supply of energy for the world in a safe and responsible way. They strive to be a world-class operator, a responsible corporate citizen and a good employer (BP, 2013). BP further offers several numbers, proving their importance for Georgian economy. In 2013 their operational expenditure totaled to USD 133 million and pipeline operations contributed approximately 8 percent of the total value of service exports in 2013. BP works with local contractors that can be testified by one of the authors of this article, as she herself used to work for a local contractor in Tbilisi. Payments to local companies

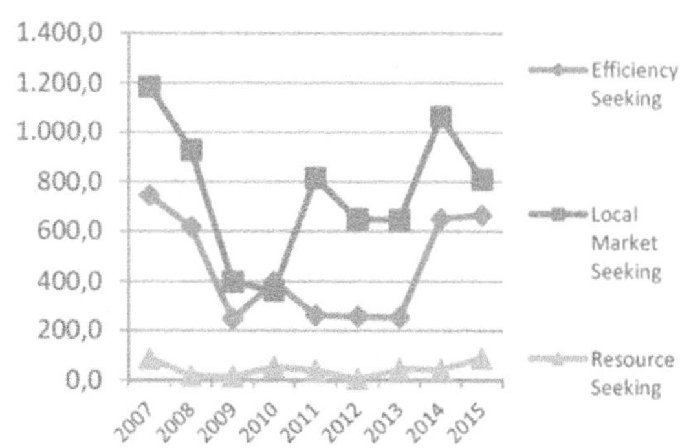

Fig. 1 FDIs between 2007 and 2015. Source: Charaia (2017)

totaled USD 77 million in 2013. BP obliges local contractors to meet their high standards thus raising standards among local companies. This is not enough, they even audit their contractors' practices to check their compliance with the social and local content requirements, examining recruitment practices, working conditions, redundancy and termination procedures, and disciplinary and grievance procedures (BP, 2013). This report suggests BP is an ideal MNE operating in Georgia fulfilling all the requirements of FDI in a developing country. A case study of a Doctor of Philosophy (Ph. D.) Student at International Black Sea University, Tamar Lazishvili in 2016 demonstrates reports on BP activities from another perspective.

The BP Baku-Tbilisi-Ceyhan (BTC) pipeline offers a good example of BP's questionable CSR practices. BP is the lead shareholder in the 1700 km oil pipeline, which runs from Baku, Azerbaijan, through Georgia to the Turkish seaport of Ceyhan. The route opened an alternative supply of oil and gas to the US, who for a long time has been in search of a substitute source that did not pass through Iran or Russia.

Georgia's important geopolitical location helped ensure it was part of the project—the biggest pipeline in the world, with 248 km of pipeline passing through Georgian territory. For the small post-Soviet country, the BTC pipeline offered great rewards but also great risk. The pipeline runs the length of a major fault line and presents a permanent risk of serious spills due to earthquakes. The pipeline also crosses the Borjomi region of Georgia—a blossoming tourist destination famous for its spectacular nature and restorative hot springs. Specifically, the pipeline crosses the heart of the region and through the 195,000-acre Borjomi/Kharagauli National Park, which is home to 1600 plant species and a handful of rare Caucasian leopards (Caucasus Nature Fund). At the time, the plan to build the pipeline through the environmentally sensitive area was not supported, for several reasons.

Firstly, locals feared the BTC pipeline would damage the environment and secondly there was concern the Borjomi region was inappropriate for the route as the Kodiana Mountains, the area near the proposed pipeline route, made the area extremely vulnerable to landslides and earthquakes. Additionally, Borjomi was also the place where Borjomi mineral water was produced and some feared the BTC pipeline would disrupt production of the water, which constituted about 10 percent of the country's exports.

Lazashvili compares putting an oil pipeline through this national park to the British putting a pipeline through London's Hyde Park.

The then Environment Minister of Georgia Nino Chkhobadze was reported in November 2002 as saying she was categorically against the route through Borjomi (selected by BP earlier the same month) because of the risk of catastrophic environmental damage in the event of pipeline rupture and cites from Chkhobadze's official letter to BP president John Brown, dated November 26, 2002:

> BP representatives are requesting the Georgian Government to violate our own environmental legislation.
>
> It is more difficult for the people of Georgia to understand why a 20 km segment of the route should challenge the sincerity of British Petroleum's worldwide commitment to environmental safety and respect of the values and norms of a host country.

Meanwhile Zaal Lomtadze, Georgia's Deputy Environment Minister at the time when the BTC project started, told environmental agency World Wildlife Fund (WWF) that his Ministry had sent BP a formal reminder on July 12, 2003 that the company must apply for construction permits for the Borjomi region. BP failed to make the application. Photographs taken by local WWF staff revealed BP illegally went ahead with construction for more than a week without permits until the government intervened on July 22, 2003 and stopped work in Borjomi. "BP has been caught red handed," said James Leaton, senior policy advisor of WWF:

> They have made all kinds of promises about how the BTC project would boost Georgian sovereignty, yet as soon as Georgian law no longer fits their schedule, they violate it without hesitation (Hopkins, 2004).

In 2004 the Georgian Government suspended work on the BTC pipeline after BP decided to begin building the pipeline in the Borjomi region. This was despite the company's repeated failures to obtain the necessary environmental certification to proceed. According to the UK-based newspaper *The Independent*, the resumption of construction of 2 weeks later came as a direct result of political pressure from the Bush administration. Washington had much to lose if the BTC pipeline project failed and it would use its political power to keep the project moving. In fact, a decision to resume the project was announced immediately after an unscheduled meeting between the then Georgian President Mikheil Saakashvili and the US Secretary of Defense Donald Rumsfeld. An article at the time by the newspaper stated that after the two officials met, the Georgian president said BP had "taken the first steps to satisfy the demands of the Georgian side", such as building the pipeline deeper and adding additional measures above ground, "with more security facilities and extra environmental safety technologies". On January 15, 2004 a piece by Green Alternative revealed towards the end of 2003 the "International Finance Corporation (IFC) and the European Bank for Reconstruction and Development (EBRD) separately agreed to finance the BTC pipeline, moves which have both provided USD 500 million of the USD 3.6 billion total and, more significantly, a priceless seal of western approval for the project." Lazishvili concludes that, in the BP-Georgia example, no more than a week was needed for the oil giant to neutralize attempts by the Georgian Government to preserve the unique ecology of Borjomi valley and get the go-ahead for construction of the BTC (Lazishvili, 2016).

3.4 Small and Medium Enterprises (SMES)

In the Journal of Small Business Strategy, Dunne and McBrayer (2019) argue that the cost of debt for small businesses decreases as firms increase their CSR disclosure transparency. Specifically, firms who disclose more social responsibility information faced reduced costs to debt financing. They argue that disclosure of Environment, Social, and Governance records provide value relevant information for lenders to use to mitigate the magnified information asymmetry inherent to lending to firms earlier in their lifecycle (Dunne & McBrayer, 2019).

Global Entrepreneurship Monitor (GEM) published Georgia's entrepreneurial Framework Conditions back in 2016 including all relevant national conditions that have an overall impact on economic development and activity, as well as specific conditions which facilitate to innovation and entrepreneurship in a society. Figure 2 demonstrates the current situation and growth potentials (GEM, 2016).

Natsvlishvili reports a couple years later (2018) that over the last years, based on successful reforms in Georgia, negative moods toward entrepreneurship are weak. Due to high unemployment, the desire of becoming self-employed is strong. As surveys show, positive attitudes of the respondents in Tbilisi toward entrepreneurship indicate their self-confidence, feelings of social and political stability, and expectations of success of market-oriented economic reforms. Subject of special interest is data about the current entrepreneurial activity of the surveyed people: 81.8 percent of respondents did not run their own businesses; 10.0 percent were self-employed; 6.1 percent were running small or medium-sized enterprises; and 1.4 percent were running large business. There are no data derived from 0.6 percent of respondents. It is noteworthy to say that, in the European Union, only 12 percent of respondents were engaged in entrepreneurial activity. In Japan, the same index was 15 percent, in the USA 21 percent, and 27 percent in China (Natsvlishvili, 2018).

As a proof to this development we introduce last year's Meliora (2019) award winning company for Responsibility in the Marketplace—*Insurance Company GPI Holding*, as small and medium sized enterprise (SME) business support Program. Meliora reports on its website: In 2017, *GPI* in partnership with the *Georgian Small and Medium Size Enterprises' Association* launched a project oriented on the development of small and medium size entrepreneurs. The project aims to popularize insurance as a financial protection mechanism, raise the awareness of entrepreneurs about insurance and engage them into the insurance system which is a necessary condition for the development and strengthening of the country's economy. The insurance program envisions a reimbursement of GEL 50,000. For the purpose of reducing the insurance fee for small entrepreneurs, *GPI Holding's* co-financing of the business risks at the first phase of the program was 50 percent and then 25–50

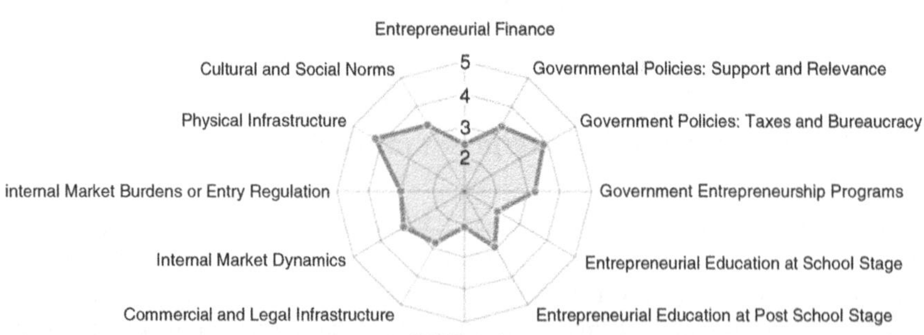

Fig. 2 Entrepreneurial framework conditions. Source: GEM (2016)

percent at the second phase. A wide audience was informed about the program's conditions and discounts through various communications campaigns. The project results were vividly revealed by the *Eliava market* fire: 70 percent of those who suffered losses and who were already insured with *GPI* received a total of GEL 600,000 in reimbursements. The attitude towards insurance has changed as well and this is reflected in almost 100 percent rate of insurance policy renewal. The program has also positively affected the company: incoming calls at the call center have increased by 300 percent and sales have increased by 500 percent.

4 Conclusion

We conclude our research citing Hoskisson et al. (2000) that emerging economies are low-income, rapid-growth countries using economic liberalization as their primary engine of growth. As we have shown in this paper, Georgia fulfills the criteria of emerging economy. The country puts much effort to attract MNEs and create favorable conditions for corporations to support Georgian economy. Furthermore, the government cooperates with international organizations and NGOs in order to support the implementation of CSR in corporations, raise awareness in the civil society as well as meet the SDGs.

We elaborated a hypothesis of interrelation of cultural specifications and CSR challenges in Georgia. Due to the characteristics, based on the GLOBE project cultural dimensions (House et al., 2004), specific challenges are comprehensive, and obstacles seem obvious. Based on our present findings, we suggest scientists in Georgia research deeper in this field. Furthermore, surveys within CSR Clubs and NGOs could be held, in order to validate or refute our hypothesis.

We recommend Georgian NGOs to define measures to win back public trust and raise awareness in the society. We consider NGOs important stakeholders to prove the linkage between cultural characteristics and current CSR challenges in specific organizations.

And finally, while working on this paper, we had our own responsible goal. No waste of paper. We are proud to be able to say that not one page has been printed and thrown away (Authors).

References

Arnold, D. J., & Quelch, J. A. (1998). New strategies in emerging markets. *MIT Sloan Management Review, 40*(1), 7.

Balarjishvili, I. (2017). Contradictions of development of civil society as economic actor in Georgia. Country experiences in economic development, management and entrepreneurship. In *Proceedings of the 17th Eurasia business and economics society conference* (pp. 171–186). New York: Springer.

British Petroleum in Georgia. (2013). *Sustainability Report 2013*. Retrieved from https://www.bp.com/content/dam/bp/business-sites/en/global/corporate/pdfs/sustainability/archive/archived-country-reports/georgia/bp-georgia-sustainability-review-2013.pdf. Consulted 3 August 2019.

Bzhalava, L., Lezhava, B., Brekashvili, P.. & Melua, I. (2017). *Global Entrepreneurship Monitor: 2016-2017 Georgia Report*. Retrieved from https://www.researchgate.net/publication/322630845_Global_Entrepreneurship_Monitor_2016-2017_Georgia_Report/citation/download. Consulted 10 August 2019.

Charaia, V. (2017). The role of multinational enterprises' investments in emerging country's economic development, case of Georgia. *International Journal of Social, Behavioral, Educational, Economic, Business and Industrial Engineering, 11*(3), 691.

CSR Club Georgia. (2019). *Overview*. Retrieved from https://csrclub.ge/en/club/overview. Consulted 3 August 2019.

Dunne, T. C., & McBrayer, G. A. (2019). In the interest of small business' cost of debt: A matter of CSR disclosure. *Journal of Small Business Strategy, 29*(2), 58–71.

East West Management Institute (EWMI). (2019a). *Advancing CSO Capacities and Engaging Society for Sustainability (ACCESS) 2014-2019*. Retrieved from https://ewmi.org/Program/AdvancingCSOCapacitiesandEngagingSocietySustainabilityACCESS. Consulted 10 August 2019.

East West Management Institute (EWMI). (2019b). *Promoting Rule of Law in Georgia (PROLoG) 2015-2020*. Retrieved from https://ewmi.org/Program/PromotingRuleLawGeorgiaPROLoGActivity. Consulted 10 August 2019.

Georgian Code of Business Conduct. (2004). Retrieved from http://dev01.icnl.org/news/2004/13-Aug-GBE.html. Consulted 10 August 2019 and http://www.conference.ge/stuff/gbcc.pdf. Consulted 10 August 2019.

Georgian Natural Tourism Administration (GNTA). (2016). http://gnta.ge/9-reasons-to-visit-georgia-now-cnn. Consulted 10 August 2019.

Global Entrepreneurship Monitor (GEM). (2016). *Global Entrepreneurship Research Association*, London Business School, Regents Park, London, UK. https://www.gemconsortium.org/economy-profiles/georgia. Consulted 10 August 2019.

Guruli, I. (2018). Current stance of entrepreneurship and SME development in Georgia: Perspectives and challenges. *Ecoforum Journal, 7*(3), 219.

Hofstede, G. (1980). *Culture s consequences: International differences in work-related values*. Beverly Hills, CA: Sage.

Hofstede, G. (2001). *Culture s consequences: Comparing values, behaviors, institutions, and organizations across nations*. Thousand Oaks, CA: Sage.

Hopkins, D. (2004). *BTC pipeline construction suspended*. Retrieved from edie.net - https://www.edie.net/news/0/BTC-pipeline-construction-suspended/8668/. Consulted 29 December 2019.

Hoskisson, R., Eden, L., Lau, C., & Wright, M. (2000). Strategy in emerging economies. *The Academy of Management Journal, 43*(3), 249–267.

House, R. J., Hanges, P. J., Javidan, M., Dorfman, P. W., & Gupta, V. (Eds.). (2004). *Culture, leadership, and organizations: The GLOBE study of 62 societies*. Thousand Oaks, CA: Sage.

Kolster, T. (2019). *In Georgia CSR-determination wins*. Retrieved from https://thomaskolster.com/in-georgia-csr-determination-wins/. Consulted 08 August 2019.

Lazishvili, T. (2016). British petroleum and corporate social responsibility case study: British petroleum in Georgia. *Journal in Humanities, 5*(1), 48.

Loew, T., & Rohde, F. (2013). *CSR und Nachhaltigkeitsmanagement: Definitionen, Ansätze und organisatorische Umsetzung in Unternehmen*. Berlin: Institute for Sustainability (Translated by Stehr, 2016).

Matten, D., & Moon, J. (2004). Corporate social responsibility education in Europe. *Journal of Business Ethics, 54*, 323–337.

Meliora, Georgian Responsible Business Awards. (2019). *About the organizers*. Retrieved from https://meliora.ge/en/about-the-organizers/. Consulted 3 August 2019.

Mghebrishvili, B. (2019). Situation of health and welfare in Georgia in the context of sustainable development and sustainable marketing. *Ecoforum, 8*(1), 18.
Miska, C., Szőcs, I., & Schiffinger, M. (2018). Culture's effects on corporate sustainability practices: A multi-domain and multi-level view. *Journal of World Business, 53*(2), 263–279.
Montero, A. G. & Le Blanc, D. (2019). *The role of external audits in enhancing transparency and accountability for the sustainable development goals.* United Nations, Department of Economic and Social Affairs (DESA) working paper no 157, January 2019.
Natsvlishvili, I. (2018). Social entrepreneurship and corporate social responsibility in the context of a moral economy: Dilemma for developing countries (case of Georgia). *Naše gospodarstvo/Our economy, 64*(4), 49–59.
Nguyen, M., & Truong, M. (2016). The effect of culture on enterprise's perception of corporate social responsibility: The case of Vietnam. *Procedia CIRP, 40*, 680–686.
Organisation for Economic Co-operation and Development (OECD). (2016). *Responsible Business Conduct in Georgia.* Retrieved from http://www.oecd.org/daf/inv/mne/RBC-in-Georgia-2016.pdf. Consulted 09 August 2019.
Palazzo, B. (2002). U.S.-American and German business ethics: An intercultural comparison. *Journal of Business Ethics, 41*, 195–216.
SAI Georgia (2018). Sharing experiences on auditing policy coherence and integration. In *Presentation at UNDESA-IDI SAI Leadership & Stakeholder Meeting*, New York.
Sadzaglishvili, S., & Kartvelishvili, M. (2018). Bridging business and nonprofit organization interests via a culture of social responsibility. In *The nonprofit sector in Eastern Europe, Russia, and Central Asia.* Leiden, Netherlands: Brill.
Takalandze, L. (2013). Social responsibility of business in Georgia: Development and problems. *Economics and Management, 18*(2), 325–330.
The Financial (2016) .*Majority of companies in Georgia misunderstood the idea of CSR, Survey* https://www.finchannel.com/world/georgia/54997-majority-of-companies-in-georgia-misunderstood-the-idea-of-csr-survey. Consulted 03 August 2019.
Tkeshelashvili, N. (2010). The effects of culture on the leadership style in Georgia. *IBSU Scientific Journal, 3*(2), 115–129.
UN. (2019a). *United Nations, knowledge platform. Sustainable Development Goals.* https://sustainabledevelopment.un.org/?menu=1300. Consulted 10 August 2019.
UN. (2019b). *United Nations, Division for Sustainable Development Goals. "Global Sustainable Development Report 2019."* https://sustainabledevelopment.un.org/globalsdreport. Consulted 10 August 2019.
UN, GEO. (2016). *United Nations, Division for Sustainable Development Goals. Voluntary National Review 2016.* https://sustainabledevelopment.un.org/memberstates/georgia. Consulted 09 August 2019.
U.S. Department of State. (2015). *2015 investment climate statement.* Georgia: U.S. Department of State,
The World Bank Group. (2019). Doing business – Measuring business regulations. Retrieved from doingbusiness.org. Consulted 10 August 2019.
World Business Council for Sustainable Development (WBCSD). (2000). *Corporate social responsibility: Making good business sense.*

Poland: CSR in an Emerging Market from Transition Until Today

Florian Urbański and Christopher Stehr

Abstract With the political and economic transformation in Central and Eastern Europe since 1989 and the increasing participation of this region into the processes of Globalisation, Poland became an emerging market. This process of economic development still continues today and as a major result of this, the concept of Corporate Social Responsibility (CSR) in Poland was and still is involved in a constant and dynamic process. This paper will focus on these changes in the field of CSR under the light of these economic and social processes by providing historical overview and an analysis of the status quo. Furthermore, the paper will examine some of the well-known case studies that will take into account Small and Medium Sized Enterprises (SMEs), Multinational Enterprises (MNEs), Civil Societies and Non-Governmental Organisations (NGO).

Keywords CSR · Strategic CSR · Corporate social responsibility · Emerging market · Transition · Poland

1 Introduction

The political and economic transformation of Poland has been one of the major challenges in Central and Eastern Europe (Długosz, 2019; Kuitto, 2016; Piatkowski, 2018) and it led to the increasing participation of Poland into the processes of Globalisation (Dančák & Hlousek, 2007; Gorynia, 2014; Gorynia, Nowak, & Wolniak, 2003). As an outcome of these developments Poland became an emerging market and still remains so today (Gorynia, 2017; McKinsey, 2019), with a Real

F. Urbański
Fundacja WrOpenUp, Wrocław, Poland
e-mail: florian.urbanski@wropenup.pl

C. Stehr (✉)
German Graduate School of Management and Law, Heilbronn, Germany
e-mail: welcome@polymundo.de

N. Mitra, R. Schmidpeter (eds.), *Corporate Social Responsibility in Rising Economies*, CSR, Sustainability, Ethics & Governance,
https://doi.org/10.1007/978-3-030-53775-3_9

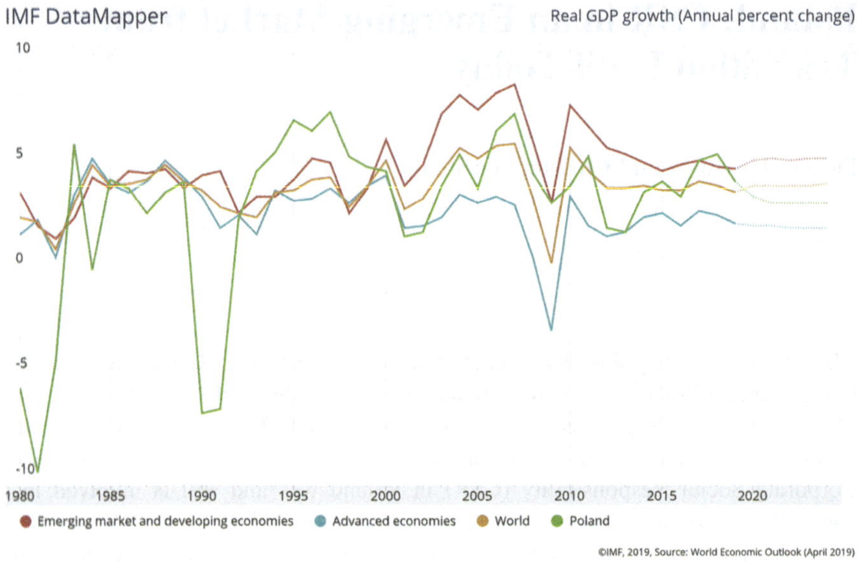

Fig. 1 Real GDP growth of Poland in comparison. Source: IMF (2016b)

GDP (Gross Domestic Product) growth (Annual percent change) in 2018 of 5.1% and an Inflation rate (Annual percent change) of 1.6% (IMF, 2016a). The latest McKinsey Report from 2019 even predicted Poland to become the new upcoming European "growth engine" until 2025 (McKinsey, 2019). The historical developments of Polish Real GDP growth including forecasts can be seen in Fig. 1.

Under the light of this economic transformation and market development of Poland, one question seems to be obvious: "How was it possible to develop concepts of Corporate Social Responsibility in Poland after 1989?" Thus, it is interesting to analyse the recent literature about Polish CSR on the basis of the following questions:

- How does the historical development of CSR in Poland look like?
- What role does Multinational Enterprises (MNEs) play in this development?
- What role are Small and Medium Sized Enterprises (SMEs) taking in it?
- What are the roles of Non-governmental Organisations (NGOs) in this process?
- What does CSR mean for the Civil Society?

To answer these questions, the article takes an integral way of viewing by analysing CSR in the context of Multinational Enterprises, Small and Medium Sized Enterprises as well as the Civil Societies mainly under the perspective of Non-governmental Organisations.

Furthermore, it will give an overview over the historical development of CSR and describe the current state in Poland by reviewing some of the recent literature (books, online and journal articles). The second part will analyse CSR under the light of

SMEs versus MNEs and understand their role in influencing the civil societies of Poland. The third part will examine several case studies and lead to the conclusion.

2 Corporate Social Responsibility

Definition of Corporate Social Responsibility

The term Corporate Social Responsibility (CSR) can be defined as a business concept for a voluntary integration of social and environmental concerns into business operations and into the interaction with stakeholders (Crowther, 2018; UNIDO, 2017), in order to achieve substantial growth and economic development for the company (Chandler, 2017; Eweje & Bathurst, 2017). Based on this definition, CSR can be also described in a broader sense as social and environmental obligations by a company which are taken additionally on top of the legal necessity to consider social expectations (Hackett, 2016; Rasche, Morsing, & Moon, 2017).

In further consequence, strategic CSR can be understood as a business model to include social, economic and environmental concerns into an organization's corporate culture, investment plans and management strategy in order to provide a larger approach of business which is described as the social model of corporations (Eweje & Bathurst, 2017; Hawkins, 2006; Wołczek, 2019). This social model postulates that the economic performance should not be the only concern of a company, as companies aim at finding a balance between two contradictory goals: the financial model and shareholders' approach to maximization of profit on the one hand; and on the other hand, considering the interests, expectations and needs of stakeholders (Chandler, 2017; Eweje & Bathurst, 2017).

The communication and cooperation between a company and its stakeholders is hereby the crucial element of a successful CSR implementation (Bhattacharya, Korschun, & Sen, 2008; Hackett, 2016). The social dialogue is directed at stakeholders as a wide range of groups such as shareholders, employees, suppliers, customers, local communities, management, citizen groups, competitors and the press and, in a much wider perspective, the society as a whole (Chandler, 2017; Freeman, 2005).

Therefore, the covered activities of CSR reflect the diversified identity of stakeholders and their various interests and values. By definition of the International Organization for Standardization (ISO) the seven main topics of CSR comprise the following (ISO, 2010): (1) Organizational Governance; (2) Human Rights; (3) Labour Practices; (4) The Environment; (5) Fair Operating Practices, (6) Consumer Issues, (7) Community involvement and Development (Bay, 2018; Hansen, 2017).

According to the European Commission (EC), these activities can also be classified into two dimensions: the internal dimension and the external dimension (COM, 2001, 2002). The Internal Dimension includes all activities which affects internal process like management (e.g. human resource management). The External Dimension focus on all outside activities by involvement of local communities and the social environment as well as of stakeholders. (Aluchna, 2015a; COM, 2001, 2002).

An additional approach to the analysis of dimensions of CSR was developed by Hiß (2006): It regards such fields of activities which can be divided into three spheres of responsibility: the internal sphere, the intermediate sphere and the external sphere (Hiß, 2009; Hiß & Nagel, 2016).

The internal sphere contains all CSR activities which are defined by the responsibilities regarding the market and law as long as it is voluntary and additional. Hereby, it is not just meant to follow rules and laws without any control by governmental institutions, but also additional commitments with social hardship clause, or the integration of international agreements of labour- and environmental standards into the company's culture. It is marked by the concept of a responsible maximization of profits (towards a responsible maximization) in terms of respecting safety standards, environmental standards, human rights etc. In this case CSR means the renunciation of profit at the expense of others (Hiß, 2006; Hiß & Nagel, 2016).

Additionally, the intermediate sphere summarizes all CSR activities which are beyond law enactments and international agreements regarding the responsibility to the value creation chain. This contains observance of labour- and environmental standards as well as Supply-Chain-Management. It involves self-commitments via various code of conducts regarding social, environmental and labour standards and their control via monitoring. Another key element is the seal of quality by independent institutions as a proof of social, environmental and labour standards in the production and business behaviour (Hiß, 2009; Hiß & Nagel, 2016).

The external sphere is defined by all activities which are beyond all regular business activities of profit maximization or the value creation chain and are aimed at social effects outside of the company. One part is the so-called Corporate Giving as activities of donation and sponsoring of social or environmental events or organizations. The second part is the Corporate Volunteering scheme (or Employee Volunteering) which is defined as the exemption of employees for community volunteering (Hiß, 2006; Hiß & Nagel, 2016).

3 CSR in Poland

3.1 Historical Development of CSR in Poland

The concept of Corporate Social Responsibility is a relatively new concept in Poland (Aluchna, 2015b; Popowska, 2016; Potocki, 2015). Early traditions of a philanthropic entrepreneurship may be found among the nineteenth century industrialist in the three Polish partitions (Rok, 2019), but the history of modern CSR in Poland began with the political change of 1989 and the transformation from planned economy into a market economy in 1990 (Magala, 2019; Wiktorska-Święcka, 2019).

Although the socialist government before 1989 declared social concerns as the official political agenda, the focus within the planned economy let on the development of the heavy and defence industry. The only kind of CSR in socialist Poland may be seen in the obligation of state-owned enterprises to provide social institutions like building kindergartens or holiday resorts for their employees (Dyczkowska, Krasodomska, & Michalak, 2016; Magala, 2019; Rojek-Nowosielska, 2019).

In the beginning of the transformation process from 1990 until 1997, the concept of CSR was nearly unknown in the Polish society. These early years were a period of market liberalization as well as an economical individualization on the one hand; and on the other hand, a time of less social contribution (Aluchna, 2015b; Potocki, 2015; Wiktorska-Święcka, 2019). This phase of low social contribution included not only an underdeveloped socially-aware society, but also an inactivity of stakeholders in terms of social commitments and performance (Dyczkowska et al., 2016; Rok, 2019; Waniak-Michałak, Macuda, & Krasodomska, 2016).

With the end of this initial phase of the Polish transformation in 1997, this picture was about to change very slowly, driven by the ongoing developments on the market (Aluchna, 2015a; Popowska, 2015a; Potocki, 2015). A share on this change of perception towards CSR was also impulsed by discussions within the academic community—mainly influenced by Gasparski (1994, 1999) and Rok (2004, 2013)—as well as by public discussions influenced by non-governmental organisations (Popowska, 2015a; Potocki, 2015; Rok, 2019).

With the Strategy *for Sustainable Development of Poland by 2025 by* the Polish government in 1999, the first official recognition of CSR in Poland appeared (Wołczek, 2019). The next major step forward was the political and economic integration of Poland into the European Union in 2004 (Aluchna, 2015a, b; Popowska, 2016; Potocki, 2015).

All these factors together did not only bring a change of perspectives to the stakeholders and the Polish society over the years but created furthermore the necessary legal basis and institutional frameworks for CSR (Aluchna, 2015a; Popowska, 2016; Waniak-Michałak et al., 2016). Studies in 2007 showed an increasing interest in CSR within Polish companies and among stakeholders, but still a major barrier did exist: the lack of appropriate legal frameworks for CSR. This picture corresponds to the fact that Poland was not included into the program by the United Nations Industrial Development Organization (UNIDO) for CSR-implementation, as well as in international CSR-Forums in 2007 and 2008 by the United Nations (UN) (Macuda, Matuszak, & Różańska, 2015; Popowska, 2016; Wołczek, 2015).

The major development regarding CSR in Poland took place in 2009; due to a recent change at the level of the Polish government which had recognized the importance of a development of CSR with respect to the influence of foreign investment (Aluchna, 2015a; Wiktorska-Święcka, 2019; Wołczek, 2015). To guarantee a constant and systematic implementation of legal frameworks for CSR, a special CSR team under direct control of the Polish Prime Minister was built (MGRP, 2010), and their conclusions have been integrated into the new Guidelines of the National Development Strategy 2020 (Aluchna, 2015a; Potocki, 2015; Urbański, 2019). Furthermore, the RESPECT Index portfolio was established by the Warsaw Stock exchange; an index to identify listed companies with responsible and sustainable behaviour and etiquette (Aluchna, 2015a; Daszyńska-Żygadło, 2019; Potocki, 2015).

While former publications came to the conclusion, to divide the history of CSR in Poland into five main phases (Dyczkowska et al., 2016; Popowska, 2015a; Potocki, 2015; UNDP, 2007), this paper combined this knowledge with the findings of the latest literature (Magala, 2019; Rok, 2019; Wiktorska-Święcka, 2019) and redefined these phases. Therefore, this paper identifies six main phases regarding the development and implementation of CSR in Poland:

1990–1997: Refusal: no social aspects of economy
1997–2000: Indifference: Silence and lack of interest towards CSR
2001–2002: Strong Opposition: Aversion and objection of CSR
2002–2004: Interest: Public declarations and first legal basis
2004–2006: Fragmentary activities: Uncoordinated CSR activities
2007–now: Strategic Activity: Interlinking projects and activities

Although the Polish ministry for Development established in 2016 a *Social Responsibility Committee* and announced in 2017 the *Strategy for Responsibility Development until 2020* to support CSR projects in Poland, a concrete and integral national vision of CSR does not exist yet. The Polish public policies towards CSR still can be described with ambiguity and disorganisation, because the state programs do not encourage enough a constructive dialogue between the government, the private sector and stakeholders (Wiktorska-Święcka, 2019; Wołczek, 2019). Nevertheless, the latest report by Forum Odpowiedzalnego Biznesu also showed a growth of 30% regarding the numbers of active companies as well as strategic CSR practices in Poland in 2019 compared to the years before (FOP, 2017, 2018, 2019).

3.2 Sector Analysis

Multinational Enterprise

The term Multinational Enterprise (MNEs) defined as a worldwide enterprise is used synonymously with the terms Transnational Corporation (TNC), Multinational Corporation (MNC), Transnational Enterprise (TNE) and International Corporation (INC) (Ietto-Gillies, 2012; Pitelis & Sugden, 2000; Voorhees, Seim, & Coppett, 1992).

All these terms describe a corporate organization with international activities based on foreign direct investment (Ietto-Gillies, 2011; Dunning & Lundan, 2008; Polzin, Kirchner, & Pollert, 2013)—as opposed to the much broader definition of an International Business Company (or also International Business Corporation) (IBC) which also includes activities of indirect investment just like import and export of goods (Dunning & Lundan, 2008; Stehr & Vodosek, 2017).

This is also valid for the Polish developments since the beginning of the political and economic changes of 1989 (Długosz, 2019; Gorynia, 2014; Tanski, 2017) and

Table 1 Categorizing SMES

Company size	Employee (maximum)	*AND*	Turnover (million EUR/year)	*OR*	Balance sheet total (million EUR/year)
Micro	9		Until 2		Until 2
Small	49		Until10		Until 10
Medium	249		Until 50		Until 43

Source: Table based on IFM-Bonn (2019) and KfW (2019)

the activities of Multinational Enterprises on the Polish market (Chechelski, 2017; Cieślik & Hagemejer, 2014). The influence on the Polish market and society (Chechelski, 2017; Prokopowicz, 2016; Siemiątkowski, 2017) can also be found in the field of Corporate Social Responsibilities because those corporations has been identified as the main drivers of CSR in Poland (Lakatoś, 2017; Skrzypczyńska, 2015).

However, under the current situation of CSR in Poland, differences between Polish-owned companies and international corporations still exist in terms of their CSR performance (Aluchna, 2015a; Wołczek, 2015). A survey by the United Nations Development Programme in Poland (UNDP) (2007) showed a significant difference between Polish-owned companies and Multinational Enterprises (MNEs) in terms of CSR strategies. According to this survey, 40% of companies have no CSR strategy at all, and these are mainly Polish businesses. The remaining 45% of companies with uncoordinated CSR Projects are represented mainly by MNEs and large Polish companies. Only 15% of companies on the Polish market have included a CSR Strategy into the overall company strategy, and these are mainly large Multinational Enterprises (Aluchna, 2015a; Jastrzębska, 2016; Potocki, 2015).

A similar picture can be found within the CSR rankings by the Forum Odpowiedzalnego Biznesu (Forum of Responsible Business/FOP) in 2017 and 2018 (FOP, 2017, 2018). When paired up with background information by Bloomberg (Bloomberg, 2019), it turns out that among the recognized companies roughly over 65% are international corporations and less than 45% Polish owned companies (Bloomberg, 2019; FOP, 2017, 2018).

Therefore, international corporations still are the main drivers of CSR in Poland (Dancewicz & Struve, 2019; Dyczkowska et al., 2016; Lakatoś, 2017).

Small and Medium Sized Enterprises

Defined by the European Commission (2003), Small and Medium Sized Enterprises (SMEs) are companies with less than 250 employees and an annual turnover of maximum 50 million EUR (Euro) or a balance sheet total of maximum 43 million EUR (EC, 2003; Eurostat, 2019; FdB, 2019). This definition of SMEs can be subdivided into micro enterprises, small enterprises and medium sized enterprises like in Table 1 (Eurostat, 2019; IFM-Bonn, 2019; KfW, 2019).

Small and Medium Sized Enterprises seem to be a very important factor within the Polish economy just by their pure numbers as well as by their business results (GUS, 2015; McKinsey, 2019; OECD, 2017, 2019), because (based on data from 2008 to 2015) the European Commission found that 99.8% of Polish companies (in the non-financial business economy sector) fits into this category: 95.7% Micro / 3.2% Small/0.9% Medium. Therefore, Polish SMEs make 51.4% of the Polish value added and account for 68.1% of employment in Poland (among non-financial business economy), as compared to EU averages of 56.8% (value added) and 66.4% (employment) (Factsheet, 2018). Also, the latest numbers by Central Statistical Office (Główny Urząd Statystyczny/GUS) from 2017 about the size of Polish companies (non-financial business economy) confirmed this picture: 96.5% Micro/ 2.6% Small/0.7% Medium/0.2% Large (GUS, 2019a, b).

In consideration of this important role SMEs play for Polish economy, it is quite surprising that surveys about CSR in Polish SMEs are relatively rare (compared to surveys among MNEs in Poland). At least uncommon are surveys with a general attempt (which could give a Poland wide overview about CSR in SMEs), towards research projects with just a sectoral perspective or with only a regional or even local scope (Bachnik, 2017; Popowska, 2015b; Sokołowska-Durkalec, 2018, 2019). But the studies like that of Deloitte (Managers-Survey, 2015) at least indicates that Polish SMEs are under-represented in Polish CSR activities anyway: 5.3% Micro/ 14.3% Small/15.0% Medium/65.4% Large (Andrejczuk, 2016; Popowska, 2015b; Przytuła, Formánková, Ubrežiová, & Dunay, 2019).

One of the less surveys which can indicate general conclusions about Polish SMEs in CSR context was the research project supported by the Polish Ministry of Science and Higher Education (Andrejczuk, 2016; Sokołowska-Durkalec, 2019). Another survey with a general approach towards SMEs in the context of CSR was made in 2016 by the Institute of Management at Warsaw School of Economics (Bachnik, 2016, 2017). Combining those two studies for an analysis, it is evident that the group of Polish SMEs, despite a more or less straight forward scientific definition, is highly heterogeneous. The specific contexts of each SME make it hard to withdraw common conclusions. Anyway, it seems possible to say, that in theory, Polish SMEs take social and environmental issues in account by announcing ethical and social declarations. But on the other hand, in practice, those companies have the tendency to avoid concrete actions. More often they seem to be content with passive and defensive interventions rather than just to avoid penalties of a pro-active, systematic and strategic CSR activity (Bachnik, 2016, 2017; Popowska, 2015b; Sokołowska-Durkalec, 2019).

Civil Society and Non-Governmental Organisation

Different definitions of the term Civil Society exists, depending on different ideological traditions (Keane, 2010; Petrie & South, 2014) and so at least three different meanings can be found: (1) normative meaning (civil society synonymously as a civilized society), (2) functional meaning (civil society as a democratized society), and at last (3) structural meaning (civil society the so called third sector) (Keane, 2010; O'Connell, 2000; Viterna, Clough, & Clarke, 2015). This paper will focus on the third meaning, the structural meaning of the "third sector", therefore civil society here is defined as "*[. . .] a sector of organized human action composed of collective actors beyond the family and distinct from the state and the market.*" (Viterna et al., 2015, p. 175).

Under the aspects of CSR the most important factor among the Civil Society are Non-Governmental Organisations (NGO). A NGO—or even more precise Non-profit Organisation (NPO)—is a group of individuals or organizations on voluntary basis which is not associated with the government and which is non-profit orientated (Ecb, 2019; Gabler, 2019). Taking in consideration the definitions of the United Nations and the European Union, NGOs aim to provide services of public concerns or aim to advocate public policies of diverse possible topics of social or ecological affairs just like environmental protection, social justice and human rights (BPB, 2019; CoEP, 2019; UN-EaSC, 2019). The field of activities of NGO are diverse in their local, national and international operations (BPB, 2019; UN-EaSC, 2019; UNRIC, 2019).

The roots of today's Polish civil society go back to the first organized Polish opposition movements in the 1970s and 1980s. Those early Polish NGOs has been described in Poland as *self-government (samorząd)*—as the equivalent to the English term of *civil society*—and focused mainly on aspects of legal rights or improving the economic situation of the Polish population (Dancewicz & Struve, 2019; Stroinska, 2013).

After the political and economic change of 1989/1990, the democratic constitution of the Republic of Poland—now in its latest version from 1997 (Polish Constitution, 2019)—set the legal framework for the civil society together with further acts of law and legal regulations which defined the legal setting for trade unions and other NGOs. Among them the law act which allows every Polish citizen to donate 1% of his income tax during the annual declaration of income to a a registered non-profit-organisation (Gumkowska & Herbst, 2006; Nowosielski, 2008, Stroinska, 2013, Mierzejewski, 2018).

Between 1989 and 1994 a rapid rise of registered NGOs in Poland started and set up the number to about 47.000 registered organisation in the year 1994 (Mierzejewski, 2018; Nowosielski, 2008; Szustek, 2008). This dynamic development and growth seem not to be completed yet, because according to the Polish Central Statistical Office (GUS), the total number of NGOs rose from 2014 with 87.5 thousand to the year 2016 with 91.8 thousand registered organizations (a rise of 4.91%). A similar conclusion of growth can be withdrawn by surveys from Jon/Klawor, because while 2012 approximately 80,000 organizations where registered, in 2018 already 143,000 registered organisations were counted (a rise of 78.75% (Charycka & Gumkowska, 2019; Przewłocka, 2013).

The field of main activities among Polish NGOs is quite diverse (Table 2, GUS 2018) and (Charycka & Gumkowska, 2019).

With this growth in the last 30 years, NGOs developed as an important stakeholder in terms of CSR in Poland: NGOs set the norms of conduct and monitor companies in their business behaviour (Dancewicz & Struve, 2019; Nowosielski, 2008; Szustek, 2008). The most influencing NGOs in that term are the RESPECT-Index (Daszyńska-Żygadło, 2019) and Forum Odpowiedzalnego Biznesu (FOP, 2019), both organisations publish annual reports and rating about companies in their level of Corporate Social Responsibility (Aluchna, 2015a; Dancewicz & Struve, 2019; Daszyńska-Żygadło 2019).

Table 2 The main focus of polish NGOS

Area of focus	Percentage
Sports, tourism, recreation, hobby	35
Culture and arts	14
Educations	13
Healthcare	8
Social services, welfare	7
Local development	6
Other	17

Source: Table based on source by Charycka and Gumkowska (2019)

The statistics of GUS does not give an exact information, how many of those registered NGOs are somehow part or supported by an official CSR project, but at least the total structure of revenues for 2016 were given. The revenue sources in 2016 were in majority 39.4% Market revenues and 38.7% public funds. Only 12.8% private funds, 6.0% membership dues and 3.1% other sources (GUS, 2018). A quite similar but nevertheless more differentiated insight was given by Klon/Jawor Association: According to this survey for Polish NGOs the national funds are becoming less important (2007: 31%; 2014: 15%) but on the other hand counting domestic and foreign public funds (e.g. from EU) together, Polish NGOs are still depending on public support on a large scale (2007: 57%; 2014: 55%) (Adamiak, Charycka, & Gumkowska, 2015; Wołczek, 2019). The numbers for 2018 by Klon/Jawor still confirmed the importance of public funding, while the influence of national public funding rose again compared to 2014. According to this survey, the total revenue came out of the following funding sources: National Public Funding: 39%; Foreign Public Funding: 15%; Commercial/Business Operations: 15%; Personal/Institutional Philanthropy: 14%; 1Percent-Income-Tax-Donation: 3%; Membership Dues: 3%; Owned Assets: 3%; Support form other NGOs: 2% and Other: 6% (Charycka & Gumkowska, 2019). All those numbers indicates, that Polish NGOs are still mainly influenced by public resources, what also reflects into their scope of activities (Dyczkowska et al., 2016; Wołczek, 2019).

Another important sector of the Civil Society are educational institutions like universities. In Poland, institutions of higher education offer programmes and courses concerning CSR, but mainly for post-graduate studies and l*ess in traditional studies* (Wołczek, 2015, 2019). From the existing papers, the picture can be withdrawn, CSR as topic of research and lectures in Poland is increasing but still undeveloped at Polish Universities (Buchta et al., 2018; Geryk, 2018; Wołczek, 2019). According to a Survey by CSR info in 2010, only 19% of students confirmed that their higher school offers classes on CSR, 28% that the institution offers classes in business ethics, 18% that CSR as topic appears in other classes and 35% declared that neither classes are offered nor CSR mentioned during any lesson (Nowak & Chowicz, 2018).

The last important sector to mention in connection with the Civil Sector is the media. According to the data by Forum Odpowiedzalnego Biznesu (FOP) (e.g. FOP,

2017, 2018) it can be concluded that media in Poland is increasingly promoting CSR in the public. Considering the years 2014 to 2016, the press articles associated with CSR rose from 2014 (4702 articles) to about 47% to 2015 (6930 articles) and about 8% to 2016 (7504 articles) (Paliwoda-Matiolańska, 2014; Wołczek, 2015, 2019).

4 Conclusions

Resume

The historical development of CSR in Poland—defining the years of political and economic change 1989/1990 as the starting point evolved with irregular period of inactivity until 1997 (Refusal), a time of indecision until 2000 (Indifference), even aversion until 2002 (Strong Opposition), a beginning of interest under the lights of first legal frameworks until 2004 (Interest), more intensive but uncoordinated projects until 2007 (Fragmentary activities) and ever since intensive and interlinking CSR-projects (Strategic Activity) by companies and their stakeholders. Meanwhile, strategic and interlinking CSR-projects became the standard, although not all the analysed sectors (MNEs, SMEs, Civil Society and NGOs) and the legal frameworks by the government are developed up to the same professional level.

The multinational corporations with their subsidiaries in Poland can hereby be still identified as the main driver and main influencer of Polish CSR concepts while small and medium sized enterprises are still under-represented in Polish CSR projects. Even more Polish SMEs still have a deficit in their very own strategic CSR Projects. In general, it is possible to say, that MNEs in Poland already reached the level of strategic CSR while this CSR level is still underdeveloped among Polish SMEs. The Civil Society with Universities and NGOs seem to be underdeveloped as well when it comes to CSR and finance out from the private sector. Furthermore, NGOs are still depending on public funding (national and international), which limits their scope of activities according to cooperation with the private sector (MNEs and SMEs) with respect towards CSR-projects. The obligation to deliver better legal frameworks and institutional structures for an integral dialogue between all involved, thereby lies in the hands of the government.

Further Research

In order to understand today's Polish Civil Society in detail it may be interesting to go back in history to understand Poland's cultural mentality towards CSR. A detailed historical overview from the beginning of the twentieth century until the development of the Polish Civil Society in socialist Poland (People's Republic of Poland) with its oppositions movement, over the political and economic transformation time into the democratic Poland (Third Polish Republic) with all social and political developments until today could be interesting. But in order to not overload the article, the analysis had to be restricted to the Status Quo with just a short historical overview. Such a socio-cultural and political-historical excursus must be left for future surveys with a more detailed focus on CSR in connection with Polish Civil Society.

Furthermore, more surveys with concrete numbers and facts about CSR by Polish SMEs seem to be necessary, also in comparison to CSR by MNEs in Poland. After all, an integral approach to examine and understand the interlinking and mutual influences within CSR in Poland with the private sector (including MNEs and SMEs) and the Civil Society as a whole (Universities, Media, NGOs and other interest groups by stakeholders) seems to be major challenge for future Polish researches.

References

Adamiak, P., Charycka, B., & Gumkowska, M. (2015). *Kondycja sektora organizacji pozarządowych w Polsce 2015 – Raport z Badań*. Warsaw, Poland: Stowarzyszenia Klon/Jawor. Retrieved June 17, 2019, from https://www.nck.pl/upload/attachments/318004/Raport_Klon_Kondycja_2015.pdf

Aluchna, M. (2015a). Corporate social responsibility in Poland: From the perspective of listed companies. In S. O. Idowu, R. Schmidpeter, & M. S. Fifka (Eds.), *Corporate social responsibility and governance – United in Sustainable Diversity* (pp. 271–289). Cham, Switzerland: Springer.

Aluchna, M. (2015b). Employee volunteering as an element of corporate social responsibility: The evidence from Polish listed companies. In S. O. Idowu, C. S. Frederiksen, A. Y. Mermod, & M. E. J. Juul Nielsen (Eds.), *CSR, sustainability, ethics and governance – Theory and practice* (pp. 117–141). Cham, Switzerland: Springer.

Andrejczuk, M. (2016). The development of CSR in Poland as seen by managers. In P. Naukowe (Ed.), *Uniwersytetu Ekonomicznego we Wrocławiu* (Vol. 423, pp. 9–22). Wrocław, Poland: Publishing House of Wrocław.

Bachnik, K. (2016). Sustainable consumption through sharing economy, w: Social Responsibility of Organizations. CSR 1.0, CSR 2.0 and what's next? In *Prace Naukowe Uniwersytetu Ekonomicznego we Wrocławiu* (Vol. 423, pp. 35–44). Wrocław, Poland: Publishing House of Wrocław.

Bachnik, K. (2017). Small and medium enterprises' approach towards CSR: Empirical study. In P. Naukowe (Ed.), *Uniwersytetu Ekonomicznego we Wrocławiu* (Vol. 464, pp. 9–19). Wrocław, Poland: Publishing House of Wrocław.

Bay, K. C. (2018). Compliance in der ISO 26000. In A. Kleinfeld & A. Martens (Eds.), *CSR und Compliance – Synergien nutzen durch ein integriertes Management*. Springer Gabler: Wiesbaden, Germany.

Bhattacharya, C., Korschun, D., & Sen, S. (2008). Strengthening stakeholder-company relationships through mutually beneficial corporate social responsibility initiatives. *Journal of Business Ethics, 85*, 257–272.

Bloomberg. (2019). Retrieved June 17, 2019, from www.bloomberg.com

BPB .(2019). *Bundeszentrale für politische Bildung: NGOs – Nicht-Regierungsorganisationen*. Retrieved June 17, 2019, from https://www.bpb.de/nachschlagen/zahlen-und-fakten/globalisierung/52808/ngos

Buchta, K., Monika, J., Skiert, M., & Wilczewski. (2018). University social Warsaw: Klon/Jawor. Responsibility – theory vs. practice. In *Prace Naukowe Uniwersytetu Ekonomicznego we Wrocławiu* (Vol. 520, pp. 22–33). Wrocław, Poland: Publishing House of Wrocław.

Chandler, D. (2017). *Strategic corporate social responsibility: Sustainable value creation*. London: Sage.

Charycka, B., & Gumkowska, M. (2019). *The capacity of NGOs in Poland – Key facts*. Warsaw, Poland: Stowarzyszenia Klon/Jawor. Retrieved January 06, 2020, from https://api.ngo.pl/media/get/110580

Chechelski, P. (2017). Changes in food industry in Poland under the impact of transnational corporations in the 21st century. *Problems of agricultural economics/Zagadnienia Ekonomiki Rolnej, 353*(4), 50–71.

Cieślik, A., & Hagemejer, J. (2014). Multinational enterprises, absorptive capacity and export spillovers: Evidence from polish firm-level data. *Review of Development Economics, 18*(4).

CoEP. (2019). *Council of Europe Publishing: Legal status of non-governmental organisations in Europe. Recommendation CM/Rec (2007)14 and explanatory memorandum*. Retrieved June 17, 2019, from https://rm.coe.int/16807096b7

COM. (2001). *GREEN PAPER – Promoting a European framework for Corporate Social Responsibility*. Commission of the European Communities (presented by the Commission). COM (2001). 366 final, (Brussels, 18.7.2001). Retrieved June 17, 2019, from https://www.europarl.europa.eu/meetdocs/committees/deve/20020122/com(2001)366_en.pdf

COM. (2002). *Corporate social responsibility: A business contribution to sustainable development*. Commission of the European Communities, Com (2002). 347 final (Brussels, 2.7.2002). Retrieved June 17, 2019, from https://www.europarl.europa.eu/meetdocs/committees/deve/20020122/com(2001)366_en.pdf

Crowther, D. (2018). The life and death of corporate social responsibility. In D. Growther & S. Seifi (Eds.), *Redefining corporate social responsibility* (Vol. 13). Bingley: Emerald Publishing Limited.

Dančák, B., & Hlousek, V. (2007). Central and Eastern Europe in the process of globalization and Europeanization: Comparing the Czech Republic and Poland. *Contemporary Studies in Economic and Financial Analysis, 89*, 227–250.

Dancewicz, B., & Struve, F. (2019). The influence of MNEss on CSR in Poland: Strategies, opportunities and challenges. In A. Długopolska-Mikonowicz, S. Przytuła, & C. Stehr (Eds.), *Corporate social responsibility in Poland - Strategies, opportunities and challenges* (pp. 149–165). Cham, Switzerland: Springer.

Daszyńska-Żygadło, K. (2019). Impact of CSR on operating financial results: The case of companies from RESPECT index: Strategies, opportunities and challenges. In A. Długopolska-Mikonowicz, S. Przytuła, & C. Stehr (Eds.), *Corporate social responsibility in Poland – Strategies, opportunities and challenges* (pp. 59–72). Cham, Switzerland: Springer.

Długosz, P. (2019). Transformation trauma in Central Eastern Europe. *Środkowoeuropejskie Studia Polityczne [Central European Political Studies], 1, 95*, –121.

Dunning, J. H., & Lundan, S. M. (2008). *Multinational enterprises and the global economy*. Cheltenham: Edward Elgar Publishing.

Dyczkowska, J., Krasodomska, J., & Michalak, J. (2016). CSR in Poland: Institutional context, legal framework and voluntary initiatives. *Accounting and Management Information Systems, 15*(2), 206–254.

EcB. (2019). *Ecyclopedia Britannica: Non-Governmental Organisation (NGO)*. Retrieved June 17, 2019, from https://www.britannica.com/topic/nongovernmental-organization

European Commission. (2003). *Commission Recommendation of 6 May 2003*. Retrieved June 17, 2019, from https://eur-lex.europa.eu/legal-content/EN/TXT/PDF/?uri=CELEX:32003H0361&from=DE

Eurostat. (2019). *Eurostat – Definiton of SME*. Retrieved June 17, 2019, from https://ec.europa.eu/eurostat/web/structural-business-statistics/structural-business-statistics/SMEs

Eweje, G., & Bathurst, R. J. (2017). Leading for corporate social responsibility and sustainability. In G. Eweje & R. J. Bathurst (Eds.), *CSR, sustainability, and leadership*. London: Routledge.

Factsheet. (2018). *2018 SBA Factsheet: Poland*, European Commission. Retrieved August 04, 2019, from https://ec.europa.eu/docsroom/documents/32581/attachments/22/translations/en/renditions/native

FdB. (2019). *Förderberatung des Bundes – Forschung und Innovation*. Retrieved June 17, 2019, from https://www.foerderinfo.bund.de/de/kmu-definition-der-europaeischen-kommission-972.php

FOP. (2017). *Forum Odpowiedzalnego Biznesu: Znamy Ranking Odpowiedzialnych Firm 2017*. Retrieved June 17, 2019, from http://odpowiedzialnybiznes.pl/aktualno%C5%9Bci/znamy-ranking-odpowiedzialnych-firm-2017

FOP. (2018). *Forum Odpowiedzalnego Biznesu: Pełne wyniki Rankingu Odpowiedzialnych Firm 2018*. Retrieved June 17, 2019, from http://odpowiedzialnybiznes.pl/aktualno%C5%9Bci/pelne-wyniki-rankingu-odpowiedzialnych-firm

FOP. (2019). *Forum Odpowiedzalnego Biznesu: In Poland responsible business is growing at a rate of 30%*. Retrieved June 17, 2019, from https://odpowiedzialnybiznes.pl/aktualno%C5%9Bci/in-poland-responsible-business-is-growing-at-a-rate-of-30/

Freeman, R. E. (2005). The development of stakeholder theory: An idiosyncratic approach. In K. G. Smith & M. A. Hitt (Eds.), *The Oxford handbook of management theory: The process of theory development*. Oxford, UK: Oxford University Press.

Gabler. (2019). *Gabler Wirtschaftslexikon; Non-Governmental Organisation*. Retrieved June 17, 2019, from https://wirtschaftslexikon.gabler.de/definition/non-governmental-organization-ngo-39218/version-262632

Gasparski, W. (1994). *Etyka biznesu. Wyb or bibliograficzny*. Warszawa: Fundacja im. S. Batorego.

Gasparski, W. (1999). Etyka biznesu – szkice do portretu. In J. Dietl & W. Gasparski (Eds.), *Etykabiznesu* (pp. 14–37). Warszawa: Wydawnictwo Naukowe PWN.

Geryk, M. (2018). Sustainable Development Goals as a Perspective for Higher Education Institutions. In *Prace Naukowe Uniwersytetu Ekonomicznego we Wrocławiu* (Vol. 520, pp. 54–63). Wrocław, Poland: Publishing House of Wrocław.

Gorynia, M. (2014). Ewolucja pozycji gospodarki polskiej w gospodarce globalnej i w gospodarce Unii Europejskiej. *Ekonomista, 3*, 287–300.

Gorynia, M. (2017). The position of Poland's economy in the economy of the European Union in 2003-2014. In *Przegląd zachodni* (pp. 157–182). Poznań, Poland: Instytut Zachodni.

Gorynia, M., Nowak, J., & Wolniak, R. (2003). Globalization of a transitional economy. *Journal of East-West Business, 9*, 29–46.

Gumkowska, M., & Herbst, J. (2006). *Basic facts on the NGO sector in Poland 2006*. Warsaw, Poland: Stowarzyszenia Klon/Jawor.

GUS. (2015). *Małe i średnie przedsiębiorstwa niefinansowe w Polsce w latach 2009-2013;* Główny Urząd Statystyczny (GUS). Studia I Analizy Statystyczne, Warsaw. Retrieved June 17, 2019, from https://stat.gov.pl/download/gfx/portalinformacyjny/pl/defaultaktualnosci/5502/22/1/1/male_i_srednie.pdf

GUS. (2018). *Sektor non-profit w 2016 r. Stowarzyszenia, fundacje, społeczne podmioty wyznaniowe, samorząd gospodarczy i zawodowy*, Główny/Urząd Statystyczny Urząd Statystyczny w Krakowie, Warsawa/Kraków 2018, Poland. Retrieved June 17, 2019, from https://stat.gov.pl/download/gfx/portalinformacyjny/pl/defaultaktualnosci/5490/12/3/1/dzialalnosc_organizacji_non-profit_w_2015.pdf

GUS. (2019a). *Atlas Przedsiębiorstw*, Główny Urząd Statystyczny, Warsaw. Retrieved August 04, 2019, from https://stat.gov.pl/download/gfx/portalinformacyjny/pl/defaultaktualnosci/5502/30/1/1/atlas_przedsiebiorstw_.pdf

GUS. (2019b). *Przedsiębiorstwa niefinansowe powstałe w latach 2013-2017*, Główny Urząd Statystyczny, Warsaw. Retrieved from https://stat.gov.pl/download/gfx/portalinformacyjny/pl/defaultaktualnosci/5502/24/4/1/przedsiebiorstwa_niefinansowe_powstale_w_latach_2013_2017.pdf

Hackett, C. (2016). *Development in an era of capital control: Embedding corporate social responsibility within a transnational regulatory framework*. Hampshire: Palgrave-Macmillan.

Hansen, K. (2017). CSR und Diversity. In K. Hansen (Ed.), *CSR und Diversity Management - Erfolgreiche Vielfalt in Organisationen*. Wiesbaden, Germany: Springer.

Hawkins, D. E. (2006). *Balancing tomorrow's sustainability and today's profitability*. Hampshire: Palgrave-Macmillan.

Hiß, S. (2006). *Warum übernehmen Unternehmen gesellschaftliche Verantwortung? Ein soziologischer Erklärungsversuch*. Frankfurt: Campus-Verlag.

Hiß, S. (2009). From implicit to explicit corporate social responsibility – Institutional change as a fight for myths. *Business Ethics Quarterly, 19*(3), 433–451.

Hiß, S., & Nagel, S. (2016). Unternehmen als gesellschaftliche Akteure. In A. Maurer (Ed.), *Handbuch der Wirtschaftssoziologie*. Wiesbanden, Germany: Springer.

Ietto-Gillies, G. (2011). The role of transnational corporations in the globalisation process. In J. Michie (Ed.), *The handbook of globalisation* (pp. 173–184). Cheltenham, UK: Edward Elgar Publishing.

Ietto-Gillies, G. (2012). *Transnational corporations and International production: Concepts, theories and effects* (2nd ed.). Cheltenham: Edward Elgar.

IFM-Bonn. (2019). *Institut für Mittelstandsforschung*. Retrieved June 17, 2019, from https://www.ifm-bonn.org/definitionen/kmu-definition-der-eu-kommission/

IMF. (2016a). *Republic of Poland – At a* glance. Retrieved June 17, 2019, from https://www.imf.org/en/Countries/POL

IMF. (2016b). *IMF DataMapper - Real GDP growth*. Retrieved June 17, 2019, from https://www.imf.org/external/datamapper/NGDP_RPCH@WEO/OEMDC/ADVEC/WEOWORLD/POL?year=2019

ISO. (2010, November). *DIN ISO 26000. Leitfaden zur gesellschaftlichen Verantwortung von Organisationen*, Bundesministerium für Arbeit und Soziales, Bonn.

Jastrzębska, E. (2016). *Zarządzanie różnorodnością jako element CSR - dobre praktyki i korzyści, Cracow*. Kraków: UE-Kraków.

Keane, J. (2010). Civil society, definitions and approaches. In H. K. Anheier & S. Toepler (Eds.), *International encyclopedia of civil society*. New York: Springer.

KfW. (2019). *Kreditanstalt für Wiederaufbau*. Retrieved June 17, 2019, from https://www.kfw.de/Download-Center/F%C3%B6rderprogramme-(Inlandsf%C3%B6rderung)/PDF-Dokumente/6000000196-KMU-Definition.pdf

Kuitto, K. (2016). *Post-communist welfare states in European context patterns of welfare policies in Central and Eastern Europe*. Cheltenham: Edward Elgar Publishing.

Lakatoś, Z. (2017). *Corporate social performance in emerging markets: Sustainable leadership in an interdependent world*. London: Routledge.

Macuda, M., Matuszak, Ł., & Różańska, E. (2015). The concept of CSR in accounting theory and practice in Poland: An empirical study. *Zeszyty Teoretyczne Rachunkowości [Accounting Theoretical Papers], 84*(140), 115–138.

Magala, S. (2019). Red roots of corporate irresponsibilities (Corporate social responsibility with a historical twist). Strategies, opportunities and challenges. In A. Długopolska-Mikonowicz, S. Przytuła, & C. Stehr (Eds.), *Corporate social responsibility in Poland – Strategies, opportunities and challenges* (pp. 31–39). Cham, Switzerland: Springer.

Managers-Survey. (2015). *CSR managers survey in Central Europe. How CSR has influenced Central European Societies and Economies. lessons learnt and future trends. Deloitte Responsible Business Forum*. Warsaw. Retrieved August 04, 2019, from http://odpowiedzialnybiznes.pl/wp-content/uploads/2015/10/CSR_Managers_Survey_2015_in_Central_Europe.pdf

McKinsey. (2019). *Poland 2025. Europe's new growth engine*, McKinsey & Company. Retrieved June 17, 2019, from https://mckinsey.pl/wp-content/uploads/2015/10/Poland-2025_full_report.pdf

MGRP. (2010). *CSR Społeczna Odpowiedzialność Biznesu w Polsce*. Ministry of Economy. Ministerstwo Gospodarki. Retrieved May 20, 2019, from http://www.urc.gov.pl/download/9/4976/CSRwPolsce.pdf

Mierzejewski, D. (2018). *Poland Socialbriefing: Non-Governmental Organizations in Poland*, Budapest, Hungary: China-CEE Institute (Vol. 12, No. 3 (PL)) (ISSN: 25601601). Retrieved January 06, 2020, from https://china-cee.eu/wp-content/uploads/2018/12/47(3)Poland.pdf

Nowak, A. K., & Chowicz, E. (2018). Social responsibility of an organization from the perspective of public universities. In *Prace Naukowe Uniwersytetu Ekonomicznego we Wrocławiu* (Vol. 520, pp. 34–45). Wrocław, Poland: Publishing House of Wrocław.

Nowosielski, M. (2008). *Revival of the civil society. Development of the third sector in Poland 1989-2008*. Poznań, Poland: Instytut Zachodni, Series: IZ Policy Papers No 2/2008.

O'Connell, B. (2000). Civil society: Definitions and descriptions. *Nonprofit and Voluntary Sector Quarterly - Nonprofit and Voluntary Sector Quarterly, 29*(3), 471–478.

OECD. (2017). *Entrepreneurship at a Glance 2017*. Paris: OECD Publishing. Retrieved June 17, 2019, from https://doi.org/10.1787/entrepreneur_aag-2017-en

OECD. (2019). *Enterprises by business size (indicator)*. Retrieved August 04, 2019, from https://doi.org/10.1787/31d5eeaf-en

Paliwoda-Matiolańska, A. (2014). Corporate social responsibility in Poland: Is it an integral part of business processand opportunity for value creation? In J. Reichel (Ed.), *CSR trends. Beyond business as usual, 2014* (pp. 7–28). Łódź, Poland: CSR Impact.

Petrie, C., & South, A. (2014). Development of civil society in Myanmar. In M. Gravers & Y. Flemming (Eds.), *Burma/Myanmar – Where now?* (pp. 86–94). Copenhagen: Nordic Institute of Asian Studies Press.

Piatkowski, M. (2018). *Europe's growth champion: Insights from the economic rise of Poland*. Oxford, UK: Oxford University Press.

Pitelis, C., & Sugden, R. (2000). The (theory of the) transnational firm: The 1990s and beyoned. In C. Pitelis & R. Sugden (Eds.), *The nature of the transnational firm* (pp. 1–9). London: Routledge.

Polish Constitution. (2019). Retrieved January 06, 2020, from https://www.sejm.gov.pl/prawo/konst/angielski/kon1.htm

Polzin, J. M., Kirchner, B., & Pollert, A. (2013). *Duden - Wirtschaft von A bis Z: Grundlagenwissen für Schule und Studium, Beruf und Alltag* (5th ed.). Mannheim: Dudenverlag.

Popowska, M. (2015a). Europe, between mandatory and voluntary approach to CSR: Some new evidence from the Polish listed companies. *Journal of Yaşar University, 10*, 38–45.

Popowska, M. (2015b). CSR and small business from the international and national perspective. *Prace Naukowe Uniwersytetu Ekonomicznego we Wrocławiu, 387*, 136–148.

Popowska, M. (2016). Shaping new generations of managers and consumers: CSR implementation and higher education system in Poland. In D. Turker, C. A. Vural, & S. O. Idowu (Eds.), *CSR, sustainability, ethics and governance* (pp. 115–138). Cham, Switzerland: Springer.

Potocki, T. (2015). Corporate social responsibility in Poland: From theory to practice. In S. O. Idowu, R. Schmidpeter, & M. S. Fifka (Eds.), *Corporate social responsibility in Europe. CSR, sustainability, ethics and governance* (pp. 245–269). Cham, Switzerland: Springer.

Prokopowicz, D. (2016). The importance of economic globalization in the context of the development of the financial system in Poland. *International Journal of New Economics and Social Sciences, 4*(2), 7–17. https://doi.org/10.5604/01.3001.0010.3862.

Przewłocka, J. (2013). *Polskie Organizacje Pozarządowe 2012*. Warsaw, Poland: Stowarzyszenia Klon/Jawor. Retrieved January 06, 2020, from https://api.ngo.pl/media/get/119192

Przytuła, S., Formánková, S., Ubrežiová, I., & Dunay, A. (2019). Corporate social responsibility in visegrad countries (Poland, Czech Republic, Slovakia, Hungary) overall landscape. In A. Długopolska-Mikonowicz, S. Przytuła, & C. Stehr (Eds.), *Corporate social responsibility in Poland – Strategies, opportunities and challenges* (pp. 325–353). Cham, Switzerland: Springer.

Rasche, A., Morsing, M., & Moon, J. (2017). *Corporate social responsibility: Strategy, communication, governance*. Cambridge: Cambridge University Press.

Rojek-Nowosielska, M. (2019). CSR level of enterprises in Poland: Before and after transition. In A. Długopolska-Mikonowicz, S. Przytuła, & C. Stehr (Eds.), *Corporate social responsibility in Poland – Strategies, opportunities and challenges* (pp. 19–29). Cham, Switzerland: Springer.

Rok, B. (2004). Państwo jako 'trzecia strona' w dialogu między sektorem biznesu a społeczeństwem obywatelskim. In K. W. Dobre państwo & J. Kubin (Eds.), *Wyższej Szkoły Przedsiębiorczości iZarządzaniaim*. Warszawa: Leona Koźmińskiego.

Rok, B. (2013). Społeczna odpowiedzialność biznesu. In W. Gasparski (Ed.), *Biznes, Etyka, Odpowiedzialność* (pp. 423–428). Warszawa: Wydawnictwo Naukowe PWN.

Rok, B. (2019). Transition from corporate responsibility to sustainable strategic management: Strategies, opportunities and challenges. In A. Długopolska-Mikonowicz, S. Przytuła, & C. Stehr (Eds.), *Corporate social responsibility in Poland – Strategies, opportunities and challenges* (pp. 3–18). Cham, Switzerland: Springer.

Siemiątkowski, A. (2017). The influence of transnational corporations on society's safety based on activity of Amazon.com in Poland and Great Britain. *Toruńskie Studia Międzynarodowe, 1*(9), 131–141.

Skrzypczyńska, K. (2015). Social responsibility of companies operating in Poland. *Journal of Corporate Responsibility and Leadership., 1*(1), 71–84. https://doi.org/10.12775/JCRL.2014.005.

Sokołowska-Durkalec, A. (2018). Methodical Dilemmas in resarch on small enterprise social irresonsiblity. *Prace Naukowe Uniwersytetu Ekonomicznego we Wrocławiu, 520*, 128–135.

Sokołowska-Durkalec, A. (2019). Social responsibility management in a small enterprise: Selected problems and good practices. In A. Długopolska-Mikonowicz, S. Przytuła, & C. Stehr (Eds.), *Corporate social responsibility in Poland – Strategies, opportunities and challenges* (pp. 135–147). Cham, Switzerland: Springer.

Stehr, C., & Vodosek, M. (2017). Chance und Herausforderung: Diversity management und CSR am Beispiel internationaler Unternehmen. In K. Hansen (Ed.), *CSR und Diversity Management: Erfolgreiche Vielfalt in Organisationen* (pp. 177–192). Wiesbaden, Germany: Springer Gabler.

Stroinska, M. (2013). Civil society, government and the opposition movements in Poland: The post-communist role reversal. *East European Review, 111*, 53–64.

Szustek, A. (2008). *Polski sektor społeczny*. Warszawa, Poland: Uniwersytet Warszawski/Oficyna Wydawnicza ASPRA-JR.

Tanski, S. (2017). Economic developments in Poland in the context of its role within the transatlantic sphere. In M. Zachara (Ed.), *Poland in transatlantic relations after 1989. Miracle fair* (pp. 311–346). Newcastle upon Tyne, UK: Cambridge Scholars Publishing.

UN-EaSC. (2019). *United Nations – Economic and social council: Resolution 1996/31*. Retrieved June 17, 2019, from https://www.un.org/documents/ecosoc/res/1996/eres1996-31.htm

UNDP. (2007). *Corporate social responsibility in Poland – A baseline study*. Warsaw, Poland: United Nations Development Programme in Poland. Retrieved June 17, 2019, from http://ekonomiaspoleczna.info/media/biblioteka/wb/spoleczna-odpowiedzialnosc-biznesu-w-pl-wstepna-analiza.pdf

UNIDO. (2017). *What is CSR? United Nations Industrial Development Organization*. Retrieved June 17, 2019, from https://www.olmun.org/uploads/2017/Documents/committeeguides/UNIDO_2017.pdf

UNRIC. (2019). *UNRIC – Regionales Informationszentrum der Vereinten Nationen für Westeuropa: Nichtregierungsorganisationen (NGOs) und die Vereinten Nationen*. Retrieved June 17, 2019, from https://www.unric.org/de/aufbau-der-uno/85

Urbański, F. (2019). Employees motivation in CSR projects: Case study of WrOpenUp: Strategies, opportunities and challenges. In A. Długopolska-Mikonowicz, S. Przytuła, & C. Stehr (Eds.), *Corporate social responsibility in Poland – Strategies, opportunities and challenges* (pp. 253–272). Cham, Switzerland: Springer.

Viterna, J., Clough, E., & Clarke, K. (2015). Reclaiming the "third sector" from "civil society". A new agenda for development studies. *Sociology of Development, 1*, 173–207.

Voorhees, R. D., Seim, E. L., & Coppett, J. I. (1992). Global logistics and stateless corporations. *Transportation Practitioners Journal, 59*(2), 144–151.

Waniak-Michałak, H., Macuda, M., & Krasodomska, J. (2016). Corporate social responsibility and accounting in Poland: A literature review. *Accounting and Management Information Systems, 15*(2), 255–303.

Wiktorska-Święcka, A. (2019). Quo Vadis, corporate social responsibility in Poland? Strategies, opportunities and challenges. In A. Długopolska-Mikonowicz, S. Przytuła, & C. Stehr (Eds.), *Corporate social responsibility in Poland – Strategies, opportunities and challenges* (pp. 311–324). Cham, Switzerland: Springer.

Wołczek, P. (2015). Development of the CSR concept in Poland - Progress or stagnation? *Prace Naukowe Uniwersytetu Ekonomicznego we Wrocławiu, 387*, 200–214.

Wołczek, P. (2019). Strategic CSR in Poland. In A. Długopolska-Mikonowicz, S. Przytuła, & C. Stehr (Eds.), *Corporate social responsibility in Poland – Strategies, opportunities and challenges* (pp. 325–353). Cham, Switzerland: Springer.

CSR in Brazil

Christopher Stehr and Martin Tobias Knopp

Abstract Brazil is a rising economy located in South America. It is the world's fifth-largest country by area but also the fifth-largest country by population. On the one hand there is the Atlantic Ocean and on the other hand the Amazon river, the Amazon rainforest, and an extensive amount of natural resources—therefore: Brazil is one of the world's most megadiverse countries.

This article presents the recent developments and the status quo within Corporate Social Responsibility (CSR) in Brazil. Our focus of attention will be mainly on the following two leading topics:

Firstly, it is the topic of environment and environment protection in Brazil. In 2015 the Mariana dam disaster and in 2019 the Brumadinho dam disaster occurred—both accounting for the worst environmental disasters in Brazilian history. Similarly, the increasing rate of deforestation of the Amazon rainforest supported by the Brazilian government is endangering the living space of indigenous tribes, the home of diverse wildlife, and the ecological system. Due to the climate crisis the ecological restoration of the Amazon rainforest—the earth's 'green lungs'—became the subject of significant global interest and consequently a part of this article.

Secondly, it is the topic of corruption in Brazil. In 2014 the 'Operation Lava Jato' started and uncovered a system of corruption developed by private companies to corrupt parts of the federal, state, and municipal governments. This article presents the current measures concerning corruption and corporate compliance in Brazil.

With a summary and outlook on the future of CSR in Brazil this article ends.

Keywords Amazon rainforest · Anti-corruption laws · Brazil · Car wash · Clean Company Act · Corporate compliance · Corruption · Environmental disaster · Indigenous tribes · Iron ore mining · Lava Jato · Soybean farming

C. Stehr · M. T. Knopp (✉)
German Graduate School of Management and Law, Heilbronn, Germany
e-mail: welcome@polymundo.de; martin.knopp@ggs.de

N. Mitra, R. Schmidpeter (eds.), *Corporate Social Responsibility in Rising Economies*, CSR, Sustainability, Ethics & Governance,
https://doi.org/10.1007/978-3-030-53775-3_10

1 Introduction

We all remember about the 2014 FIFA World Cup in Brazil as well as the 2016 Summer Olympics in Rio de Janeiro. Brazil hosted successfully the world sports community and their supporters. All around the globe people got an impression about the Brazilian people, their culture, economy, and its guest-friendly atmosphere.

Undoubtedly, everybody could view Brazil as one of the most rising economies in the world. With more than 210 million people and 8.5 million km^2 Brazil is both the world's fifth largest country by population and the world's fifth largest country by area. Furthermore, Brazil is a country located in South America with a unique environmental heritage: on the one hand there is the Atlantic ocean and on the other hand the Amazon river, the Amazon rainforest, and an extensive amount of natural resources—hence, Brazil is also one of the most megadiverse countries in the world (CIA, 2019; IBGE, 2019a, 2019b).

The discourse about CSR in Brazil in the area of science and research but also in politics and society is dominated mainly by the following two dimensions:

Firstly, it is the dimension of environment and environment protection. Brazil has current issues concerning deforestation in the Amazon basin. The Amazon habitat is being destroyed. As a consequence, a multitude of plant and animal species indigenous to the area is being endangered seriously. But there are also current issues like land degradation and water pollution caused by improper mining activities of some iron ore mines (CIA, 2019).

Secondly, there is the dimension of corruption and corporate compliance. In 2014 the 'Operation Lava Jato' started and uncovered a system of corruption developed by private companies to corrupt parts of the federal, state, and municipal governments. In the Transparency Internationals 'Corruption Perceptions Index 2018' Brazil is currently ranking on position 105 out of 180 countries. To combat corruption in general, serious efforts have to be made both by the Brazilian government and also by the companies in Brazil (Ferreira, 2019, 244–245; Transparency International, 2019b).

Following the preface about CSR in Brazil this article goes on to explain the recent developments (Sect. 2), the status quo of environment protection in close cooperation with private companies as well as corruption and corporate compliance (Sect. 3). Finally, the article concludes with a short summary and outlook on the future of CSR in Brazil (Sect. 4).

2 Recent Developments Concerning CSR in Brazil

2.1 Improper Mining Activities and Deforestation

The first recent development—the national and international 'CSR in Brazil'—discourse is focusing on improper mining activities in Brazil and their consequences for the Brazilian environment and society:

On November 5, 2015 the Mariana dam disaster occurred where an iron ore tailing dam collapsed near the city of Mariana, Minas Gerais. As a result, a torrent of sludge flooded, destroyed, and wiped out the village of Bento Rodrigues. The deluge not only cost the lives of 19 people but also was spilling contaminated water through the Duce river into the Atlantic Ocean. As a result of the failure of the dam, people became homeless. In consequence of the pollution of the water, people of indigenous tribes were no longer able to use the Duce river on which they depended. Moreover, other people like fishermen lost their livelihood. At the end, the Mariana dam disaster was one of the worst environmental disasters in Brazilian history (Dias Carneiro, 2016). Finally, the Brazilian government started a criminal investigation against the iron ore mine Samarco Mineração S.A., a joint venture of the Brazilian Vale S.A. and the British-Australian BHP Billiton plc., because of the collapse of the dam. In the end, the Samarco Mineração S.A. was sentenced (a) to pay a fine over (United States Dollar) US $4.8 billion for the incident (the pollution of water and damages included) and (b) to establish an autonomous and independent foundation (named the Renova Foundation today) in order to repair the damages caused by the burst of the dam. Furthermore, the Samarco Mineração S.A. had to compensate the people separately who were affected by the disaster and suffered damage (Reuters, 2016; Samarco, 2019).

But the Mariana dam disaster was not the last collapse of a Brazilian tailing dam that could be ranked in a list of the worst mining disasters in the last decades:

On January 25, 2019 occurred the Brumadinho dam disaster. Yet another iron ore tailing dam collapsed in the Brazilian state Minas Gerais. A sea of mud killed at least 248 people, flooded the city of Brumadinho, polluted the water of the Paraopeba river, and contaminated the whole ecosystem of that region. It was a dam used by Córrego do Feijão S.A., another iron ore mine owned by the Vale S.A. In the meantime, a court has frozen US $29 billion of Vale S.A.'s assets. The judge said that the funds should be used to compensate the families and businesses affected by this big industrial disaster (BBC, 2019; Reuters, 2019a). In a press release published on July 19, 2019 Vale S.A. informed:

> Since the breach of the B1 Dam at the Córrego do Feijão Mine, Vale has been dedicated to quickly repairing the damage in Brumadinho and other municipalities affected along the Paraopeba River, with actions that include indemnification, donations, medical and psychological assistance, the purchasing of medicines and the construction of safety structures, among other initiatives. After 6 months, the company has already agreed on the final individual and labour indemnities, structured and implemented monthly financial transfers to more than one hundred thousand people, started the main tailings removal and environmental recovery works, formalized donations to local governments and state public agencies, ensured the care of the animals and set up the entire system for monitoring the water quality of the Paraopeba river.
>
> The causes of the breach are still being investigated. Since the moment the dam breached, Vale has submitted all the relevant documentation and information requested and, as a major interested party in the factual outcome of the investigation, will continue contributing in every way possible (Vale, 2019a).

In this context it is to mention: In the course of criminal investigation the state prosecutors arrested three Brazil mining company employees, but also two engineers

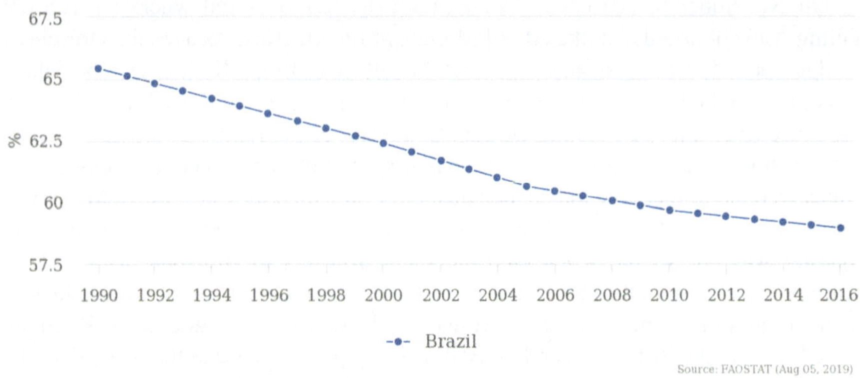

Fig. 1 Forest land—share in land area (in %) from 1990 to 2016. Source: FAO (2019)

of the TÜV Süd, a German technical inspection association, who certified the safety of the dam after its inspection in 2018. In the meantime, TÜV Süd lost, until further notice, in Brazil the permission to issue safety securities for dams. Furthermore, a court has frozen US $15 million of TÜV Süd's Brazilian assets for possible claims for indemnification (BBC, 2019; Merkur, 2019; Reuters, 2019a).

The second recent development—the national and international 'CSR in Brazil'—discourse is focusing on, is the deforestation of the Amazon rainforest in Brazil and its consequences for the Brazilian environment and the world's climate:

As depicted in Fig. 1 the share of forest land in the Brazilian land area is steadily diminishing from 65.41% in 1990 to 58.93% in 2016 (FAO, 2019). The new President of Brazil, Jair Bolsonaro, who denies the climate change, reinforced this trend with his current agricultural policy. In July 2019, over 2254 km^2 of Brazilian rainforest were cleared. As compared with July 2018, the deforestation was only 597 km^2. Normally the newly reclaimed land will be used as meadowland, but also as farmland for the expansion of export-oriented agriculture industries, for example: to produce soybeans and meat (Zeit, 2019).

The destruction of the Brazilian rainforest has serious consequences for the earth's 'green lungs': One fifth of the world's oxygen is produced by the Amazon rainforest—as a result of converting more than 60 billion tons of Carbon Dioxide (CO_2) a year. Approximately 60% of the Amazon rainforest is located in Brazil. Currently, the flora and fauna, the wildlife habitat—the ecosystem of the Brazilian rainforest will be destructed step by step. In the meantime, indigenous tribes are already threatening seriously to have to leave the Brazilian rainforest involuntarily—because of deforestation in their former living environment. In addition, the deforestation of the Amazon rainforest is demonstrably one of the drivers for the current world's climate crises (Greenpeace, 2019a; IPCC, 2019; Zeit, 2019).

2.2 Corruption

As already mentioned in Sect. 1, yet another recent development in the national and international 'CSR in Brazil' discourse focusses on the corruption in Brazil and its consequences for the Brazilian economy and society.

Transparency International, an international non-governmental organization with the mission "*to stop corruption and promote transparency, accountability, and integrity at all levels and across all sectors of society*" (Transparency International, 2019e), uses the following definition of the term '*Corruption*':

> Corruption is the abuse of entrusted power for private gain. It can be classified as grand, petty and political, depending on the amounts of money lost and the sector where it occurs (Transparency International, 2019a).

In the Transparency Internationals 'Corruption Perceptions Index 2018' Brazil is ranked on position 105 out of 180 countries (Fig. 2):

A country's score indicates the perceived level of public sector corruption on a scale of 0 (highly corrupt) to 100 (very clean). With a score of 35 in 2018, Brazil belongs to countries with high corruption. Following the results of the Brazilian scores over the last few years, there is no fundamental turnaround of that negative trend visible (Transparency International, 2019b). But what hinders anti-corruption efforts? In general, "*corruption is much more likely to flourish where democratic foundations are weak and, as we have seen in many countries where undemocratic and populist politicians can use it to their advantage*", argues Delia Ferreira Rubio, Chair of Transparency International (Transparency International, 2019b, 2019c).

One impressive example for corruption in Brazil is the so called "'Operation Lava Jato': Clean cars, dirty money". The case is also listed on Transparency International's compilation of "25 corruption scandals that shook the world" (Transparency International, 2019d).

The 'Lava Jato' investigation was carried out by the Brazilian federal police in 2014. They uncovered a sophisticated scheme of corruption by analyzing petrol station financial transactions. It was a system of corruption developed by private companies to corrupt relevant parts of federal, state, and municipal governments in exchange for economic benefits, financing political campaigns, and illegally

Rank	Country	Region	2018	2017	2016	2015
1	Denmark	Western Europe & EU	88	88	90	91
2	New Zealand	Asia Pacific	87	89	90	91
3	Finland	Western Europe & EU	85	85	89	90
...	...	...	...	...	...	...
105	*Brazil*	*Americas*	*35*	*37*	*40*	*38*
...	...	...	...	...	...	...
180	Somalia	Sub-Saharan Africa	10	9	10	8

Fig. 2 Transparency Internationals 'Corruption Perceptions Index 2018'. Source: Transparency International (2019b)

enriching politicians and governmental employees (Ferreira, 2019, 244–245). On the one side, more than 20 corporations were involved in that network that also included the Brazilian giants Petrólea Brasileiro S.A. (oil) and Odebrecht S.A. (construction). On the other side, at least 12 countries in Latin America and Africa were affected by and more than 150 politicians and businesspeople were convicted in this tremendous case of corruption. With payments of nearly US $1 billion in bribes and more than US $6.5 billion in fines by now the 'Operation Lava Jato' developed to one of the most unprecedented and biggest corruption scandals in Brazilian history (Cavazotte, Cohen, & Brunelli, 2019; Smith, Valle, & Schmidt, 2017; Transparency International, 2019d).

On October 28, 2018 Jair Bolsonaro, a far-right member of the Social Liberal Party (PSL), was elected as the 38th President of Brazil. One of his most important campaign promises was to "*free the country from the yoke of corruption*" (Economist, 2019). His presidency started on January 1, 2019, but his popularity is falling rapidly. Brazilian people feel baffled by his actions and his speeches. There are also protests, scandals, corruption claims, and allegations of mafia links—"*even the right [are] dismayed*" after his first 6 months as President of Brazil reports the Guardian (Phillips, 2019). In particular Bolsonaros administration seems to be as scandal-prone as the administration before his presidency: There are investigations against his tourism minister, but also against his son Flávio Bolsonaro who is a senator from Rio de Janeiro—for money laundering (Economist, 2019).

Hopes rest on Sérgio Moro. He is the Brazilian Justice Minister and in charge of fighting corruption and crime. But his reputation is also damaged because of leaked messages concerning his actions as the judge in charge of the 'Lava Jato' investigation: On the one hand, he brought many businesspeople and politicians—including the former president Luiz Inácio Lula da Silva—in prison because of corruption. Therefore, he became a national hero of the Brazilian people. But on the other hand, leaked messages uncovered that he, as the judge in charge of the 'Lava Jato' investigation, also collaborated improperly with prosecutors (Economist, 2019; Winter, 2019).

As depicted in Fig. 3 the actual developments in Brazil led Transparency International to put Brazil on the current list of countries to watch (Transparency International, 2019b).

3 Corporate Social Responsibility

3.1 Definition

Over the last decades 'Corporate Social Responsibility' is widely-spread in research and practice. As a result, many definitions and approaches about CSR have been developed in literature till date. One example how to define CSR is the pragmatic approach chosen by Matten & Moon in 2008: CSR refers to "*clearly articulated and*

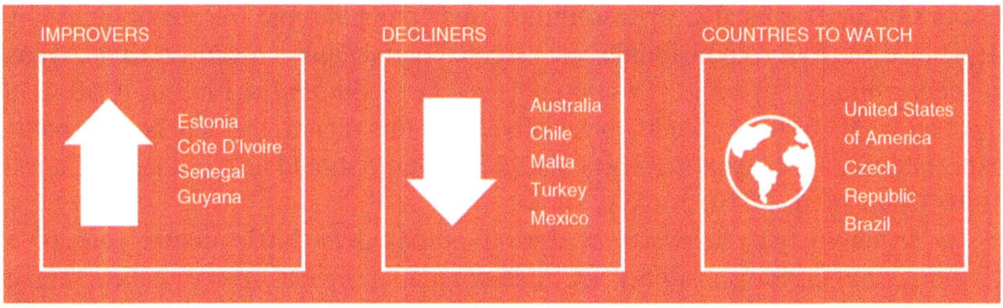

Fig. 3 Highlights of the Transparency Internationals 'Corruption Perceptions Index 2018'. Source: Transparency International (2019b)

communicated policies and practices of corporations that reflect business responsibility for some of the wider societal good" (Matten & Moon, 2008, 405).

However, there is no common definition for Corporate Social Responsibility in research and practice yet (Garriga & Melé, 2004; Salazar & Husted, 2008, 141–142). Votaw already said about CSR: "*The term is a brilliant one; it means something, but not always the same thing, to everybody*" (Votaw, 1973, 11).

But what is the nature of Corporate Social Responsibility in general? Carroll initially proposed and subsequently refined a multilayer concept—the so called 'Four-Part Model of Corporate Social Responsibility'—depicted in Fig. 4 (Carroll, 1991; Crane, Matten, Glozer, & Spence, 2019, 50–53):

As one of the most established and accepted models, it distinguishes Corporate Social Responsibility into four interrelated aspects: economic responsibilities, legal

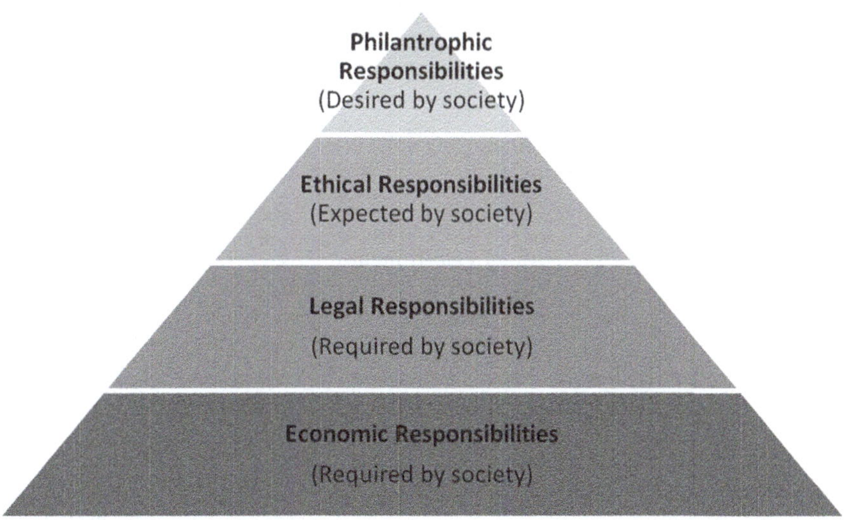

Fig. 4 Carroll's 'Four-Part Model of Corporate Social Responsibility'. Source: Adapted from Carroll (1991) (Fig. 3); Crane et al. (2019) (Fig. 2.2)

responsibilities, ethical responsibilities, and philanthropic responsibilities. As depicted these four responsibilities are essential parts of his consecutive multilayered concept within a pyramid. In consequence, the requirement for true CSR is to meet all levels of the pyramid consecutively. In this regard, the dependence on the expectations of society at that particular point in time should be considered (Carroll, 1991; Crane et al., 2019, 50–53).

As an alternative, Schwartz & Carroll proposed in 2003 another concept of Corporate Social Responsibility—a three-domain approach—the so called 'Three-Domain Model'—as depicted in Fig. 5 (Schwartz & Carroll, 2003):

In this alternative approach, there are only three core domains: economic responsibilities, legal responsibilities, and ethical responsibilities. As illustrated, it is a Venn model framework with no hierarchical relationships among the core domains. Contrary to the 'Four-Part Model of CSR' in the 'Three-Domain Model of CSR' the philanthropic responsibilities are subsumed under ethical and/or economic responsibilities. As a result of the overlap of the three core domains, seven CSR categories emerged (Schwartz & Carroll, 2003).

With the 'ISO 26000 Social Responsibility' the International Organization for Standardization created an international standard that provides guidance to all types of organizations (not only to corporations) regarding social responsibility (ISO 26000:2010, Article 1). The intentions of this international standard are inter alia (a) to encourage all organizations to go beyond legal compliance, recognizing that compliance with law is a fundamental duty of any organization and an essential part

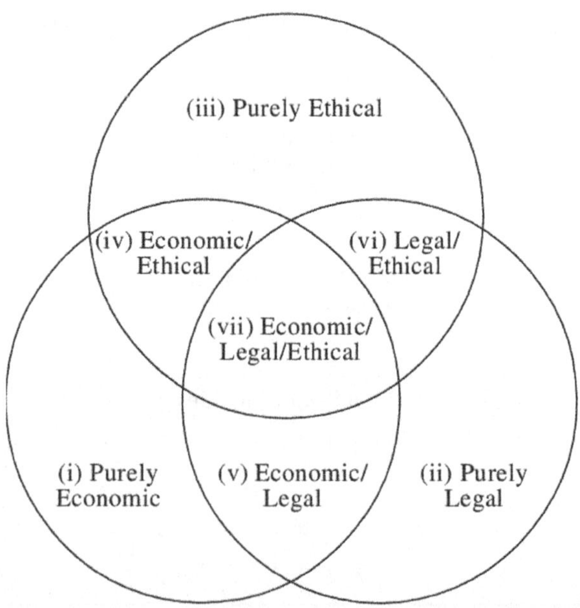

Fig. 5 The 'Three-Domain Model of Corporate Social Responsibility'. Source: Schwartz and Carroll (2003)

of their social responsibility (ISO 26000:2010, Article 1), but also (b) to promote a common understanding in the field of social responsibility, and to complement other instruments and initiatives for social responsibility (ISO 26000:2010, Article 1). The 'ISO 26000 Social Responsibility' defines 'Social Responsibility' as follows:

> Social Responsibility [is the] responsibility of an organization for the impacts of its decisions and activities on society and the environment, through transparent and ethical behaviour that
> - contributes to sustainable development, including health and the welfare of society;
> - takes into account the expectations of stakeholders;
> - is in compliance with applicable law and consistent with international norms of behaviour (2.11); and
> - is integrated throughout the organization (2.12) and practised in its relationships
>
> Note 1 to entry: Activities include products, services and processes.
> Note 2 to entry: Relationships refer to an organization's activities within its sphere of influence (ISO 26000:2010, Article 2.18).

Furthermore, the 'ISO 26000 Social Responsibility' follows seven 'Principles of Social Responsibility': Accountability, transparency, ethical behavior, respect for stakeholder interests, respect for the rule of law, respect for international norms behavior, and respect for human rights (ISO 26000:2010, Article 4 ff.).

As a result, this international standard includes all recent basic characteristics of Corporate Social Responsibility. The 'ISO 26000 Social Responsibility' is also a global convergence of defining CSR (Schneider, 2015, 27). Therefore, this article applies the definition of 'Social Responsibility' set out in Article 2.18 of the 'ISO 26000 Social Responsibility' as its reference CSR definition.

3.2 Environment and Environment Protection

In this chapter the focus of interest is on the status quo concerning environment and environment protection in close cooperation with private companies in Brazil.

As a consequence of the Mariana dam disaster in 2015, the Renova Foundation, an autonomous and independent non-profit organization, was established by Samarco Mineração S.A, one of Vale S.A.'s iron ore mines, in order to repair the damages caused by the burst of the Fundao dam—an iron ore tailing dam used by Samarco Mineração S.A. The scope of action of the Renova Foundation is defined by a legal commitment called 'Transaction and Conduct Adjustment Term'. There are 42 programs unfolded in many projects to be implemented in the impacted area along the Doce river and its tributaries. The Renova Foundation expects that these ongoing actions take up to 10 years (Renova Foundation, 2019a; Reuters, 2019a; Samarco, 2019). Finally, the 42 programs were divided in three thematic axes: AXIS 1—People and Communities, AXIS 2—Land and Water, and AXIS 3—Reconstruction and Infrastructure (Renova Foundation, 2019b).

The Renova Foundation already achieved noticeable success, inter alia: It has spent on repair actions (Brazilian Real) R $6.06 billion of the provided budget over R $11.6 billion since 2016 (Renova Foundation, 2019a).

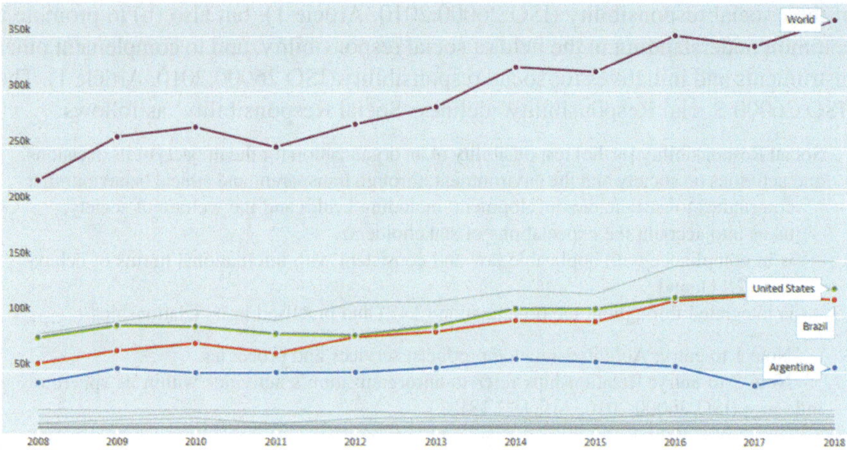

Fig. 6 Soybean production, in thousand tonnes, from 2008 to 2018. Source: OECD (2019)

Concerning the Brumadinho dam disaster, Vale S.A. remains focused on repair fronts in Brumadinho. So far, Vale S.A. "*has already agreed on the final individual and labour indemnities, structured and implemented monthly financial transfers to more than one hundred thousand people, started the main tailings removal and environmental recovery works, formalized donations to local governments and state public agencies, ensured the care of the animals and set up the entire system for monitoring the water quality of the Paraopeba river*" (Vale, 2019b).

So far, the environment respectively the environment protection in close cooperation with private companies—like Vale S.A.—has developed well. The companies who caused two of the worst environmental disasters in Brazilian history take their ecological responsibility seriously.

With regard to the recent developments concerning the deforestation of the Amazon Rainforest in Brazil and its consequences for the Brazilian environment and the world's climate, the status quo is quite alarming:

As depicted in Fig. 6, Brazil is one of the world's leading countries in soybean production and export. Over the last 10 years the Brazilian export expanded from 57,200 tonnes in 2008, to over 86,100 tonnes and 115,300 tonnes in 2013 and 2018. Compared to the world's export of soybeans in 2018 (365,300 tonnes), Brazil's share was close behind the United States of America (world leading country with 125,200 tonnes), but with a great distance in front of Argentina (third-placed country with 54,200 tonnes) (OECD, 2019).

With a view to strengthening and developing the Brazilian economic activities President Bolsonaro wants to open reservation lands that falls even in the Amazon rainforest for agriculture and mining. He and the Brazilian farm sector leaders are going to push the agriculture frontier deeper into the Amazon. They add to their argumentation that the 13% of Brazilian territory in question is home to only less than 1% of the national population—namely the indigenous people (Reuters, 2019b).

But there are also other regions in Brazil already threatened by the expansion of cattle and soya farms, for example: the Savanna region of the Cerrado (Ferreira Gomes de Assis et al., 2019; Greenpeace, 2019b).

Finally, as a reaction to the lasting destruction and deforestation of the Amazon rainforest supported by the Brazilian government, the German government suspended—until further notice—the promotion of forest and biodiversity conservation projects in Brazil. The Amazon Fund (Fig. 7) affected by this German decision raises donations for non-reimbursable investments in efforts to prevent, monitor, and combat deforestation as well as to promote the preservation and sustainable use in the Brazilian Amazon (Amazon Fund, 2019a; Ismar, 2019). Since 2008, the Amazon Fund received donations of US $1.3 billion (93.8% from the Norwegian Government, 5.7% from the Germany Government, and 0.5% from the Petróleo Brasileiro S.A.) and supported in total 103 projects (Amazon Fund, 2019b).

With regard to the German government's decision Bolsonaro said to the press: "*Brazil does not need German money to preserve the Amazon*" (Petrov, 2019).

3.3 *Corruption and Corporate Compliance*

Brazil belongs to the rising economies in the world. But as already mentioned earlier, corruption is still one of the biggest obstacles to further economic development in Brazil (France, 2019; Transparency International, 2019f, 1).

On the one hand, Brazil signed the international anti-corruption conventions—like the Organisation for Economic Co-operation and Development (OECD) Anti-Bribery Convention, the (United Nations) UN Convention Against Corruption, and the Inter-America Convention against Corruption as well as enacted several national laws like the Brazilian Law No. 8.429/92 that sanctions public agents who use their position for personal gain. On the other hand, the enforcement of the implemented international standards and the national laws by Brazil were traditionally very lax (Picanço, Prado, & Allen, 2018).

However, in the recent years Brazil has taken several steps to prevent and combat corruption. One of these steps was very effective: the Brazilian Law No. 12.846/2013—the so called 'Clean Company Act' which is Brazil's new anti-bribery law. It entered into force on January 29, 2014 (Flesch et al., 2014, 1).

Under the 'Clean Company Act' business organizations in Brazil, Brazilian foundations or associations, and foreign companies with any presence in Brazil can be strictly liable for prohibited acts committed in their interest or for their benefit. Due to the fact that the 'Clean Company Act' only applies to the above-mentioned entities, its charges are restricted to companies. Nevertheless, Brazil's Criminal Code or other Brazilian laws are still applicable for individuals involved in related misbehavior. The 'Clean Company Act' established a strict liability

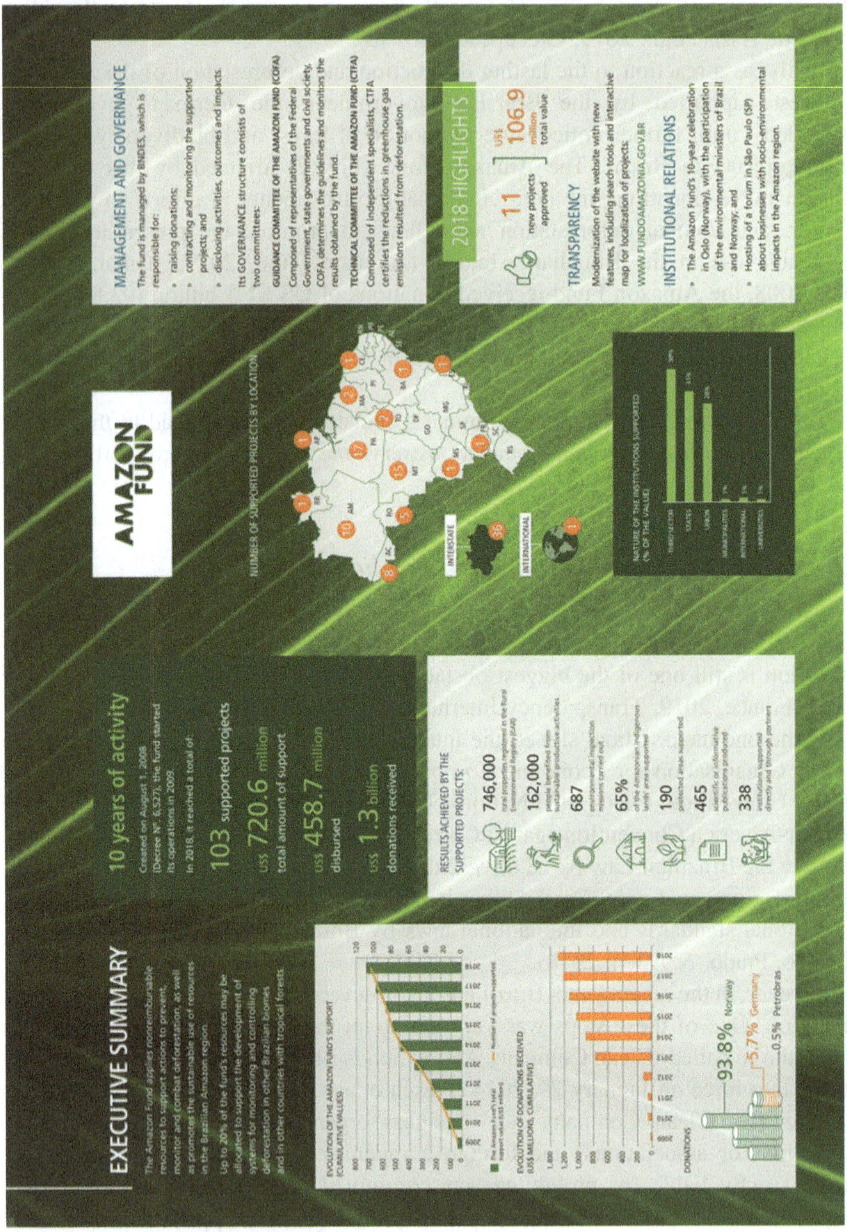

Fig. 7 Executive summary 2018 of the Amazon Fund. Source: Amazon Fund (2019b)

violation, i.e. it is sufficient to demonstrate that a prohibitive act was done by a company or any individual officer of that company. The strategy behind this lower threshold in the 'Clean Company Act' was to create an effective incentive for Brazilian authorities to undertake actively corporate investigations (Baker & McKenzie, 2016; Flesch et al., 2014, 1f; Global Legal Insights, 2019).

The 'Clean Company Act' covers corporate corruption, but also other prohibited acts committed against local Brazilian or foreign public officials, inter alia: "*(1) to promise, offer, or to give, directly or indirectly, an undue advantage to a public agent or a related third person, (2) to finance, pay, sponsor or, in any way, subsidize the performance of a prohibited act, (3) to make use of any individual or legal entity to conceal or disguise its real interests or the identity of the beneficiaries of acts performed or (4) to hinder an investigation or audit by a public agency, or to otherwise interfere with this work*" (Flesch et al., 2014, 2). In this respect, it has to be noted that Brazilian authorities—like the 'Office of the Federal Comptroller General'—are also authorized to pursue the above-mentioned entities and their individuals for prohibited acts taken abroad—i.e. the 'Clean Company Act' covers both foreign and domestic bribery—hence, there is an extraterritorial jurisdiction of this new Brazilian law (Flesch et al., 2014, 3f).

In comparison with the 'Foreign Corrupt Practice Act' in the US and the 'Bribery Act' in UK, the Brazilian 'Clean Company Act' also has an alternative resolution mechanism (for a high-level comparison of the 'FCPA', the 'Bribery Act', and the 'Clean Company Act' see Fig. 8). A company that wants to cooperate with the Brazilian authorities can enter into a so called 'Leniency Agreement'. If all related legal requirements are fulfilled by this company, the company's fine can be reduced (up to 2/3 of the total) and the company will also be exempt from certain judicial and administrative sanctions (Flesch et al., 2014, 6).

Five years after the Brazilian 'Clean Company Act' entered into force, this new Brazilian law has been the basis for numerous corruption investigations—particularly in conjunction with the 'Lava Jato'. Consequently, many companies involved in these investigations entered into leniency agreements to reduce their fines, i.e. SBM Offshore (R $1.22 billion) and Odebrecht (R $2.72 billion). In summary, the 'Clean Company Act' not only demonstrated a positive effect on the Brazilian combat against corruption, but also on the steadily improving business environment in Brazil. Nevertheless, there is still a long way to go (DLA Piper, 2018).

For doing business in general, a corporation has to comply with several requirements, e.g. economic and legal requirements. Therefore, to regulate all relevant corporation activities and also to ensure that the corporation is compliant with all these relevant requirements, corporations implement a compliance management system. Nevertheless, a corporation also has to take the economic, legal, and ethical responsibilities for its business activities. Thus, this is making it clear that 'Corporate Compliance' and 'Corporate Social Responsibility' are based on the same ground (Carroll, 1991; Schwartz & Carroll, 2003; Wieland, 2014, 15–40).

'Corporate Compliance' in a narrow sense relates only to legally orientated compliance. But in contrast to a legal department, a compliance office has to translate legal requirements, economic requirements as well as ethical requirements

Legal Element	FCPA	U.K. Bribery Act	Clean Company Act
Bribery of Foreign Officials	YES	YES	YES
Bribery of Local Officials	NO	YES	YES
Bribery in Private Context	NO	YES	NO
Extraterritorial reach	YES	YES	YES - Only if the violation relates to Brazilian entity
Books and Records	YES	NO - Covered under other legislation	NO - Covered under other legislation
Other prohibited acts	NO	NO	YES - Acts against Pub. Admin. (e.g., fraud in public tender process, bid rigging)
Exception for Facilitation Payments	YES	NO	NO
Corporate Criminal Liability	YES	YES	NO - Civil and Administrative liability only
Strict Liability	NO	YES - For "failure to prevent bribery"	YES - But for certain sanctions it is necessary to prove intent or fault
Credit for Compliance Program	YES - Via relevant U.S. Sentencing Guidelines	YES - Can be full defense for corporate offense of "failure to prevent bribery"	YES - Amount of credit not yet determined
Credit for Self-Disclosure and/or Cooperation	YES	YES - But somewhat limited and yet to be tested	YES - Under leniency program, fines can be reduced up to 2/3 and other sanctions can be excluded

Fig. 8 Comparing the Brazilian 'Clean Company Act' with the US 'FCPA' and UK 'Bribery Act'. Source: Flesch et al. (2014, 3)

into ethics and/or compliance programs. Consequently, 'Corporate Compliance' has to be understood in a wide sense because of its legal, economic, and ethical orientation (Wieland, 2014, 15ff).

As depicted in Fig. 9, there is one example how to create and implement a compliance office into the company's organization. This company uses an 'Integrity & Compliance Management' system—that means: integrity serves as the reference point for that kind of compliance management system (Wieland, 2014, 18f, 2018, 108):

In connection with the 'Clean Company Act', on March 18, 2015 a 'Brazilian Compliance Guide' (Decree 8.420/2015) was set in force by the former Brazilian President Dilma Rousseff. Under her decree several criteria were established by

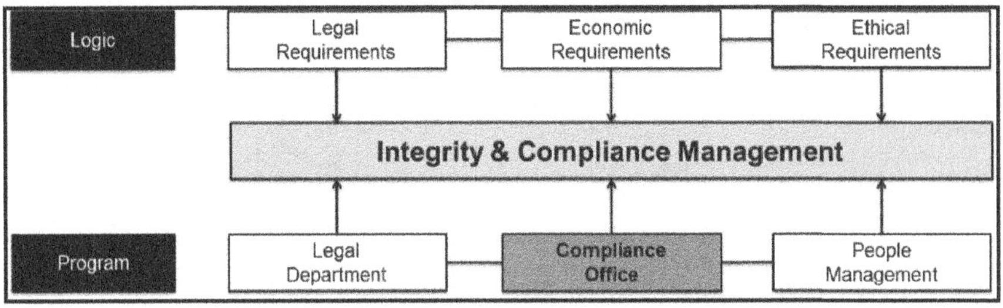

Fig. 9 Integrity & compliance management. Source: Wieland (2018, 108)

which a company's compliance system will be evaluated in case of a sanction. If an affected company has a compliance program in accordance with these criteria, its administrative sanctions can be reduced significantly. As mentioned in the decree, not only the size of the company, but also the following criteria are factors that form part of the compliance program's evaluation: top-level commitment; risk assessment; compliance policies; due diligence; internal monitoring, testing and review; transparency; reporting and disciplinary measures; and training (Ferreira, 2019; Gan Integrity, 2019).

As a result, the 'Clean Company Act' provides a further positive development concerning the combat against corruption in Brazil (Baker & McKenzie, 2016; DLA Piper, 2018; Flesch et al., 2014; Global Legal Insights, 2019).

4 Conclusion

4.1 CSR in Brazil: Quo Vadis?

In recent years the focus on the national and international discourse about 'CSR in Brazil' was dominated by the following two topics:

1. Environment protection in Brazil.
2. Corruption in Brazil.

So far, Brazilian corporations like Vale S.A. take their responsibilities concerning the reparation of the damages caused by environmental disasters, e.g. the Mariana dam disaster and the Brumadinho dam disaster. Nevertheless, corporations like Petrobras and Odebrecht are still clearing their corruption scandals.

But CSR goes beyond the laws. It is not enough for a corporation to start with 'Corporate Social Responsibility' after a self-convicted environmental disaster or a corruption scandal occured. 'Corporate Social Responsibility' has to influence the core business, culture, mission, and vision of a corporation in general.

A fortiori this also applies for the Brazilian government and its national and international policies. The government of a country is responsible for the sustainable

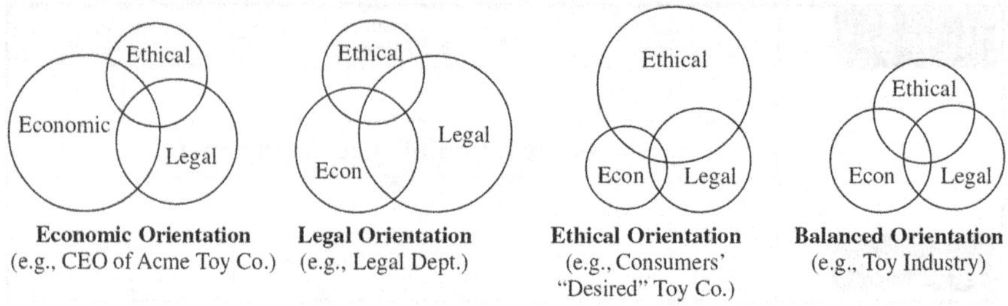

Fig. 10 Corporate social responsibility—'portraits'. Source: Schwartz and Carroll (2003, Fig. 4, 524)

development of its economy, environment, and society. Because of the great importance of the Amazon rainforest for the Brazilian and world's climate, the Brazilian government also needs to balance national and international interests wisely.

As depicted in Fig. 10, the big challenge for both the Brazilian government and the Brazilian corporations will be to moderate the turn away from a very dominant 'economic orientation' towards to a more 'balanced orientation' portrait of 'Corporate Social Responsibility'. Thus, it is still a long way to go.

Quo vadis 'CSR in Brazil'—if the Brazilian government and the Brazilian corporation will manage the above-mentioned turnaround very well? The rise of the Brazilian economy would go on and could lead to a sustainable development of Brazil's economy, environment, and society. At the end, not only Brazil but also the whole world would benefit from that development: The protection and reforestation of the Amazon rainforest could improve the world's climate significantly.

But *Quo vadis 'CSR in Brazil'*—if the Brazilian government and the Brazilian corporation will *not* manage the above-mentioned turnaround well? At first the rise of Brazilian economy would go on in equal measure. But recent developments like corruption, exploitation and pollution of the environment would not be defeated successfully but strengthened significantly. This applies also to the current rise of populism and the weakening democracy in Brazil. In the long term this dominant 'economic orientation' tends to an unbalanced development of Brazil's economy, environment, and society. At the end, not only Brazil but also the whole world would feel the effects of this. The world's climate crisis is a first teaser.

4.2 CSR in Brazil: Esperanca!

Not only the Brazilian economy but also the 'Corporate Social Responsibility' in Brazilian corporations is rising in recent years. More and more Brazilian corporations are taking up environmental, social, and community practices (Crisóstomo, de Souza Freire, & Nobre Parente, 2014; Damiano-Teixeira & Pompermayer, 2007; Galego-Álvarez, Formigoni, & Pompa Antunes, 2014, 1). Because of Brazil's long tradition in philanthropy and its great relevance in Brazilian society, it is not surprising that Brazilian corporations have still made positive experiences with social and responsibility programs. It is fair to say that Brazil is the pioneer and leader of 'Corporate Social Responsibility' in South America. As a result, 'CSR in Brazil' is more than just a trend—the understanding of CSR is anchored in the Brazilian culture and its values (Galego-Álvarez et al., 2014, 15; Scharf, 2008).

But also the current resistance of the Brazilian society, Brazilian indigenous tribes, Brazilian politicians, as well as Brazilian non-governmental organizations against President Bolsonaro's policy to open reservation lands to agriculture and mining is a powerful sign that 'CSR in Brazil' is already on the right track (Ismar, 2019; Petrov, 2019; Reuters, 2019b).

Finally, with the 'Clean Company Act' Brazil has one of the toughest anti-corruption laws in the world. But it must be recognized that more needs to be done by the Brazilian government and authorities to make the enforcement of that law more consistent (Backsmann & Backsmann, 2019; Gan Integrity, 2017).

Anyhow, if the Brazilian corporations are ready to deal with the challenges of implementing, establishing, and developing a serious and effective 'Corporate Compliance' system (if needed in conjunction with environmental governance), they also could combat corruption in their own corporation very successfully (Ferreira, 2019; Küster de Oliveira, Andreoli, & da Mata Cavalcante, 2019).

References

Amazon Fund. (2019a). Amazon Fund: Brazil protects it. The world supports it. Everybody wins. Retrieved August 14, 2019, from http://www.amazonfund.gov.br/en/home/

Amazon Fund. (2019b). Executive summary. Retrieved August 14, 2019, from http://www.amazonfund.gov.br/export/sites/default/en/.galleries/imagens/rafa-capa/Rafa_eng_2018_Executive_Summary.jpg

Backsmann, T. A., & Backsmann, C. (2019). Evolution of corruption in Brazil. In C. Stehr, N. Dziatzko, & F. Struve (Eds.), *Corporate social responsibility in Brazil—The future is now.* Cham: Springer International Publishing AG.

Baker & McKenzie. (2016). Anti-corruption in Brazil. Retrieved August 16, 2019, from https://globalcompliancenews.com/anti-corruption/handbook/anti-corruption-in-brazil/

BBC. (2019, July 11). Brazil's Vale ordered to pay compensation for dam disaster. *BBC Online.* Retrieved August 9, 2019, from https://www.bbc.com/news/world-latin-america-48935651

Carroll, A. B. (1991). The pyramid of corporate social responsibility: Toward the moral management of organizational stakeholders. *Business Horizons, 34*(4), 39–48.

Cavazotte, F., Cohen, M., & Brunelli, M. (2019). Business ethics in Brazil: Analyzing discourse and practice of the Brazilian contractors involved in the Operation Lava Jato. In C. Stehr, N. Dziatzko, & F. Struve (Eds.), *Corporate social responsibility in Brazil—The future is now.* Cham: Springer International Publishing AG.

CIA. (2019). The World Factbook: South America—Brazil. Retrieved August 11, 2019, from https://www.cia.gov/library/publications/the-world-factbook/geos/br.html

Crane, A., Matten, D., Glozer, S., & Spence, L. (2019). *Business ethics. Managing corporate citizenship and sustainability in the age of globalization* (5th ed.). Oxford: Oxford University Press.

Crisóstomo, V. L., de Souza Freire, F., & Nobre Parente, P. H. (2014). An analysis of corporate social responsibility in Brazil: Growth, firm size, sector and internal stakeholders involved in policy definition. *Pensamiento & Gestión, 2014*(37), 126–150.

Damiano-Teixeira, K. M., & Pompermayer, M. M. (2007). Corporate social responsibility: Profile and diagnosis of 797 programs developed in Brazil. *Business and Society Review, 112*(3), 343–367.

Dias Carneiro, J. (2016). Brazil dam burst: Six months on, the marks left by sea of sludge. Retrieved August 8, 2019, from https://www.bbc.com/news/world-latin-america-36230578

DLA Piper. (2018, December 5). Five years of the Brazilian clean companies act: Lessons learned. *DLA Piper Online*. Retrieved August 15, 2019, from https://www.dlapiper.com/en/korea/insights/publications/2018/12/global-anticorruption-newsletter-dec-2018/five-years-of-the-brazilian-clean-companies-act/

Economist. (2019, July 25). Jair Bolsonaro has given up on his anti-graft crusade: The president is breaking his main campaign promise. *Economist Online*. Retrieved August 13, 2019, from https://www.economist.com/the-americas/2019/07/25/jair-bolsonaro-has-given-up-on-his-anti-graft-crusade

FAO. (2019). Faostat: Land use. Retrieved August 9, 2019, from http://www.fao.org/faostat/en/#data/EL/visualize

Ferreira, M. L. (2019). Challenges of implementing corporate compliance in contemporary Brazil. In C. Stehr, N. Dziatzko, & F. Struve (Eds.), *Corporate social responsibility in Brazil—The future is now*. Cham: Springer International Publishing AG.

Ferreira Gomes de Assis, L., Ferreira, K. R., Vinhas, L., Maurano, L., Almeida, C. A., Nascimento, J. R., et al. (2019). Terrabrasilis: Spatial data infrastructure for disseminating deforestation from Brazil. Retrieved August 14, 2019, from https://proceedings.science/sbsr-2019/papers/terrabrasilis%2D%2Da-spatial-data-infrastructure-for-disseminating-deforestation-data-from-brazil?lang=pt-br

Flesch, E. M., Maeda, B. C., Sarubbi, E., Ayres, C., Cunningham, J. P., & Martin, G. (2014). Brazil's Clean Company Act: How U.S., U.K., and global models may influence enforcement. Retrieved August 14, 2019, from https://www.bakermckenzie.com/-/media/files/insight/publications/2015/10/global-issue-spotting-for-automotive-parts/brazilcleancompanyact.pdf?la=en

France, G. (2019). Brazil: Overview of corruption and anti-corruption. Retrieved August 14, 2019, from https://knowledgehub.transparency.org/assets/uploads/helpdesk/Brazil-Country-Profile-2019_PR.pdf

Galego-Álvarez, I., Formigoni, H., & Pompa Antunes, M. T. (2014). Corporate social responsibility practices at Brazilian firms. *Revista de Administração de Empresas, 54*(1), 12–27.

Gan Integrity. (2017). Brazil corruption report. Retrieved August 15, 2019, from https://www.ganintegrity.com/portal/country-profiles/brazil/

Gan Integrity. (2019). Compliance guides: Brazilian compliance guide. Retrieved August 15, 2019, from https://www.ganintegrity.com/portal/compliance-quick-guides/brazil/

Garriga, E., & Melé, D. (2004). Corporate social responsibility theories: Mapping the territory. *Journal of Business Ethics, 53*, 51–71.

Global Legal Insights. (2019). Bribery & corruption in Brazil. Retrieved August 16, 2019, from https://www.globallegalinsights.com/practice-areas/bribery-and-corruption-laws-and-regulations/brazil#chaptercontent7

Greenpeace. (2019a, August 8). Deforestation, meat production driving climate crisis. *Greenpeace Online*. Retrieved August 9, 2019, from https://www.greenpeace.org/international/story/23685/deforestation-meat-production-driving-climate-crisis/

Greenpeace. (2019b). Restore forest: Restore hope. Retrieved August 6, 2019, from https://www.greenpeace.org/international/act/restore-forests-restore-hope/

IBGE. (2019a). Cidades e Estados. Retrieved August 11, 2019, from https://www.ibge.gov.br/cidades-e-estados.html

IBGE. (2019b). Projeção da população do Brasil e das Unidades da Federação. Retrieved August 11, 2019, from https://www.ibge.gov.br/apps/populacao/projecao/index.html?utm_source=portal&utm_medium=popclock&utm_campaign=novo_popclock

IPCC. (2019). Climate change and land. Retrieved August 9, 2019, from https://www.ipcc.ch/report/srccl/

Ismar, G. (2019, August 9). Bundesregierung legt Brasilien-Projekt auf Eis. *Tagesspiegel Online*. Retrieved August 10, 2019, from https://www.tagesspiegel.de/politik/regenwald-rodung-bundesregierung-legt-brasilien-projekt-auf-eis/24889568.html

ISO. (2010). ISO 26000:2010(en)—Guidance on social responsibility. Retrieved August 13, 2019, from https://www.iso.org/obp/ui/#iso:std:iso:26000:ed-1:v1:en

Küster de Oliveira, R., Andreoli, C. V., & da Mata Cavalcante, P. (2019). Curbing corruption in Brazilian environmental governance: A collective action and problem-solving approach. In C. Stehr, N. Dziatzko, & F. Struve (Eds.), *Corporate social responsibility in Brazil—The future is now*. Cham: Springer International Publishing AG.

Matten, D., & Moon, J. (2008). 'Implicit' and 'explicit' CSR: A conceptual framework for a comparative understanding of corporate social responsibility. *Academy of Management Review, 33*(2), 404–424.

Merkur. (2019, Mai 17). TÜV Süd darf in Brasilien nach Unglück keine Dämme mehr prüfen. *Merkur Online*. Retrieved August 16, 2019, from https://www.merkur.de/welt/hunderte-vermisste-nach-dammbruch-in-brasilien-zr-11491503.html

OECD. (2019). Crop production. Retrieved August 14, 2019, from https://data.oecd.org/agroutput/crop-production.htm

Petrov, A. (2019, August 12). Bolsonaro claims Brazil does not need German funds to preserve the Amazon. *The Rio Times Online*. Retrieved August 14, 2019, from https://riotimesonline.com/brazil-news/brazil/politics-brazil/bolsonaro-claims-brazil-can-do-without-german-funds-to-preserve-the-amazon/

Phillips, T. (2019, July 3). 'A bad trip'—Jair Bolsonaro's first six months leave even the right dismayed. *The Guardian Online*. Retrieved August 5, 2019, from https://www.theguardian.com/world/2019/jul/03/jair-bolsonaro-brazil-first-six-months-right-dismayed

Picanço, L. B., Prado, M. N., & Allen, A. (2018). Anti-corruption efforts—Brazil 2018 understanding the issues. Retrieved August 14, 2018, from https://www.wilsoncenter.org/article/anti-corruption-efforts-brazil-2018-understanding-the-issues

Renova Foundation. (2019a). The Foundation. Retrieved August 13, 2019, from https://www.fundacaorenova.org/en/the-foundation/#

Renova Foundation. (2019b). Discover the programs. Retrieved August 13, 2019, from https://www.fundacaorenova.org/en/discover-the-programs/

Reuters. (2016, January 29). Samarco, Brazil move closer on $ 4.8 B dam-disaster settlement. *CBC Online*. Retrieved August 8, 2019, from https://www.cnbc.com/2016/01/21/samarco-brazil-move-closer-on-48b-dam-disaster-settlement.html

Reuters. (2019a). 3 Brazil mining company employees, 2 contractors arrested in dam disaster. Retrieved August 9, 2019, from https://www.cbc.ca/news/world/brazil-dam-disaster-mining-arrests-1.4996923

Reuters. (2019b, June 20). Brazil's Bolsonaro hands indigenous land decision back to farm sector. *Reuters Online*. Retrieved August 14, 2019, from https://www.reuters.com/article/us-brazil-politics-indigenous/brazils-bolsonaro-hands-indigenous-land-decisions-back-to-farm-sector-idUSKCN1TK37O

Salazar, J., & Husted, B. W. (2008). Principals and agents. Further thoughts on the Friedmanite critique of corporate social responsibility. In A. Crane, A. McWilliams, D. Matten, J. Moon, & D. S. Siegel (Eds.), *The Oxford handbook of corporate social responsibility*. Oxford: Oxford University Press.

Samarco Mineração S.A. (2019). Renova Foundation. Retrieved August 8, 2019, from https://www.samarco.com/en/renova-foundation/

Scharf, R. (2008, Winter). Why Brazil leads the region in CSR. *Americas Quarterly Online*. Retrieved August 15, 2019, from https://www.americasquarterly.org/node/288

Schneider, A. (2015). Reifegradmodell CSR – eine Begriffsklärung und -abgrenzung. In A. Schneider & R. Schmidpeter (Eds.), *Corporate social responsibility* (2nd ed.). Berlin: Springer Verlag.

Schwartz, M. S., & Carroll, A. B. (2003). Corporate social responsibility: A three-domain approach. *Business Ethics Quarterly, 13*(4), 503–530.

Smith, M., Valle, S., & Schmidt, B. (2017, June 8). No one has ever made a corruption machine like this one—There's a graft, and then there's Odebrecht graft. *Bloomberg Businessweek*. Retrieved August 5, 2019, from https://www.bloomberg.com/news/features/2017-06-08/no-one-has-ever-made-a-corruption-machine-like-this-one

Transparency International. (2019a). What is corruption? Retrieved August 5, 2019, from https://www.transparency.org/what-is-corruption#define

Transparency International. (2019b). Corruption Perceptions Index 2018. Retrieved August 5, 2019, from https://www.transparency.org/cpi2018#world-map

Transparency International. (2019c). Americas—Weakling democracy and rise in populism hinder anti-corruption efforts. Retrieved August 5, 2019, from https://www.transparency.org/news/feature/cpi-2018-regional-analysis-americas

Transparency International. (2019d). 25 Corruption scandals that shook the world – 23. Operation Lava Jato: Clean cars, dirty money. Retrieved August 5, 2019, from https://www.transparency.org/news/feature/25_corruption_scandals

Transparency International. (2019e). Mission, vision and values. Retrieved August 5, 2019, from https://www.transparency.org/whoweare/organisation/mission_vision_and_values/0

Transparency International. (2019f). Brazil: Overview of corruption and anti-corruption. Retrieved August 14, 2019, from https://knowledgehub.transparency.org/assets/uploads/helpdesk/Brazil-Country-Profile-2019_PR.pdf

Vale. (2019a, July 19). Vale remains focused on repair fronts in Brumadinho. *Vale Online*. Retrieved August 9, 2019, from http://www.vale.com/EN/aboutvale/news/Pages/vale-segue-focada-nas-varias-frentes-em-brumadinho.aspx

Vale. (2019b, July 19). Vale remains focused on repair fronts in Brumadinho. *Vale Online*. Retrieved August 13, 2019, from http://saladeimprensa.vale.com/en/Paginas/Articles.aspx?r=Vale_remains_focused_on_repair_fronts_in_Brumadinho&s=Mining&rID=1274&sID=6

Votaw, D. (1973). Genius becomes rare. In D. Votaw & S. P. Sethi (Eds.), *The corporate dilemma: Traditional values versus contemporary problems* (pp. 11–45). Englewood Cliffs, NJ: Prentice Hall.

Wieland, J. (2014). Integritäts- und Compliance-Management als Corporate Governance – konzeptionelle Grundlagen und Erfolgsfaktoren. In J. Wieland, R. Steinmeyer, & S. Grüninger (Eds.), *Handbuch Compliance-Management: Konzeptionelle Grundlagen, praktische Erfolgsfaktoren, globale Herausforderungen* (2nd ed.). Berlin: Erich Schmidt Verlag.

Wieland, J. (2018). *Relational Economics. Ökonomische Theorie der Governance wirtschaftlicher Transaktionen*. Marburg: Metropolis Verlag.

Winter, B. (2019, July 22). What Latin America's "corruption busters" got right—And wrong. *Americas Quarterly Online*. Retrieved August 15, 2019, from https://www.americasquarterly.org/content/what-latin-americas-corruption-busters-got-right-and-wrong

Zeit. (2019, August 7). Abholzung des Amazonas-Regenwalds stark ausgeweitet. *Zeit Online*. Retrieved August 9, 2019, from https://www.zeit.de/wissen/2019-08/brasilien-regenwald-abholzung-rodung-amazonaswald-weltrauminstitut

Understanding Integrated Reporting: A Study of Selected Companies in India

Sumona Ghosh and Arabinda Bhattacharya

Abstract Even though there has been a growing importance of Integrated Reporting (IR) globally, there has been limited research conducted with respect to IR in India. Hence the study investigated the extent to which the companies in India are integrating financial and non-financial data in their reporting. It employed Longitudinal Qualitative Document Analysis for the period 2010–16 using an Integrated Reporting Index (IRI) in examining annual reports of 102 most valuable companies ranked on the basis of market capitalization. Exploratory Factor Analysis (EFA) was applied for extraction of factors. Multiple Regression analysis was performed in order to determine the impact of the independent variables i.e. factors so generated from factor analysis on Integrated Reporting Index. The study revealed an average IRI of 70%. Strategic Environment, Internal Uncertainty, Internal Environment and Internal Design emerged to be important for the years under consideration. Regression results highlighted the fact that overall, internal design comprising manufacturing capital and business model proved to have the most significant impact on IRI.

Keywords Integrated reporting · Sustainability reports · Global Reporting Initiative (GRI) · The International Integrated Reporting Framework · Longitudinal Qualitative Document Analysis · Factors · Integrated Reporting Index · Functional relationship

---

S. Ghosh (✉)
Department of Commerce, St. Xavier's College, Kolkata, India

A. Bhattacharya
Department of Business Management, University of Calcutta, Kolkata, India

N. Mitra, R. Schmidpeter (eds.), *Corporate Social Responsibility in Rising Economies*, CSR, Sustainability, Ethics & Governance,
https://doi.org/10.1007/978-3-030-53775-3_11

1 Introduction

Integrated reporting can be described as: "*a process founded on integrated thinking that results in a periodic integrated report by an organization about value creation over time and related communications regarding aspects of value creation*" (Integrated Reporting, 2016). The main aspect of integrated reporting is value creation and impact of an organization. Integrated Reporting communicates effectively to the stakeholders, a holistic picture of a company's future targets and links between financial performances and reporting on corporate social and environmental responsibilities, thus enables stakeholders to fully evaluate the economic, environmental, and social performance of a business and effectively assess a company's ability to create value over the long-term. Integrated reporting is not only a valuable form of corporate reporting but it is also an effective approach to sound business management. Allen White, one of the co-founders of the Global Reporting Initiative (GRI), in June 2005, had observed that integrated reporting would be the future of corporate reporting. As on February 7, 2017 Securities Exchange Board of India (SEBI) have issued guidelines to top 500 listed companies to follow Integrated Reporting framework as given by International Integrated Reporting Council in 2013. However this is on a voluntary basis, hence in India some companies have been proactive enough to adopt this new form of reporting but others have not. Therefore, our study would not only contribute to the existing literature but also enhance the understanding of integrated reporting in the context of India. With the inclusion of this introduction, the paper has been structured into six sections. Section 2 gives a brief understanding of the work that has been done in this area globally. Section 3 outlines the objectives. Section 4 states the methodology. Section 5 delves into empirical results. Section 6 presents the conclusion and implications of this study and Sect. 7 deals with future research and limitations.

2 Literature Review

Research on integrated reporting was observed to be much more in the global context as compared to India. A brief summary of the work carried on in this area globally as well as in India is highlighted below.

Eccles and Krzus (2010) in their study found that the integrated reporting had improved the credibility and accuracy of sustainability information due to an improvement in the management information systems and control procedures related to the sustainability data.

Adams and Simnett (2011) in their study considered Integrated Reporting to be a more meaningful reporting that could be relevant for Australia's reporting organizations, including not-for-profits. Azcárate, Carrasco, and Fernández (2011) analyzed the role of integrated indicators included in sustainability reporting initiatives in exhibiting business contribution to Sustainable Development. Eccles and

Serafeim (2011) in their study described the concept of integrated reporting by providing a brief history of the development of integrated reporting and it also reviewed the current state of its practice. It presented a strategy for institutional change that would accelerate the adoption of integrated reporting.

Jensen and Berg (2012) in their study analyzed the similarities and differences between companies with traditional sustainability reporting (TSR) and those that publish integrated reports. Their analysis showed that investor and employment protection laws, the intensity of market coordination and ownership concentration, the level of economic, environmental and social development, the degree of national corporate responsibility and the value system of the country of origin proved to be relevant. Solomon and Maroun (2012) in their paper made an attempt to explore the emerging themes and reporting trends from 2009 to 2011. The observation was that the introduction of integrated reporting has resulted in an increase in social, environmental and ethical information disclosures.

Abeysekera (2013) in his research study examined the concept of integrated reporting and proposed a template for integrated reporting to be used in organizations. Frías-Aceituno, Rodríguez-Ariza, and García-Sánchez (2013) in this paper examined the influence of one of the most important institutional factors, the legal system, on the development of integrated reports. The results showed that companies located in civil law countries, and where indices of law and order are high, are more likely to create and publish a broad range of integrated reports. Dragu and Tudor-Tiron (2013) in their study argued that the emerging determinants of the voluntary adoption of an integrated reporting system were the political, cultural, and economic factors. Ioana and Adriana (2013a, 2013b) in their paper provided a very brief history of integrated reporting and identified three stages in the evolution of the integrated report: The emergence of non-financial reporting initiatives, the sustainability era and Contemporary integrated reports. Lyons (2013) focused on addressing issues like integrated thinking, integrated intelligence, value creation and value preservation in integrated reporting. The author suggested that improved corporate reporting was required to safeguard stakeholders and integrated reporting could be the answer to it. Owen (2013) reports on ACCA's support of and response to the latest initiatives in IR, particularly the impact this will have on the education and training of accountants. According to the author in order to reflect these new principles the twenty-first-century accountant have to be prepared for a much more challenging role in the near future.

Bavagnoli, Comoli, Gelmini, and Riva (2014) investigated the mutual relationship between materiality and conciseness from a theoretical and empirical perspective and it showed that they had an effective and positive effect on integrated reporting. Cheng, Green, Conradie, Konishi, and Romi (2014) in their paper introduced the concept of integrated reporting as described by the International Integrated Reporting Council (IIRC). They discussed on the key issues affecting integrated reporting and also identified a range of potential research issues relating to this area.

De Villiers, Rinaldi, and Unerman (2014) in their paper made an attempt to study and synthesize the insights from accounting and accountability research into the rapidly emerging field of integrated reporting and suggested many areas where further robust academic research was needed to guide developments in policy and practice. Eccles and Serafeim (2014) in their paper presented the two primary functions of corporate reporting (information and transformation), identified the drawbacks of isolated financial and sustainability reporting, described the concept of integrated reporting and explained the fact that while financial reporting was more focused on the information function and sustainability reporting on the transformation function, integrated reporting would accomplish both. Hao (2014) through their study showed the development of integrated reporting in Canada. The research showed that the Canadian business had not adequately prepared itself in terms of knowledge, mindset and resources for a more integrated model of corporate reporting. The study puts forward a series of suggestions for corporate directors to accelerate the move of integration.

Ioana and Adriana (2014) in their study defined integrated reporting, discussed the main fundamental theories (the institutional and legitimacy approach) that apply to integrated reporting research as well as various methodological approaches like descriptive/empirical studies, comparative/content analysis, or field studies such as interviews and questionnaires for testing the emergence of integrated reports. Smith (2014) in his paper discussed about the relationship that existed between the three pillars i.e. Stakeholder engagement, corporate governance, and integrated financial reporting and how these pillars had a very significant impact on the way businesses operated and reported the results to market participants. Stubbs, Higgins, Milne, and Hems (2014) studied about the adoption of integrated reporting in Australia and concluded that the gap between the information supplied by companies and the information required by providers of financial capital to make investment decisions was a significant issue and Integrated Reporting had the potential to bridge this information gap. Villiers (2014) focused on the concept of integrated reporting as a sustainable development mechanism. The study recommended a greater involvement of stakeholders, NGOs (Non-Governmental Organizations) and civil society in the development of the framework for integrated reporting.

Serafeim (2015) studied the relationship that existed between Integrated Reporting and the composition of a firm's investor base. It was found that, firms that practiced Integrated Reporting had a more long-term oriented investor base with more dedicated and fewer transient investors. It was also seen that firms that report more information about the different forms of capital as described in the Integrated Reporting Framework of the IIRC exhibit a more long-term oriented investor base. Adams (2015) analyzed integrated reporting and its potential to change the outlook of the corporate sector which in the long run would result in further integration of sustainability actions into corporate strategic planning and decision making. Eccles and Spiesshofer (2015) observed that corporate and financial reporting was an essential element of capitalism which rewarded companies for creating negative externalities however integrated reporting could help in changing this since such reporting was focused on the material issues that affected a company's ability to create value over the short, medium, and long term. Flower (2015) in his study traced the history of the International Integrated Reporting Council (IIRC) over the 4 years since its formation in 2010. He argued that IIRC's concept of value was primarily 'value for investors' and not 'value for society'. The author felt that the IIRC's proposals would have little impact on corporate reporting practice, because of their lack of force. Havlová (2015) focused on the early adopters of integrated reporting. He investigated how reporting had changed since the adoption of Integrated Reporting, the benefits that arose from the adoption and the usage of information technology.

Lee and Yeo (2016) in their paper examined the association between Integrated Reporting and firm valuation by taking a sample of listed firms in South Africa, which turned out to be positively associated. They further predicted that Integrated Reporting reduced the information processing costs in firms with complex operating and informational environment. Oprisorak (2015) studied auditing of integrated reports in the form of a literature review. His study showed that a high or reasonable level of assurance was difficult to obtain in the case of integrated reports because of the lack of audit regulations, company specific traits of integrated reports and key performance indicators for non-financial information.

Demirel and Erol (2016) in their paper looked at the development of integrated reporting and Corporate Reporting (CR) and tried to reveal the basic principles, theoretical background and development process of integrated reporting. The study concluded that in 2012 most large businesses preferred integrated reporting. This study also revealed that integrated reporting was made in the European region the most and financial services sector was the sector publishing integrated report the most. Burke and Clark (2016) discussed the business case for integrated reporting, as well as the multitude of challenges a firm might face when beginning its integrated reporting journey, drawing upon transcripts from 19 unstructured panel interviews at a global symposium on the subject. Dumay, Bernardi, Guthrie, and Demartini (2016) reviewed the various researches to date that have been conducted on integrated reporting and the authors concluded that most published integrated reporting research presented normative arguments for integrated reporting and there was little research examining the integrated reporting practice. The paper suggested future research possibilities on such an area.

Kurochkina, Shuvalova, and Novozhilova (2016) in their study tried to build information blocks of an integrated reporting of transport and communication enterprises by linking three key approaches from perspectives of intrinsic value of a firm; value embodied in the capitals' value and changes therein; created value, which is influenced by the stakeholders. Ruiz-Lozano and Tirado-Valencia (2016) in their study wanted to understand the level of attention given to the principles of Integrated Reporting by the industrial companies and the results showed that they still had to improve a lot especially in relation to the principle of "conciseness". Perego, Kennedy, and Whiteman (2016) presented an exhaustive literature review of integrated reporting. They also studied the managerial perceptions concerning integrated reporting and it was observed that the experts perceived the field to be fragmented and believed that most companies currently had a weak understanding of the business value of integrated reporting. Mio, Marco, and Pauluzzo (2016) analyzed the case of Generali, an Italian insurance company that implemented Integrated Reporting (IR) principles internally, creating an Internal Integrated Report

(IIR). They found that by merging management control systems and integrated reporting literature, several mechanisms that could potentially lead to an evolution in management control systems could be identified. Wilburn and Wilburn (2016) analyzed the scandal of Volkswagen AG which had demonstrated weak corporate social responsibility and they suggested that there has to be an integrated model that could help in standardizing as to what is meant by being socially responsible and ensuring that the consumers believe in the importance of corporate social responsibility. Zhou, Simnett, and Green (2016) studied the benefits that the disclosures of integrated reporting have by looking into the Johannesburg Stock Exchange integrated reporting listing requirements. They observed that the analysts' forecast error and dispersion reduces as the level of alignment with the integrated reporting framework increases.

Melloni, Caglio, and Perego (2017) examined performance determinants to gain insights into the factors associated with conciseness, completeness and balance in integrated reporting. They observed that when a firm's financial performance was weak, the integrated reports tend to be less concise and more optimistic. They additionally found that firms with poor social performance provided reports that were foggier and with less information on their sustainability performance. Bhasin (2017) analyzed the content and structure of the corporate integrated reports published in 2013 and available on the International Integrated Reporting Council (IIRC) Emerging Examples Database. The study indicated that early integrated reports were mostly lengthy, had failed to adhere to all the guiding principles and covered only four of the six capitals suggested. The author suggested that integrated reporting should be made mandatory for all the global listed companies within the next 5–10 years. De Villiers and Sharma (2017) in their paper made an attempt to examine the future of Intellectual Capital Reporting by presenting a critical reflection on the different forms of reporting, with a particular focus on Integrated Reporting. Maroun (2017) addressed the issue of integrated reports being the subject matter of a conventional assurance engagement and three possible assurance models—restricted; integrated and Delphi-inspired assurance model was brought into focus. Pavlopoulos, Magnis, and Iatridis (2017) in their paper examined the association between integrated reporting disclosure quality and corporate governance mechanisms. They observed that Integrated Reporting disclosure quality was positively associated with corporate governance variables. Rupley, Brown, and Marshall (2017) in their study highlighted both corporate social responsibility reporting and integrated reporting. They pointed out that the integrated reports covered indicators of economic and social performance but with little focus on governance. It also failed to provide the information most highly desired by investors (i.e. market share, executive compensation, and product safety).

3 Indian Perspective

From the Indian perspective we find very limited research has gone in to the aspect of integrated reporting. Athma and Laxmi (2013) in their study created awareness about integrated reporting and its importance as a better communication tool between the companies and the investors which would enhance the company's reputation and long-term sustainability of the business. Jhunjhunwala (2014) discussed about the international integrated reporting framework. Thiagarajan and Baul (2014) provided a comprehensive overview and argument for the implementation of integrated reporting or value reporting, with a specific focus on intellectual capital. Dhingra, Singh, and Magu (2014) in their study concentrated on determining the disclosures required if integrated reporting is adopted to counter the different limitations of the current financial reporting and sustainability reporting. Kiran and Goud (2015) studied integrated reporting amongst banks. Raju (2015) studied the integrated reporting practices followed by the Tata Steel Company Ltd. Thus, from the above brief outline of the research done on this area we can observe that integrated reporting has not been deeply ventured into by the researchers in India as compared with the global scenario. Das (2015) studied the relationship between integrated reporting and firm performance. The study revealed that integrated reporting affected firm performance and the shareholders wealth in long run. Basu and Wats (2015) through their study wanted to find out if there was any association between integrated reporting and enterprise performance management systems. The authors found a very strong association between integrated reporting and enterprise performance management systems. They suggested that integrated reporting through enterprise performance management systems could be useful to external value investors by providing a more comprehensive overview of opportunities and risks from the perspective of the economy, environment and society at large. Sunder (2017) presented a theoretical rationale for adopting integrated reporting. The study concluded by stating that such an integrated system of reporting will furnish better data for corporate, governance, regulatory, and macro-economic decision making. Ghosh (2019) in her study had observed that Indian companies are nearly well equipped to adopt and implement "integrated reporting" as required by the IIRC framework but preparation of "Integrated Report" needs its promotion amongst such companies in the Indian context so that it encourages them to step forward and adopt this method of reporting.

4 Objectives

On 7 February 2017, SEBI (Securities and Exchange Board of India) had issued a circular advising top 500 listed companies to adopt integrated reporting on a voluntary basis from the financial year 2017 to 18. The information related to integrated reporting (IR) may be provided either as part of annual report with a separate section on IR or incorporating in management discussion and analysis, or preparing a separate report as per IR framework. However, from the current scenario we observe that presently annual reports contain financial information and some content prescribed by the Integrated Reporting framework but in an un-organized manner. Thereby users of the annual reports would be facing problems to reconcile the non-financial information with financial information to understand the true, fair and strategic picture of organization's affairs. Additionally, from the literature review we observe that even though there has been a growing importance of integrated reporting globally, there has been limited research conducted on this area. These works were basically conceptual or case study based. With these in the background, the present study will be concerned with the following objectives:

- Objective 1: To construct Integrated Reporting Index (IRI) for different time periods across all companies and to differentiate the companies on that basis.
- Objective 2: To investigate the extent to which the companies in India are integrating financial and non-financial data in their reporting by using the constructed Integrated Reporting Index (IRI).
- Objective 3: To ascertain the factors emerging out of the parameters defined by IIRC in the context of integrated reporting for different periods.
- Objective 4: To estimate the functional relation between the factors and the Integrated Reporting Index for different time periods in order to examine the extent of influence of the factors on the Integrated Reporting.

5 Methodology

5.1 Data Source and Study Design

An empirical and analytical study was undertaken for the financial years 2010–11 till 2015–16 to give us an overview about integrated reporting for said period by analyzing the company's annual reports. Annual reports have been analyzed because on 7 February 2017, SEBI (Securities and Exchange Board of India) had issued a circular advising top 500 listed companies to adopt integrated reporting on a voluntary basis from the financial year 2017 to 18 and the information related to integrated reporting (IR) was to be provided either as part of annual report with a separate section on IR or incorporating in management discussion and analysis or preparing a separate report as per IR framework. Data was then generated from such an analysis using Longitudinal Qualitative Document Analysis for the 6-year period. Consistent with Popa, Blidişel, and Bogdan (2009), the presence or absence of an item was the measure for the extent of integrated reporting. As it is exhibited in Annexure 1, there are 14 items of disclosure as provided by the IIRC (The International Integrated Reporting Council). All these items were equally weighted as such if the item was disclosed in the annual report; it was awarded a score of 1 and if not a score of 0.

5.2 Selection of Companies

Top 500 companies were selected from the ET 500 list published by Economic Times for the years 2015–16 and 2016–17. From the list of 500 most valuable companies for the years 2015–16 and 2016–17 the common companies which had succeeded in maintaining its rank and position within the list of '500 most valuable companies' for the 2 years were selected and from this the top 135 companies were considered for the study. Banks were excluded from the list of 135. The final select data set consisted of 102 companies. These companies were ranked on the basis of market capitalization. The annual reports of these companies were analyzed on the basis of the study design specified above for the time period 2010–11 to 2015–16 i.e. 6 years.

5.3 Method

Longitudinal Qualitative Document Analysis was employed for the period 2010–11to 2015–16. An Integrated Reporting Index (IRI) was constructed by examining the annual reports of 102 most valuable companies ranked on the basis of market capitalization. The IRI was calculated in the following manner:

$$\mathrm{IRI} = \left(\sum \mathrm{di}/\mathrm{n}\right) \times 100 = (\mathrm{TS}/\mathrm{n}) \times 100$$

where:

IRI= Integrated Reporting Index
di: 1 if item i is disclosed; 0 if item i is not disclosed
n = number of items = Maximum Score
TS = Total Score

Mission and strategy, management approach, performance tracking, risk management stakeholder engagement, format public reporting are the main criteria that are used for measuring the integration level. In our study we have taken the 14 items of disclosure as provided by the IIRC (The International Integrated Reporting Council). They are financial capital, manufactured capital Intellectual capital, Human capital, Social and relationship capital, Natural capital, Organizational overview and external environment, Governance, Business model, Risks, Opportunities, Strategy and resource allocation, Performance, Outlook. Since there are 14 items of disclosure, the maximum score for each sampled company will be 14. Therefore, the maximum IRI score is "100" and the minimum score is "0". Hence a score of 100 or closer to it suggests high level of integration by the company. A score of "0" or closer to it suggests low level adoption of integration. We also calculated the grand mean score for each of the years.

From here we identified the four levels of integration which are as follows:

- Companies with scores above the grand average score for each year reflected high integration.
- Companies with scores below grand average score for each year reflected low integration.
- Companies with scores gradually improving over the time period considered for the analysis reflected progressive companies in respect of integration.
- The remaining companies reflected moderate integration.

The variables for factor analysis were obtained through Longitudinal Qualitative Document Analysis. Exploratory Factor Analysis (EFA) was applied for extraction of factors. Multiple Regression analysis was performed in order to determine the impact of the independent variables i.e. factors so generated from factor analysis on Integrated Reporting Index. This estimation of multiple regression models has been done for all the 6 years under study.

6 Results and Discussions

Table 1 focused on the individual Integrated Reporting Index (IRI) for the companies for the time period 2010–16. The study revealed an average IRI of 70% (Table 1, Annexure 2). Table 2 showed the extent of integration whereby the companies were differentiated on the basis of their IRI into high integration, low integration, progressive integration and moderate integration. Companies with score above the grand average score for each year reflected high integration. Hence companies with a score above 67% for 2010–11, 68% for 2011–12, 70% for 2012–13, 70% for 2013–14, 72% for 2014–15 and 73% for 2015–16 respectively were companies with high integration Similarly companies with score below grand average score for each year reflected low integration, companies with scores gradually improving over the time period considered for the analysis reflected progress companies in respect of integration and the remaining companies reflected moderate integration. Hence from Table 2 we observe that 39 companies fell into the category of high integration, 21 companies fell into the category of moderate integration, 15 companies fell into the category of progressive integration and 27 companies fell into the category of low integration (Table 2, Annexure 2).

Factor analysis was carried out for the years 2012–13 to 2015–16. Results proved to be insignificant for 2010–11 and 2011–12, hence we had to leave out these 2 years from the aforesaid analysis. Reporting was 100% for ‘performance’, ‘governance’ and ‘financial capital’ for the years under consideration. So, these were not considered for carrying out factor analysis. IC, NC, SC, STRA, RISK, OPPOR, OUTLOOK, HC, ORGREV, MC, BM are the factors which emerged from the analysis (Table 3, Annexure 2).

We grouped these factors into four broad groups as described in Table 4, Annexure 2. IC, NC, SC, STRA was grouped under ‘Strategic Environment’,

RISK, OPPOR, OUTLOOK was grouped under 'Internal Uncertainty', HC, ORGREV fell under the group 'Internal Environment' and MC, BM fell under the group 'Internal Design'. From Table 5 we observe that Strategic Environment, Internal Uncertainty, Internal Environment and Internal Design emerged to be important for the years under consideration.

Multiple Regression analysis was performed in order to determine the impact of the independent variables i.e. factors so generated from factor analysis on Integrated Reporting Index. For the year 2012–13 we observed that 'Internal Design' comprising MC, BM proved to be highly significant with $p = 0.002$. For the year 2013–14 we observed that 'Internal Design' comprising MC, BM proved to be highly significant with $p = 0.000$. For the year 2014–15 we observed that 'Internal Design' comprising MC, BM proved to be highly significant with $p = 0.000$. For the year 2015–16 we observed that both 'Internal Design and Internal Environment' comprising MC, ORGREV (with $p = 0.002$) and 'Internal design, Strategic Environment and Internal Environment' comprising BM, STRA and HC ($p = 0.000$) proved to be significant out of which 'Internal design, Strategic Environment and Internal Environment' proved to be highly significant (Table 6, Annexure 2).

Table 5 summarized the whole regression results for us and we observed that overall, internal design comprising manufacturing capital and business model proved to have the most significant impact on IRI (Table 5, Annexure 2).

7 Conclusions

An integrated report is a concise communication about how an organization's strategy, governance, performance and prospects, lead to the creation of value over the short, medium and long term. It provides a more holistic, multidimensional and lucid representation of the business. Integrated reporting would help businesses to think holistically about their strategy and plans, it would help in making more informed decisions and managing key risks so as to build investor and stakeholder confidence and improve future performance. From our study we can conclude on a positive note that Indian companies are nearly well equipped to adopt and implement "integrated reporting" as required by the IIRC framework. The study revealed an average IRI of 70%. 38.24% of the companies chosen for our analysis, fall under "highly integrated companies". But at the same time 26.47% of the companies chosen for our analysis falls under "low integrated companies". Hence preparation of "Integrated Report" needs its promotion amongst such companies in the Indian context so that it encourages them to adopt this method of reporting.

Our analysis has shown that 'Business Model' and 'Manufacturing Capital' for all the years and 'Strategy & resource allocation' along with them for the last year have turned out to be absolutely important in respect of integrated reporting. Hence effective disclosure of the same which has such a significant impact on Integrated Reporting Index needs to be encouraged.

Business model can be looked upon as to how an organization generates value over the longer term. A good business model is critical as it contextualizes the rest of the information about a company. Investors use business model information in their initial investment appraisal process. Business model information is fundamental to an investor's analysis and understanding of a company and its prospects. Investors will often compare business models and form views on the quality and sustainability of the business model. The world in which companies operate is increasingly complicated. The success of today's companies is determined by their interaction with, and their impact on, a growing number of stakeholders, who expect more from them keeping in mind that business environment is rapidly changing due to new technologies stepping in, growing of smaller and more agile competitors and environmental factors, such as climate change. The need for investors to better understand a company's business model has never been greater. Companies therefore need to clearly demonstrate how they create value, their resilience to change, and the quality and sustainability of the business and its performance. Companies need to be specific in their communication as to how they are differentiating themselves from their peers and how they are creating value for their investors. According to Ghosh (2019) companies in the Indian context have failed to disclose their business models and strategy as required by IIRC which would affect any stakeholder from understanding how the organizations are creating value over time and how are they going to achieve it. Since our analysis has shown that 'Business Model' is essential in respect of integrated reporting effective disclosure of the same needs to be encouraged.

Manufactured capital which refers to the material goods and infrastructure owned, leased or controlled by an organization that helps in production or service provision, but do not become embodied in its output is important for the sustainable development of an organization in two ways. Firstly, the efficient use of manufactured capital enhances flexibility of an organization, helps an organization to be responsive to market or societal needs, and be innovative and faster in getting its products and services to market. Secondly, manufactured capital and technology can reduce the use of resources specially non-renewable resources and focus more on human creativity, thus enhancing both efficiency and sustainable development. Companies in the Indian context have not shown an encouraging response towards disclosure of the same in the annual reports. Since our analysis has shown that 'Manufacturing capital' is essential in respect of integrated reporting effective disclosure of the same needs to be promoted.

'Strategy & resource allocation' informs us as to where does the organization wants to go and how does it intend to get there. An organization should be communicating about their short, medium and long-term strategic objectives, the strategies it has in place, or intends to implement, to achieve those strategic objectives, the resource allocation plans it has in place, or intends to put in place, to implement its strategy and how it will measure achievements and target outcomes for the short, medium and long-term. Such communication will enable stakeholders to assess whether companies are making progress towards achieving their ambitions. However According to Ghosh (2019) information about strategy and resource allocation was the least well reported content element in the annual reports. Companies should be made to realize the importance of communications and its impact on the investors.

8 Future Research and Limitations

This study would help future researchers or practitioners to understand integrated reporting in more details. More empirical work on this area instead of case study-based approach can be attempted. However, in this paper we have focused only on India but a comparative study with the other countries already advanced in integrated reporting could help us understand our position with respect to integrated reporting.

Annexure 1

There are 14 parameters required to be disclosed by IIRC:

- Financial capital—FC
- Manufactured capital—MC
- Intellectual capital—IC
- Human capital—HC
- Social and relationship capital—SC
- Natural capital—NC
- Organizational overview and external environment—ORGREV
- Governance—GOVERNAN
- Business model—BM
- Risks—RISK
- Opportunities—OPPOR
- Strategy and resource allocation—STRA
- Performance—PERFORMANCE
- Outlook—OUTLOOK.

Annexure 2

Table 1 Individual IRI for the companies for the time period 2010–16

Company	2010–11	2011–12	2012–13	2013–14	2014–15	2015–16	Average	Integration level
Indian Oil Corporation Ltd	79	79	79	79	79	79	79	HI
Reliance Industries Ltd	86	79	79	79	86	100	85	HI
Tata Motors	79	79	79	79	79	79	79	HI
Bharat Petroleum Corporation Ltd	71	71	79	79	79	79	76	HI
Hindustan Petroleum Corporation	50	50	50	71	71	71	61	LI
Rajesh Exports Ltd	50	36	36	36	36	36	38	LI
ONGC Ltd	79	79	79	79	79	79	79	HI
Tata Steel Ltd	86	86	100	100	100	100	95	HI
TCS Ltd	79	57	79	71	71	71	71	PI
Bharti Airtel Ltd	64	64	71	71	71	71	69	MI
Larsen and Toubro Ltd	86	86	86	71	71	71	79	MI
Hindalco Industries Ltd	71	79	79	79	79	79	77	HI
Coal India Ltd	79	79	86	86	86	86	83	HI
NTPC Ltd	86	86	86	86	86	86	86	HI
Mahindra and Mahindra Ltd	79	79	79	79	79	79	79	HI
Vedanta Ltd	64	79	79	100	100	100	87	PI
Infosys Ltd	86	86	86	86	86	86	86	HI
Maruti Suzuki India Ltd	71	71	71	71	71	71	71	MI
Gail India Ltd	64	64	79	79	79	79	74	PI
Wipro Ltd	79	79	79	79	79	100	82	HI
HDFC	64	64	64	50	57	57	60	LI
Adani Enterprises Ltd	64	71	71	71	100	79	76	PI
HCL Technologies Ltd	71	71	71	71	71	79	73	PI
JSW Steel Ltd	71	79	79	79	79	79	77	HI
ITC Ltd	50	57	57	64	64	64	60	LI
Mangalore Refinery and Petrochemicals Ltd	79	79	79	79	79	79	79	HI
Steel Authority of India Ltd	86	86	86	86	86	86	86	HI
Tata Power Co Ltd	79	79	79	79	79	79	79	HI

(continued)

Table 1 (continued)

Company	2010–11	2011–12	2012–13	2013–14	2014–15	2015–16	Average	Integration level
Motherson Sumi Systems Ltd	79	79	79	79	79	86	80	HI
Grasim Industries Ltd	79	79	79	79	79	79	79	HI
Idea Cellular Ltd	50	50	64	64	64	64	60	LI
Redington India Ltd	43	43	43	43	79	79	55	PI
Hindustan Unilever Ltd	71	71	86	86	86	86	81	HI
Ruchi Soya Industries Ltd	79	79	79	93	86	86	83	HI
Hero Motocorp Ltd	71	71	71	71	71	71	71	MI
Sun Pharmaceutical Industries Ltd	43	43	57	57	71	79	58	PI
Bharat Heavy Electricals Ltd	93	93	93	93	93	93	93	HI
Power Finance Corporation Ltd	71	71	71	71	71	71	71	MI
Petronet LNG Ltd	57	64	64	64	64	64	63	LI
Tech Mahindra Ltd	71	79	79	79	79	79	77	HI
Chennai Petroleum Corporation Ltd	79	79	79	79	79	79	79	HI
Ultra Tech Cement Ltd	71	71	71	71	79	79	74	HI
Adani Power Ltd	50	50	50	50	43	71	52	LI
Rural Electrification Corporation Ltd	79	79	79	71	71	71	75	MI
Aditya Birla Nuvo Ltd	71	79	79	79	79	86	79	HI
Bajaj Auto Ltd	43	43	43	43	43	43	43	LI
Jet Airways India Ltd	43	43	43	43	43	43	43	LI
Reliance Communication Ltd	79	79	79	79	79	79	79	HI
Power Grid Corporation of India Ltd	71	71	71	71	71	71	71	MI
Ashok Leyland Ltd	57	57	50	50	64	64	57	LI
Tata Communication Ltd	71	71	71	64	64	71	69	MI
Reliance Infrastructure Ltd	57	57	64	64	64	64	62	LI
MMTC Ltd	50	36	36	36	64	64	48	LI
Jindal Steel and Power Ltd	79	79	71	100	93	93	86	HI
Tata Chemicals Ltd	79	79	71	71	71	86	76	PI

(continued)

Table 1 (continued)

Company	2010–11	2011–12	2012–13	2013–14	2014–15	2015–16	Average	Integration level
Jai Prakash Associates Ltd	71	71	71	71	71	71	71	MI
Hindustan Zinc Ltd	71	71	86	86	86	86	81	HI
Asian Paints Ltd	64	64	64	57	64	64	63	LI
Dr Reddy Laboratories Ltd	71	71	79	86	86	86	80	HI
EID Parry India Ltd	50	50	86	71	71	71	67	MI
Lupin Ltd	71	71	79	79	79	79	76	HI
Videocon Industries Ltd	71	71	71	71	71	71	71	MI
Amtek Auto Ltd	50	50	50	50	50	50	50	LI
Gitanjali Gems Ltd	50	36	50	57	64	64	54	LI
Aurobindo Pharma Ltd	71	71	79	79	79	79	76	HI
PTC India Ltd	36	36	36	36	36	36	36	LI
Cipla Ltd	57	57	57	64	79	79	65	PI
GMR Infrastructure Ltd	71	79	79	71	71	71	74	PI
MRF Ltd	79	79	79	79	79	79	79	HI
Bajaj Finserv Ltd	50	50	50	50	50	43	49	LI
UPL Ltd	64	79	79	86	79	71	76	MI
Alok Industries Ltd	64	93	93	86	86	64	81	PI
Bharti Infratel Ltd	64	64	57	64	64	64	63	LI
Sundaram Clayton Ltd	64	64	64	64	64	64	64	LI
Eicher Motors Ltd	57	57	57	57	57	71	60	LI
LIC Housing Finance Ltd	64	64	71	64	64	79	68	MI
CESC Ltd	50	50	50	50	50	50	50	LI
Torrent Power Ltd	71	71	71	71	43	43	62	MI
ACC Ltd	86	86	86	86	86	86	86	HI
Apollo Tyres Ltd	71	71	79	79	79	79	76	HI
Bhushan Steel Ltd	50	57	64	43	50	50	52	LI
Max Financial Services Ltd	86	86	86	86	86	86	86	HI
Coromandel International Ltd	71	64	57	71	79	86	71	PI
TVS Motor Company Ltd	64	57	57	57	57	57	58	LI
Siemens Ltd	50	64	57	57	50	71	58	LI
Titan Company Ltd	43	50	64	71	71	64	61	MI

(continued)

Table 1 (continued)

Company	2010–11	2011–12	2012–13	2013–14	2014–15	2015–16	Average	Integration level
Godrej Industries Ltd	79	79	79	79	79	79	79	HI
Oil India Ltd	71	79	79	71	71	71	74	MI
Reliance Power Ltd	50	50	57	57	57	57	55	LI
Bosch India Ltd	79	79	79	79	79	79	79	HI
Suzlon Energy Ltd	86	64	71	79	79	79	76	PI
State Trading Corporation of India	50	50	50	50	50	50	50	LI
United Spirits Ltd	43	43	57	57	86	79	61	PI
Chambal Fertilisers and Chemicals Ltd	71	71	71	71	71	71	71	MI
Cairn India Ltd	79	79	79	79	79	79	79	HI
Rain Industries Ltd	64	71	71	71	71	71	70	MI
JSW Energy Ltd	57	86	86	71	79	86	77	PI
Shriram Transport Finance Company Ltd	50	57	79	57	71	71	64	MI
NHPC Ltd	71	86	79	79	79	79	79	HI
Zuari Agro Chemicals Ltd	50	50	57	43	50	64	52	LI
Reliance Capital	57	57	57	71	71	71	64	MI
Cadila Health Care Ltd	57	79	64	64	64	64	65	MI
Total	**67**	**68**	**70**	**70**	**72**	**73**	70	

Source: Authors own computation

Note: *HI* high integration, *MI* moderate integration, *PI* progressive integration, *LI* low integration

Thus, from the above table we can summarize the extent of integration of our select data set in the following manner:

Table 2 Classification of companies by extent of integration for the time period 2010–16

High integration	Moderate integration	Progressive integration	Low integration
Indian Oil Corporation Ltd	Bharti Airtel Ltd	TCS Ltd	Hindustan Petroleum Corporation
Reliance Industries Ltd	Larsen and Toubro Ltd	Vedanta Ltd	Rajesh Exports Ltd
Tata Motors	Maruti Suzuki India Ltd	Gail India Ltd	HDFC
Bharat Petroleum Corporation Ltd	Hero Motocorp Ltd	Adani Enterprises Ltd	ITC Ltd
ONGC Ltd	Rural Electrification Corporation Ltd	HCL Technologies Ltd	Petronet LNG Ltd
Tata Steel Ltd	Power Grid Corporation Of India Ltd	Redington India Ltd	Adani Power Ltd
Hindalco Industries Ltd	Tata Communication Ltd	Sun Pharmaceutical Industries Ltd	Bajaj Auto Ltd
Coal India Ltd	Jai Prakash Associates Ltd	Tata Chemicals Ltd	Jet Airways India Ltd
NTPC Ltd	EID Parry India Ltd	Cipla Ltd	Ashok Leyland Ltd
Mahindra and Mahindra Ltd	Videocon Industries Ltd	GMR Infrastructure Ltd	Reliance Infrastructure Ltd
Infosys Ltd	UPL Ltd	Alok Industries Ltd	MMTC Ltd
Wipro Ltd	LIC Housing Finance Ltd	Coromandel International Ltd	Asian Paints Ltd
JSW Steel Ltd	Torrent Power Ltd	Suzlon Energy Ltd	Amtek Auto Ltd
Mangalore Refinery and Petrochemicals Ltd	Titan Company Ltd	United Spirits Ltd	Gitanjali Gems Ltd
Steel Authority of India Ltd	Oil India Ltd	JSW Energy Ltd	PTC India Ltd
Tata Power Co Ltd	Chambal Fertilizers and Chemicals Ltd		Bajaj Finserv Ltd
Motherson Sumi Systems Ltd	Rain Industries Ltd		Bharti Infratel Ltd
Grasim Industries Ltd	Shriram Transport Finance Company Ltd		Sundaram Clayton Ltd
Hindustan Unilever Ltd	Reliance Capital		Eicher Motors Ltd
Ruchi Soya Industries Ltd	Cadila Health Care Ltd		CESC Ltd
Bharat Heavy Electricals Ltd	Power Finance Corporation Ltd		Bhushan Steel Ltd
Tech Mahindra Ltd			TVS Motor Company Ltd
Chennai Petroleum Corporation Ltd			Siemens Ltd

(continued)

Table 2 (continued)

High integration	Moderate integration	Progressive integration	Low integration
Ultra Tech Cement Ltd			Reliance Power Ltd
Aditya Birla Nuvo Ltd			State Trading Corporation Of India
Reliance Communication Ltd			Zuari Agro Chemicals Ltd
Jindal Steel and Power Ltd			Idea Cellular Ltd
Hindustan Zinc Ltd			
Dr Reddy Laboratories Ltd			
Lupin Ltd			
Aurobindo Pharma Ltd			
MRF Ltd			
ACC Ltd			
Apollo Tyres Ltd			
Max Financial Services Ltd			
Godrej Industries Ltd			
Bosch India Ltd			
Cairn India Ltd			
NHPC Ltd			

Source: Authors own computation

Table 3 Factor analysis for the years 2012–16

Year 2012–13				
KMO and Bartlett's Test				
Kaiser-Meyer-Olkin Measure of Sampling Adequacy.				0.600
Bartlett's Test of Sphericity	Approx. Chi-Square			143.375
	df			55
	Sig.			0.000
Rotated component matrix[a]				
	Component			
	1	2	3	4
NC3	0.814	0.161	0.096	−0.016
STRA3	0.658	0.010	0.237	−0.104
SC3	0.653	0.308	−0.314	0.267
IC3	0.544	−0.288	−0.036	0.151
OPPOR3	−0.117	0.760	−0.148	−0.280

(continued)

Table 3 (continued)

Rotated component matrix[a]

	Component			
	1	2	3	4
RISK3	0.040	0.643	0.194	0.381
OUTLOOK3	0.213	0.561	0.260	−0.034
HC3	−0.059	0.134	0.839	0.004
ORGREV3	0.278	0.047	0.651	0.330
MC3	−0.066	0.023	0.068	0.837
BM3	0.084	−0.064	0.050	0.495

Extraction Method: Principal Component Analysis.
Rotation Method: Varimax with Kaiser Normalization.

[a]Rotation converged in 6 iterations
Factor 1 = NC, STRA, SC, IC (Strategic Environment)
Factor 2 = OPPOR, RISK, OUTLOOK (Internal Uncertainty)
Factor 3 = HC, ORGREV (Internal Environment)
Factor 4 = MC, BM (Internal Design)
The total variance explained here is 57.421%

Year 2013–14

KMO and Bartlett's Test

Kaiser-Meyer-Olkin Measure of Sampling Adequacy.		0.555
Bartlett's Test of Sphericity	Approx. Chi-Square	125.332
	df	45
	Sig.	0.000

Rotated component matrix[a]

	Component			
	1	2	3	4
NC4	0.831	0.071	0.091	0.032
SC4	0.776	0.199	−0.206	0.025
STRA4	0.580	−0.145	0.215	0.121
OPPOR4	−0.015	0.814	0.008	0.035
OUTLOOK4	0.194	0.658	0.221	0.170
IC4	0.418	−0.444	0.167	0.189
HC4	−0.094	0.128	0.868	−0.097
ORGREV4	0.236	0.000	0.676	0.235
MC4	−0.029	0.130	0.003	0.823
BM4	0.164	−0.022	0.082	0.678

Extraction Method: Principal Component Analysis.
Rotation Method: Varimax with Kaiser Normalization.

[a]Rotation converged in 6 iterations
Factor 1 = NC, SC, STRA (Strategic Environment)
Factor 2 = OPPOR, OUTLOOK, IC (Internal Uncertainty and Strategic Environment)
Factor 3 = HC, ORG REV (Internal Environment)
Factor 4 = MC, BM (Internal Design)
The total variance explained here is 60.003%

Year 2014–15		
KMO and Bartlett's Test		
Kaiser-Meyer-Olkin Measure of Sampling Adequacy.		0.638
Bartlett's Test of Sphericity	Approx. Chi-Square	112.377
	df	55
	Sig.	0.000

Rotated component matrix[a]

	Component		
	1	2	3
NC5	0.750	0.111	0.074
SC5	0.704	0.042	−0.137
STRA5	0.546	−0.102	0.394
ORGREV5	0.500	0.307	0.314
IC5	0.399	−0.169	0.337
RISK5	0.273	0.609	−0.085
OPPOR5	−0.356	0.599	0.088
OUTLOOK5	0.030	0.590	0.293
HC5	0.036	0.569	−0.035
BM5	0.043	−0.010	0.727
MC5	0.044	0.184	0.629

Extraction Method: Principal Component Analysis.
Rotation Method: Varimax with Kaiser Normalization.

[a]Rotation converged in 5 iterations
Factor 1 = NC, SC, STRA, ORGREV, IC (Strategic Environment and Internal Environment)
Factor 2 = RISK, OPPOR, OUTLOOK, HC (Internal Uncertainty and Internal Environment)
Factor 3 = BM, MC (Internal Design)
The total variance explained here is 45.214%

Year 2015–16		
KMO and Bartlett's Test		
Kaiser-Meyer-Olkin Measure of Sampling Adequacy.		0.613
Bartlett's Test of Sphericity	Approx. Chi-Square	126.180
	df	55
	Sig.	0.000

Rotated component matrix[a]

	Component			
	1	2	3	4
NC6	0.757	0.148	0.184	−0.031
IC6	0.699	−0.195	0.039	−0.183
SC6	0.514	0.370	−0.077	0.334
RISK6	0.161	0.739	0.035	0.125
OPPOR6	−0.287	0.687	0.015	−0.175
OUTLOOK6	0.118	0.448	0.408	−0.224

(continued)

Rotated component matrix[a]				
	Component			
	1	2	3	4
MC6	−0.058	−0.048	0.830	0.098
ORGREV6	0.275	0.128	0.668	0.120
BM6	−0.035	0.071	0.198	0.776
STRA6	0.505	−0.022	0.144	0.530
HC6	0.156	0.336	0.123	−0.499

Extraction Method: Principal Component Analysis.
Rotation Method: Varimax with Kaiser Normalization.

[a]Rotation converged in 9 iterations
Factor 1 = NC, IC, SC (Strategic Environment)
Factor 2 = RISK, OPPOR, OUTLOOK (Internal Uncertainty)
Factor 3 = MC, ORGREV (Internal Environment and Internal Design)
Factor 4 = BM, STRA, HC ((Internal Design, Strategic Environment and Internal Environment)
The total variance explained here is 56.169%

Table 4 Summary of the factors emerging from the analysis for the companies for the time period 2012–16

Strategic environment	Internal uncertainty	Internal environment	Internal design
Intellectual capital—IC	Risks—RISK	Human capital—HC	Manufactured capital—MC
Social and relationship capital—SC	Opportunities—OPPOR	Organizational overview and external environment—ORGREV	Business model—BM
Natural capital—NC	Outlook—OUTLOOK		
Strategy and resource allocation—STRA			

Table 5 Regression analysis for the years 2012–16

Year 2012–13				
Model summary				
Model	R	R square	Adjusted R square	Std. error of the estimate
1	0.317[a]	0.101	0.064	0.13483

[a]Predictors: (Constant), internal design, internal environment, internal uncertainty, strategic environment

ANOVA[a]

Model		Sum of squares	df	Mean square	F	Sig.
1	Regression	0.197	4	0.049	2.716	0.034[b]
	Residual	1.763	97	0.018		
	Total	1.961	101			

[a]Dependent Variable: IRI
[b]Predictors: (Constant), internal design, internal environment, internal uncertainty, strategic environment

Coefficients[a]

Model		Unstandardized coefficients		Standardized coefficients	t	Sig.
		B	Std. error	Beta		
1	(Constant)	0.020	0.013		1.469	0.145
	Strategic environment	0.011	0.013	0.079	0.819	0.415
	Internal uncertainty	0.001	0.013	0.004	0.041	0.967
	Internal environment	0.005	0.013	0.034	0.349	0.728
	Internal design	0.043	0.013	0.306	3.173	0.002

[a]Dependent Variable: IRI

Year 2013–14

Model summary

Model	R	R square	Adjusted R square	Std. error of the estimate
1	0.540[a]	0.291	0.262	0.11969

[a]Predictors: (Constant), internal design, internal environment, internal uncertainty, strategic environment

ANOVA[a]

Model		Sum of squares	df	Mean square	F	Sig.
1	Regression	0.571	4	0.143	9.966	0.000[b]
	Residual	1.390	97	0.014		
	Total	1.961	101			

[a]Dependent Variable: IRI
[b]Predictors: (Constant), internal design, internal environment, internal uncertainty, strategic environment

Coefficients[a]						
		Unstandardized coefficients		Standardized coefficients		
Model		B	Std. error	Beta	t	Sig.
1	(Constant)	0.020	0.012		1.654	0.101
	Strategic environment	0.014	0.012	0.103	1.211	0.229
	Internal uncertainty and strategic environment	0.004	0.012	0.030	0.348	0.729
	Internal environment	0.007	0.012	0.048	0.557	0.579
	Internal design	0.073	0.012	0.527	6.162	0.000

[a]Dependent Variable: IRI

Year 2014–15

Model summary				
Model	R	R square	Adjusted R square	Std. error of the estimate
1	0.549[a]	0.301	0.280	0.11825

[a]Predictors: (Constant), internal design, internal uncertainty and internal environment, strategic environment and internal environment

ANOVA[a]						
Model		Sum of squares	df	Mean square	F	Sig.
1	Regression	0.590	3	0.197	14.072	0.000[b]
	Residual	1.370	98	0.014		
	Total	1.961	101			

[a]Dependent Variable: IRI
[b]Predictors: (Constant), internal design, internal uncertainty and internal environment, strategic environment and internal environment

Coefficients[a]						
		Unstandardized coefficients		Standardized coefficients		
Model		B	Std. error	Beta	t	Sig.
1	(Constant)	0.020	0.012		1.675	0.097
	Strategic environment and internal environment	0.001	0.012	0.007	0.087	0.931
	Internal uncertainty and internal environment	0.003	0.012	0.024	0.282	0.779
	Internal design	0.076	0.012	0.548	6.491	0.000

[a]Dependent Variable: IRI

Year 2015–16				
Model summary				
Model	R	R square	Adjusted R square	Std. error of the estimate
1	0.490[a]	0.240	0.209	0.17350

[a]Predictors: (Constant), internal design strategic environment and internal environment, internal environment and internal design, internal uncertainty, strategic environment

ANOVA[a]						
Model		Sum of squares	df	Mean Square	F	Sig.
1	Regression	0.923	4	0.231	7.666	0.000[b]
	Residual	2.920	97	0.030		
	Total	3.843	101			

[a]Dependent Variable: IRI
[b]Predictors: (Constant), internal design strategic environment and internal environment, internal environment and internal design, internal uncertainty, strategic environment

Coefficients[a]						
		Unstandardized coefficients		Standardized coefficients		
Model		B	Std. error	Beta	t	Sig.
1	(Constant)	0.039	0.017		2.283	0.025
	Strategic environment	0.009	0.017	0.048	0.545	0.587
	Internal uncertainty	0.023	0.017	0.119	1.343	0.182
	Internal environment and internal design	0.056	0.017	0.285	3.222	0.002
	Internal design strategic environment and internal environment	0.074	0.017	0.377	4.264	0.000

[a]Dependent Variable: IRI

Table 6 Summary results of the regression analysis for the time period 2012–2016

Year	Significant factors	Components
2012–2013	Internal design	Manufactured capital—MC, Business model—BM
2013–2014	Internal design	Manufactured capital—MC, Business model—BM
2014–2015	Internal design	Manufactured capital—MC, Business model—BM
2015–2016	Internal environment and internal design	Internal design, strategic environment and internal environment Organizational overview and external environment—ORGREV, Manufactured capital—MC, Business model—BM, Strategy and resource allocation—STRA, Human Capital—HC

Dependent variable: Integrated Reporting Index (IRI)
Note: Results proved to be insignificant for 2010–2011 and 2011–2012, hence we had to leave out these two years from the aforesaid analysis

References

Abeysekera, I. (2013). A template for integrated reporting. *Journal of Intellectual Capital, 14*(2), 227–245.

Adams, A. (2015). The international integrated reporting council: A call to action. *Critical Perspectives on Accounting, 27*(C), 23–28. Elsevier.

Adams, S., & Simnett, R. (2011). Integrated reporting: An opportunity for Australia's not-for-profit sector. *Australian Accounting Review, 2*(3), 292–301.

Athma, P., & Laxmi, N. (2013). Integrated reporting: The global scenario. *The IUP Journal of Accounting Research & Audit Practices, XII*(3), 7–18.

Azcárate, F., Carrasco, F., & Fernández, M. (2011). The role of integrated indicators in exhibiting business contribution to sustainable development: A survey of sustainability reporting initiatives. *Spanish Accounting Review, 14*, 213–240.

Basu, P. C., & Wats, S. (2015). Management tools that make corporate reporting key part of business strategy. *The Management Accountant, 50*(5), 22–26.

Bavagnoli, F., Comoli, M., Gelmini, L., & Riva, P. (2014). An open question in the integrated reporting: Materiality or conciseness? In *CSEAR Conference, Padova, Italy, September 2014*.

Bhasin, M. (2017). Integrated reporting: The future of corporate reporting. *International Journal of Management and Social Sciences Research, 6*(2), 17–30.

Burke, J., & Clark, C. (2016). The business case for integrated reporting: Insights from leading practitioners, regulators and academics. *Business Horizons, 59*, 273–283.

Cheng, M., Green, W., Conradie, P., Konishi, N., & Romi, A. (2014). The international integrated reporting framework: Key issues and future research opportunities. *Journal of International Financial Management & Accounting, 25*(1), 90–119.

Das, M. (2015). *Integrated reporting: Some research issues*. This paper was presented in 38th All India Accounting Conference and International Seminar on Accounting Education and Research. Retrieved from https://ssrn.com/abstract=2700517

De Villiers, C., Rinaldi, L., & Unerman, J. (2014). Integrated reporting: Insights, gaps and an agenda for future research. *Accounting, Auditing & Accountability Journal, 27*(7), 1042–1067.

De Villiers, C., & Sharma, U. (2017). A critical reflection on the future of financial, intellectual capital, sustainability and integrated reporting. *Critical Perspectives on Accounting*. https://doi.org/10.1016/j.cpa.2017.05.003.

Demirel, B., & Erol, I. (2016). Investigation of integrated reporting as a new approach of corporate reporting. *International Journal of Business And Social Research, 6*(10), 32–46.

Dhingra, P., Singh, A., & Magu, G. (2014). Limitations of current financial reporting: A case study of integrated reporting. *Business Analyst, 35*(1), 1–10.

Dragu, I., & Tudor-Tiron, A. (2013). New corporate reporting trends. Analysis on the evolution of integrated reporting. *Annals of the University of Oradea, Economic Science Series, 22*(1), 1221–1228.

Dumay, J., Bernardi, C., Guthrie, J., & Demartini, P. (2016). Integrated reporting: A structured literature review. *Accounting Forum, 40*(3), 166–185.

Eccles, R., & Krzus, M. (2010). *One report: Integrated reporting for a sustainable strategy*. Hoboken, NJ: Wiley.

Eccles, R., & Serafeim, G. (2011). Accelerating the adoption of integrated reporting. In F. de Leo & M. Vollbracht (Eds.), *CSR Index*. InnoVatio Publishing. Retrieved from https://ssrn.com/abstract=1910965

Eccles, R. G., & Serafeim, G. (2014). Corporate and integrated reporting: A functional perspective, Chapter 9. In E. Lawler, S. Mohrman, & J. O'Toole (Eds.), *Corporate stewardship: Achieving sustainable effectiveness*. Sheffield: Greenleaf, 2015.

Eccles, R., & Spiesshofer, B. (2015). *Integrated reporting for a re-imagined capitalism*. Harvard Business School General Management Unit Working Paper No. 16-032.

Flower, J. (2015). The international integrated reporting council: A story of failure. *Critical Perspectives on Accounting, 27*, 1–17.

Frías-Aceituno, J., Rodríguez-Ariza, L., & García-Sánchez, I. (2013). Is integrated reporting determined by a country's legal system? An exploratory study. *Journal of Cleaner Production, 44*, 45–55.
Ghosh, S. (2019). Integrated reporting in India: Research findings and insights. In S. Idowu & M. Del Baldo (Eds.), *Integrated reporting. CSR, sustainability, ethics & governance*. Cham: Springer.
Hao, S. (2014). *Corporate integrated reporting in Canada: Are the businesses ready?* Retrieved from https://ssrn.com/abstract=2531522 or https://doi.org/10.2139/ssrn.2531522
Havlová, K. (2015). What integrated reporting changed: The case study of early adopters. *Procedia Economics and Finance, 34*, 231–237.
Integrated Reporting. (2016). *Integrated reporting*. Retrieved April 25, 2017, from http://integratedreporting.org/
Ioana, D., & Adriana, T. (2013a). New corporate reporting trends: Analysis on the evolution of integrated reporting. *Annals of Faculty of Economics, 1*(1), 1221–1228.
Ioana, D., & Adriana, T. (2013b). The integrated reporting initiative from an institutional perspective: Emergent factors. *Procedia – Social and Behavioural Sciences, 92*, 275–279.
Ioana, D., & Adriana, T. (2014). Research agenda on integrated reporting: New emergent theory and practise. *Procedia Economics and Finance, 15*, 221–227.
Jensen, J., & Berg, N. (2012). Determinants of traditional sustainability reporting versus integrated reporting: An institutionalist approach. *Business Strategy and the Environment, 21*(5), 199–316.
Jhunjhunwala, S. (2014). Beyond financial reporting-international integrated reporting framework. *Indian Journal of Corporate Governance, 7*(1), 73–80.
Kiran, U. V., & Goud, M. M. (2015). A study of integrated reporting in Indian banks. *The Management Accountant, 50*(5), 29–33.
Kurochkina, I., Shuvalova, E., & Novozhilova, I. (2016). About formation of the integrated reporting performance in the process of building a sustainable business of transport and communication companies. *Procedia Engineering, 178*, 267–277.
Lee, K. W., & Yeo, G. H. H. (2016). The association between integrated reporting and firm valuation. *Review of Quantitative Finance and Accounting, 47*(4), 1221–1250.
Lyons, S. (2013). Integrated Reporting—International Framework: Response to the IIRC Consultation Draft, IIRC Consultation Draft: Integrated Reporting International Framework, April 2013.
Maroun, W. (2017). Assuring the integrated report: Insights and recommendations from auditors and preparers. *British Accounting Review, 49*(3), 329–346.
Melloni, G., Caglio, A., & Perego, P. (2017). Saying more with less? Disclosure conciseness, completeness and balance in integrated reports. *Journal of Accounting & Public Policy, 36*(3), 220–238.
Mio, C., Marco, F., & Pauluzzo, R. (2016). Internal applications of IR principles: Generalli's internal integrated reporting. *Journal of Cleaner Production, 139*, 204–218.
Oprisorak, T. (2015). Auditing integrated reports: Are there solutions to this puzzle? *Procedia Economics and Finance, 25*, 87–95.
Owen, G. (2013). Integrated reporting: A review of developments and their implications for the accounting curriculum. *Accounting Education, 22*(4), 340–356.
Pavlopoulos, A., Magnis, C., & Iatridis, G. (2017). Integrated reporting: Is it the last piece of the accounting disclosure puzzle? *Journal of Multinational Financial Management, 41*(C), 23–46. Elsevier.
Perego, P., Kennedy, S., & Whiteman, G. (2016). A lot of icing but little cake? Taking integrated reporting forward. *Journal of Cleaner Production, 136*, 53–64.
Popa, A., Blidişel, R., & Bogdan, V. (2009). *Transparency and disclosure between theory and practice: A case study of Romania*. Retrieved from http://kgk.bmf.hu/fikusz
Raju, K. K. (2015). Communicating value to the stakeholders: A case study of Tata Steel Company Ltd. *The Management Accountant, 50*(5), 34–35.

Ruiz-Lozano, M., & Tirado-Valencia, P. (2016). Do industrial companies respond to the guiding principles of the Integrated Reporting framework? A preliminary study on the first companies joined to the initiative. *Revista de Contabilidad – Spanish Accounting Review, 19*(2), 252–260. Elsevier.

Rupley, K., Brown, D., & Marshall, S. (2017). Evolution of corporate reporting: From stand-alone corporate social responsibility reporting to integrated reporting. *Research in Accounting Regulations, 29*(2), 172–176. Kelley School of Business Research Paper No. 17-73.

Serafeim, G. (2015). Integrated reporting and investor clientele. *Journal of Applied Corporate Finance, 27*(2), 34–51.

Smith, S. S. (2014). Integrated reporting, corporate governance, and the future of the accounting function. *International Journal of Business and Social Science, 5*(10), 58–63.

Solomon, J., & Maroun, W. (2012). Integrated reporting: The new face of social, ethical and environmental reporting in South Africa? In ACCA (ed.), London: The Association of Chartered Certified Accountants.

Stubbs, W., Higgins, C., Milne, M. J., & Hems, L. (2014). Financial capital providers' perceptions of integrated reporting. Retrieved from https://ssrn.com/abstract=2473426 or https://doi.org/10.2139/ssrn.2473426

Sunder, S. (2017). Value creation, distribution, and integrated financial reporting. *Indian Accounting Review, 21*(1), 1–18.

Thiagarajan, A., & Baul, U. (2014). Value reporting and integrated reporting in the era of intellectual capital. *International Journal of Computational Engineering and Management, 17* (1), 44–56.

Villiers, C. (2014). Integrated reporting for sustainable companies: What to encourage and what to avoid. *European Company Law, 11*(2), 117. University of Oslo Faculty of Law Research Paper No. 2014-25.

Wilburn, K., & Wilburn, H. (2016). The growing importance of integrated reporting for corporate social responsibility. *Review of Business & Finance Studies, 7*(2), 75–89.

Zhou, S., Simnett, R., & Green, W. (2016). Does integrated reporting matter to the capital market? *Abacus, 53*(1), 94–132.

Part III
Book Review

Book Review: Corporate Social Responsibility in India: Cases and Developments After the Legal Mandate

Umashankar Venkatesh

The term Corporate Social Responsibility (CSR) usually evokes very strong emotions among various stakeholders of the society and today more so. For instance, many corporate executives and their companies look at CSR with a degree of skepticism—as something that is essentially an extra burden for them to carry and hence, largely seen as a cost; the employees many a times look at it with a modicum of guilt and embarrassment due to what they have become party to as employees in 'profiteering' companies that routinely cut corners of all kinds; the consumers frequently feel that the corporations are either their adversaries or do not have their welfare in mind, as they frequently feel shortchanged due to the misrepresentation and miscommunication from corporations in their daily transactions. Institutions and corporations in the business-to-business world often look at their relationship with their upstream and downstream partners as a zero-sum proposition that they must exploit forcing the vendors to circumvent conventions of good business (say, by reducing safety norms; or material quality etc.) in the name of 'cutting' costs; and finally the regulators, who time and again sees the corporation as merely a recalcitrant and mercenary partner in the developmental and governance goals envisaged by the government of the day.

As the earth's finite resources increasingly gets exploited and depleted at an ever faster rate; and the physical environment of the world in which we live-in deteriorates in an accelerated manner, tougher questions are being asked - especially by those who are impacted by such retrogressive change. On the other hand as technology evolves rapidly, enabling the individual today to be easily heard far and wide, in a manner possible never before, transparency and the power of knowledge is no more the preserve of an elite few. In fact, in the realm of marketing the locus of control as far as marketing communication is concerned is said to have already

U. Venkatesh (✉)
Great Lakes Institute of Management, Gurgaon, India
e-mail: umashankar.v@greatlakes.edu.in

N. Mitra, R. Schmidpeter (eds.), *Corporate Social Responsibility in Rising Economies*, CSR, Sustainability, Ethics & Governance,
https://doi.org/10.1007/978-3-030-53775-3_12

shifted from the brand owner to the consumers and other stakeholders (Schultz, 2012), due to enabling technologies that empower stakeholders to easily disseminate information and assessments that may be contrary to the claims of the brand owners. Another example is how the investors have become increasingly assertive in a developing country like India. A study reveals that shareholders today in India are regularly raising their voices and successfully defeating board resolutions which they perceive as—either prejudicial to their interests; or seemingly dodgy on aspects of governance. Traditionally such activism was not seen so often and board resolutions of all kinds used to pass without much fuss (Harsh, 2018).

Different countries are engaging differently with the conceptualization and modeling of systems that will shape and govern the practice of CSR, both unilaterally as well as through multilateral agreements and compacts. India is no different and has devised a mandated way forward as far as the practice of CSR is concerned, by enacting the watershed Companies Act 2013, which mandates companies falling within a defined set of criteria to compulsorily spend, in every financial year, at least 2% of its average net profits made during the three immediately preceding financial years. This most probably is the first such mandated regime adopted by any country, making it the object of research and analysis.

Thus this new reference title edited by two experienced professionals, namely—Dr. Nayan Mitra from India and Dr. René Schmidpeter from Germany—"Corporate Social Responsibility in India: Cases and Developments after the Legal Mandate," is a topical addition to the corpus of CSR literature especially in the context of developing economies. The unique position that India currently assumes because of this new CSR regime, makes it a cynosure of researchers globally. This is especially of interest to researchers in developing countries who may be keen to understand and evaluate how efficacious such a regime is in shaping CSR and with what effects. For societies grappling with large deficits in parameters of human development and civil infrastructure and access (say) in a myriad of areas such as—education; healthcare (preventive disease control; primary healthcare; diagnostics etc.); sanitation; potable water etc.—CSR could be a clear force multiplier for governments to augment program creation and implementation.

The contributors in this book represent a diverse set of people drawn variously from the realm of academia, research, consulting, civil services, social enterprises; corporations as well as not for profit entities—across Asia and Europe. The book unfolds itself in three parts. The first part titled—"CSR Mandate and its Implications" is devoted to delineating and understanding the meaning and specifications of this new Indian CSR mandate; the antecedents and evolution of CSR in India; the various models that have been evident over time including how India has tried to fit-in in the global scene as far as CSR is concerned. The most interesting part of this section is the opening chapter based on an interview aptly of the person who is considered to be the Father of CSR in India and the author of the 'Chatterjee Model' of CSR, Dr. Bhaskar Chatterjee. The chapter clarifies why and how the CSR Policy in a developing country like India had to be distinct from existing models of CSR, due to the uniqueness of the context for which it is proposed. The differentiating aspects of the Indian CSR regime and its conceptualization is lucidly brought out through a series of well-founded questions and answers. From conceptualizing a new meaning for CSR as against the existing models and discussing the rationale for what and how to implement; who is responsible and what to measure and why—the chapter provides a backdrop for the following chapters in the book. This arguably is the pièce de résistance of this title, as it captures the antecedents and essence of this new Indian CSR mandate.

This section also provides a critical evaluation of the Indian CSR mandate; discusses the state of CSR implementation in India; and the challenges faced by companies in implementing their CSR strategies and how they are lagging behind their global peers. Another chapter investigates the CSR effort in the realm of education, wherein through a case based methodology the author categorizes the efforts made by Indian corporations specifically in the field of education and identifies the antecedents of professionalization of the process of CSR in education.

The second part of the book titled—"CSR Mandate and its Implementation," provides through select commentary and case studies, the practice and evolution of CSR in India to answer the implementation question of how corporations can go about integrating CSR in their internal design and operating principles and processes. This section also tries to identify priority areas that can be targeted by corporations through their CSR outreach and initiatives. The case studies included are from the core sector of steel and of a large fast moving consumer goods (FMCG) company. The case study on ITC Ltd. highlights how CSR in India at least for some companies predates the 2013 mandate while describing the nature of the diverse CSR strategy of the company in question, ranging from—the use of technology for knowledge empowerment of disenfranchised sections of the population (read rural); integrated watershed development; sustainable agronomy; social forestry; livestock development. The Jindal Steel case focuses upon their efforts in gender equality and women empowerment space along with environment conservation; education and health.

The third part of the book is devoted to delineating the future roadmap for CSR. The opening chapter of this part sets the context of the debate by elucidating how the recent focus on (mandated?) CSR in India, should not be seen as an endeavor to shift the responsibility of sustainable development from governments to corporations. And how Social Entrepreneurship may provide a new way of engagement in CSR for both governments and organizations. This conclusion is also validated in the last chapter of the book through a case study on Tata Group, which through its arm based upon the principles of a Social Enterprise, namely—Tata ClassEdge, provides curriculum support; teacher development assessment; and analytics—in the Indian school education system through Information and Communications Technology (ICT) based products. Another chapter in this section identifies three ways in which Indian CSR may be or is being rolled out, namely—enhancing transparency between the corporation and all stakeholders; acknowledging rights of stakeholders and how that can be manifested in all corporate strategies and practices; and finally how being the purveyors of eco-social sustainability is profitable for the corporation.

Given that this new CSR mandate is currently applicable to a defined set of companies, that qualify based upon minimum limits on parameters ranging from their—net worth; turnover; or net profit; a one-size-fits-all approach, as far as CSR strategies are concerned, may not work. Further, going forward tweaking the existing classification may add more companies to the mandated fold. On the other hand, as discussed in the opening paragraphs of this review, stakeholders are becoming increasingly aware and demanding and rightly so. Thus the book under review is an important addition to the literature available in the space of CSR, especially in the Indian context and is certainly the precursor for ongoing research and research based practices, enabling corporations and other enterprises to engage with sustainability needs by designing truly beneficial and hence meaningful CSR initiatives, and truly manifesting leadership beyond mere compliance.

References

Harsh, H. V. (2018). Watch out corporate India, 'active activism' by institutional investors is next. *Mint*, (Dec 31, 2018), p. 02.

Schultz, D. (2012). International marketing communication as the global marketing change agent. In T. C. Melewar & S. Gupta (Eds.), *Strategic international marketing*. Basingstoke: Palgrave Macmillan.

The manufacturer's authorised representative in the EU is Springer Nature Customer Service Centre GmbH, Europaplatz 3, 69115 Heidelberg, Germany. If you have any concerns regarding our products, please contact ProductSafety@springernature.com

Printed and bound by CPI Group (UK) Ltd, Croydon, CR0 4YY
28/09/2026
02224090-0009